IDOLS, ICONS, AND ILLUSIONS:
THE MOVIES WE LOVE - AND LOVE TO HATE - AND THE PEOPLE WHO MADE THEM

Bill Mesce, Jr.

STEPHEN F. AUSTIN STATE UNIVERSITY PRESS

NACOGDOCHES, TEXAS

Copyright 2015 Bill Mesce

All rights reserved
Printed in the United States of America

No part of this book may be used or reproduced in any manner whatsoever without written permission except in the case of brief quotations embodied in critical articles or reviews.

Stephen F. Austin State University Press
1936 North Street, LAN 203
Nacogdoches, TX 75962

sfapress@sfasu.edu

LIBRARY OF CONGRESS CATALOGUING-IN-PUBLICATION DATA

Mesce, Bill
Idols, Icons, and Illusions/Bill Mesce, Jr.—1st ed.
p.cm.

ISBN: 978-1-62288-096-6

I. Title

First Edition: 2015

To Big Bill —

Thanks for always being there for me, Pop.

Smooches,

Li'l Bill

CONTENTS:

12 Movies to Get You Through the Election Day Blues	9
Charles Durning (1923 – 2012): Open Wounds	14
Hollywood's First War	18
10 Terrific War Movies You Probably Never Heard Of	27
7 Anti-007 Movies You Haven't Seen	38
The Master: Alfred Hitchcock (1899 – 1980)	45
All Hail the King: Stephen King Movies	53
11 Commonly Overlooked Horror Films Worth Seeing	57
Under the Radar: Roger Corman	67
10 (Kind of) Classic Sci-Fi Flicks You May Have Never Heard Of	72
Ray Harryhausen (1920 – 2013): Master of Illusion	82
Them!	85
My Love/Hate Affair with *Star Trek*	88
Richard Matheson (1926 – 2013): "Just" a Great Storyteller	96
Jack Klugman (1922 – 2012): Everyman	98
George Lucas: One (Mega)Hit Wonder?	100
The Studio Auteur: Stanley Kubrick (1928 – 1999)	106
Breaking the Bank: 6 of Hollywood's Lost Old-School Epics	109
Michael Gough (1916 – 2011): Oh, Yeah! *That* Guy!"	119
Post Sandy Thoughts: 7 Disaster Films Done Right	121
Train Wrecks: My Favorite Stinkers	126
Tony Scott (1944 – 2012): Love 'Im or Hate 'Im, It'll Be a Long Time Before Anyone Forgets Him	135

Move Over, *Total Recall*: 10 More Remakes You'll Want to Avoid	139
Richard Zanuck (1934 – 2012): "Good" Sells	155
Cliff Robertson (1923 – 2011): Utility Player	159
Elmore Leonard (1925 – 3013): "I Don't Remember All the Bad Ones"	162
Don and *Dirty*: The Career of Don Siegel (1912 – 1991)	164
Kingdom of Darkness: RKO and Film Noir	172
Robert Mitchum (1917 – 1997): "Baby I Don't Care"	178
9 Great Crime Movies You've Probably Never Seen	184
Sidney Lumet (1924 – 2011): The Quintessential New Yorker	191
James Gandolfini (1961 – 2013): One of Our Own	194
Dennis Farina (1944 – 2013): Coming By It Honestly	196
8 Counts of Grand Theft Cinema	199
Peter Falk (1927 – 2011): Working Harder Than Everybody Else	206
Blake Edwards (1922 – 2010): Mr. Cool	210
7 Great Rebel Portraits of the '60s and '70s	213
Ben Gazzara (1930 – 2012): Greater Than the Sum of His Parts	219
Lee Remick (1935 – 1991): "Uncommonly Gifted"	221
John Calley (1930 – 2011): A Class Act	225
Nora Ephron (1941 – 2012): She Was Her Greatest Work	230
Peter Yates (1929 – 2011): We Are Where We Live	232
Elia Kazan's *America, America* and *Man on a Tightrope*	234
Great Locations: *The Prisoner* and *Local Hero*	237
Sofia Coppola's *Lost in Translation*	240
Anne Bancroft (1931 – 2005): "The Consummate Everything"	241

Andy Griffith (1926 – 2012): The Yokel as Shrewdie	245
Barbara Stanwyck (1907 – 1990): The Dame from Brooklyn	248
William Holden (1918 – 1981) and Glenn Ford (1916 – 2006): A Pair of Aces	251
The Magnificent Seven	258
Jane Russell (1921 – 2011): The Good Girl	265
9 Overlooked Classic Westerns	268
Throwback: Clint Eastwood	277
Arthur Penn (1922 – 2010): "A Really Nice Guy"	289
Ernest Borgnine (1918 – 2012): "Keep Going"	291
5 Forgotten Gems from 5 Great Movie Music Composers	294
Holiday Thoughts: *It's a Wonderful Life* and *Miracle on 34th Street*	300
Memento Mori: Remembering Those We Lost in 2011	302
Acknowledgments	308

12 MOVIES TO GET YOU THROUGH ELECTION DAY BLUES

November 2, 2012

Election Day is just around the corner, and depending on your view of the current state of The Republic, you can look at that day in one of two ways:

> It's a national celebration of history's greatest, most successful democracy, demonstrating our ability to freely choose our leadership and peacefully see the baton of power passed to the next man;

Or –

> It's a national embarrassment, history's greatest, most successful democracy squandering it's hard-won freedoms in a campaign for leadership poisoned by oversimplification, appeals to gut-level fears rather than the intellect, claims and charges plagued by inflation, distortion, and outright falsehood, and warped and distorted by the infusion of tens of millions of dollars from vested interests.

Either way, we still have to get through the day.

So, for those of you who just want to pull the shades and wait for the noise to die down, yet still feel part of the democratic process, here's enough government fodder to get you through those 24 hours.

Mr. Smith Goes to Washington (1939)
Directed by Frank Capra
Written by Sidney Buchman, Lewis R. Foster, and an uncredited Myles Connolly

This is the granddaddy of American political films, and it's wonderfully surprising — and simultaneously depressing – at how well this film holds up. James Stewart, in all his Jimmy aw-shucks Stewart glory, is a naïve young senator thrown into the lion's den of the Senate. Maybe all the behind-closed-doors wheeling and dealing isn't shocking news anymore, but it's hard not to root for Stewart's battered but unbowed idealism in the face of seamy reality. In a day where moneyed interests and inflexible ideologues on both sides of the aisle have brought government to a near standstill, a reminder of what this country is supposed to be about – rather than what it often seems to be – isn't a bad thing.

All the President's Men (1976)
Directed by Alan J. Pakula
Adapted from the Robert Woodward/Carl Bernstein book by William Goldman

This is the Mr. Hyde to Mr. Smith's Dr. Jekyll. Over 40 years after the fact, it's hard to remember how the Watergate scandal shattered Americans' faith in government as a paranoid, ambitious president cast aside his inaugural vow to uphold and protect the Constitution in order to uphold and protect his place of power. Goldman deservedly one his second Oscar for wrestling Woodward/Bernstein's dense, detailed journalistic account of the snowballing political disaster which brought about, for the first time in American history, a presidential resignation. Pakula musters together a masterful, mammoth cast and turns what could've/should've been a boring, static piece (the action climax? Robert Redford's Woodward and Dustin Hoffman's Bernstein... *typing*) into a master class in suspense.

The Candidate (1972)
Directed by Michael Ritchie
Written by Jeremy Larner

It's frightening how contemporary this dissection of a fictional California senatorial campaign remains current and on point. Its portrait of media hype, playing to the crowd, grubbing for funding all combining to compromise a young idealist's (Redford again) attempt to make a positive impact is just as potent today as it was 40 years ago. That's probably the most disturbing aspect of the movie; that we knew what was compromising the political process then, and don't seem to have done much about it since.

The Seduction of Joe Tynan (1979)
Directed by Jerry Schatzberg
Written by Alan Alda

Tynan could very well be taken as a sequel to *The Candidate* which ends as its dazed title character wins the election he'd planned on losing. Alda plays a young, newbie senator who now finds himself exposed to the back room horse-trading and power-brokering that's an everyday part of government. The question of the movie isn't, Do you sell your soul to move yourself ahead? It's, How much of your soul do you think you can afford to sell, and still have something left to let you look in the mirror at night without throwing up?

The President's Analyst (1967)
Written and directed by Theodore J. Flicker

Most agree this year's *The Campaign* brought the laughs, but most also agree it did so by taking some fairly easy, not especially provocative shots. *Analyst* may be one of the most ruthless eviscerations of the American socio-cultural-political landscape to ever come out of a major studio. James Coburn is the eponymous analyst whose privileged knowledge of the Chief Executive's private life becomes a prize wanted by, well, almost everyone, from foreign governments to the phone company. Audiences today might need to sit with their laptops set to Wikipedia to get all the period references (how many of you remember there used to be only one phone company?), but a smarter political comedy you won't find.

Seven Days in May (1964)
Directed by John Frankenheimer
Adapted from the Fletcher Knebel/Charles W. Bailey II novel by Rod Serling

Smart, intelligent, adult drama about an attempted military coup, led by super patriotic general Burt Lancaster, to overthrow the government of the United States led by president Frederic March. Kirk Douglas, in his fifth (and the best) of the seven movies he made with his buddy Lancaster, is the conscientious military officer who exposes the conspiracy. What still remains disturbing about this flick is how much the movie's right v. left antagonism echoes today's Tea Party v. The Left yowling.

The Missiles of October (1974)
Directed by Anthony Page
Adapted from the Robert F. Kennedy book by Stanley R. Greenberg

Made as a three-part video production for network TV, *Missiles* is the docudrama account of the closest this country has come to nuclear war in the defining event of the Kennedy presidency. Smart, nuanced, gripping, you can't help but ask, by the end, "Who the hell would ever want to be president?"

Path to War (2002)
Directed by John Frankenheimer
Written by Daniel Giat

Frankenheimer returns to his TV roots with this pungent, true-life, made-for-HBO drama which follows, step-by-step, Lyndon Johnson's disastrous series of decisions which embroiled the U.S. deeper and deeper into the sanguinary mess of Vietnam. Johnson emerges not as the cold-hearted villain so many anti-war protestors of the '60s thought him to be, but as a monumentally tragic, if misguided, figure who did wrong by trying to do right. *Missiles of October* showed a flawed president at his best; *Path* shows a flawed president giving in to his flaws. A perfect, and ultimately melancholic illustration of, the road to hell is paved with good intentions.

The Best Man (1964)
Directed by Franklin J. Schaffner
Adapted by Gore Vidal from his stage play

Cliff Robertson is a slimy, no punches-pulled contender vying for his party's presidential nomination against Henry Fonda's Mr. Nice Guy. Vidal admitted he'd based Robertson's character on Richard Nixon, and Fonda's on lefty intellectual Adlai Stevenson, but it's hard to think of a presidential contest that hasn't had at least two contestants of similar ilks. As one might expect of Vidal, it's a sharp, vital drama that, sadly, hasn't lost a step in the decades since.

The Contender (2000)
Written and directed by Rod Lurie

Calling this Lurie's best film is not exactly setting a high bar, but this is the only time Lurie came close to matching his ambitions. Jeff Bridges is a wily Chief Exec who needs a replacement vice president and has decided to make his mark in history by picking a woman (Joan Allen). But right wing ideologue Gary Oldman will have none of it, and, over the course of the hearings to determine Allen's suitability, the mud-slinging and dirty fighting is relentless. Up until the movie unravels in its last minutes, this is a contemporary rarity: a sharp-edged, well-played piece of modern-day political drama.

Twilight's Last Gleaming (1977)
Directed by Robert Aldrich
Adapted from Walter Wager's novel *Viper Three* by
Ronald M. Cohen and Edward Huebsch

Burt Lancaster plays a disaffected Air Force general threatening to launch nuclear missiles at Russia if President Charles Durning doesn't release a secret document explaining the Machiavellian decision-making behind the country's involvement in Vietnam. Part conspiracy thriller, part nuclear thriller, part history and political science lesson, the parts don't always integrate smoothly, but it is one of the most frank approaches in mainstream movies to not only Vietnam but the whole Cold War mindset. It also touches on an oft-forgot aspect of the presidency; that each president inherits the sins (and their consequences) of the men who held the office before him. The buck stops with the last guy in the leather chair.

Advise & Consent (1962)
Directed by Otto Preminger
Adapted from the Allen Drury novel by Wendell Mayes

No one ever accused Preminger of being a director with a soft touch, and much of *Advise* is overwrought and over-the-top, particularly its frightfully dated depiction of homosexuality and the gay community. Still, if you can wince your way through those passages, there's a colorful ensemble cast (Walter Pidgeon, Henry Fonda, George Grizzard, Lew Ayers, Franchot Tone, Charles Laughton, just to name a few) that gives one of the few, full portraits of the workings of the congressional machine, both at its best…and worst.

CHARLES DURNING (1923 – 2012): OPEN WOUNDS

December 28, 2012

Some acting careers are made by a single role. Think Brando's Stanley Kowalski in *A Streetcar Named Desire* (1951), Robert De Niro's Johnny Boy in *Mean Streets* (1973), Leonardo DiCaprio's Jack in the box office behemoth *Titanic* (1997).

A similar connection can happen on a more personal basis. You watch a movie and an actor — for whatever magical, alchemical reason – clicks with you. You suddenly remember the other times you've seen him or her, you want to know more about what they've done, what they're going to do. From that moment on, their name in the credits means something to you.

And in that great, romantic way Hollywood dream-making works, they may not even be stars; never were, never will be. But they are somebody you respond to, somebody whose work touches you.

For me, Charles Durning was one of those actors. At the news of his passing on Christmas Eve, it came back to me that the role of his which did it for me came in 1977. By then, Durning had already been acting in movies and on TV for 15 years, and his stage career went back even further. He'd been nominated for a Golden Globe for his outstanding work in *Dog Day Afternoon* (1975) as the very picture of a New York cop: frumpy, rough around the edges, and a bit fried trying to keep the Big Apple's latest episode of Gotham insanity in check.

As great as he was in *Dog Day*, that wasn't the movie where he clicked for me. It came, ironically, in a movie that was a flat-out box office flop: *Twilight's Last Gleaming*.

A disaffected Air Force general takes over a missile silo and threatens to send nukes toward Russia if the president – Durning – doesn't publicly release a secret document detailing the brutal *realpolitik* thinking behind the country's decision to become engaged in Vietnam.

Up until then, I'd seen presidents in movies portrayed as either sly old-timey political maestros (i.e. Lee Tracy in *The Best Man* [1964]; Franchot Tone in *Advise and Consent* [1962]), or saintly public servants pledged to the highest ideals of the office (Henry Fonda in *Fail-Safe* [1964]; Fredric March in *Seven Days in May* [1964]). Durning's David Stevens was neither, nor did he fold into the later more cynical models that came with a more cynical age: the buffoon (Robert Culp in *The Pelican Brief* [1993]; Dan Aykroyd in *My Fellow Americans* [1996]), or the big-headed, self-justifying villain (Gene Hackman in *Absolute Power* [1997]; Donald Moffatt in *Clear and Present Danger* [1994]).

Durning's president was simply…human. Smart, yet a bit naïve;

understanding of the unpleasant pragmatics of the job, yet not so inured to them as to execute them without pause or regret.

In an early introductory scene, Durning sits with an old college professor of his (Roscoe Lee Brown) who has come to ask Durning to intercede on behalf of one of his young protégés, guilty of assassinating a foreign dictator. There's no question of the young man's guilt; Durning cannot move on his behalf. But as soon as his old friend leaves, Durning sinks into a mope over the unconfessed truth of the matter; the boy was given up to secure overseas missile bases.

Stephens is a decent man but no committed idealist, chafing under the sins-of-the-father-visited-on-the-son circumstances of being asked to atone for the missteps of his predecessors, just as afraid as anybody else at the possibility of dying. When Durning's advisors tell him his only option is a face-to-face meeting with Lancaster which could very well get him killed, Durning angrily balks. "I will not be crucified for the sins of others…period!" he declares before storming out of the room.

But there were two other moments I've never forgotten, two moments that particularly stirred me then, and still do.

Durning is re-reading the document Lancaster wants released; a transcript of a conversation between the then president and his advisors during the early days of the country's Vietnam involvement (FYI: the policy espoused in the movie is loosely based on a 1957 book by future Secretary of State Henry Kissinger in which he promoted the idea of fighting limited wars to avoid larger, potentially nuclear conflicts). He reads the transcript aloud to his own advisory team; the advocating of continuing to fight an acknowledged unwinnable war to prove to North Vietnam's Soviet backers that the U.S. could be just as "capable of inhuman acts" as our enemies.

As he reads, Durning simmers, then begins to boil, his outrage barely suppressed…and then he detonates in a tirade of moral outrage. He turns to one of his advisors, a Washington veteran who'd been part of that long ago decision-making, and, almost quaking with anger, demands, "What in the name of the Holy Father were you thinking of?"

He retreats from the meeting to his private office where his aide and only friend in the White House (Gerald S. O'Loughlin) finds him staring at a painting on the wall, drink in hand. "My wife painted that," he says quietly, the rage gone, his voice soft and wistful. He turns to another wall: "She painted that one the following year. She might've been a really fine painter some day."

In just those few lines, Durning brings home the isolation, the loneliness of the Man at the Top, and with it, the desire to be in some other place, in some other time, the sense of loss that comes with knowing those other places and times are gone forever.

Durning knew both feelings: the outrage over wasteful carnage, and painful loss.

He was a decorated veteran of World War II: a Silver Star and Bronze Star for gallantry under fire, and three Purple Hearts for wounds received in action. He'd been the only man in his unit to survive landing on Omaha Beach on D-Day. Wounded, he'd been shipped back to England, recovered and was returned to duty just in time to be swept up in the Battle of the Bulge where he was taken prisoner and was one of a handful of captured Americans to survive the infamous Malmedy Massacre. The emotional wounds never quite healed; Durning would rarely speak of his military service.

And as for loss? He'd been born into a poor Irish family, one of ten siblings. His five sisters didn't survive childhood, taken by illness and disease.

"There are many secrets in us," the actor once said, "in the depths of our souls, that we don't want anyone to know about… horrifying things we keep secret. A lot of that is released through acting."

And it was there in those two moments, tapped and released, and I guess that's what scored with me: their authenticity.

Call them what you will – character actors, supporting players, familiar faces – we often don't quite fully appreciate their artistry, eclipsed as they are by the front-and-center stars. Often, they're asked to do only one thing in a movie: be the funny guy, be the best friend, be the cuddly dad. It is only in looking at their body of work as a whole that we can appreciate the range — for some of them, their extraordinary range — and there was little Durning couldn't do: he played cops and bad guys and dads and even, on several occasions, Santa Claus. He could go over the top for the big laugh (*To Be or Not to Be* [1983]), or dial it down for a more life-sized chuckle (*Tootsie*[1982]), or break into song and dance (*The Best Little Whorehouse in Texas* [1982]). And then he could turn around and wrap himself in the darkness of an ice-blooded thriller (*When a Stranger Calls* [1979]), or cop a Tony for playing Big Daddy in the 1989 Broadway revival of Tennessee Williams' classic *Cat on a Hot Tin Roof*. He was just as comfortable on the small screen, playing it heavy as Denis Leary's dad on the firefighter drama *Rescue Me*, or bringing the laughs as the exasperated priest trying to corral the craziness of the Barrone family on *Everybody Loves Raymond*.

What struck me – and still does – about *Twilight's Last Gleaming*, was it was one of the few times he was asked to play more than one note, to present a three-dimensional, flawed human being who eventually stumbles his way to the moral high ground.

In his book on writing, *On Moral Fiction*, novelist and essayist John Gardner stated, "Art begins in a wound." In the deepest of wounds, Charles

Durning found his art. I'd like to think that in the decades of laughs and poignancy and all that lies in between that he gave us, he found some measure of healing. He'd certainly earned it.

HOLLYWOOD'S FIRST WAR

November 11, 2010

As happens every year around this time, the cable spectrum has been heavily laced with programming throughout the week commemorating Veterans Day. HBO trundled out its full epic and brutal miniseries *The Pacific* for a one-day re-run broken up by the debut of the James Gandolfini-hosted documentary *War Torn 1861-2010*, a disturbing look at the psychological scars America's soldiers have suffered in every conflict since The Civil War; The History Channel ran an all-day marathon of *WW II in HD*, sprinkling its commercial breaks for the week with commemorative spots; AMC ran a day of war movies like *The Enemy Below* (1957) and *A Few Good Men* (1992) under the umbrella, "Vets Best"; and so on.

The bulk of memorializing programming focused on World War II; unsurprising, in that it remains, to this day, America's greatest, defining, and least morally problematic war. Even 65 years later, despite a half-century of demythologizing takes on the brutality of WW II combat, it remains, as Studs Terkel dubbed it in his 1984 oral history, "The Good War."

The same can't be said of any of America's military engagements since, and with each new commitment of U.S. forces, Hollywood has searched, and often struggled, to find an appropriate voice with which to connect with the audience perception and understanding of a particular conflict. Hollywood is *still* struggling to find a successful key to the country's complex, multi-faceted, and seemingly endless involvement in the Middle East.

The fate of 2008's *The Hurt Locker* is emblematic. Even with a modest budget of $12 million, and despite near-universal acclaim, a host of award nods, and an Oscar for director Kathryn Bigelow, the film barely crawled to breakeven. Behind *The Hurt Locker* stands a line of modest earners, underperformers and flat-out flops including *Three Kings* (1999), *In the Valley of Elah* (2007), *Red Sands* (2009), *Charlie Wilson's War* (2007), *Syriana* (2005), *Lions for Lambs* (2007), *Jarhead* (2005), *The Kingdom* (2007), *Rendition* (2007), and *Brothers* (2009). Even the man who found a hit in the Holocaust with *Schindler's List* (1993), Steven Spielberg, couldn't do better than an underperformer in *Munich* (2005) with a domestic gross of $47.4 million against a budget of $75 million.

At this time of remembrance for the service and sacrifice of America's men and women in uniform, it is worth comparing that near-universal rejection of the country's most recent conflict with the response to Hollywood's grappling with its first war nearly a century ago. It was, perhaps, the American movie industry – and its audience – at their most courageous...and their most honest.

*****

It was a combination of timing and the circumstances of both the movie industry and the U.S. involvement in World War I which guaranteed the greatest conflict in history up to that time would make only a modest impact on American movies during the war years. As an industry, American movies were still in a nascent, half-formed state, the movie-making technology of the time crude and physically awkward, and there was some question as to just how interested the American audience would be in a war for which, over much of its duration, the country was only a sideline observer.

On June 28, 1914, a Serbian nationalist assassinated Archduke Franz Ferdinand, heir to the Austro-Hungarian throne. For decades prior, the major powers of Europe had been constantly angling for position on the global stage, each trying to secure and advance their own expansionist designs while containing and/or disadvantaging the others. The end product of all this often covert diplomatic maneuvering was an interlocking network of secret treaties and alliances which turned the single radical act of a lone assassin into a lit match tossed into a pool of gasoline. Within two months of the archduke's death, those crisscrossing commitments had drawn nearly all of Europe's major powers into war with each other, each seeing in the conflict an opportunity for imperial self-aggrandizement, and each arrogantly assuming a quick war and sure victory.

Across the Atlantic in the U.S., sentiments about the war, at least at the outset, were mixed. There was an understandable inclination to support the democratic powers of the west (i.e. Britain, France) against militarist Germany and its allies, the fading Ottoman and Austro-Hungary empires. On a more pragmatic level, the U.S. also had significant financial interests in the western European countries which would be at risk in the event of their defeat.

But to others, the war in Europe was no more than the latest, if grandest, in a centuries-long line of bloody duels between European empires jockeying for supremacy; a competition in which the U.S. had no clear stake or interest. In fact, U.S. aversion to direct involvement in the war was so strong, Woodrow Wilson won his second presidential term in 1916 on the campaign promise of maintaining the course of neutrality the country had been steering since the outbreak of hostilities.

However, as the massive clash of European superpowers ground on, U.S. sentiment – stoked by, among other things, American civilian losses at the hands of marauding German U-boats, as well as surging pro-war propaganda — began to lean toward involvement, and, in April 1917, Wilson called for a declaration of war against Germany and its allies. Despite the declaration, the country was ill-prepared for war and it would be more than a year before significant numbers of American troops saw combat during the summer of 1918. Even then, while America's numbers helped tipped the scales in what had early on deteriorated into a horrifyingly sanguinary war of attrition, the U.S. was something of a junior partner.

By war's end, a little over three million men would serve in the American Army during WW I (far fewer than were fielded by the British or French), with casualties numbering just under 117,000 killed (more than half by disease), and almost 206,000 wounded. These numbers paled next to the casualty counts of the other major combatants whose losses tallied higher than the total number of American soldiers in service. Forty-four percent of the almost 5-1/2 million men Great Britain mobilized during the war were killed or wounded; more than half of Germany's 11 million servicemen; a shattering 75% of the French Empire's 7.5 million troops (final tally: 37 million people were killed or wounded in the war, 40% of whom were civilians).

The U.S.' late entry into and limited engagement in the war, the movie industry's inchoate state, the technological limitations of the medium – all these worked against a significant timely or even desired response to the war by American movie companies.

This is not to say the movie industry ignored the conflict. Some of the then-growing majors had films about the war on movie screens by 1917. Paramount put out several propagandistic efforts such as the luridly titled *The Claws of the Hun* (1918), boasting in a full-page ad that it was using its moviemaking muscle as a "weapon of victory." Universal, as well, produced a number of films about the war including *Treason* (1917), and *The Kaiser, Beast of Berlin* (1918). *The Birth of a Nation* (1915) maestro himself, D.W. Griffith, turned out the flag-waving *Hearts of the World* (1917), while Charlie Chaplin starred in what was probably the first so-called "service comedy," *Shoulder Arms* (1918). Still, compared to the torrent of war-related films which would pour out of the studios during WW II, the movie industry's response to the cataclysmic events of 1914-1918 could only be characterized as underwhelming, and the generally unimpressive box office performance of these releases suggests the movie-going public was, at best, ambivalent about features concerning the war.

However, in the years following the armistice, the terrain of both the movie industry and the psychology of its ever-growing audience changed substantially.

The unprecedented bloodletting of WW I resulted from a perfect storm of tragic elements: 19th century strategic thinking combined with new 20th century technologies of mass slaughter. The last major war on European soil had taken place during the 19th century, in an era of muzzle-loading cannon, horse cavalry, and single-shot muskets. Commanders went into the so-called Great War still thinking in last century terms of overwhelming enemy positions with frontal assaults. But, on the battlefields of the Western Front, those waves of charging infantry were pummeled by fast-firing breach-loading artillery, then channeled by concertina wire into killing zones where they were massacred by machine guns. If an assault did manage to close with the enemy, attacking troops faced a hail of fire from bolt-action, magazine-fed rifles and semi-automatic pistols and even, in the last year of the war, hand-carried automatic weapons. The new generation of military hardware also included poison gas, submarines, armed aircraft, flamethrowers, tanks, and massive, heavily armored and armed battleships – the "dreadnaughts."

The exponentially growing violence of combat on the Western Front was made all the worse by the miserable physical conditions under which the war was fought. Barely a month after hostilities had begun in the west, the opposing armies had battled to a stalemate, digging in along an unbroken 400-mile line of heavily fortified trenches extending from the Swiss border across northern France to the Belgian coast; a battle line which shifted only modestly through years of brutal attacks and counterattacks. Life in the dank, rat-infested trenches was supremely dismal, and disease and ailments like trench foot were as much a danger to troops as enemy fire.

Because of its late arrival on the scene, the American Expeditionary Force (AEF) did not suffer as long or as extensively as its British and French allies, or its German opponents. Still, Americans were no more prepared for the high-tech carnage of the Western Front than any other army. Besides a rather one-sided 10-week romp against Spain in 1898, the country's most significant conflict – and, up until WW I, its largest in scale (and still its bloodiest) – had been The Civil War which had ended a half-century before the Great War. In sum, the general populace's notions of war were uninformed at best, horribly naïve and antiquated at worst, with the few movies made during the war doing little to enlighten them.

American wartime war movies 1917-1918 typically didn't deal with the circumstances of front line combat, Griffith's drum-beating *Hearts of the World* – featuring footage Griffith had actually shot on the Western Front — being a notable exception. Rather, they were drama-driven, or, more accurately, *melo*drama-driven, set away from the battle front and featuring broad caricatures of threatening Teutonic villainy, damsels in distress, nefarious plottings of sabotage and espionage, and so on.

It was not until years after the war that the American movie industry and American moviegoers began to take a long, serious look at what was assumed, until the Second World War, to be the great tragedy of the 20th century.

Beginning in the 1920s, Hollywood kicked off a successful cycle of World War I films, often grand in scale, which extended through the coming of sound and even into the 1940s. It was a long line, but a thin one. The war movie of the 1920s-1930s was never the box office staple it would be during WW II and for decades thereafter; the number of war movies produced during those two decades would total only a fraction of the war-related movies the studios produced during the 44 months of the US involvement in WW II.

Although WW I films dominated the war movie genre, other types of war films were also produced during the period. There was, however, a marked difference between the character of WW I and non-WW I war films of the time.

WW I movies might be action-packed, but there were no pure action adventures where the war served mainly as a vehicle for breathtaking thrills. Nor, despite sometimes heavy doses of humor in some WW I titles, were there true service comedies in the vein of Chaplin's *Shoulder Arms* aside from a small number of shorts. It was almost as if there was a shared sense by moviemakers and moviegoers alike that The Great War had been such a monumental tragedy it would somehow be disrespectful to exploit it for mere escapist thrills and/or laughs. It was a code of conduct articulated in an opening title card of 1930's *All Quiet on the Western Front*:

> *This story is neither an accusation nor a confession, and least of all an adventure, for death is not an adventure to those who stand face to face with it...*

But there was, evidently, no such tacit taboo among other types of war movies. If the setting was exotic enough (French colonial North Africa for two versions of *Beau Geste* [1926, 1939] and the Laurel & Hardy slapstick comedy, *The Flying Deuces* [1939]), or historically removed enough from the still-fresh impressions of The Great War (19th century British Colonial India in *The Four Feathers* and *Gunga Din* [both 1939], the American Civil War for Buster Keaton's *The General* [1926], the Crimean War for *The Charge of the Light Brigade* [1936]), movies could be as packed with adventure, exciting action, high-spirited derring-do and/or laughs as moviemakers could make them. Although these movies varied tremendously in tone — from the serious drama of *Beau Geste* and *The Four Feathers*, to the sweeping action of *The Charge of the Light Brigade*, to the cheekiness of *Gunga Din*, to the laugh-out-loud comedy of *The Flying Deuces* and *The General* – as a rule, they all provided handsomely mounted entertainment and big-scale action without treading on Great War sensitivities.

The WW I movies Hollywood turned out between the world wars also vary considerably in tone and style. John Ford's *Four Sons* (1928) concentrates on the drama of a German family torn apart by the war, while the strongest elements of *Hell's Angels* (1930) – directed by eccentric tycoon Howard Hughes – are its screen-filling air battles. The screen adaptation of Maxwell

Anderson's 1924 stage play, *What Price Glory?* (1926), breaks up front line despair with the laugh-out-loud comedy of two soldiers competing for the attention of a French innkeeper's daughter, while *All Quiet on the Western Front* commits to a relentless depiction of life and death in the trenches.

For all their differences, and despite being produced over a period of two decades by different moviemakers at a variety of studios, the WW I movies of the 1920s-1930s are strikingly unified in their vision of the war, so much so that, looked at collectively, they all seem of a piece; like different colored tiles in a mosaic of a single, grand panorama of The Great War. All share the same brooding sense of tragic waste. "(For) what?" asks one pilot on learning yet another comrade has failed to return from *The Dawn Patrol* (1938), "What have all these deaths accomplished?"

There are no tributes to famous battles among post-WW I combat movies, nor is there that WW II feeling of a compelling purpose behind the fighting. These movies tend to be apolitical, and recognize no victory worth saluting. The war in movies like *The Big Parade* (1925), *Four Sons*, *The Dawn Patrol* (1930, remade in 1938), *Journey's End* (1930), *The Legion of the Condemned* (1928), *All Quiet on the Western Front*, *The Four Horsemen of the Apocalypse* (1921), *Wings* (1927), *Hell's Angels*, *The Eagle and the Hawk* (1933), *A Farewell to Arms* (1932), and *What Price Glory?* seems pointless, drenched in a heavy air of unnecessary-ness. Trying to puzzle out the reasons for the war, one German soldier in *All Quiet...* can only come up with, "I think it's more a kind of fever. Nobody wants it in particular, and then all at once, there it is. We didn't want it. The English didn't want it. And here we are fighting." A flyer from *The Dawn Patrol* speculates the cause was something more elemental: "Man is a savage animal, who, periodically, to relieve his nervous tension, tries to destroy himself."

True to the static nature of combat on the Western Front, the war in these movies comes off as a quasi-permanent state with no sense the fighting and dying is moving the men toward some ultimate war-ending triumph. Rather, the front line *was*, *is*, and *always will be*, an insatiable, eternal Moloch into which are chain-fed a generation of young men from all sides. Boiled down to its essence, the shared thesis of this body of work is that of good men dying in an ugly war run by generals removed and insulated from the miseries of the front in service of national aims so abstract as to be meaningless. Observes one droll infantryman from *All Quiet...*: "Me and the Kaiser, we are both fighting. The only difference is the Kaiser isn't here."

It's a testament to both the universality and adamancy of this grim vision of The Great War, as well as its persistence, that most of the war films turned out over those two decades feature central characters who either die (*The Four Horsemen of the Apocalypse*, *All Quiet on the Western Front*, *Wings*, *The*

Eagle and the Hawk, *Hell's Angels*, *The Dawn Patrol*) or are maimed (*The Big Parade*) before the final fade-out. And, in the rare event the main character manages to physically survive the war, he is still so *psychologically* damaged as to be beyond repair, as in 1937's *They Gave Him a Gun* with Franchot Tone as a good man turned gun-crazy hood by his frontline experiences. Says the opening title card of *All Quiet...*, they were "...a generation of men who, even though they may have escaped its shells, were destroyed by the war..."

Replacing the ambivalence of the war years, Hollywood's perception of The Great War was one that was, by the 1920s, also widely shared by the American audience as indicated by the consistently strong box office tallies of these releases. Perhaps the public had needed a few years to gain some perspective on and understanding of the war, to get far enough beyond the wartime sloganeering and propaganda for a clear-eyed, curious look through a cinematic window to see what had destroyed, spiritually as well as physically, so many young men. Whatever the cause for the attitudinal change, many of these movies were among the top performers of their release years, with *The Four Horsemen...*, *The Big Parade*, *What Price Glory?*, and *Four Sons* ranking as some of the biggest moneymakers of the silent film era, while *All Quiet...* was among the top 75 earners of the 1930s.

WW I was a war of mass actions, so, consequently, most of these productions are epic in scale. In those days before Computer-Generated Imagery (CGI), any credible depiction of WW I combat on either the ground or in the air had to be recreated full-sized. In *Hell's Angels*, Howard Hughes' efforts to capture the sky-filling violence of the air war not only made the film the most expensive film production up to that time, but cost the lives of three stunt pilots. The U.S. War Department provided over 4,000 soldiers, 200 trucks and 100 aircraft for the shooting of *The Big Parade*. In an interview for *The Parade's Gone By*, film historian Kevin Brownlow's 1968 tribute to the days of silent film, *Wings* director William Wellman – himself a veteran of the Lafayette Escadrille (a French air squadron of American volunteers) – tells of taking his production to Texas where he had the space to film his grand scale air battles over an enormous recreation of the Western Front trenches. At one point, Wellman had 165 aircraft tangling in a mock dogfight over a *faux* battlefield populated with thousands of extras – all to get just three and a half minutes of film.

The focus of these movies is the front line soldier (or the combat pilot), and perhaps his immediate superiors who share with him, at least to some degree, the same discomforts and dangers. The higher echelons are rarely glimpsed, their distance from the front line never respected. Like a malevolent deity, they are the often unseen power on high calling for a regular (*What Price Glory?*) or even daily (*The Dawn Patrol*) sacrifice of Abraham from their subordinates on the line through their directives which accomplish little more than a lengthening of the casualty lists. "Orders! Orders!" cries despairing John Gilbert in *The Big Parade*, "Who the hell is fighting this war — men or orders?"

The front line soldier or pilot in these movies is no superman. The best soldier can crack under the unbearable pressures and miserable conditions of the front as does German infantryman Paul Baumer (Lew Ayres) in *All Quiet…*. Even a veteran officer's considerable poise can erode under the stress of too much time on the line (Captain Flagg [Victor McLaglen] in *What Price Glory?*; *The Dawn Patrol's* squadron leader Brand [Neil Hamilton in the 1930 version; Basil Rathbone in 1938]; the alcoholic Lieutenant Stanhope in *Journey's End*). One too many brushes with death and a soldier might permanently lose his nerve (flyer Monte Rutledge [Ben Lyon] in *Hell's Angels*; Fredric March's psychologically gutted pilot in *The Eagle and the Hawk* who commits suicide rather than face another round of war in the air). For most, knowing their odds of survival diminish with each action, it's a heroic act simply to pull themselves "over the top" in the next assault; to climb into the cockpit for the next mission. However idealistically they may have begun the war, they come to view patriotism as an affliction of either the sociopathically rabid, or the dangerously naïve.

On leave, *All Quiet…*'s Paul Baumer returns to visit his old teacher, Professor Kantorek (Arnold Lucy), who doomed Paul's entire class by rousing them to enlist *en masse* in the German army. Kantorek pushes Baumer to tell some tale of front line heroism to stir up yet another classroom of potential cannon fodder, but the angry Baumer tells him in front of his pupils, "You still think it's beautiful to die for your country…The first bombardment taught us better." Such patriotism, *All Quiet…* and its fellow combat movies posits, serves only as fuel to keep the killing machines killing.

It is a not uncommon motif in these movies to show men in the opposing armies having more commonalities than differences, suggesting this had not been a war of peoples, but as the product of the failures of their respective governments. In *All Quiet…*, Paul shares a shell hole in No Man's Land with the corpse of a French soldier. Battle fatigued, Paul goes on a delirious rant to the dead man, begging his forgiveness, thinking that in another time, another place they could've been friends. In *Hell's Angels*, two British brothers flying for the RAF unknowingly attack a zeppelin on which a German friend of theirs from before the war is the bombardier.

Some movies took this brother-against-brother theme to a more emphatic level by making it more literal. In *The Four Horsemen of the Apocalypse*, two cousins – one French, the other German – end up facing each other on the battlefield, only to both be killed by the same stray shell. *Four Sons* focuses on the heartbreak of a mother with sons on both sides of the conflict; three on the side of her native Germany, a fourth who had emigrated to the U.S. years before fighting for the Allies.

Perhaps no movie made the case in such extreme fashion as *Hell's Angels*. Ben Lyon and James Hall play brothers flying in the same RAF squadron. After they're shot down and captured by the Germans, Lyon loses his nerve when they're threatened with execution, and Hall is compelled to kill his brother to keep him from divulging valuable information.

There is a pervasive fatalism connecting all of these movies, a feeling the war is so ultimately all-devouring that there is no surviving combat at the front. The seemingly never-ending war will always outlast any soldier's amount of skill or luck, no matter how considerable. In *What Price Glory?*, company commander Flagg is haunted by the battle which decimates his unit, and even more so by the inevitable next battle which will bleed his outfit even more. Similarly, *The Dawn Patrol's* squadron commander Brand is close to cracking as he is regularly forced to feed unseasoned replacements directly into flight assignments from which few return. "You know what this place is? It's a slaughterhouse," declares a fraying Brand, "and I'm the butcher." In *All Quiet on the Western Front*, death eventually finds "Kat" Katczinsky (Louis Wolheim), the wily, resourceful and seemingly indestructible older soldier who has been a mother hen through most of the film to Paul and his cadre of friends new to the front. In the climactic scenes of *Wings*, an American airman played by Richard Arlen survives a crash landing and escapes the Germans in one of their own aircraft, only to be misidentified as the enemy and shot down and killed by his best friend.

The WW I combat movies of the 1920s-1930s featured a war without victors populated solely by victims. The Western Front comes off as a Land of the Damned where men are sentenced to fight for no discernable purpose until they die or crack. Coming away from the full body of these films with their shared Boschian vision, it's hard not to agree with Kat Katczinsky's prescription for how wars *should* be fought:

"I'll tell you how it should all be done. Whenever there's a big war comin' on, you should rope off a big field…And on the big day, you should take all the kings and their cabinets and their generals, put 'em in the center dressed in their underpants, and let 'em fight it out with clubs."

10 TERRIFIC WAR MOVIES YOU PROBABLY NEVER HEARD OF

February 27, 2012

I've always been a war film buff, maybe because I grew up with them at a time when they were a regular part of the cinema landscape.

From the 1920s into the 1980s or so, movies about men and the combat experience were a Hollywood staple, from *The Big Parade* (1925) to *A Walk in the Sun* (1945) to *The Bridges at Toko-Ri* (1954) to *The Longest Day* (1962) to *Platoon* (1986) and *Top Gun* (1986). But some time after the 1980s, the popularity of the war movie began to wane. The last war movies to cross the $100 million line in domestic grosses were Roland Emmerich's simplistic *The Patriot* (2000 — $113.3 million), Ridley Scott's sanitized *Black Hawk Down* (2001 — $108.6 million), and Michael Bay's incredibly bad *Pearl Harbor* (2001) which pulled down an equally incredible $198.5 million. You have to go all the way back to Spielberg's *Saving Private Ryan* (1998 — $216.1 million) to find a movie that clicked with both audiences and critics.

A gauge of just how out-of-favor the combat movie is can be found in Oscar-winner *The Hurt Locker* (2008) which finished at the domestic box office #116 for the year ($17 million) in a field of 521 releases behind movies like *Astro Boy* and *Saw VI*. *Locker's* entire worldwide gross of $49.2 million was just a hair better than the opening weekend domestic haul for *Alvin and the Chipmunks: The Squeakquel*.

One of the most honest movies about front line combat to be produced during the WWII years: *A Walk in the Sun* (1945), based on the novel by Harry Brown, himself a veteran of the war. Counterclockwise from left front: Norman Lloyd, Dana Andrews, John Ireland, Lloyd Bridges, Richard Conte, George Tyne, Steve Brodie.

It occurrs to me that there are war movies most of us know: the classics (*All Quiet on the Western Front* [1930]) and the evergreens that never seem to lose their popularity (*The Dirty Dozen* [1967]). But then I get to recalling the not-so-classics; the small movies unnoticed in their time, the good-but-not-great flicks, the high-profile efforts that missed their mark in their day with appreciation only coming with time and retrospection. They pretty much run the gamut from the novel and unique to those that do the familiar, but do it exquisitely well.

1. *Men in War* (1957)
Directed by Anthony Mann
Adapted from Van Van Praag's novel *Day without End* by Ben Maddow and Philip Yordan

Like its worn-out infantrymen, *Men* does not cry out in anguish nor anger, but is, rather, a sigh of grim resignation.

Few war movies have ever distilled combat to such an elemental level. Although a title card at the beginning of the film tells us this is Korea in 1950, the war and the parties involved don't matter. In fact, Mann largely keeps the enemy off-screen because while this is a movie set in Korea, it's not about Korea. It's about all men in every war. There are no causes, no patriots, no heroes, no reasons…nothing beyond making it to the end of the day alive. Maddow/Yordan's simple story of a platoon's day-long walk to illusory safety reminds one of the WW II classic *A Walk in the Sun* (1945) crossbred with the legend of The Flying Dutchman; these men seem damned to an eternity of marching from nowhere to nowhere, with nothing but a dozen different kinds of death lying in wait, melded into the seemingly deserted country around them.

Robert Ryan, at his world-weariest, commands a cut off, decimated platoon he's trying to lead through hostile country to the supposed haven of an American-held hill. He hooks up with a renegade sergeant (Aldo Ray) working to get his shell-shocked commander out of the war zone. Ryan is a humanist, pledged to getting at least one of his men back alive. Ray is an ugly combination of brutal survivor's instincts and equally brutal killer's instincts, pledged only to himself and his beloved colonel. Between them are a dwindling number of men looking to this Jekyll/Hyde coupling to get them home.

Deliberately paced, intentionally episodic, supported by an artfully thin Elmer Bernstein score, Men feels both realistic and ethereal (a friend of mine hit it on the head when he said, "It almost feels like a *Twilight Zone* episode), literal and poetic. There are no great actions: wind in the tall grass turns out to be an enemy creeper; a tired soldier walking through woods stumbles and finds himself staring at the detonator of a mine poking up through the carpet of fallen leaves.

When Ryan has to face the fact that the hill they've struggled toward all day is occupied by the enemy, his commander's reserve finally falters and he spouts the truth of his unit's damnation: "Battalion doesn't exist. Regiment doesn't exist. Command HQ doesn't exist. The U.S.A. doesn't exist. We're the only ones left to fight this war." And then somehow, he pulls himself together to plan an assault on the hill with his few remaining men for no other reason than, "We've got no place else to go."

The combat story reduced to eternal elementals: Anthony Mann's *Men in War* (1957). Left to right: Aldo Ray, Robert Ray, L.Q. Jones.

2. *Attack!* (1957)
Directed by Robert Aldrich
Adapted from James Poe's play *The Fragile Fox* by Norman Brooks

If *Men in War* is a resigned sigh, the WW II-set *Attack!* is an hysterical scream of rage. *Men in War* is combat at its most elemental; *Attack!* is a three-ring nightmare of self-interest, revenge, loyalty, and cowardice elevated to manic levels by the life-and-death pressures of combat.

Eddie Albert is Cooney, a spineless company commander who has already cost the lives of one of platoon leader Costa's (Jack Palance) squads. Shielding Cooney is battalion CO Bartlett (Lee Marvin) looking to curry favor with Cooney's politically powerful father back home. Trying to keep all the excesses in check is company exec Woodruff (William Smithers) who gains a promise from Bartlett that with the war so close to ending, Cooney's outfit will probably never see combat again.

But it's December 1944, and the Germans' surprise Ardennes offensive – what will come to be called The Battle of the Bulge – puts Cooney's company literally under the gun one more time. Again, Cooney falters, and, again, costs Costa men. The story comes to a bitter head in a shadowy basement as rabidly vengeful Costa, his arm mangled by a German tank, finds Cooney hiding with Woodruff and other company survivors as the enemy occupies the town above. Costa is slowly bleeding to death, emboldening the gutless Cooney who smirks and giggles as he nudges a pistol just out of reach of the belly-crawling Costa.

The movie never lets up, not even in its closing image of the bodies of Cooney and Costa lying side by side on stretchers. Cooney lies peacefully, released from the pressure of having to be a hero for his father; while Costa, his body frozen in a silent cry like something from Edvard Munch's "The Scream," seems to still call for blood justice even in death.

3. *Hell Is for Heroes* (1962)
Directed by Don Siegel
Written by Robert Pirosh and Richard Carr

It is the closing months of WW II and an under-strength squad is assigned to defend a sector facing the German Siegfried Line normally manned by a company. The squad's only edge comes in the form of Reese (Steve McQueen), a born hunter/killer who is only in his element on the front line.

It's a simple, familiar plot juiced by a disturbing mix of honest desperation and equally honest brutality. One of the most haunting sequences in the film comes when Reese leads two of the squad against a German pillbox in a nighttime foray which goes horribly bad when one of them, laden with a flamethrower, trips a mine. As Reese and the other man (Mike Kellin) make a mad dash for their own lines, Kellin is hit. Reese gets the screaming Kellin back to their lines but it's too late. Frantically, with his last breaths, Kellin, knowing he's dying and imagining his wife getting the news, gasps out, "Don't tell her it was like this!"

McQueen, not yet a major star, is a standout in a uniformly strong ensemble in one of war movies' first portraits of an adrenaline junkie who only comes apart when he's off the front line. He's all fire and ice dished out in disciplined bursts until Kellin's ugly death leaves him cradling his submachine gun for comfort, like a child holding on to his teddy bear. When his platoon leader asks him if he'd made the right call in making the run at the pillbox, McQueen, looking lost for the first time, forlornly says, "How the hell do I know?"

4. *Castle Keep* (1969)
Directed by Sydney Pollack
Adapted from William Eastlake's novel by Daniel Taradash and David Rayfiel

The Cuban Missile Crisis had taken us to the brink of nuclear war, the U.S. was, for the second time since WW II, sinking into another confused conflict for reasons so abstract as to be pointless to the people at home asked to support it, and the men tasked with fighting it. It seemed the only lesson learned from WW II and its loss of 50 million souls was to make wars smaller.

That postwar disillusionment stirred by the growing morass in Vietnam spawned a number of impressive novels which dealt with the absurdities and insanities of war with darkly comic absurdity and insanity, among them Joseph Heller's *Catch-22*, Kurt Vonnegut's *Slaughterhouse-Five*, and William Eastlake's *Castle Keep*. All were set in the so-called "Good War" — WW II – to make Studs Terkel's point that there is no such thing as a good war.

Movie audiences at the time didn't click with the film adaptation of Eastlake's novel; it's odd, highly symbolic, comedy-colliding-with-tragedy, often surreal texture was too alien a sensibility, and it didn't help that it's hardly a flawless movie. Sometimes it works too hard at being offbeat, the symbols have all the subtlety of a poke in the eye, and the film's whorehouse scenes shot in a '60s oh-wow style have aged into an oh-oh. But it's hard to imagine anyone doing a better job considering the challenges of Eastlake's novel with its episodic structure, multiple narrators, and dream-state prose.

Tuning in to the film's frequency means understanding it to be a WW

II fairy tale with GIs falling in love with Volkswagens, beauty v. war, caped princesses (a countess, actually) on horseback galloping through snowy woods. Burt Lancaster commands the motliest of motley crews, a group of GIs battered in both mind and body assigned to occupy a strategically-placed castle. If the movie seems to ramble through its first two-thirds, it still grounds us in its principals: Lancaster, the warrior incarnate; Patrick O'Neal, the art lover who would rather lose the battle than destroy the castle and its treasures; Peter Falk as the life-loving soldier cum baker, and the rest of Eastlake's bizarre ensemble.

Like the novel, the film finally coheres into a driving narrative line when the castle's occupiers find themselves astride the German line of advance. Pollack's battle scenes gain their power not just from their impressive mounting – and they are impressive — but also from their deftly blended undertone of the oddly comic and the poignantly heartbreaking. Imagine the final battle of *Saving Private Ryan* – but with jokes…bitter jokes that fit.

The film's strongest and most affecting scene, taken almost line-for-line from Eastlake's novel, has three soldiers dying in a rose garden, while the narrator imagines them still alive, entering the castle and marching "…up the wide marble stairs clear to the high alone turret on top where they could see all the way home."

5. *Murphy's War* (1971)
Directed by Peter Yates
Adapted from Max Catto's novel by Stirling Silliphant

If Castle Keep is a WW II fairy tale, *Murphy's War* is a WW II version of *Moby Dick*. The vengeance-crazed Ahab is Peter O'Toole's Murphy; the white whale a German U-boat which torpedoed his ship and massacred the crew before hiding out in the muddy waters of Venezuela's Orinoco River to wait out the last days of the war.

Few directors had as strong a gift for a sense of place as Yates, and he captures an edge-of-the-civilized-world remoteness which emphasizes both the global range of the contagion of war, as well as the pointlessness of this particular duel. Murphy may occasionally pay lip service to the war to the affable French caretaker (Philippe Noiret) he cajoles into helping him, but this is a personal vendetta and nothing more. As with Ahab, the collateral damage his obsession brings down on the innocents around him – the natives who rescued Murphy – only fuels rather than curbs his mania.

Murphy's defining moment comes during the third act face-off as he tries to ram the sub with an abandoned work barge, his wide, blue eyes filled with mad determination. The Frenchman brings Murphy the radio news that the war is over. "Their war!" Murphy spits back, "Not mine!"

6. *The Train* (1964)
Directed by John Frankenheimer
Adapted from Rose Valland's book, Le front de l'art by Franklin Coen and Frank Davis (as well as seven other uncredited writers)

WW II and the Allies are close to taking Paris. Paul Scofield is an aristocratic German officer charged with delivering a trainload of art looted from Paris museums to the Reich while Burt Lancaster is the emotionally exhausted, cynical leader of what's left of a Resistance cell ordered by their London handlers to stop the train without damaging its cargo. Ironically, Scofield – the looter, the brutal conqueror – is the one cultured enough to appreciate the aesthetic value of his cargo, whereas Lancaster sees it only as exacting a needless cost in blood.

Few war movies work in such heady philosophical terrain. What's a culture worth? Is there a value to the aesthetic soul of a nation? There is no clear answer, and the movie ends provocatively unresolved, juxtaposing the abandoned crates of Picassos and Monets and Gaugins against the jumbled corpses of the civilian hostages used as shields against sabotage, then murdered when they were no longer needed.

Frankenheimer, as good at action as at drama, plays this moral debate against some incredible pre-CGI action sequences, all the more powerful for our knowing that what we are seeing is exactly what we are seeing, and not a realistic cartoon generated by a computer: real trains colliding at 60 mph, an entire rail yard disappearing in a cascade of enormous explosions.

And yet the most powerful moment in the film is the dead quiet final standoff between Scofield and Lancaster, alone among the litter of bodies and crates around the abandoned train, and hovering over them that question which echoes so often among the best movies about men and war: was it worth it?

The war movie as philosophical debate: how much blood is a nation's cultural identity worth? *The Train* (1964) with Burt Lancaster.

7. *Secret Invasion* (1964)
Directed by Roger Corman
Written by R. Wright Campbell

If you're in a lighter, impossible-mission-*Guns-of-Navarone* kind of mood, holding its own against such big-budget *Navarone*-sized spectacles is B-movie maestro Corman's surprisingly engaging contribution to the genre.

Three years before action classic *The Dirty Dozen* featured an American special ops team of convicted criminals sent against the Germans, Corman/Campbell had Stewart Granger as a British officer putting together a team of elite convicts for a special op in Nazi-occupied Yugoslavia.

At first, it seems like a behind-the-lines thriller, but then the plot takes a turn and *Invasion* becomes a POW escape flick, and then, after another turn, it becomes a wide-open WW II actioner, with still another zig and zag left before its holy-crap! climax.

Not the least of the film's unexpected gifts is Campbell's touch with character, particularly Raf Vallone as a cerebral Mafiosi who passes up a chance at escaping the mission simply out of the intellectual curiosity in seeing how things will play out; and icy B-movie regular Henry Silva as a cold-blooded killer, shattered after accidentally smothering a baby, finding atonement through a final, ultimate sacrifice.

It's not great cinema, but it is, like so much Corman, infinitely fun storytelling; the celluloid equivalent of stopping at a back road diner, ordering a cup of coffee and a wedge of pie, then afterward sitting back satisfied thinking, "I know it was only coffee and pie, but ya know? That was damned good coffee and damned good pie!"

8. *Go Tell the Spartans* (1978)
Directed by Ted Post
Adapted from Daniel Ford's novel *Incident at Muc Wa* by Wendell Mayes

With the exception of John Wayne's jingoistic, simple-minded *The Green Berets* (1968), Hollywood studiously avoided dealing with the war in Vietnam in any major way from the time the U.S. committed ground troops in 1965 until years after the fall of South Vietnam ten years later. Do an anti-war movie, and one risked alienating the older audience and antagonizing the powers that be who oversaw media regulation. Do a movie supporting the war, and one risked putting off the young, draft-age audience so critical to the box office. And, there was the underlying question of just how open any audience was to a movie dealing frankly with a conflict that had left the national psyche morose and traumatized.

Made on a shoestring budget, *Spartans* was one of the first combat movies to take on Vietnam, using the experiences of a small group of pre-1965 advisors as representing the war in microcosm. Sometimes the movie is a little too complete, touching too many bases, yet it tragically brings home why and how the war would go so badly in the years to come.

9.   *Ulzana's Raid* (1972)
Directed by Robert Aldrich
Written by Alan Sharp

Hey, that's not a war movie! That's a Western!

Well, it is and it isn't, and back in 1972, quite a number of reviewers picked up on what the always subversive Aldrich was up to.

A fresh-faced cavalry lieutenant (Bruce Davison), advised by seasoned scout Burt Lancaster (don't ask me why he's in so many movies on this list), is charged with hunting down a small band of Apaches who've gone off the reservation on a killing spree.

It's a gutty, grim Western, but, in the early '70s, reviewers saw in Davison's stumbling idealism and white man's arrogance and complete mystification by the alien brutality of his enemy the same missteps and lack of understanding that was going on in Southeast Asia. Davison is first appalled, then enraged by the Apaches' wake of torture and murder, and then is even more appalled when he sees his own men vindictively mutilate the corpse of a dead brave. After Davison reprimands his men, he turns on the placid old scout. "Well, killing I expect, Mr. McIntosh, but mutilation and torture? I cannot accept that as readily as you seem to be able to."

"What bothers you, Lieutenant," Lancaster replies quietly, "is you don't like to think of white men behaving like Indians. It kind of confuses the issue, don't it?"

Ulzana's Raid is a Western, and is also a war movie, a movie about all wars, and how the moral fiber of the best men can be tested by the abrading effect of extreme violence and an environment where – as Lancaster's McIntosh advises the young lieutenant – "The first one to make a mistake gets to buryin' some people."

10. "Hills Are for Heroes"
Directed by Vic Morrow
Written by Gene L. Coon

Ok, I cheated. This isn't really a movie. It's a two-part episode of the 1960s WW II TV series *Combat!*, but I couldn't resist. Airing in the series' fourth '65-'66 season, it's a cast and fan favorite for reasons obvious to anyone who sees it; take out the commercial breaks and it is a hell of a movie.

In the early to mid-1960s, before Vietnam had grown into the national soul-breaker it would become, TV was still looking back nostalgically at The Good War with series like *The Gallant Men, 12 O'Clock High, The Rat Patrol, Garrison's Guerillas,* and *Combat! Combat!* was the longest running and most popular of the bunch, and arguably the best despite that, over the course of its five seasons, episodes tended to fall into a regular pattern. One of its two rotating leads (Morrow and Rick Jason) would lead the same squad of regulars on a mission into enemy territory that involved a lot of shooting and pyrotechnics, ending with our handful of heroes always triumphing over greater numbers usually suffering nothing more than a wound to the arm or leg. Over five seasons, some of the regulars must have been shot in the same arm a half-dozen times.

But on a fairly regular basis, the show would rise above its format, using the setting of the war for strong, sometimes affecting adult drama. And, maybe once or twice a season, the show would rise still higher and tease at reaching the profound. "Hills Are for Heroes" was one time they definitely made it.

It doesn't look like TV, it doesn't feel like TV, and much of that credit goes to Morrow who took the directing chair on this one to give "Hills" a visual panache rarely seen on TV then or now. And even though the same cast of regulars fills out most of the roles, Morrow gets a level of performance from them they were rarely given the opportunity to display.

Rick Jason is Lieutenant Hanley whose platoon is ordered to take two hills, each topped by a machine gun bunker, which command an important road. But the hills offer absolutely no cover and the crossfire from the two bunkers is murderous. Hanley's CO will not accept, "It's impossible." Again and again, Hanley sends his men up the hill, trying one clever stratagem after another, but all it gets him is more dead and wounded and more hounding from his seniors.

The men grow resigned, then fatalistic; they'll keep being sent up the hill until they're all dead. In his best performance on the show, Jason's Hanley, for the only time on the series, begins to crack.

Finally, Hanley's people do manage to take the hill but that doesn't end their Sisyphusian nightmare.

The triumphal cheers are still echoing up the hillside when Hanley orders his men off the hill. The situation elsewhere on the battle line has changed and Hanley's been ordered to withdraw from the hill.

"Remember it," he orders what's left of his men. "Remember every bit of it. Because we'll be back."

7 ANTI-007 MOVIES YOU HAVEN'T SEEN

December 20, 2012

Author's note: this was part of Sound on Sight's celebration of 50 years of James Bond.

The Bond franchise, which has been with us so long, has become so deeply entrenched in popular culture, that we often forget what it was that first distinguished the Bonds a half-century ago. *Skyfall* might be one of the best of the Bonds, and even, arguably, one of the best big-budget big-action flicks to come along in quite a while, but it's not alone. The annual box office is – and has been, for quite some time – dominated by big, action-packed blockbusters of one sort of another. The Bonds aren't even the only action-driven spy flicks (Mr. James Bond, I'd like you to meet Mr. Jason Bourne and Mr. Ethan Hunt).

That's not to take anything away from the superb entertainment *Skyfall* is, or the sentimentally treasured place the Bonds hold. It's only to say that where there was once just the one, there are now many.

The dawn of the Bonds is now long enough ago that perhaps that's been forgotten, at least certainly by many in a younger generation of Bond fans. Everything about the Bonds in those first years was novel, unique, one-of-a-kind: a sophisticated, urbane, gimmick-laden, oversexed yet cold-blooded assassin jet-setting from one exotic spot on the globe to another to foil some evil grand-scale plot by an operatic villain usually in a third-act over-the-top action finale. It may by routine now, but in the early 1960s, nothing like that had ever hit the screen before, and except for some wannabes (a spoofy Derek Flint; a trashy Matt Helm), it would be years before the Bond flicks had much competition in the action-driven blockbuster arena.

Part of what burnished the Bonds singularity was how deeply it cut against the grain of the typical spy movie of the day. James Bond may have been the first movie super spy, but he was not the movies' first spy; he was just the movies' first unbelievable spy.

****

Movies about intrigues and spy capers go back to the days of the silents. Almost without fail, however, they played out in a life-sized arena set in a real world context. The spies were not particularly super, nor the villains' perfidy all that grand.

World War I sparked the likes of *Treason* (1917) and *The Claws of the Hun* (1918), and any number of movies would be made about one of the most famous spies in spydom, WW I's Mata Hari, the first naturally enough titled

Mata Hari (1920). The early career of suspense maestro Alfred Hitchcock is filled with stories of nasty people skulking around trying to lie, cheat, steal and kill in the national interest in movies like *The 39 Steps* (1935), *The Man Who Knew Too Much* (1934), *Sabotage* and the singularly appropriate *Secret Agent* (both 1936).

The spy movie naturally enough blossomed during the years of WW II. In the wartime spy movies, behind-the-lines skullduggery was another front in the war against Axis villains, and spy movies maintained the same kind of moral clarity battlefield war movies did: Bad Guy spies extorted, blackmailed, bribed, and assassinated, while Good Guy spies didn't. Good Guy spies stole a few state secrets which saved lives, foiled some dastardly plots to save lives, and maybe fibbed a bit about their real names to save lives (their own). But, as spies go, they were a pretty honorable lot.

That changed during the postwar Cold War years. If anything, the new communist menace (with the occasional neo-Nazi scheme providing a little variety) was viewed as an even more ruthless and malevolent threat than the old wartime villains. In time, the Cold War spy movies took on a different tone from the spy flicks of the 1940s. As early as the late '40s, the Cold War was jelling as a war without end or triumph. It was move/countermove, foiling one plot knowing there was another gestating somewhere down the road. The moral ambiguity and ambivalence of the postwar film noirs found a natural home in the spy movie, digging in deeper and deeper into its substance year by year as the often covert duel between East and West ground on…and on and on and on, getting ever dirtier in the process.

Whether the postwar spy movie dished up its tales of intrigue with gritty realism (*The Street with No Name*, 1948) or high style and a priority on providing thrilling McGuffin-driven entertainment (*North by Northwest*, 1959), the mass audience was well-aware of the nuke-backed real-world players and the global stakes they played for. Even as a dashing Cary Grant unbelievably scrambled around the schnozzes of the presidential greats of Mt. Rushmore in *North by Northwest*, the movie was still grounded, in the collective mind of movie-goers, in the real-life parry-and-thrust every ticket-buyer knew was going on between one side of the world and the other.

The Bonds, in contrast, were a refreshing breath of topically irrelevant escapism, a spy fantasy rather than a spy story, and that, undoubtedly, was part of their early, airy charm. I love James Bond. Always have, and Daniel Craig has given me reason to speculate I always will. But sometimes I like something with a bit more real-world gravitas. A *Munich* (2005), say, or an *Argo* (2012), a *Syriana* (2005). Or even go back to the kind of flicks that inspired them.

If you're ever in the mood for the like, let me offer seven personal favorites of the kind of spy movies the early Bonds were rebelling against:

1. *Night People* (1954)
Directed by Nunnally Johnson
Written by Johnson, Jed Harris, Tom Reed, and an uncredited W.R. Burnett

Over a long, tense night, Army intelligence officer Gregory Peck wheels, deals, and connives to get back a young GI serving on the East/West Berlin border abducted by the Soviets, all the while having also to deal with a possible mole in his own network of agents and the GI's abrasive VIP businessman dad (Broderick Crawford).

Night People is a transitional step between the patriotic spy tales of WW II and the bleak cynicism that would pervade the genre by the 1960s. This East/West business is a dirty one, and Peck realizes the only rule is to win, but there's still a Good Guy echo of reluctance and bad aftertaste to his efforts. Reluctant or not, Peck doesn't hesitate to nearly poison himself, drug his double-dealing girlfriend, or fob her off on the Russians, all to get back that poor, hapless pawn of a GI.

It's a smart, ever-accelerating spy drama that shows a growing, unhappy awareness that this new kind of under-the-table war wasn't going to be like any other.

2. *The Spy Who Came in from the Cold* (1965)
Directed by Martin Ritt
Adapted from the John Le Carre novel by Paul Dehn and Guy Trosper

Ian Fleming had worked for British Naval Intelligence during World War II and out of that somehow came up with the high-flying, ultra-debonair James Bond. John Le Carre came up with a much different take on the spy game, one firmly grounded in his experiences working for the British intelligence services MI5 and MI6 in the late 1950s and early 1960s. More than any other author, Le Carre changed the flavor of the spy novel for a generation, and, in turn, the spy movie.

Richard Burton plays a burned-out, supposedly disillusioned British agent who defects to East Germany and ingratiates himself with his East German interrogator (Oskar Werner) but it turns out to be a ploy to expose suspected double agent Peter van Eyck. But Burton, too, is a pawn in an even more byzantine plot actually designed to protect van Eyck and disgrace Werner. Adding another unpalatable flavor to the mix is that van Eyck is something of a slime-bucket; a cruel, anti-Semitic mercenary, while Werner is actually a comparatively decent sort.

Spy is the first novel to catch that unsettling scent of postwar disillusionment; that the spy war between East and West wasn't between freedom loving democracies and oppressive communist regimes, but a basic, primal, anything-but-altruistic Us vs. Them fight for survival. The reticence of *Night People* is long dead and gone; moral quandary has no place in this arena. At one point, after his idealistic young girlfriend castigates him for setting Werner up for execution, Burton snarls back: "What do you think spies are?…They're a bunch of seedy, squalid bastards like me, little drunkards, queers, henpecked husbands, civil servants playing cowboys and Indians to brighten their rotten little lives."

3. *The Deadly Affair* (1966)
Directed by Sidney Lumet
Adapted from John Le Carre's novel *Call for the Dead* by Paul Dehn

Undoubtedly trying to capitalize on the success of *The Spy Who Came in from the Cold*, *The Deadly Affair* went back to Le Carre's first, more mystery-driven novel, with James Mason playing Le Carre's signature creation, George Smiley (here renamed Dobbs). Mason is tasked with investigating the suicide of a government official, but finds the suicide was no suicide.

In Le Carre's spy world, intelligence agencies are no more immune to all the pettiness, turf wars, jealousies and ego pissing matches of any other human organization. The personal and the professional often intersect, usually with tragic consequences, and *The Deadly Affair* is no exception. Dobbs thinks he's investigating a break in national security, while trying to keep his foundering marriage afloat, but the two have an unhappy nexus at the old German friend (Maximilian Schell) Dobbs had recruited into working for British intelligence years before.

It is that blend of the personal and the professional that, in some ways, makes *Affair* an even bleaker occasion than *Spy*, but like its predecessor, it's smart, adult drama all the way.

4. *The Ipcress File* (1965)
Directed by Sidney J. Furie
Adapted from the Len Deighton novel by W.H. Canaway and James Doran

Len Deighton's antihero Harry Palmer was the anti-James Bond (ironically, Harry Saltzman, one of the Bond series' co-producers, was one of the producers of the Harry Palmer movies). Featured in four novels, three of which were adapted to the screen (*Ipcress* was the first), Palmer (played in all three by then rising star Michael Caine) is a Brit soldier convicted of black marketing and arm-twisted into working for the intelligence services to work off his sentence. He's underpaid, lives a decidedly unglamorous, working-class life, has a lousy relationship with his boss, and looks like a dweeb in his much-needed glasses.

In this debut outing – the best of the lot — Palmer is caught in a turf war between two of his bosses (a deliciously effete Guy Doleman, and hard-charging Nigel Greene) as they investigate the kidnapping and brain-erasing of a number of top Brit scientists. It's an open question as to who is going to victimize Palmer first and most: his bosses, the bureaucracy on which they're all choking, or the enemy spies draining the brains of Britain's scientific elite.

By the mid-'60s, the kind of cynicism and amorality Le Carre had popularized had become de rigueur for the spy story, and Deighton and his adapters exercise it as well as anybody. It all comes home in a discussion between Palmer's two bosses. When Palmer is framed for the killing of a CIA agent, his chiefs suspect the agency will look to exact revenge. Their opinion: that's Palmer's tough luck.

5. *The Quiller Memorandum* (1966)
Directed by Michael Anderson
Adapted from Elleston Trevor's novel *The Berlin Memorandum* by Harold Pinter

Quiller was a rather murky character Trevor featured in over a dozen spy thrillers. Played in this adaptation by George Segal, he's sent by an equally murky government agency to try to uncover a neo-Nazi ring in West Berlin.

Memorandum has all the earmarks of the typical '60s non-Bond spy movie: a grim, hardboiled tenor, the supposed Good Guys operating in a moral twilight zone that leaves one wondering just how good the Good Guys really are. But, what makes this a particular favorite of mine is Pinter's odd-rhythmed screenplay.

Pinter is to English what Mamet is to American; an orchestrator who works pauses and repetition to hypnotic effect. It all creates a sense of unease, of a bent world filled with crooked characters none of whom ever mean what they say, or say what they mean.

Except in one scene; the beating black heart of the movie. Alec Guiness is Pol, Quiller's handler. Sitting in a café, Pol explains Quiller's eminently disposable role. He sets two muffins down on the table representing two armies separated by a fog. Quiller, Pol explains, setting a raisin down between the muffins, is like a scout trying to spot the enemy without giving away the position of his own people. "That's where you are," Pol says flatly, "In the gap," and pops the raisin into his mouth.

6. *The Odessa File* (1974)
Directed by Ronald Neame
Adapted from the Frederick Forsyth novel by George Markstein and Kenneth Ross

A one-time globe-trotting journalist who provides novels like *The Dogs of War* and *The Day of the Jackal* with an in-depth, fact-based plausibility, Forsyth's *Odessa File* was one of the author's first hits.

Set in the early 1960s, Jon Voight plays a young German journalist trying to run down the hidden lair of a wanted war criminal (Maximilian Schell). Helped by Israel's Mossad intelligence service, Voight penetrates ODESSA – an organization which helps ex-SS men on the run from the authorities. In a neat twist, Voight is not the usual Holocaust avenger, but has a more personal reason for his obsessive quest: Schell had killed Voight's father, a German army officer.

Without diminishing the horrific slaughter of the Jews by the Nazis, Forsyth's bang-along thriller reminds one that the Nazi murder rolls didn't end with them, and, in turn, paints a portrait of an evil so ravenous it even turned on its own.

Curio: Schell's character, in typical Forsyth fashion, was based on the real "Butcher of Riga," Eduard Roschmann. The release of the movie brought attention to the real Roschmann hiding out in Argentina. Roschmann managed to escape the country and died three years later in Paraguay.

7. *The Doomsday Gun* (1994)
Directed by Robert Young
Written by Walter Bernstein and Lionel Chetwynd

Produced for HBO, this true story concerns arms designer Gerald Bull's (Frank Langella) building of a super cannon for Saddam Hussein in the 1980s; a weapon that would not only make Hussein a major power in the Middle East, but which would directly threaten Israel.

It's a morally infuriating story as the British and the U.S. turn a blind eye toward the project; the Brits because it's good for some U.K. manufacturing concerns, the Americans because they see Hussein as a check on militant Iran. And Bull is equally disturbing; a genius so focused on building the world's biggest cannon that he's willfully blinded himself to the malevolent purpose for which the gun will be used.

Backing up Langella is a particularly strong cast: Kevin Spacey as a caustic, seen-it-all CIA operative who is roused from his usual so-what·cynicism by the insanity of the U.S. policy; Tony Goldwyn as Spacey's naifish, overbearing boss who confuses moronic shortsightedness with Machiavellian shrewdness; James Fox as a British intelligence chief brimming with a Le Carre brand of pragmatic amorality; and Alan Arkin as a Mossad agent who sounds like the one sane voice amidst a gallery of *realpolitik* dilittantes utterly convinced they're much smarter than they really are.

Special Mention:

Tinker, Tailor, Soldier, Spy (1979)
Directed by John Irvin
Adapted from John Le Carre's novel by Arthur Hopcraft
&
Smiley's People (1982)
Directed by Simon Langton
Adapted by John Le Carre from his novel

The 2011 big screen version of *Tinker, Tailor* was a delight, but it just couldn't do what the more expansive 1979 miniseries did aired on PBS in the U.S. in seven episodes. The miniseries format allowed viewers to become steeped in Le Carre-created intelligence arcana, to feel enveloped by the same insular, alien world of his grand gallery of characters.

Alec Guiness beautifully underplays the plodding George Smiley as he tries to uncover a mole in The Circus (MI6), but this *TTSS* is as much about mood and atmosphere as it is about plot. Living in their hermetic world of deceit and subterfuge, it's easy to see where the twisted, moral vacuum that was the trademark of Le Carre's work (and those who followed his lead) derives from.

Smiley's People is a direct sequel to *TTSS* as Smiley continues to press home the hunt for the Russian masterspy "Karla," architect of the plot in *Tinker*. Like its forerunner, *Smiley's People* is a deliberately-paced, gloomy excursion through an espionage netherworld, and plays seamlessly back to back with its partner. Want the feeling in a nutshell?

Says one character to Smiley, "I'm still on the side of the angels."

Says Smiley, "I didn't know we had any angels."

THE MASTER: ALFRED HITCHCOCK (1899 -- 1980)

September 9, 2010

There have been enough books and articles on Alfred Hitchcock and his work to fill a library wing. Doubtless little can be said here about one of the most examined careers in movies which hasn't already been said several times over elsewhere. Still – and sadly, to those of us of a certain age — the director's familiar rotund silhouette inevitably becomes *less* familiar with each new generation as, no doubt, does his work. It therefore remains a worthwhile endeavor to stir the memory to remember why Hitchcock holds such a revered place in the cinema canon, and why 30 years after his passing so many in the critical community still widely acknowledge him as the Master of Suspense.

By 1950, Hitchcock had already become a force in commercial American cinema. By the end of the decade, he was the premier maker of big studio suspense pictures, advancing his position enough to become a recognizable brand, seen as synonymous with the thriller genre with his name on a marquee as familiar to moviegoers as those of the stars in his movies. The same circle of French critics who had developed the concept of *film noir* were so impressed with Hitchcock's mastery of cinematic vocabulary they included him in their pantheon of Hollywood *auteurs* as a moviemaker with a unique, idiosyncratic style imprinting a personal vision on even his most commercial movies.

Hitchcock, however, had a more humble view of his work, denying *auteur* status for himself: "When I'm asked how I feel about Truffaut and other French critics describing me as a metaphysician and so on, I can only say that it's very nice…(but) all these 'philosophical' theories hold no water at all." He was, in his own eyes, not an artist but an entertainer. His material was generally populist, his movies, particularly in the 1950s, increasingly directed toward the box office mainstream.

His commercial instincts were as acute as his aesthetic ones. Of the eleven pictures he made 1950-1959, two – *North by Northwest* (1959) and *Rear Window* (1954) — were among the 60 top performing pictures of the decade. Understandably, it is his work from the 1950s and early 1960s – his most popular films – with which he is usually identified, but, in fact, his career went through several evolutionary cycles.

In his native England, though he made a variety of films, even during the earliest years of his career Hitchcock had begun gravitating toward thrillers. With their restrictive budgets, his English work doesn't have the big studio high gloss of his later Hollywood films, but he was already demonstrating a unique technical expertise, and many of his recurring themes and tropes – well-mannered villains, accused innocents, ordered worlds tipping into chaos

– had emerged. American producer David O. Selznick brought Hitchcock to the U.S. for a string of – ironically – English-set mysteries including the gothic romance/mystery *Rebecca* (1940) and the courtroom suspenser *The Paradine Case* (1947).

His strongest work during his early Hollywood years, however, was done out from under Selznick's legendary controlling hand where Hitchcock could more fully express himself in more thematically *noir*-ish works like *Rope* (1948) and, one of his best films, *Shadow of a Doubt* (1943). Set in a small, sun-kissed town beautifully detailed by *Our Town* playwright Thornton Wilder (working with Sally Benson and Alma Reville from Gordon McDonell's story), *Shadow* is full of the moral muddles which are the *noir* trademark as a teenaged girl (Teresa Wright) begins to suspect the charming, worldly uncle (Joseph Cotton) she idolizes and who has come for a visit might be a serial killer.

With its contrast between idyllic small-town Americana and a cynical serial-killing visitor, Hitchcock considered *Shadow of a Doubt* (1943) a favorite among his films. Left to Right: Charles Bates, Henry Travers, Edna May Wonacott, Teresa Wright, Joseph Cotton.

Hitchcock's career took yet another turn in the early 1950s as he cast off the gloomy airs of his *noirs* to embrace color and the wide screen, and even dabble with 3-D in *Dial M for Murder* (1954). There was a simultaneous change in the dramatic substance of his work as well as he leaned away from the real world moral confusion and unease of *Shadow of a Doubt* toward stories with an almost escapist affirming moral clarity. His Good Guys were unquestionably good, his Bad Guys, despite their unctuous charm, inarguably bad, and clearly defined good, with rare exemption, triumphed over equally well-defined evil. He cared little for the interior lives of his characters, and he had little interest in stories reflecting or responding in any fashion to the circumstances of the world around him.

That said, there were noteworthy exceptions. The starkly shot *I Confess* (1953) deals with the intriguing moral conundrum of a priest (Montgomery Clift) who hears the confession of a murderer, but then, bound by the strictures of the confessional, is unable to defend himself when falsely accused of murder; James Stewart's ex-cop turned private eye in *Vertigo* (1958) is straight out of the *noir* mold of damned and haunted souls, tormented by his failure to stop a woman's suicide, then trying to "resurrect" her in the woman he meets years later who resembles the dead woman, finally discovering he's been a dupe in an elaborate spouse murder scheme and ultimately losing the woman he's become obsessed with a second time; Hitchcock shot the gritty docudrama *The Wrong Man* (1956) in bleak black-and-white on the locations where the true story of a musician (Henry Fonda) wrongly accused of robbery had played out; behind *Rear Window*'s front story of a photojournalist confined to his Manhattan apartment with a broken leg who suspects one of his neighbors of murdering his wife is a subtext of urban isolation, with Hitchcock (working from John Michael Hayes' elegant adaptation of a Cornell Woolrich story) flitting about several independent stories playing out around an apartment building's inner court, all told in vivid non-verbal vignettes framed by apartment windows – a compassionate mosaic of human loves, frustrations, and loneliness.

As a rule, however, the credibility of the elements which catalyzed his plots, and the reasoning of his characters and their actions were of little importance to him. For Hitchcock, what he referred to as "the MacGuffin" – a bit of microfilm *(North by Northwest)*, an assassination plot *(The Man Who Knew Too Much*, 1934 remade in 1956), an incriminating bit of evidence *(Strangers on a Train*, 1951) – was, in his own words, "…the least important…" part of the plotting. To the director, it was nothing more than a spark to get the suspense machinery moving and provide a venue for him to indulge his considerable technical gifts. The other *noirs* of that time were all about human frailty and foible, but *Rope* is less about the psychology of two young thrill killers than it is about Hitchcock's virtuoso display of technique in filming the entire picture in a single take (although Hitchcock's ambition was to shoot *Rope* in one take, film magazines at the time could only hold ten minutes of film, so the director choreographed the shooting to be done in ten takes with some object blocking the camera to conceal each cut as the magazines were changed, giving the movie the appearance of being filmed in a single 80-minute shot).

Double Indemnity (1944) and *The Postman Always Rings Twice* (1946) – two prototypical *noirs* – have simple spouse murder schemes triggering elaborate webs of moral, emotional, and psychological repercussions. Conversely, Hitchcock's *Strangers on a Train* (1951) offers an elaborate spouse murder scheme with little emotional resonance at all, and *Rear Window* conceals the banality of its spouse murder with an impressive studio recreation of the interior court of a Manhattan city block and Hitchcock's dexterity at moving from one peripheral vignette to another.

He preferred plots which twisted and turned and looped back on themselves not in any organic, natural, or even credible progression, but in ways which managed to deliver his heroes into artfully crafted peril. *Strangers on a Train* and *Vertigo* involve enormously elaborate methodologies to accomplish what adulterer John Garfield managed in *Postman* with a simple conk on Cecil Kellaway's head. The espionage/chase plot of *North by Northwest* was so tangled, even bewildered leading man Cary Grant publicly confessed during shooting, "…I still can't make head or tail of it!"

Hitchcock's stories deal regularly with murder, kidnapping, assassination, extortion, and assorted other misdeeds, but in an abstract, undisturbing way. He could compose a violent act for shock value i.e. *North*'s murder in broad daylight in the lobby of the United Nations; and/or for stylish visual effect i.e. the dying "Moroccan" in 1956's *The Man Who Knew too Much* whose make-up comes off in James Stewart's hands revealing the non-Arab spy beneath. Yet, for all this mayhem, the acts of violence in Hitchcock's movies are rarely violent. There is little or no actual brutality, nor does witnessing bizarre murders seem to have any lasting emotional effect on the "civilian" protagonists regularly sucked into a Hitchcock movie's intrigues. There might be an initial moment of shock, but then the hero resourcefully moves on to the next bit of adventure with little thought to or reflection on the trail of bloodletting left behind. Malevolent acts are simply another tool propelling the plot forward.

Any grim effects of violence are further undercut by the liberal exercise of a droll and often morbid comic sensibility. Said screenwriter Ernest Lehman, who worked on several Hitchcock pictures including *North by Northwest*: "There had to be a certain amount of wit…No matter how melodramatic the goings-on were, the characters had to have a sense of humor…"

Characters were "designed" for function. Hitchcock cast his heroes with an eye toward the innate charisma as well as box office appeal of stars like Stewart and Grant which compensated for the fact that, on the script page, his heroes had little life outside the central plot. Hitchcock heroes have labels – Farley Granger is a tennis pro in *Strangers on a Train*, Robert Cummings a thriller writer in *Dial M for Murder*, Cary Grant an ad agency executive in

North – but other than sometimes supplying a plot device (Granger must desperately hurry the playing of a match in a race against time with the man that, at that moment, is framing him for a murder) there is little of substance to their identities. Though the director often extracted compelling performances from leads and supporting performers alike, despite being accused of dismissing actors as "cattle," actors and their characters were just parts in his "...elaborate machine..."

The exceptions are his villains, and here he seemed to delight in providing a breathing space he did not grant his heroes. Yet, like his heroes, his villains are built for entertaining effect rather than believability: well-spoken, charming, witty in a black comic way...all in all, wonderful cocktail company. There is Robert Walker, the mother-oppressed psychopath of *Strangers* misanthropically popping a child's birthday balloon; Ray Milland in *Dial M* never losing his suave urbanity even while being arrested for murder, pouring himself a drink and offering one to the "guests" placing him under arrest; James Mason, the elegant antique dealer/spy of *North* and his weary condescension in dealing with Cary Grant whom he's mistaken for an American espionage agent – "Games, Mr. Kaplan? Must we?" Mason's silky, chatty spy is, said Ernest Lehman, a perfect example of the Hitchcock villain. However murderous and manipulative he may be, he is, said Lehman, always "...a gentleman about it."

In a Hitchcock profile, film critic Stephen Whitty pointed out that the director was often considered "...a cold, callow craftsman..." Yet even the director's detractors have always agreed on his technical mastery of the medium, a skill matched by few, if any, directors in American cinema. His unquestioned ability to capture the attention of an audience and subject them to exquisite constructions of suspense is best exemplified – from his work in the 1940s/1950s – by *North by Northwest*. Typical of some of Hitchcock's most entertaining pictures, *North*'s plot is one which trades logic for surprise. Yet Hitchcock keeps the increasingly tangled threads of his plot moving through his suspense machine in so rapid and stylish a fashion one never gets a moment to question its improbabilities.

Cary Grant is an ad man mistakenly identified as an American spy by a ring of agents of an unnamed foreign power led by James Mason. The spy Grant is supposed to be is, himself, a fiction created by the Americans to confuse the enemy. Grant becomes romantically involved with Eva Marie Saint, Mason's mistress who, it turns out, is also an American agent. Grant's interest in Saint threatens to expose the woman's true identity which she can only protect by feigning antipathy toward the fate of Grant at the hands of Mason et al. To save her, Grant pretends to be the non-existent spy the enemy agents have assumed him to be.

All the Hitchcock tropes are there: unpredictable twists in the plot (Grant trying to locate the spy he's been mistaken for only to discover the man doesn't exist), black humor (Grant, cornered by Mason's henchmen at an antique auction, escapes by bidding crazily to the point where the management has him escorted out by police), and a shocking murder or two. *North* also contains some of the most memorable set pieces in the Hitchcock *oeuvre:* a climactic chase across the faces of Mt. Rushmore, and – one of the director's most famous sequences – the crop duster scene. It is this last which shows Hitchcock at his manipulative best.

Grant has been summoned to a meeting on a country road cutting across an expanse of empty fields. There's a sense of expectant threat, but Hitchcock goes to great pains to visually "explain" there is no place in such open country for a threat to conceal itself. Grant watches first one car pass by from horizon to horizon, then another. The shots are long, relaxed, bordering on the tedious for the purpose of putting the viewer at ease. The first indication of lurking danger comes when a passing farmer points to a crop dusting plane flitting back and forth in the distance. "That's funny," says the farmer. "He's sprayin' where there ain't no crops." Soon, the plane evolves from background detail to hounding threat as the scene's deliberately restrained pace gives way to rapid acceleration and lethal action. Writes Louis Giannetti in his seminal work on film aesthetics, *Understanding Movies:* "Even with a visually uninteresting setting, Hitchcock's mise-en-scene…is exemplary."

Hitchcock's creative direction veered yet again with two hits in the early 1960s. Not only did the new work cut against the grain of his preceding films, but they flouted most of the conventions of mainstream moviemaking at the time.

In *Psycho* (1960), Hitchcock turned away from the high gloss of most of his 1950s work. Shot on a quick 36-day schedule in black-and-white with the unit from his *Alfred Hitchcock Presents* TV series, most of the story takes place at the decidedly non-exotic location of a seedy, back road motel. Unusual for Hitchcock, the film is character-driven, erotic, overtly violent, and simply laid out, the story's twists taking place not in a gimmicky plot but in the damaged psyche of shy motel manager Norman Bates (Anthony Perkins). Hitchcock shocked audiences by killing off his presumed main character (Janet Leigh) early in the story, then daring viewers to sympathize with a mother-smothered serial killer. Though it was reviled by critics at the time, *Psycho* was a tremendous success and, in time, would be reconsidered as one of Hitchcock's best works.

Breaking all the rules with *Psycho* (1960). Anthony Perkins and Janet Leigh.

He followed *Psycho* with *The Birds* (1963), his one, true horror film which pulls off the trick of being a monster movie without a monster. Instead of some massive, stalking creature, Hitchcock finds menace in seemingly innocuous gatherings of birds. Evan Hunter's precisely constructed expansion of Daphne du Maurier's short story lays out a favored Hitchcock paradigm: an insulated, secure enclave of ordinariness – the seaside village of Bodega Bay – descending into fear and chaos as the avian threat escalates in meticulously crafted stages. By the time Hitchcock was done with his audience, no one could ever look at birds sitting innocently on a phone wire the same way again.

Thereafter, Hitchcock's career veered yet again, but this time with less than glowing results. Going into the mid- and late 1960s, amidst the social turmoil of the time, the graphic on-screen violence of movies like *Point Blank* (1967), *Bonnie and Clyde* (1967), *The Dirty Dozen* (1967), and *The Wild Bunch* (1969), the in-the-street realism of movies like *Mean Streets* (1973) and the topical relevance of films like *Fail-Safe* (1964), Hitchcock's work seemed out-of-step, stale and artificial.

He attempted two projects which uncharacteristically reflected real-world milieus: the Cold War thriller *Torn Curtain* (1966), and *Topaz* (1969), an espionage tale set against the Cuban missile crisis. The results were widely considered unimpressive. The audience already had available to them James Bond derring-do at one end of the espionage thriller scale, and the informed real-world cynicism and Cold War weariness of John Le Carre and Len Deighton at the other. Measured against them, Hitchcock's films seemed hollow and forced.

He would have one more late-career hit with *Frenzy* (1972), a surprisingly graphic story of a serial sex murderer on the loose in London, but it was clear The Master's heyday was over.

Still…

Most of Alfred Hitchcock's pictures – particularly those from his 1950s/early 1960s peak — remain entertaining and exciting decades later. This may come, paradoxically, from their oft-criticized emotional aloofness. There are no topical matters to date them, no provocative elements or wincing brutality to alienate or distance an audience. Emotionally superficial, morally simplistic, yet wonderfully crafted, they remain perpetually untroubling, reassuring, and infinitely entertaining. They are confections, set in a real-but-unreal Hollywood realm which, because of its very unreality, remains a timeless and eternal place of fantasy and fable. Hitchcock had been right: he had, after all, been nothing more than an entertainer…but a Masterful one.

ALL HAIL THE KING: STEPHEN KING MOVIES

September 2, 2010

Though primarily a literary figure, Stephen King has enjoyed one of the most successful symbioses between publishing and Hollywood of any popular author, if not in box office and critical respect (those trophies would most likely have to go to Harry Potter creator J. K. Rowling), certainly in terms of sheer *quantity.*

King's first novel, *Carrie,* was published in 1974, and the breakout success of *Salem's Lot,* published two years later – the same year the movie version of *Carrie* was released – elevated him into the major commercial publishing ranks and ignited a revived interest in literary horror fiction as a whole. King's ascension to bestseller status roughly coincided with a surge in Hollywood horror fare (this was, after all, the era of *The Texas Chain Saw Massacre* [1974], *Halloween* [1978], *The Exorcist* [1973], *The Omen* [1976], just to name a very few), and his early-won, long-held prominence in both print and film – with each venue reinforcing King's status in the other – quickly combined to cement his reputation as one of modern horror's leading lights.

Since the screen adaptation of *Carrie,* King-based horror movies have been so much a regular feature of studio slates it wouldn't be unfair to consider the King-inspired creep fest as a genre unto itself. Since 1980, hardly a year has gone by without a theatrical release or TV project connected to the author. According to the Internet Movie Data Base, as of this writing there have been some 120 theatrical releases, shorts, TV movies, series and mini-series, including sequels and remakes, built around King's novels, novellas, short works, and original screenplays, beginning with *Carrie* and up to and including over a half-dozen projects currently in various stages of development or production including adaptations of his most recent novels, *Cell* and *Under the Dome,* both tentatively scheduled for a 2011 release. "Stephen King" is considered such a brand commodity among the major studios that the novelist's name is not infrequently incorporated into the titles of screen adaptations and originals as a marquee draw i.e. *Stephen King's Graveyard Shift* (1990), *Stephen King's Silver Bullet* (1985), *Stephen King's The Green Mile* (1999), etc.

What makes King so representative of movie horror over the last 35 years is that the extensive canon of King screen adaptations and originals encompasses nearly every approach, trend, and permutation of horror cinema the studios have explored over that period, from the industry's 1960s/1970s surge in elegant, adult-oriented horror *(The Shining,* 1980) to the 1980s tidal wave of more modestly-produced shockers *(Pet Sematary,* 1989), and so on. Stephen King thriller movies range from the insipid *(Graveyard Shift* [1990] – giant rat preys on mill workers; *Maximum Overdrive* [1986] – alien force takes over the world's trucks) to the intentionally kitschy *(Creepshow* [1982] – anthology salute to the horror comics of the 1950s and 1960s) to the intellectually intriguing *(Apt Pupil* [1998] – disaffected teen becomes interested in elderly neighborhood man who might be a Nazi war criminal). There have been King thrillers which were exhausted rehashes of the familiar (werewolf tale *Silver Bullet,* 1985), while others were refreshingly novel *(Carrie* and its portrait of adolescent frustration manifesting as telekinetic catharsis). Some stories have been all "hook," hung on a promotable premise but little else *(Thinner* [1996] — nasty lawyer is cursed by a gypsy to become thinner and thinner) while others have been so effectively drama-driven one is loathe to even consider them thrillers *(Dolores Claiborne* [1995] and its front story of a fractured mother/daughter relationship).

Productions have been similarly variegated. Some King features have been prestige productions helmed by the strongest directors in the horror genre *(Creepshow*'s George Romero; *Christine*'s [1983] John Carpenter; *The Dead Zone*'s [1983] David Cronenberg), as well as some of the most notable directors in the commercial mainstream *(Carrie*'s Brian DePalma; *The Shining*'s Stanley Kubrick; *Misery*'s [1990] Rob Reiner).

Hollywood's consistent interest in the "Stephen King" genre is understandable beyond the obvious hope the brand will bring a built-in fan base to movie houses. King's stories are mainstream-friendly as they are often clearly-defined morality tales with boldfaced villains and Everyman heroes who find some deep, inner, uplifting resource to take them to an ultimate triumph. As well, by King's own admission, many of his horror stories provide just the kind of grotesqueries – "…the gross-out" — which appeals to the horror genre's youthful fan base and its appetite for visual shocks.

Also appealing to Hollywood in much of King's work is his ability to take bankably familiar horror icons – vampires *(Salem's Lot,* 1979), werewolves *(Silver Bullet),* the undead *(Pet Sematary),* hauntings *(The Shining, Christine, Rose Madder* [2002]), paranormal powers *(Carrie, The Shining, The Dead Zone, Firestarter* [1984], *The Green Mile),* hexes and curses *(Thinner), Jaws*-like monster tales *(Cujo* [1983], *Graveyard Shift)* -- and revive them by marrying them firmly to recognizably everyday milieus.

King has a penchant for returning to certain story ideas and elements and reworking them into new but familiar shapes. Thus, the homicidal blocked aspiring writer of *The Shining* becomes the homicidal blocked established writer of *Secret Window* (2004); the haunted hotel corrupting its caretaker in *The Shining* becomes the haunted vintage sedan corrupting its owner in *Christine;* The Faustian *Needful Things* (1993) becomes the Faustian *Storm of the Century* (1999); the relationship between a young boy and old hotel cook with whom he shares a special psychic connection in *The Shining* becomes the relationship between a young boy and middle-aged boarder with whom he shares a special psychic connection in *Hearts in Atlantis* (2001); childhood bullies are faced down tragically in *Carrie* and *Christine*, more triumphantly in *Sometimes They Come Back* (1991) and *Hearts in Atlantis;* in *Salem's Lot*, a fatigued novelist returns to his sleepy town to find it plagued by vampirism, while in *The Tommyknockers* (1993), an alcoholic poet discovers *his* sleepy town is plagued by an alien force. Such recyclings have only attracted a Hollywood enamored of sequels, remakes and knockoffs, and which often seems less interested in forging iconoclastic successes than in cloning past ones.

Hollywood execs have no doubt also been attracted to the fact that most King theatricals have been produced for moderate budgets. Up until *The Green Mile* ($60 million budget), the average budget for a King theatrical over a 20-year period stood at a little over $11 million. Subtract the few top-of-the-line King adaptations from the roster – *The Shining, The Running Man* (1987)*, Misery* (1990)*, The Shawshank Redemption* (1994) – and the average budget over the same period drops to a lean $8.7 million.

While these elements go a long way toward explaining Hollywood's ceaseless mining of King's material, there remains something paradoxical about the major studios' fealty to the brand; a fact which, in itself, reveals something indicative about today's Hollywood mindset.

King's literary success has *never* found parity on the big screen. While, as an author, he has been a consistent bestseller for decades, the canon of King screen works can boast only very few major box offices success. Of 41 Stephen King theatrical movies released between 1976-2007 (including non-thrillers like the elegiac boyhood tale *Stand By Me* [1986], and prison drama *The Shawshank Redemption)*, 19 either fell short of breakeven on their domestic release or were outright flops. Most of the remainder were modest or mid-range performers with the average box office for those same 41 releases standing at a little over $30 million domestic gross per. Only four Stephen King adaptations over that same period grossed more than $60 million: *The Shining* ($65 million), *Misery* ($61.3 million), *The Green Mile* ($136 million – best performance of a Stephen King movie to date), and *1408* ($72 million). The record becomes even more uninspiring the more parsed it gets: only seven of these 41 features have grossed more than $40 million domestic; 18 grossed less than $20 million; seven earned less than $10 million. The most recent big screen King feature: 2007's *The Mist*, adapted and helmed by Frank Darabont (who had previously adapted/directed *Shawshank* and *Green Mile)*, turning in a disappointing $25.6 million box office on a budget of $18 million (Hollywood rule of thumb: a movie typically has to gross at *least* twice its budget to achieve breakeven).

To be fair, this performance rate may say more about Hollywood thriller-making than King's material. Many King adaptations pare down the pop culture texture and character drama which have helped the author connect so widely with readers, and, instead, emphasize the horror and gross-out aspects of his work. Going one step further, some projects seemed to have been picked primarily for their quotient of bizarreness and the grotesque *(Silver Bullet, Graveyard Shift,* and *Thinner* offering prime examples), rather than their ability to sustain a movie feature.

Still, despite a box office record which could only be described as erratic, Hollywood's devotion to Stephen King as a brand name franchise has been unflagging and surprisingly consistent over the last thirty-odd years, regardless of whether the industry has just experienced a King triumph or a string of King disappointments. In this, Stephen King movies are a testament to an industry dedication bordering on religious fanaticism to the concept of the brand name franchise. Particularly as time has gone by, the major studios have seemed less concerned about selecting just the right Stephen King property and matching it with just the right cast and director, then they have been in getting *anything* on a cinema marquee which begins with the descriptive, *Stephen King's*....

11 COMMONLY OVERLOOKED HORROR FILMS WORTH SEEING

March 31, 2012

When I was a kid, I used to love a scary movie. I remember catching the original *The Haunting* (1963) one night on Channel 9's *Million Dollar Movie* when I was home alone. Before it was over, I had every light in the house on. When my mother got home she was screaming she'd been able to see the house glowing from two blocks away. The only thing screaming louder than her was the electricity meter.

That was something of an accomplishment, scaring me like that. Oh, it's not that I was hard to scare (I *still* don't like going down into a dark cellar). But, in those days, the movies didn't have much to scare you with. Back as far as the '50s, you might find your odd dismemberment and impaling, even an occasional decapitation, but, generally, the rule of the day was restraint. Even those rare dismemberments, impalings, and decapitations were, by anatomical standards, surprisingly bloodless. If you were going to scare somebody, all you had available to you were mood and suspense. Storytelling. *Style*. *The Haunting* – one of the best and most adult haunted house movies ever – did it with some spooky noises out in the hall and a turning doorknob. Yup, a doorknob. Try to pull that one off, Eli Roth!

True, the early '60s saw the first "splatter" films: gorefests like *Blood Feast* (1963) from splatter master Herschell Gordon Lewis. But those kinds of sensationalistic bloodbaths didn't make it to my neck of the woods. For the most part, splatter was a rural drive-in phenomenon.

I think most critics agree the turning point was George A. Romero's *Night of the Living Dead* (1968). The explosive popularity of Romero's people-eating zombies cracked open the gore door to the commercial mainstream, and by the '70s, blood-drenched moneymakers like *The Last House on the Left* (1972), *The Texas Chain Saw Massacre* (1974), and *Halloween* (1978) permanently took the goriest gore in from the drive-in cold and made a warm, snug home for it in mainstream moviemaking.

Gore goes mainstream in George Romero's *Night of the Living Dead* (1968)

I think a more pivotal turning point was *Friday the 13th* (1980). Though the early work of Romero and Wes Craven *(Last House)*, Tobe Hooper *(Chain Saw)*, and John Carpenter *(Halloween)* was often dismissed as just another strain of splatter flick, the more perceptive critics saw that Romero et al had something more on their mind than just trying to jolt a young audience with a splash of red goo. Some sensed, in their films, a reflection of the violence and moral chaos of a violent and morally chaotic time. Others noted, sometimes belatedly, that *Chain Saw* and *Halloween* unsettled audiences more with a skillfully manipulated sense of dread and suspense and the *threat* of gruesomeness rather than with actual gruesomeness. But Sean S. Cunningham's *Friday the 13th*?

Friday the 13th taught Hollywood that you didn't need Romero's social commentary subtext, or Carpenter's gift for mood to make money with a horror flick. All you needed was a cast of forgettable young people, some dark woods, a serial killer armed with the contents of the Sears Tool & Garden catalogue, and then some appallingly graphic mayhem to ice the cake. The blood-letting hasn't stopped since.

It was at that point I feel like the horror film stopped being scary and simply became horrifying. I'm not saying some terrific horror films haven't been made since then. Just to name a few: *Scream* (1996), *28 Days Later* (2002), *The Blair Witch Project* (1999), *Shaun of the Dead* (2004), this last managing the impressive hat trick of being gory, oddly sweet, and hysterically funny all at the same time.

But for every *Scream*, it seems there've been more along the lines of

The Devil's Rejects (2005), *Dreamcatcher* (2003), *House of 1,000 Corpses* (2003), *Cabin Fever* (2002), *Saw* (2004 + sequels), *Hostel* (2005 + sequels) *ad infinitum ad nauseum* – so called "torture porn" which equates an assault of the grotesque with a good scare. Will they give you the creeps? Give you nightmares? Yeah, sure. So will witnessing a 10-car pile-up with the EMS crews scraping body parts off the pavement.

All of which gets me thinking about those flicks which did give me a serious case of the creepy-crawlies without necessarily having to rely on a tidal wave of Karo syrup.

1. The Abominable Dr. Phibes (1971)
Directed by Robert Fuest
Written by James Whiton and William Goldstein

Camp is about as hard a tightrope for a filmmaker to walk as there is. Lean too far one way and it comes off as forced, lame humor. Too far the other way and it falls into sheer silliness. *Phibes* manages to walk that walk without a quiver of imbalance. Fuest – who supposedly rewrote much of the Whiton/Goldstein script – delivers up an off-kilter funny-gross horror flick the likes of which you don't see again until *Shaun of the Dead*.

Vincent Price is the ingenious inventor Phibes, horribly disfigured in the same automobile accident which cost him his beloved wife. Phibes decides to take vengeance on the surgical team he believes botched his wife's operation by killing them one by one, each through some horrible application of one of the Biblical plagues of Egypt.

Phibes is a unique mix of the near-surreal (Phibes' palatial underground lair; part Egyptian tomb, part ballroom complete with automaton orchestra), gruesome horror (if you remember the plagues of Egypt, you know what I'm talking about), and some wonderfully outrageous black humor carried off by a rogues gallery of some of the UK's finest character actors i.e. Terry-Thomas, Peter Jeffrey, Hugh Griffith and others.

How gruesome and how funny? British cops looking at one of Phibes' victims impaled on the twisted horn of a brass unicorn head ponder: "How we gonna get him off this? You take his head and I'll take his feet. Let's unscrew him."

Phibes was a big enough hit to generate a 1972 sequel, *Dr. Phibes Rises Again,* which pushed the ick and humor both a bit harder and a bit further. *Phibes 2.0* has a somewhat less compelling story, but the horrors are horrible enough (how does the idea of a scorpion crawling down your pants grab you?) and the funny is plenty funny. If you like your horrors cut with a grim grin and high style, this is the double bill for you.

2. *Don't Look Now* (1973)
Directed by Nicolas Roeg
Adapted from Daphne Du Maurier's story by Allan Scott and Chris Bryant

Sparked by the box office success of *Rosemary's Baby* (1968), the late '60s and '70s became a golden time for adult horror stories; top-drawer productions made with top-ranked talent intended to be as compelling dramatically as they were creepy. Think *The Exorcist* (1973) and, toward the end of the period, *The Shining* (1980). One of the best while being probably the least well-remembered is *Don't Look Now*.

Donald Sutherland and Julie Christie are a married couple trying to get past the drowning of their little girl with a trip to Venice. They meet a pair of sisters, one of whom claims to be psychic asserting she's seeing flashes of the couple's dead daughter in Venice.

Don't Look Now is a brooding, melancholic story, as much about a marriage breaking under the strain of grief as it is a (maybe) ghost story, and it is that human drama which drives the story. Venice, usually thought of as one of the world's great romantic cities, in Roeg's hands becomes a gloomy maze peopled with dark forces and lost souls, and in which – as Sutherland's character says at one point – "Nothing is what it seems."

The movie's final twist provides one of those shocks that is both complete in its surprise, and, on reflection, tragically inevitable.

3. *The Night Stalker* (1972)
Directed by John Llewellyn Moxey
Adapted from Jeff Rice's unpublished novel by Richard Matheson and Max Hodge

Back in those pre-cable days, made-for-TV horror didn't have a lot of tools in its toolbox. If you were going to scare people with a TV movie, the standard shock effects – graphic violence, gore, etc. – were off the table. You were left with the basics: telling a good story, and telling it well.

How well did *The Night Stalker* tell its story? At the time, *Stalker* was the highest-rated TV movie ever with a 33.2 rating and a 54 share (it still remains one of the all-time top-rated made-fors). In English, that means over one-third of the sixty-odd million TV households in the U.S. at the time – and over half of households watching TV that night – tuned into *The Night Stalker*. You want a comparison? The TV universe has grown by more than one-third since then, but only absolutely *huge* TV events – like the Super Bowl or the Oscars – pull more viewers.

Darren McGavin plays Carl Kolchak, a sleazy, annoying reporter on the story of a serial killer plaguing modern day Las Vegas who evidently thinks he's a vampire. The more McGavin follows the story, the less it becomes about a guy who *thinks* he's a vampire, and the more about a guy who *is* a vampire.

The pace is brisk, and to make up for the lack of gore there are some nicely put-together action set pieces. Punching it along is McGavin, playing seedy, sensation-seeking Kolchak to the hilt, and never better than when he's working against his fuming boss, the great character actor Simon Oakland. Take this bit from the 1973 sequel, *The Night Strangler:*

Oakland, fed up with McGavin's having stumbled into another series of bizarre murders, begins mumbling to himself: "'Go to journalism school,' my father said. 'It's a good, sound, down-to-earth profession.'"

"Do you want to hear this?" McGavin nags.

"What I want to do," says Oakland, "is raise tulips for a living, but there's not enough demand."

The real *auteur* here is producer Dan Curtis who was sort of the Chris Carter of his day. Curtis had created the cult classic TV series *Dark Shadows,* then followed it up with a number of made-for-TV horror flicks (see below). But *Night Stalker* was easily his most popular, spawning a sequel (not quite as good but a lot of fun) and a short-lived series. While the series' monster-of-the-week routine grew stale rather quickly, it's often considered the precursor for *The X-Files* which, in turn, begat *Fringe*. So, even if you prefer your gruesomeness appropriately grotesque in the 21st Century fashion, you still might want to visit the grandpappy of them all and see this early bud on the TV horror family tree.

4. *The Strange Case of Dr. Jekyll and Mr. Hyde* (1968)
Directed by Charles Jarrott
Adapted from Robert Louis Stevenson's novel by Ian McLellan

For TV connoisseurs, *J&H* – another bit of Curtis manufacture – is an enlightening artifact from a period in network TV sadly dead and gone. The security that came to the then three broadcast networks (ABC, CBS, NBC) from their monopolizing the attention of 90% of all TV viewing (today, their share is a bit less than half) bought them the latitude to break up their routine scheduling on a regular basis with special events, original movies, miniseries and the like. *J&H* was originally aired over three consecutive nights in one-hour installments; the only time the broadcast nets preempt regular programming like that anymore is for the World Series.

And, it was worth it. Although shot on video, Jarrott filmed the story cinematically. For those who've only seen video used for three-camera sitcoms, you'd be surprised how visually accomplished this effort is, and how lush the physical period production.

In the many adaptations of Stevenson's classic horror tale, Hyde is usually portrayed as something animalistic, a monster rather than that dark, integrated side of ourselves. But in this shrewd rendering, the physical changes are subtle; it's the psyche that changes. Jack Palance – an often underrated actor too often cast based on his battered boxer's looks rather than his ability – carries off the dual role of the meek, well-meaning Dr. Jekyll and the manic, id-on-the-loose Hyde with aplomb. Palance is backed by an extremely strong cast of fine actors: Denholm Elliott, Billie Whitelaw, Leo Genn, and Oskar Homolka.

This is easily one of the best of the myriad adaptations of *J&H,* and also one of the smartest. This isn't a horror story for the Saturday matinee crowd or for the late-night *Living Dead* gore hounds. Curtis' *J&H* is a drama-driven tale of a man liberated and damned by, in essence, an addiction. A taste of that drama:

In the climactic face-off between Jekyll/Hyde and Denholm Elliott, Jekyll's friend, the wily Hyde tries to talk Elliott out of killing him:

"If you kill me, you'll be killing Henry Jekyll!"

"You don't understand, do you?" Elliott replies defiantly. "Jekyll deserves to die!"

5. *Bram Stoker's Dracula* (1974)
Produced and directed by Dan Curtis
Adapted from Bram Stoker's novel by Richard Matheson

Ok, last Dan Curtis flick, I promise. I would guess having scored so heavily with *The Night Stalker,* Curtis felt emboldened to take the helm himself and go back to the prototype: the 1897 Bram Stoker novel that started it all.

There'd been a long line of vampire movies before Curtis' made-for-TV effort, and an equally long line since. To name just a very few: F.W. Murnau's 1922 expressionistic grotesque, *Nosferatu* with Max Schreck playing the vampire as a hideous, other-wordly thing; Tod Browning's 1931 *Dracula* with Bela Lugosi's iconic performance in a movie that has, sadly, rigor mortised with age; Frank Langella tapping into the count's sex appeal in an adventurous but ultimately limp 1979 version; and then there was Gary Oldman chomping on the scenery as well as arteries in Francis Ford Coppola's overheated, FX-laden 1992 take.

But I give this one the Blue Ribbon. It's got all of Curtis' signatures: a handsome production, an energetic pace, a strong cast (Jack Palance as Dracula chased down by Simon Ward and, as vampire-killer Van Helsing,

Nigel Davenport). At the same time it stays relatively close to Stoker's original. This was also the first *Dracula* to wed Stoker's literary creation to the historical Vlad the Impaler, giving the count a sense of lonely immortality.

It's also, for its time, surprisingly graphic and even erotic. There's one scene I've never forgotten: Palance baring his midriff, then cutting himself with a fingernail so one of his female victims can lap up his blood and thus be bound to him.

Ew!

6.   *The Changeling* (1980)
Directed by Peter Medak
Written by Russell Hunter, William Gray and Diana Maddox

The elements are familiar: a big, old house with a sketchy history, strange noises in the night, a mysterious sealed room, a very nasty decades-old secret, clue-furnishing psychics, a psychologically damaged hero. But Medak — ably supported by cinematographer John Coquiilon and editor Lilla Pedersen, and working with a rather smart script and a strong cast – executes so exceptionally well, that even if *Changeling* feels a bit been-there/done-that, most other haunted house stories still seem like poor relations.

George C. Scott is a composer who rents a rambling country house as a place both to work and to retreat a bit from the world as he tries to grapple with the recent death of his wife and daughter in an accident. But soon there are strange goings-on in the house; signs of some past, buried tragedy, and it is Scott's wounded nature which seems to make him susceptible to the message.

While there's a strong dramatic line – Scott trying to heal his own wounds by healing those of a soul not at rest — *The Changeling* is all about mood, and as Scott slowly peels back one layer of mystery after another to find the truth of the house, that mood becomes all the more oppressive.

One of the best examples in the film of how Medak recharges the familiar is a scene with a medium. She tries to contact the spirit world through "automatic writing," asking her questions as she scribbles on one piece of paper after another, the scribbles taking rough shape as words as the spirits respond through her. The questions are asked in a soft drone, there is no other sound in the room other than that of her pencil on the paper, the shuffle of sheets as her assistant pulls away one full page and feeds another in under her ever-moving pencil. The subtle sounds, the regular pace of the page shifting are all slowly, subtly unnerving, building to a sudden climax as the medium frantically begins scribbling a page-filling "HELP" over and over and over.

7. *I Bury the Living* (1958)
Directed by Albert Band
Written by Louis Garfinkle

Despite its lurid title, this is a neat little gem of a psychological horror story starring Richard Boone as the newly-elected director of a cemetery who comes to think he can cause the deaths of those who own plots in the graveyard.

Boone, in one of his few leading roles, catches just the right tone of a man haunted by what he knows is incredible but seems to be true nonetheless, and Band – normally a director of low-budget throw-away sci fi and horror – is surprisingly deft here at walking the line between suggesting the supernatural, or an equally grim but mortal explanation. What Robert Wise did with a doorknob in *The Haunting*, here Band pulls off with a map of the cemetery – almost a face taunting the tortured Boone with an unsaid, "But you know it's true!"

8. *The Body Snatcher* (1945)
Directed by Robert Wise
Adapted from Robert Louis Stevenson's short story by Philip MacDonald and Val Lewton

The Body Snatcher was just one of a crop of moody drama-driven horror tales turned out at RKO in the '40s by legendary producer Val Lewton. Lewton's unit turned out to be a training ground for some of RKO's future directorial luminaries, like Wise and Jacques Tourneur (who would go on to direct the classic *noir, Out of the Past* [1947]). Made on small budgets, all of Lewton's horror relied on atmosphere, style, and literate scripts. *Body Snatcher* is arguably the best of the bunch.

Loosely based on the 19th century Burke & Hare murders, Boris Karloff is a carriage driver providing corpses for Doctor Henry Daniell so that he can perfect his surgical techniques. When circumstance no longer provides enough cadavers for Karloff, he gives misfortune a little help. Daniell tries not to think about where these uncomfortably fresh bodies are coming from until one comes across his table that he recognizes.

In truth, *The Body Snatcher* is less a horror story than a brooding drama about two men, neither particularly evil, who become corrupted by their mutual needs and weaknesses. That dynamic gradually pushes the men to reversed roles, where the servant becomes the master.

In the movie's best scene, Daniell begs Karloff to leave him be, and demands to know why he won't do so. Replies Karloff, "I am a small man, a humble man. Being poor I have had to do much that I did not want to do. But so long as the great Dr. McFarlane comes to my whistle, that long am I a man. If I have not that, then I have nothing. Then I am only a cabman and a grave robber. You'll never get rid of me..."

9. *Ritual of Evil* (1970)
Directed by Robert Day
Written by Robert Presnell, Jr., and Richard Alan Simmons

This made-for-TV flick is actually a sequel to *Fear No Evil* (1969), which, I confess, I have not seen. Both feature Louis Jourdin as a psychiatrist specializing in the occult. In *Ritual* he's looking into the death of one of his patients, and the deeper he probes, the more it appears the woman's death might be connected to a cabal of devil worshipers.

It is not a particularly novel movie, but an adult story told with style delivering its sense of the creeps not through shocks but through an increasingly pervasive feeling that something dark is at work. A fun watch late at night...with the lights on.

10. *Curse of the Demon* aka *Night of the Demon* (1957)
Directed by Jacques Tourneur
Adapted from M.R. James' story, "Casting the Runes,"
by Charles Bennett, Hal E. Chester, and Cy Endfield

After Tourneur left RKO, he spent the 1950s as a freelance director, but his output was never quite as consistent as it had been when he had been one of RKO's house directors. *Curse of the Demon,* however — a return to his horror roots -- comes damned close.

Dana Andrews is an American psychologist come to London to expose fraudulent (he thinks) devil-worshipper Niall MacGinnis. You probably won't be surprised to hear that MacGinnis isn't the fraud Andrews comes to wish he was.

Typical of Tourneur's work, the strength of *Curse* is in his ability to unsettle an audience with mood, inference, suggestion. In fact, the weakest part of the movie is during its climax when the demon MacGinnis has been unleashing on people is finally revealed. It's such a criminally bad effect it comes close to eclipsing the previous ninety-odd minutes of carefully constructed dread and suspense, of MacGinnis' hypnotic performance, of a strong, smart script...I said "comes close," but not quite. This is still worth a watch, even though that ending comes with a caution Dana Andrews utters at one point: "Maybe it's better not to know."

11. *Below* (2002)
Directed by David Twohy
Written by Lucas Sussman, Darren Aronofsky, and David Twohy

Full disclosure: this is not a great horror film. It's not even a particularly good horror film. It is, however, two-thirds a terrific war movie. There's so much to like about *Below* that even with its weaknesses in mind, I couldn't convince myself not to include it.

It's the North Atlantic, World War II, and three survivors from a torpedoed British hospital ship are brought aboard an American submarine commanded by Bruce Greenwood. One of the survivors, a nurse (Olivia Williams) comes to suspect – rightly, as it turns out – that the senior officers on the sub are concealing a big, dark secret connected to the badly explained death of the boat's original commander.

Up until the story becomes overtaken by supernatural events, Twohy & Co. render one of the strongest portraits of wartime sub life since *Das Boot* (1981): the close quarters, the lack of privacy, the particular terror of a depth charge attack portrayed as vividly as I've ever seen it. The most frightening parts of *Below* are the all-too-real combat sequences against which the later spooky goings-on can't hold a candle.

Twohy is also working with a universally strong ensemble led by Greenwood and including Holt McCallany, Dexter Fletcher, Nick Chinlund, Scott Foley, Zach Galifianakis, Jason Flemyng. Even the smallest of parts ring true.

The underlying mystery is potent enough, and it's hard not to wonder — a bit ruefully considering how well-executed so much of the movie is – about the movie this could've been if those concerned had found a natural way to tell their story about good men damned by trying to cover up one natural but tragic mistake.

UNDER THE RADAR: ROGER CORMAN

September 21, 2010

There have always been moviemakers who operated just outside the major studio spotlight: showmen, hucksters, exploiters working on small budgets. Before the advent of home video and the multiplex, they could sometimes be found hand-carrying their single print from one movie house to another. Post-World War II, many of them found small, survivable niches specializing in the kinds of material – mostly horror, chillers, and science fiction – which could always find a ready home with the burgeoning youth audience. There were some whose ability to spin their thread-bare, pulp fiction-caliber productions into a small but lucrative box office return was so exceptional they came to be looked upon as masters of cinema's minor leagues, *maestros* of the "B"-movie. Among them were producers like William Allan and Sam Katzman, writer/producer/director William Castle, directors Edgar G. Ulmer and Bert I. Gordon, producing partners James H. Nicholson and Samuel Z. Arkoff, and the man often referred to as the King of the Bs, writer/producer/director Roger Corman.

Corman has outlasted everyone in his generation of drive-in/grindhouse circuit peers and is still turning out films today (Syfy channel will soon be premiering his latest: *Sharktopus*). The sheer bulk of his output – over 300 movies produced since the 1950s of which he's directed more than 50, all endlessly recycled on DVD and cable – has kept his oldies alive for generation after generation of connoisseurs of low-budget thrills. Last year, Corman received the Academy of Motion Pictures Arts and Sciences' Governor's Award in recognition of a half-century-long career consistently marked with "…ingenuity, boundless energy and a deep love of movies." Next week, at the Fantastic Fest in Austin, Corman, along with his wife, Julie, will receive a Lifetime Achievement Award. In less flowery language than that of the Motion Picture Academy, Fantastic Fest's announcement may actually hit closer to the heart of every Corman aficionado, saluting him for "…(making) sure audiences have a blast at the cinema every time."

Corman became as famous, if not more so, for those who made movies with or for him then for his own work. In pictures he directed as well as produced from the late 1950s onward, serving their Hollywood apprenticeships on titles like *Boxcar Bertha* (1972), *The Wild Angels* (1966), *Dementia 13* (1963), *Teenage Caveman* (1958), and *The Little Shop of Horrors* (1960), could be found what would become the most prominent talents of a generation of American cinema including actors Jack Nicholson, Robert De Niro, Sylvester Stallone, Peter Fonda, Robert Vaughn, Bruce Dern, screenwriter Robert Towne, and directors Francis Ford Coppola, Nicolas

Roeg, Monte Hellman, Jonathan Demme, Peter Bogdanovich, Ron Howard, Joe Dante, and Martin Scorsese.

Corman had begun dabbling in movies in the early 1950s, but his career only began in earnest when he hooked up with legendary schlock producers Sam Arkoff and James Nicholson who were heading a company which became American International Pictures. Throughout the late 1950s, Corman ground out an incredible number of low-budget movies for AIP, most of them sci fi and horror titles. From 1955, when he joined AIP, through 1959, he directed and/or produced no less than 34 movies, many boasting more bombast in their titles than in their skimpy productions i.e. *The Beast with a Million Eyes* (1956), *Saga of the Viking Women and Their Voyage to the Waters of the Great Sea Serpent* (1957), *Attack of the Crab Monsters* (1957), and *She Gods of Shark Reef* (1958). Corman's incredible profligacy was maintained through an efficient production formula film historian Joel Finler describes as "…a sixty-minute running time, a ten-day shooting schedule, a minimal crew, an even more minimal cast (and) a monster in a rubber suit…". He shaved still more dollars off budgets by casting hungry young beginners (i.e. Jack Nicholson in *The Little Shop of Horrors)*, and past-their-peak "B"-players like Boris Karloff, Vincent Price, and Peter Lorre. To inflate the production values of *The Masque of the Red Death* (1964), he cadged sets leftover from Paramount's opulent *Becket* (1964).

His economic shooting style remains the stuff of legend. He rarely invested time in his actors, relying, instead, on the craft of the veterans who headlined his better work. Boris Karloff, who top-lined several of Corman's 1960s horror films, would remember, "If you asked (Corman) about advice on a scene he'd say that's your pigeon," while whirlwinding the crew through an incredible number of camera set-ups.

His speed in shooting could be blinding. *The Little Shop of Horrors* was shot in an amazing two-and-a-half days. He would often rush straight from one production into another to take advantage of locations and cast already in place from the previous shoot. In one instance, having Karloff on hand after shooting *The Raven* (1963), Corman quickly ran the actor through two days' filming on *The Terror* (1963) using the very same *Raven* sets. Karloff would remember Corman hurrying his crew through the *Terror* shoot "…two steps ahead of the wreckers…" bringing down the *Raven* sets (Corman had been in such a rush on *The Terror* that it wasn't until he'd begun to assemble his footage he realized the movie didn't make any sense; solving the problem in typical Corman fashion, he called back two of his supporting actors and shot them in close-up – the sets having been struck by then – while they delivered blocks of exposition explaining the plot). It's worth pointing out, however, there was a method in Corman's rapid-fire madness. To carry out his short schedules, pre-production was meticulous and thorough, so much so that as quickly as the shoots were executed, they were rarely rushed.

Despite the short schedules, acting ranging from the hammy to the amateurish, and often slapdash plots, what elevated Corman from among so many other grind-'em-out "B" purveyors was his ability to still turn out movies with a sense of visual flair. As Corman's directorial hand grew more sure, he was even able to pull off his monster movies without the benefit of a monster. In *The Beast with a Million Eyes* (1955), there is no beast – just an invisible force. *Not of This Earth* (1957) managed a genuinely creepy feel in its story of a vampire-like alien though the threat was nothing more than "B" actor Paul Birch in a business suit and sunglasses. His cinematic fluency and self-assurance grew project by project, and he became more playful with his material, working an ironic and often humorous social commentary into his movies. At a time when one low-budget horror movie seemed indistinguishable from the next, Corman became a drive-in circuit *auteur*, a cult hero to the teenagers who were AIP's primary target audience.

By the 1960s, Corman was confident enough in both his ability and his rapport with his young audience to convince AIP it was time for an upgrade. With bigger budgets, a gallery of a higher class of fading stars i.e. Karloff, Lorre, Basil Rathbone, Ray Milland, Lon Chaney, Jr., and perennial Corman leading man Vincent Price, Corman embarked on the work for which he is probably most fondly remembered, a series of movies inspired by the literary work of Edgar Allan Poe: *The House of Usher* (1960), *The Pit and the Pendulum* (1961), *The Premature Burial* (1962), *Tales of Terror* (1961, an anthology movie using Poe's "The Case of M. Valdemar," "The Black Cat," and "Morella" as source material), *The Raven, The Haunted Palace* (1963), *The Masque of the Red Death,* and *The Tomb of Ligeia* (1964), of which *Masque* is generally considered the best of the lot.

Some of Corman's Poes, like *Masque,* actually pillaged a number of Poe stories, while most took little more than the title and possibly a dramatic "hook" (as in *The Pit and the Pendulum)* from their source material. Still, to some extent, they usually managed to capture some semblance of Poe's feel for the macabre, and for a malevolence lying not in the supernatural or in bizarre creatures, but within the human psyche.

There are usually no monsters in Corman's Poe movies, other than the one manifesting itself in some fatal flaw in their central characters. In *The Pit and the Pendulum* and *The Haunted Palace,* the protagonist is haunted (supernaturally? psychologically?) by the actions of a morally corrupt ancestor. In *The Premature Burial,* tragedy arises from Ray Milland's obsessive fear of being buried alive.

The most dramatically ambitious of Corman's Poes is *The Masque of the*

Red Death. Price plays Satan-worshiping Prince Prospero whose castle is an isolated island of safety in a land scourged by a plague called The Red Death. His fellow noblemen allow Prospero to debase and toy with them to gain the safety of his castle, but Prospero reserves his greatest amusement for his attempts to corrupt a virginal village girl (Jane Asher) pleading for mercy on behalf of her father and fiancé whom Prospero has imprisoned. The screenplay, by Charles Beaumont and R. Wright Campbell, paints Prospero as more than a simple sadist or despot; as an essayist in a self-justifying malignant sophistry. When the village girl brings up belief in God, Prospero sneers back:

>**Prospero:** Believe? If you believe you are gullible. Can you look around this world and believe in the goodness of a god who rules it? Famine, pestilence, war, disease and death... *They* rule this world.
>
>**Francesca:** There is also love and life and hope.
>
>**Prospero:** Very little hope I assure you. No. If a god of love and life ever did exist...he is long since dead. Someone...something rules in his place.

Corman's use of color *(Masque*'s cinematographer was future director Nicolas Roeg) is, at times, stunning. Prospero takes Francesca on a tour of several small apartments, each done completely in a single color: purple, black, yellow, etc. A macabre story is attached to each, the most unsettling one perhaps being that attached to the room of bright yellow. Prospero tells of a man held prisoner there until the sight of sunshine – "...or even a daffodil" -- became repugnant to him.

While Corman's movies could hardly be considered classic cinema – or, often, even among the best of their respective genres – what continues to impress is how much dramatic muscle and directorial flair he could bring to his projects despite all their restrictions and even his own artistic limitations. A good example is one of his better contemporary sci fi efforts, *X – The Man with the X-Ray Eyes* (1963). Again, the "monster," as such, is the protagonist, in this case Ray Milland's surgeon experimenting with a chemical compound endowing him with X-ray vision.

Corman and screenwriters Robert Dillon and Ray Russell throw an AIP-typical sop to the young audience with a scene at a student party and a bevy of teen dancers revealed in the buff thanks to Milland's enhanced vision, but the cheap jokes and titillation are soon left behind. An accidental killing puts Milland on the run through a series of *Les Miserables*-like episodes as he looks for some safe haven in which he can make enough money to continue researching some way to control the visual ability which is devouring him.

He can't sleep as he sees through his closed eyelids and on through the floors of the apartments above him. Trying to rest, his vision is plagued by a strange light – God, he wonders, or far-off suns? He sees "cities of the dead," his x-ray powers stripping buildings of their concrete shells and their inhabitants of their flesh.

He takes a job as a carnival mind-reading act to make money, eventually allowing himself to be exploited by a crude midway barker (Don Rickles) who sets him up in a slum office as a "healer." In one of those pithy dramatic moments Corman consistently included in his pictures, Milland asks the sweaty hustler what Rickles would want to see had he Milland's power, and gets the repugnant answer: "All the undressed women my poor eyes could stand!"

In the movie's disturbing final scene, Milland, pursued by police, drives off into the Nevada desert and crashes. He staggers into a religious revival tent meeting, his eyes now completely turned a necrotic black. He speaks of visions of far off worlds smashing together. The evangelist preacher proclaims them false visions: "If thy eye offend thee, pluck it out!" The preacher's disciples join in the chant – "Pluck it out! Pluck it out!" – and Milland, with a pained cry, plunges his fingers into his eyes and tears them out.

Corman did not expand the genres in which he worked, and few, if any, of his titles could be considered among the best of their kind. He quite consciously walked a line between mercenary commerce and creative craftsmanship. According to Corman alumnus Jonathan Demme, Corman, with no self-consciousness at all, referred to himself "…as being 40% artist and 60% businessman…". At the same time, there can be seen in his work a clear delight in moviemaking. "My prime goal," Corman has said, "was to make movies and have a good time doing that…" while trying to do the best possible job no matter how little money or time he had to work with.

Existing successfully between economic necessity and his own modest creative ambitions, Corman proved budget has, at best, only a tenuous connection to good movie-making; that one could interweave entertainment with the threads of the occasionally, intelligently provocative. He trusted his instincts and his adolescent audience – perhaps the most fickle, least serious-cinema-minded of ticket-buyers – and turned out a succession of surprisingly entertaining and stylish fantasies, often turning what should have been disposable and forgettable teen fodder into– according to film historian John Baxter — "…the picturesque and the profound…"

10 (KIND OF) GREAT CLASSIC SCI-FI FLICKS YOU MAY HAVE NEVER HEARD OF

March 17, 2012

We know the greats; movies like *Metropolis* (1927), *Invasion of the Body Snatchers* (1956), *2001: A Space Odyssey* (1968), *Star Wars* (1977).

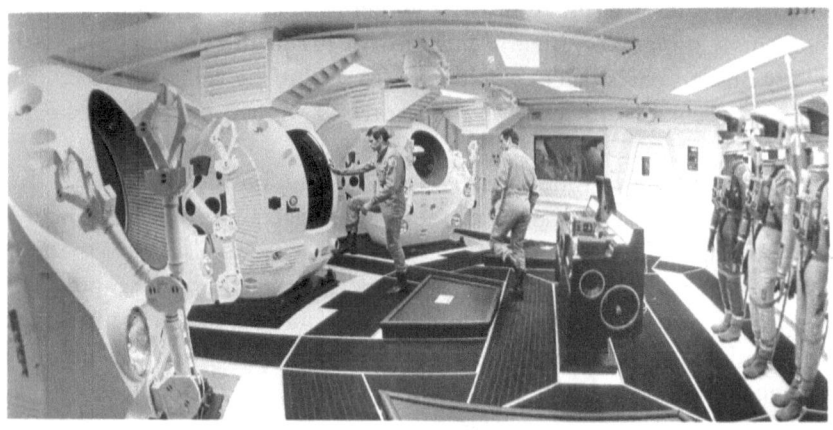

Science fiction as cinematic poetry: Stanley Kubrick's *2001: A Space Odyssey* (1968). Gary Lockwood and Keir Dullea.

And there are those films which maybe didn't achieve cinematic greatness, but through their inexhaustible watchability became genre touchstones, lesser classics but classics nonetheless, like *The War of the Worlds* (1953), *Godzilla* (1954), *Them!* (1954), *The Time Machine* (1960).

In the realm of science fiction cinema, those are the cream (and below that, maybe the half and half). But sci fi is one of those genres which has often too readily leant itself to – not to torture an analogy — producing nonfat dairy substitute.

During the first, great wave of sci fi movies in the 1950s, the target audience was kids and teens. There wasn't a lot in the way of "serious" sci fi. Most of it was churned out quick and cheap; drive-in fodder, grist for the Saturday matinee mill.

By the early 1960s, that wave had crested, and it wouldn't be until later in the decade – when films like *2001* and *Planet of the Apes* (1968) not only revived the genre commercially, but earned it an adult stature it had never before enjoyed – that Hollywood would, again, begin turning out sci fiers in significant numbers.

But where I lived in New Jersey, the space aged, monster-riddled, mutant-filled, alien-infested thrills never stopped. That great reservoir of 1950s/early '60s cheapies helped fill the hours for our local independent TV stations (being part of the humongous New York City market, we had three indies along with three network affiliates). There were even dedicated sci fi/horror slots on Saturday night when the kids were sure to be home which meant, come Sunday, we were together on the streets, laughing about the goofy bits, awed by the cool parts, and recreating them both. Saturday afternoon we got the new stuff in matinees at the Elwood Theater just a few blocks away, and Saturday night we got the oldies in our living rooms.

Every great once in a while, one of those made-on-a-shoestring memories resurfaces on TCM. Some are as corny as I remember them, some considerably worse. But some, well, I realize the reason the memories have hung with me so strongly was that somehow – despite their threadbare budgets, the often outrageous plots, and the painfully, plainly awful special effects – something clicked. Maybe a director, for all the limits he had to work within, showed a bit of style, or maybe it was the actors, B-talent to be sure, but taking the proceedings seriously enough to sell it to an undiscriminating young mind. Whatever; something *worked*. And maybe it's no more than nostalgia, but when I see them again, whatever it was that worked then still works for me.

And even if it is nostalgia, well, that's ok, too. Herewith 10 of my favorites that didn't make the great and near-great lists, but I think might still give you a little kick some Saturday night.

1. *Colossus: The Forbin Project* (1970)
Directed by Joseph Sargent
Adapted from D.F. Jones' novel *Colossus* by James Bridges

After all that reflective talk about low-rent sci fi cheese and drive-in fodder, I feel a bit hypocritical bringing in this slickly produced, intelligent, Computer Age take on *Frankenstein*. Still, it was a movie overlooked in its time (Universal, unsure of how to market the pic, dumped it on the market with little support dooming it to a came-and-went release) and undeservedly forgotten.

Colossus is a massive supercomputer created by Dr. Forbin (Eric Braeden) to handle the country's national defense. But Forbin has built his thinking machine *too* well. Given the goal of preventing war, Colossus calculates the most effective way of doing so is by subjugating mankind, threatening nuclear destruction if the nations of the world don't obey, promising The Millennium if they do.

What keeps *Colossus* from being just another computer-goes-berserk *Star Trek* episode is the smarts and style with which Sargent and Bridges come at the project (no surprise: Sargent would go on to win several Emmys and DGA awards for his work in TV and also direct that tangy paean to dysfunctional New York, *The Taking of Pelham One Two Three* [1974], while Bridges would move up to director with films like *The Paper Chase* [1973] and *The China Syndrome* [1979]). Sargent/Bridges lean heavy on the adult drama and avoid the cheap thrills to turn in a taught thriller about cold-hearted logic run riot.

2. *X: The Man with the X-Ray Eyes* (1963)
Directed by Roger Corman
Written by Robert Dillon and Ray Russell

Nobody got more bang on screen for his few bucks than that maestro of the matinee, the doyen of the drive-in, the godfather of grindhouse cinema, the King of the Bs himself, Roger Corman. *X* is one of his best.

Despite its obvious budget limitations (you can tell the overturned cheap sedan Milland crawls from is not the flashy Lincoln he supposedly wrecked), *X*'s screenplay by Dillon & Russell is an unsettling, sometimes near poetic platform which Corman ably runs with. *X* is a movie you'll still see playing behind your eyes when you try – unsuccessfully – to sleep that night.

3. *The Lost Missile* (1958)
Directed by William Berke*
Written by John McPartland, Jerome Bixby, and Lester William Berke

(* The director's son, he took over directing when his father died after the first day of filming.)

An alien missile becomes trapped in Earth orbit. The atmospheric friction from its incredible speed throws off enough heat to incinerate everything within a five mile-wide track. Conventional weapons are useless, prematurely detonating against the million degree heat wave. With New York in the missile's path and just hours from destruction, scientists race to launch a nuclear warhead whose blast can reach through the heat track and destroy the missile.

I don't know what the budget on this pic was, but when I was talking about sci fi cheese, this is what I was talking about. *Missile* was evidently made as cheaply as you can make a movie without it looking like some Ed Wood monstrosity. It's 70-minute running time is padded out with more Defense

Department stock footage than a "Why We Fight" documentary, the plot is held together with stretches of somber narration, and the bargain basement not-so-special effects include obvious paintings and puffs of smoke blown in front of the camera. And that's not even getting into the cornball turns the script takes, like a nuclear warhead escorted by a single jeep being waylaid by a bunch of leather-jacketed toughs. Seriously?

But even as a kid, I thought there was something...*haunting* about this modest little thriller. Maybe it was the unknown nature of the threat (we never learn the origin of this stray missile, or even if it's manned – I used to toy with that thought; a trapped crew just as appalled by the destruction they're causing as those on the ground), or its inexorability; its steady, unstoppable progression around the globe, a countdown of destruction ending with Earth a cinder. One of the times that grim voiceover (by an overwrought Lawrence Dobkin) works is when it projects the missile's timeline forward, counting down the days the major cities of the world have left before they're incinerated.

Or maybe it was its unique feeling of melancholy. I remember the people of Ottawa (the missile's first urban casualty) hunkering down for the missile's arrival, there being no time for an evacuation. One guy on the street hears some whimpering, finds a couple of lost kids, and huddles down with them to await the inevitable. It's also the wedding day for rocket scientist Robert Loggia (in one of his earliest roles); a wedding that never happens. Loggia has to abandon his wife-to-be (Ellen Parker) to take the "baby warhead" whose protective case has been compromised to the rocket base and install it even though it means exposing himself to lethal radiation. The movie climaxes with Parker standing alone in an open field, shrieking as she witnesses the atomic blast which will destroy the alien missile...and which signifies the death of the man she was to have married that day.

4. *First Men in the Moon* (1964)
Directed by Nathan Juran
Adapted from H.G. Wells' novel by Nigel Kneale

For whatever reason, people remember *The War of the Worlds,* they remember *The Time Machine,* but somehow this rich-looking, utterly charming Wells adaptation seems to have slipped down a black hole.

A modern day moon landing (or rather a not-bad 1964 guess at what the 1969 moon landing would look like) discovers that English explorers have already been there – over 60 years earlier! Space agency officials run down lone, aged survivor Edward Judd. As a young, wannabe playwright dodging creditors, he found himself living next to an obsessive, eccentric inventor (wonderfully kooky Lionel Jeffries) who invents a substance which can block the effects of gravity. They venture to the moon where they find an underground civilization of insect-like beings. The exuberant adventure takes a darker turn when Jeffries has to explain mankind's warlike existence to the head moon bug ("This isn't an audience!" Judd warns him, "It's a *trial!*"), and inadvertently brings about an extinction level event…through a case of the sniffles.

A strong cast, a still impressive production (even more so for being rendered on a fairly modest budget), special effects which still hold up (particularly stop-action master Ray Harryhausen's "moon cow" and master bug inquisitors), and the delightfully winsome details of a Victorian era trip to the moon make this an unjustly forgotten class act.

5. *Wizards* (1977)
Written and directed by Ralph Bakshi

This one's a bit of a cheat, coming from my college days (I can't think of it without remembering a certain pungent, herbal scent wafting through the theater; FYI, I did not inhale), but it does qualify as a neglected if not forgotten bit of fantastical fun.

If you know anything about animation, you know Bakshi is the man who single-handedly made the medium grow up with his feature debut, the X-rated *Fritz the Cat* (1972). Bakshi's career has had more misses than hits, though oddly, his biggest hit – an uncharacteristically turgid, animated version of the first half of *The Lord of the Rings* (1978) – seems to have been forgotten. Just as well because as ambitious as his *LOTR* was, and as provocative and controversial as *Fritz* was, I think *Wizards* is his most enjoyable flick.

Wizards is a wonderfully chaotic blend of *LOTR* fantasy tropes, sci fi, 1970s pothead grooviness, street corner humor, war movie clichés, casual eroticism, parody, satire, allegory, God knows what else. I wouldn't call it great cinema, or even great animation, but it's a hell of a lot of fun.

In a post-apocalyptic world, fairies, elves, and the whole magical tier of existence has reasserted itself on Earth. Two brother wizards, one good (the cigar-chomping Avatar, voiced by Bob Holt), one evil (Blackwolf, voiced by Steve Gravers) have already fought one war for dominion over the earth ending with Blackwolf's defeat and his banishment to the land of Scortch. To rally his army of demons and monsters, Blackwolf uses Nazi propaganda films dug up from the ancient ruins. Energized by images of a fanatical Hitler and the WW II blitzkrieg, Blackwolf and his minions again go to war against his brother.

With his limited budget, Bakshi relied heavily on rotoscoping for his battle scenes – drawing over live footage culled from movies like *Zulu* (1964), *El Cid* (1961), *Patton* (1970), and *The Battle of the Bulge* (1965) – but his additions (devil's horns on tankers, glowing eyes in the dark silhouette of a WW I pilot) turn what could seem like a cheat into a series of striking animated images.

What gives *Wizards* a feel like few other fantasies – a distinctly *adult* feel, by the way – is Bakshi's streetwise sensibility which reaches its defining moment in the movie's climax. Avatar's long quest ends with a face-off with Blackwolf. The austere, towering evil brother seems ready to zap away his pudgy little brother. Avatar flashes his sleeves with a magician's flourish, announces "Here's a trick mom showed me when you weren't around." He pulls an automatic pistol from his sleeve – "Oh, yeah, one more thing: I'm glad you changed your last name you sonofabitch" – and puts two bullets through his brother's heart.

Ok, it ain't exactly Tolkien or even Lucas, but I still consider it a great "Oh *yeah!*" movie moment. I can just see Avatar saying, "Hey, Frodo, ya don't like it? Then just kiss my dimpled wizard's ass!"

6. *X: The Unknown* (1956)
Directed by Leslie Norman
Written by Jimmy Sangster

There's something about Brit cinema from the '50s and early '60s. Think of *The Entertainer* (1960), or *The Loneliness of the Long Distance Runner* (1962). It always looked, especially in black and white, a bit grimier and grittier than American cinema, a bit tougher, more bleak. Even when it was sunny, it always seemed to be a damp fall day, the farm fields empty and trees bare. That same gray pall is at work in *X* giving it a marked visual contrast to its Southern California, antiseptically sun-baked American counterparts.

A radioactive, possibly sentient mud (yeah, you read that right) has found its way from deep in the earth to the surface, and it falls to scientist Dean Jagger, assisted by investigator Leo McKern, to try to destroy it.

Sangster was one of the engines behind the success of the legendary Hammer Studios. After a stint as assistant director, he turned screenwriter with *X,* then went on to write many of Hammer's signature redos of classic gothic horrors like the Frankenstein and Dracula tales. Despite its out-there concept, Sangster delivers a smart, well-built script. It may not be saying much, but if you're going to do a sci fier about thinking mud, this is as good as it gets.

Another refreshing difference between Brit sci fi of the period and its American opposite numbers: there's not a lantern-jawed hero scientist to be had, nor is there any curvy girlfriend or hotsie-totsie helpmate wife to conveniently turn her ankle in the path of the oncoming goo. Instead, the Good Guys are led by bald, middle-aged Jagger backed up by stout, rubber-faced McKern; both of them first rank character actors. Sangster's script, low-key performances eschewing the usual sci fi hysteria, and that raw-November-day look: *X* never feels as slight as it is.

7. *4D Man* (1959)
Directed by Irvin S. Yeaworth, Jr.
written by Jack H. Harris, Theodore Simonson, and Cy Chermak

Yeaworth and Simonson had previously scored a surprising success with *The Blob* (1958). Though they never had another hit as big (how do you compete with a pile of Day-Glo pink ooze?), this is actually the better film (which, I grant, isn't saying much).

Robert Lansing is a scientist at a private research lab. His brother (James Congdon), another scientist, takes a job alongside, bringing with him his own pet project: a device – which has only worked successfully once — allowing solid objects to pass through each other. Lansing gets the device to work, allowing him to pass through objects, but he can't control the process. It begins aging him and any attempt to touch another human being is lethal.

What makes this small-scale thriller work is Lansing. *Star Trek* fans might remember him as Gary Seven in the episode "Assignment Earth" which had been intended as the launch for a spinoff series which never happened. Lansing always had a quiet intensity about him, and no matter the material – as the lead in the TV version of *12 O'Clock High*, the mysterious "Control" in the series *The Equalizer*, Gary Seven, or here as a driven but not mad scientist – he played with absolute conviction. It's his performance more than anything else which sells this diverting piece of decidedly human-sized sci fi.

8. *Fantastic Voyage* (1966)
Directed by Richard Fleischer
Written by Harry Kleiner, David Duncan, Otto Klement, and Jerome Bixby

With sci fi and fantasy such a cornerstone of the current studio theatrical business, it might be hard to fathom there was a time when it was hardly the go-to genre for the majors. It was often bargain basement stuff ground out for the kids. But every great once in a while, a studio would see the potential in the genre to showcase the movies' ability to take us *anywhere*. And that's the case with this lavishly-produced tale about a journey into *inner* space.

It's the Cold War and both Our Side and Their Side have the technology to miniaturize anything: missiles, ships, whole armies. The catch is neither side has found a way to keep things shrunk for more than an hour. The one scientist who knows that secret defects to the U.S., but, before he can share his knowledge he's critically injured in an assassination attempt which leaves him comatose, his life threatened by a blood clot inoperable through conventional means. But a special team, shrunk to microscopic size, traveling through the scientist's blood stream in their itty-bitty sub, might be able to save his life from the *inside!*

Fleischer was a solid craftsman whose filmography includes A-caliber releases ranging from Disney's family adventure *20,000 Leagues Under the Sea* (1954), to the Kirk Douglas bit of sword-swinging swagger *The Vikings* (1958), to the provocative adult drama of *The Boston Strangler* (1968) and *Compulsion* (1959), and he's helped out here with an exceptional cast of pros including Stephen Boyd, Arthur Kennedy, Edmond O'Brien, Arthur O'Connell, and the always fun-to-watch Donald Pleasance.

I concede this A-caliber feature isn't exactly cheese factory stuff, but I include it here as a reminder of what pre-CGI Hollywood could do. For me, *Fantastic Voyage* still inspires awe when you realize this journey through the body had to be made with incredibly detailed miniatures, some amazing full-sized recreations of a "landscape" every bit as bizarre and alien as the surface of some foreign planet, and an enormous amount of technical skill.

No offense, computer geeks, but next to what these guys accomplished with hammers and nails, CGI razz-dazzle loses some of its dazzle.

9. *The Crawling Eye* (aka *The Trollenberg Terror*)(1958)
Directed by Quentin Lawrence
Written by Jimmy Sangster and Peter Key

Mr. Sangster is at it again, taking some sci fi hokum and making it play through sheer craftsmanship.

Forrest Tucker is a scientist called to the Swiss Alps by an old associate (Warren Mitchell) who thinks a situation might be developing on Mt. Trollenberg similar to one Tucker found (and was professionally discredited by) in the Andes several years earlier. Mountaineers have been disappearing or found decapitated, and seemingly stuck in place on the upper slopes is a radioactive cloud. What's hiding in that cloud? Surprise! Crawling Eyes (the title didn't give it away for you?) – aliens that look sort of like giant-sized, one-eyed octopi.

Alright, it sounds silly, but Sangster's script and Lawrence's disciplined direction give the film a deliciously restrained, moody build-up, and the actors, particularly Tucker, give nicely shaded performances. Lawrence really nails it the first time we see one of the invaders; Tucker has run back to the evacuated village to grab a little girl left behind, scoops her up in the lobby of the local inn just as the front doors come crashing down to reveal one of the veiny-eyed uglies.

The short money kills the third act climax and it's hard not to laugh at the stupendously awful miniatures, but up until then, you're surprised at just how well this creeper plays out.

10. *Rodan* (1956)
Directed by Ishiro Honda
Written by Takeshi Kimura, Ken Kuronuma, and Takeo Murata
(screenwriter David Duncan contributed to the U.S. version)

You can't do a piece like this and not include at least *one* Japanese monster bash. Made two years after *Godzilla* (and released the same year the U.S. version of *Godzilla* opened on this side of the Pacific), *Rodan* was one of the earliest *Godzilla* clones, the first Japanese beastie flick shot in color, and arguably the last one where the involved parties tried to take the goings-on seriously. After this, it was flame-eating flying turtles, and 12-inch high girls singing to giant moths and... Well, you know.

Out in Japanese mining country, a particularly deeply-dug shaft is bringing trouble: disappearances in the mine, mangled bodies. The authorities eventually find the mine has released some Buick-sized prehistoric insects, but that's just the start of this poor little hill town's troubles. Turns out the insects are, in turn, food for a pair of gigantic, prehistoric reptiles which have been resurrected in caverns beneath a dormant volcano.

Like the *Godzilla* prototype, *Rodan* has a disciplined, slow build up with a pretty good mystery going in the first act: people disappear from the area, a strange flying object is sighted high in the skies over Japan (one of the screenwriters was supposedly inspired by a late 1940s true story of an American fighter pilot who died in a crash while trying to pursue a reported UFO). Of course, once the Rodans reveal themselves, the flick looks like any other Japanese creature feature: guy in a rubber suit kicking the hell out of an H-O-sized model city while toy tanks and jets bang away at it with fireworks. Actually, all the city-razing and tiny blasting tanks are impressive in a chintzy, low-rent kind of way.

But the finale takes an oddly melancholic tack (again, just like *Godzilla*). The military tries to seal the Rodans up in their home caves, but the explosions jumpstart the nearby volcano. One of the Rodans is crippled and can't fly away. Its mate, rather than escape, flies circles above, the reptiles calling back and forth to each other. The volcanic fumes become too much for the flying Rodan and it falls to earth where it's consumed by flaming lava along with its partner. Over this, one of the bystanders provides an awed voiceover, something like, "And I wondered if I, a twentieth century man, could die as well."

Despite the toy missiles going off, the volcano looking like backyard fireworks, and all this pseudo-majestic drivel about how bravely the two rubber monsters are dying, there's still something, well, *affecting* about it… at least there is when you're 12, you're susceptible in that way that happens when you've stayed up too long trying to catch the end of the late movie, and you're still open enough to take the emotional ride with damned near anything.

The fun wasn't over when "The End" came up. Even before you stumbled off to bed, your head was already looking forward to that next-day get-together with The Guys; the one where you'd rehash the cool parts, mock the bad ones, then replay the whole thing out in someone's backyard under the summer sun.

RAY HARRYAUSEN (1920 – 2013): MASTER OF ILLUSION

May 19, 2013

The most honest magicians never use the word "magic" – they're illusionists; they make believable that which can't possibly be, and that's what Harryhausen was: a master illusionist who made us believe that his table-top constructions of fabric and clay and metal were massive, mighty creatures out of legend, out of fantasy, out of our nightmares. He was a master of stop-motion animation; moving his creations a fraction of an inch per frame to create the illusion of flying saucers toppling the Washington Monument (*Earth vs. the Flying Saucers*, 1956), a tremendous octopus threatening the Golden Gate Bridge (*It Came from Beneath the Sea*, 1955), or an impossible prehistory of cave men battling dinosaurs (*One Million Years B.C.*, 1966). When he passed, a generation of filmmakers who'd grown up watching his work at movie house matinees and Saturday night monster movie TV slots saluted him, acknowledging how his work had inspired them. We're talking the likes of James Cameron and Tim Burton. George Lucas said, "Without Ray Harryhausen, there would likely have been no *Star Wars*."

Born, fittingly enough, in the movie capital of the world – Los Angeles – Harryhausen became enamored of the possibilities of stop-motion when he was just a 13-year-old kid, sitting enthralled through *King Kong* (1933) over and over. Harryhausen reached out to the genius behind *Kong*, the legendary stop-motion pioneer Willis O'Brien, and eventually found work as O'Brien's technician on *Mighty Joe Young* (1949).

Harryhausen had already been experimenting at home with stop-motion, but possibly one of the greatest lessons he learned from his apprenticeship with O'Brien was that it took more than good animation technique to bring their little creatures to life; they had to have *character*.

Think of O'Brien's Kong, a combination of animal savagery and childlike mystification. Think of Kong standing over the prostrate T. Rex he's beaten in battle, not quite understanding death, toying with the reptile corpse's broken jaw. Harryhausen would apply that lesson time and again. Think of his Rhedosaurus in his first solo effort, *The Beast from 20,000 Fathoms* (1953), as it finds itself dying and trapped amid the burning latticework of a Coney Island roller coaster. There's a grand sadness to this creature trapped out of time and place slowly lying down to die.

If familiarity with Harryhausen's name is limited to aficionados, it's a testament to the man's integrity. "Modesty is a four-letter word in Hollywood, I'm afraid," he told *The Star-Ledger* film reviewer Stephen Whitty some years ago. "I never fought for credit…"

But even had he done so, on many of his early films there might not have been much credit to be had. Harryhausen often worked on small-budgeted sci fi and fantasy flicks like *It Came from Beneath the Sea, 20 Million Miles to Earth* (1957), and *Earth vs. the Flying Saucers;* matinee fodder for the kiddies in which Harryhausen's effects work was often the most – and sometimes only — impressive thing about them.

But he did work on some projects that were pure gold, and that we of a certain age count as treasured movie memories. My favorite – and the favorite of a lot of fantasy gourmets – was his 1963 effort, *Jason and the Argonauts*, which also showcased one of his finest pieces of work: a sword fight between three of the Argonauts and seven stop-motion animated skeletons. Those few minutes of screen time took Harryhausen four months to shoot, but see that scene as a kid and it stays in your memory for a lifetime. Harryhausen himself knew it was one of his best pictures, and always considered it his favorite.

Harryhausen retired after the 1981 *Clash of the Titans*. While the effects work was unsurprisingly impressive, too much of the movie seemed to be working overly hard – and unsuccessfully — to recapture the magic of *Jason*. Though the movie was a moneymaker, the bad reviews stung and Harryhausen never made another movie.

See his films today, even in this age of CGI marvels, and they still entrance. Sometimes the very illusion of reality that's the gift of CGI works against it. "If you make things too real," Harryhausen once said, "sometimes you bring it down to the mundane." The fluid, lifelike behemoth of the 1998 *Godzilla* can't hold a candle to the few minutes (which was all Harryhausen could afford to produce on the movie's skimpy $200,000 budget) of monster footage in *The Beast from 20,000 Fathoms*.

And even if you hold that CGI outclasses the old stop-motion techniques, that Peter Jackson's 2005 *King Kong* is more credible than Willis O'Brien's and the dinosaurs of *Jurassic Park* (1993) look so much more lifelike than Harryhausen's Rhedosaurus, you still have to respect – hell, be in *awe* – of what Harryhausen did. His work required he be a master engineer of miniatures, a master sculptor and make-up artist, an expert in materials and textures, a master model maker, a skilled cinematographer and lighting designer, and also possess an expert enough eye to match the movements of his pint-sized creations with real world settings and real world people. And in those days, folks, it was all done by hand; no computers to help.

Maybe I'm being overly nostalgic because I sat in theaters as a kid, slack-jawed with awe, with wonder, with the sheer fun of what this, in Steven Spielberg's words, "artist magician" accomplished with his little dolls and models. They were part of what made me fall in love with the movies.

And if, as I grew older, I couldn't help but realize some of the movies were silly or even just plain bad, it didn't change what they'd been for me years ago. Spielberg hit it right and spoke for so many of our generation when he said, on Ray Harryhausen's passing, "All those so-called 'B movies' were the A movies of my childhood."

Ray Harryhausen's creatures may have been able to fit on a table-top, but the magic he created on-screen was big enough.

THEM!

July 6, 2013

THEM! (1954)
Directed by Gordon Douglas
Written by Ted Sherdeman

In that filled-to-bursting canon of 1950s science fiction cinema, movies range from true film classics – like the Hawksian *The Thing from Another World* (1951), and that alarm bell about human desensitization, *Invasion of the Body Snatchers* (1956) – to cheapie craptasmagoriums like *Beginning of the End* (1957 – giant grasshoppers crawling over photographs of downtown Chicago), and *It Conquered the World* (1956 – "It" being an alien that looks like a devil-faced carrot with lobster claws). I'd go as far as to say the consensus is probably there's just a few of the former, and a whole stinking pile of the latter. But scattered (thinly, I'd have to say) between those poles are movies neither classic nor crap, but made with enough craftsmanship to be eminently and repeatably watchable. You know: just good, damned fun! One of my faves from that group: *Them!* (1954).

A small girl is found wandering through the New Mexico desert, mute with shock. Her vacationing family's trailer is found torn apart, her mother and father missing. Since her dad was an FBI agent, that brings Fed James Arness out to help local cop James Whitmore with the investigation. One thing leads to another and they find themselves confronted with a nest of 12-foot-long ants; mutants created by the first desert nuke tests. The nest is destroyed but not before a queen ant escapes and sets up housekeeping in the storm sewers of Los Angeles which leads to a bing-bang-boom climax as Army troops go head-to-head with the ant army.

Ok, in synopsis, it sounds like just another Giant Bug Movie (actually, *Them!* was the first Giant Bug Movie, and its success instigated a parade of giant spiders, grasshoppers, scorpions, Gila monsters, crabs, shrews, leeches, praying mantises, and even – I swear, I'm not lying – giant mutated bunny rabbits rampaging across drive-in screens). But a lot of what keeps *Them!* so easily watchable 60 years later owes a lot to screenwriter Ted Sherdeman (who took over adapting George Worthing Yates original treatment when the first screenwriter, Russell Hughes, died suddenly) and director Gordon Douglas.

Sherdeman (who was also the prime mover in getting the film made) treats the story about as intelligently as you can treat a story about big bugs, and shrewdly as well. The ants are kept off-screen for nearly the whole first third of the film which plays out more like a terse, hard-edged *Dragnet*-like police procedural than a monster pic. And even after, Sherdeman keeps his script smart…and witty.

As Whitmore and Arness accompany lady bug professor Joan Weldon through the desert nest, she points out how the ants secured their tunnel walls with saliva. "Spit's all that's holding me together right now, too," cracks Whitmore.

Sherdeman's efforts to keep *Them!* from being the usual Saturday matinee juvenilia would've been for nought without Gordon Douglas at the helm. Neither a great director nor a major one, Douglas was, however, a solid, capable craftsman whose later career would include respectable efforts like Rat Pack musical *Robin and the 7 Hoods* (1964), the *noir*-ish Western *Rio Conchos* (1964), James Bond parody *In Like Flint* (1967), and gritty cop drama *The Detective* (1968).

Douglas catches that tight-lipped, fast-paced *Dragnet* rhythm perfectly, and he also nailed himself strong leads in Arness and Whitmore (who'd already earned an Oscar nod for his supporting role in the 1949 WW II classic, *Battleground)*, backed up by such reliable Familiar Faces as Onslow Stevens, Sean McClory, William Schallert, Dub Taylor, a young Fess Parker (supposedly, Walt Disney's seeing Parker in this flick led to him casting Parker as Daniel Boone), and, in one of his earliest roles, Leonard Nimoy.

Giant Bug Movie or not, according to *Twenty All-Time Great Science Fiction Films*, by Kenneth von Gunden and Stuart H. Stock, Douglas gave the flick his best. The desert sequences were shot on location in the Mojave Desert in 110 degree heat, and the entrances to the L.A. nest were also shot on location in that concrete-lined channel that passes for the Los Angeles River. For the set of a destroyed general store, Douglas had the set fully stocked, then set his crew loose tearing it apart to get the right effect. And, while Douglas may not have a seat in the lodge of all-time great helmsmen, he did have an eye.

My favorite shot: Arness, Whitmore & Co. have finally found the desert nest by helicopter search and come upon the giant ant mound just as one of the bugs is getting rid of some leftovers: a rib cage which Douglas' camera tracks in its tumble down the mound to where it comes to rest among other bones and the skull and gun belt of Whitmore's missing partner.

Douglas is at his best during the climactic shoot-out in the L.A. sewers; frantic, desperate, wonderfully cathartic, it's a satisfying Big Finish delivered with no small amount of style, an especially commendable accomplishment considering Warner Bros. cut the film's already tight budget to under a million – scrapping plans for color and 3-D — before shooting.

Even in its time, *Them!* stood above the usual sci fi swill, receiving universally positive notices, becoming Warners' biggest earner of the year, and topping out at #51 in the national box office race.

Look, it ain't Shakespeare, it ain't even *Planet of the Apes* (1968). But if you're looking for a fun way to spend an hour and a half, *Them!* beats out any number of the nine-figure sci fi blockbusters that steamroll into the plexes every summer.

MY LOVE/HATE AFFAIR WITH *STAR TREK*

March 20, 2013

Star Trek – and we're talking the original 1966-69 series here – was a lousy TV show. I was 11 years old when the series debuted on NBC and I thought it was a lousy show then.

That's why I couldn't stand the Trekkies even back before there was a name for them. My first run-in with a pre-Trekkie Trekkie was Vincent DePalma. In seventh grade, Vincent had his mother make a sparkly Star Fleet emblem for a corduroy pullover to make it look like the uniform blouses on the show. He wore it to school which I thought was him begging to get his ass beat. He'd built a full-sized replica of the helm/navigation console from the Enterprise bridge in his basement. His father worked for Bell Telephone and had gotten him banks of light-up buttons that really worked. His dream was to eventually recreate the entire bridge in his basement. He was a friend of mine and even I thought he was dweeb, at least when it came to *Star Trek*.

There were things about the show that drove me bats, even at 11, and drove me still battier when guys (and it was always guys) like Vincent DePalma treated *Star Trek* like a fifth gospel delivered by St. Gene of Roddenberry. For instance…

Those cheap-ass high school play-looking sets when they were shooting exterior scenes in a studio. The paper mache boulders were the worst, right after the caves with smooth linoleum floors.

And those God-awful uniforms. For the guys, those tidewater pants and unflatteringly-tight corduroy tops made me chafe just watching them. If series star William Shatner'd had a big lunch that day, it showed. And while, as an 11-year-old boy, I appreciated the micro-mini skirts the ladies had to wear, you'd think 300 years into the future servicewomen wouldn't have to deal with wrestling into pantyhose to go to work. That'd be like our present day women soldiers having to go to war in Daisy Dukes while the guys wear body armor and cammo.

Or that heap of a spaceship, the Enterprise, a vehicle only a crooked used car dealer could love. Oh, it looked cool, I give you that, but it only proved that three centuries hence government contractors were still wasting taxpayers' money on high tech junk that didn't work. Jeez, it seemed like every other week some damned thing on the United Starship Hunkajunk broke down.

Or the way Enterprise skipper Captain Kirk seemed to solve most dilemmas by punching some alien's lights out and/or getting into an intergalactic hottie's pants, only to have some snotty superbeing show up and condescendingly tell us that because ol' Kirkie had stopped short of caving somebody's skull in with a rock there was hope for our species in a few kajillion years.

I could go on...and on and on and on.

And yet I watched every damned one of those 79 original episodes, kept watching it no matter where NBC bounced it on the schedule, watched it right to the end when the network finally pulled the plug. And when it showed up in syndication not long after, I was there, again. In fact, where I lived, Channel 11 ran *Star Trek* twice a day: in the early evening, and another episode at 11, and I watched both. When Syfy picked up the original series some years ago and was bragging about running it uncut (in syndication it had often been trimmed to jam in another commercial or two), sure enough, there I was watching it again.

And you know something? I *still* thought it was a lousy show!

That was part of the attraction; it was often a show I loved to hate.

But another part of the attraction was – especially as I grew older and, I like to think, more perceptive – being able to see the show *Star Trek* could have been, and that, on rare, compelling, as-good-as-anything-else-on-TV-ever occasions, it managed to be.

*****

Star Trek has been idolized and adored so long and so adamantly, with the Trekkies as the high priests leading the services, that a lot of cracks and blemishes in the *Trek* saga have been spackled and painted over by time, nostalgia, the success of subsequent spin-offs and films, and, in some quarters, blind worship. Take the role of series creator Gene Roddenberry for instance.

Roddenberry is *Star Trek's* daddy, no question, and to fans, whether a fevered Trekkie or someone a bit more passively enthused, he's the statue people pray to in the *Trek* church. Some view him as kind of a martyr: the guy who took it on the chin fighting NBC for his vision, who kept the *Trek* flame alive after cancellation, who gave the brand its philosophical heart.

All of which is true.

But – and this doesn't take anything away from Roddenberry because no Roddenberry, no *Star Trek* — the long-term success of *Trek* owes as much to others as it does to Roddenberry who hardly had a golden touch.

He'd been a cop with the Los Angeles Police Department in the 1950s when he'd started writing for TV under a pen name. The cops didn't pay that well and Roddenberry eventually left the force to focus fulltime on TV writing. He ran up a respectable tally of credits including work for some of the more notable shows of the late 1950s/early 1960s i.e. *Have Gun — Will Travel, Naked City,* and *The Virginian*. What he had a harder time doing was trying to land a series of his own. He kept pitching, but nobody wanted to catch. In 1963, he finally got a series he created on the air – *The Lieutenant*, starring Gary Lockwood (who would guest star on the *Trek* episode, "Where No Man Has Gone Before") – but the show was cancelled after one season.

Even after *Star Trek* and its evolving into one of the all-time great TV/film cults, Roddenberry couldn't seem to hit the sweet spot a second time. He holds a position not unlike George Lucas with *Star Wars*, his one major hit becoming a money-making machine through the shows, films, and merchandise it spun off, but who couldn't find success outside the brand (nor did Roddenberry share in the *Star Trek* riches; unlike Lucas, Roddenberry didn't retain ownership of the property). A number of pilots stiffed, and after the disappointing response to the first *Trek* feature film – *Star Trek: The Motion Picture* (1979), on which Roddenberry is listed as one of the producers – Roddenberry was relegated by Paramount, rights-holder to the franchise, to a creative consultant's role.

And then there's NBC, often portrayed as the villain in the demise of the original series; considered a network which neither understood nor appreciated what Roddenberry & Co. were trying to do.

Also true.

Be that as it may, in its original run, *Star Trek* was an unqualified flop. The show debuted a ratings winner, but then, over the course of just the first season alone, submarined, finishing out the 1966-67 season a feeble #51 out of a field of 94 shows. That was bad enough, but the show continued to slide throughout its remaining two seasons. Say what you will about NBC not really understanding *Star Trek* and monkeying around with its scheduling in the most lethal of ways, finally putting a stake through the show's heart by sticking it in the graveyard Fridays at 10 slot, but give them this: they stuck with a proven loser for three seasons.

One of the problems was the show never accomplished what Roddenberry had hoped for: to use sci fi – usually dismissed as kiddie fodder – as a platform for adult drama. The adults – even during the show's first season with choice scheduling at 8:30 on Tuesdays – didn't buy it, and even fewer bought it week by week.

I don't know what the problem was. Maybe grown-ups of the time – despite the leggy *Trek* ladies (for the men) and a then buff Shatner losing his shirt on a regular basis (for the women) — couldn't get past thinking ray guns and space ships were for kids, no matter how adult the themes were. Maybe they couldn't look past the paper mache rocks and other cheesy bits which went with the tight budgets.

One thing I'm sure of: the numbers continued to steadily slide from the show's very first airing because the longer you stuck with the show, the more apparent the series' crippling flaws became.

*****

A wannabe independent producer I bumped into some years ago once told me that when your funds were as limited as his were, you made the movie you *could* make rather than the one you *wanted* to make.

Gene Roddenberry had come up with an admirably ambitious vision for *Star Trek* inculcated in the famous lines which series star William Shatner intoned at the beginning of each episode:

> *"These are the voyages of the starship Enterprise. Its five-year mission: to explore strange new worlds, to seek out new life and new civilizations, to boldly go where no man has gone before."*

But Roddenberry didn't curtail his ambitions just because the money to realize them wasn't there. He only had $200,000 each week to create those strange new worlds and civilizations, and, for the kind of show he wanted *Trek* to be, that was chump change. Extrapolating for inflation, that'd be the equivalent today of the budget for a typical one-hour drama with no special effects or model work, no special make-up and costumes or weird sets. *The Outer Limits*, which was cancelled the year before *Trek* debuted, had had a similar budget and they had regularly struggled although the show was set in the present day. For two hundred grand, *Trek* couldn't help but often look cheesy. That explains the crappy sets, the goofy alien costumes and make-up, and a steady reliance on strange new worlds and civilizations which often looked an awful lot like some aspect of *this* one.

There were times when *Trek's* adventures were like a trip through Disneyland. Where Disneyland has its Tomorrow Land and Frontier Land, *Star Trek* had Nazi Land ("Patterns of Force"), Contemporary Roman Empire Land ("Bread and Circuses"), Native American Land ("The Paradise Syndrome"), Gay '90s Land ("Return of the Archons"), Roaring '20s Land ("A Piece of the Action"), and Davy Crockett Land ("A Private Little War"). Then there's the two times the Enterprise traveled back in time to Earth in the then present ("Tomorrow Is Yesterday," and "Assignment: Earth" which was intended as the launch for a spinoff series which never happened), and a third trip back, this time to the Great Depression ("City on the Edge of Forever"). And then there's "Miri" in which, camouflaged by some doubletalk about "parallel development," the Enterprise visits a planet that's the spitting image of 20th Century Earth, right down to the shape of its continents.

It also explains why most *Star Trek* aliens looked, well, just like us. And always spoke English.

For me, one of the episodes where the show's threadbare quality really showed through was the third season ep, "Mark of Gideon," and its story about a frighteningly overpopulated planet. The only part of the planet

Gideon we get to see is the office of boss Gideonite David Hurst and what we can see out his window: a bunch of people in green tights bumping into each other against a black backdrop. Even as a symbolic image, it looked worse than bad; it looked ridiculous.

Ok, they had money problems. But with a depressing frequency, neither was the show up to Roddenberry's expansive vision creatively either.

Roddenberry had boxed the show in with the very devices meant to make planet-hopping storytelling easier. You've got this super-cool, faster than light spaceship, but now you have to keep it from whizzing our heroes out of trouble at warp speed. Thusly, every other week you had poor Scottie (James Doohan), the ship's chief engineer, foaming at the mouth about how some gizmo or another was going to overheat, break down, shut off, or blow up.

The only piece of space junk that misbehaved more than that hoopty the Enterprise was that damned transporter. Anything that could get characters into a situation so easily could also get them out of trouble with equal ease. So, the transporter had to fizz, spark, and break on a regular basis, too. Communicators and phaser pistols were always getting lost, confiscated, or neutralized, subspace radio was getting interfered with… Hell, if flush toilets had ever been a key plot element on *Star Trek*, guaranteed they'd back up.

Ok, so they had money problems and maybe they hadn't quite thought through some of the founding principles of the show.

But it gets worse.

David Gerrold's is a name familiar to devoted *Star Trek* fans. Gerrold penned "The Trouble with Tribbles," one of the series' most memorable episodes, and thereafter became a regular chronicler of all things *Trek*. While Gerrold has always been an unabashed fan of the show, he can also be impressively clear-eyed on how and why the series didn't deliver on its creator's vision. In *The World of Star Trek: The Show the Network Could Not Kill!* (Ballantine, 1973), Gerrold offers a fairly brutal autopsy of the show's failures, and illustrates them hysterically in a scenario which combines all of those recurring lapses which represented the "…format's degeneration into formula."

Writes Gerrold, "A 'formula' story is the pat story, the easy story, the one that gets written by the book. It's a compilation of all the tried and true tricks. It's six devices in search of a plot…It's generally a waste of time."

In Gerrold's hoot of a scenario – a veritable Greatest Hits of the shortcuts and cheap tricks *Star Trek* writers came to over-rely on, "…Kirk, Spock and McCoy get captured by six foot green women in steel brassieres. They take away the spacemen's communicators because they offend the computer-god that these women worship…Scott discovers that he's having trouble with the doubletalk generator, and…the Enterprise will shrivel into a prune in two hours…it's been more than two hours since Kirk's last piece of ass and he starts getting twitchy…So (he) seduces the cute priestess – there always is at least one…the girl he has seduced decides that she has never been laid so good in her life and discards all of her years-long training and lifetime-held beliefs to rescue him…" And so on.

Put it another way. The first time our intrepid space explorers manage to turn a super computer's logic in on itself, that's kind of nifty ("The Return of the Archons"). But keep going back to that well ("The Changeling," "I, Mudd," "The Ultimate Computer") and the show begins to have a been-there-done-that stale feel. The noisy finale of "The Apple" plays out an awful lot like the noisy finale of "Who Mourns for Adonis?" which lends "Plato's Stepchildren" some ideas about aliens visiting ancient Greece. When Spock (Leonard Nimoy) loses his Vulcan cool in "The Naked Time," it's appropriately disturbing, but then he loses it again in "This Side of Paradise," "Amok Time," and "All Our Yesterdays," and it gets to feel like "Here we go, again." Superior aliens keep testing the Enterprise gang's moral mettle with life or death versions of the SATs ("Arena," "Spectre of the Gun," "The Empath," "The Savage Curtain"), while other E.T.s play with them the way a kid plays with ants and a magnifying glass ("The Squire of Gothos," "The Gamesters of Triskelion," "Bread and Circuses" "Day of the Dove").

The Enterprise wasn't exploring strange new worlds and going places where no man had gone before. *Au contraire*; it kept going to places that seemed way too damned familiar.

And that wasn't the worst of it, not by a long shot. The worst shows were the moralizers, the episodes with a message that was often simplistic, heavy-handed, and about as subtle as a poke in the eye. "Let me see… Hmm, the one guy is black on one side of his body, and the other guy is white on that side, and they hate each other, and — … Oh, I get it! Prejudice is stupid!" ("Let That Be Your Last Battlefield"). "Oh, so these tribes, the Yangs and the Kohms, that's really Yankees and communists and if we don't learn to live nicely together, we're going to bomb each other back into the stone age" ("The Omega Glory").

The only episodes worse than the moralizers were the ones where *Star Trek* tried to be topical, using its futuristic sci fi vantage point to comment on the present day. Only for all its sage blabbing about cruising through the galaxy on a state-of-the-art battlewagon to make peaceful contacts, in episodes like "A Private Little War" and "The Enterprise Incident," *Star Trek* fell right into line with atavistic Cold War thinking.

One of the most embarrassing of the topical eps was *Star Trek's* take on the hippy movement with "The Way to Eden." The show's take on what will be groovy 300 years in the future is painful to watch (and was painful back in 1969 when it aired), and more pained was its superficial grasp of what was going on in the 1960s. The moral of "Eden" seemed to be a *Father Knows Best*-like, "You can have your rock 'n' roll, kids, but listen to your parents."

So, all this in mind, was that why I watched it? Just so I could make fun? Just so I could give Vincent DePalma a hard time every Wednesday during lunch about how Captain Kirk had boinked his crew to safety for the thirty-third time?

The thing about *Star Trek* was there were times when the show got it right, when it did what it aspired to do and did it beautifully. It didn't happen often, but that's what kept me hanging in there; hoping they'd do it again.

*****

Most of my favorites come from the series' first season. It was the only season where you actually got a sense of life on a starship: the crew get physicals ("The Corbomite Maneuver"), some fall in love and get married ("Balance of Terror"), they spend time in the gym and hang out in the rec lounge ("Charlie X"). There's a wonderful background flow to those episodes that gets lost in subsequent seasons.

What also gets lost is a sense of adventure; in living up to the promise of "going where no man has gone before." "The Corbomite Maneuver" was as intelligent an exercising of that mandate as the show ever produced. The ship has, indeed, gone where no ship has gone before, has contacted a wholly alien being, and is locked in a psychological poker game which ultimately leads to a meaningful contact. Similarly, "Devil in the Dark" combined suspenseful monster flick with the tragedy of the limitations of our human points of reference in trying to understand a life form as different from us as air is from earth.

Other episodes triumphantly did what sci fi rarely does: provide a platform for human drama but in a way that could only be told through sci fi. I'm thinking here of "The Enemy Within," with a sharp screenplay by sci fi master Richard Matheson in which through a malfunctioning transporter (surprise!), Kirk is split into a good Kirk and a bad Kirk, with the interesting twist that much of the bad Kirk is what makes Kirk the capable skipper he is. Or "Charlie X" with its painfully acute portrait of adolescent angst in a vehicle that presaged Stephen King's *Carrie* by almost a decade.

But my favorite episode, and the one that I think was not only *Star Trek* at its best, but was just damned sharp television, was "The Naked Time." The ship's crew becomes infected with a disease that suppresses inhibitions and allows all their secret wants and fears to rise to the surface. Bit by bit, the infection spreads through the ship and the episode becomes a potent revelation of the difference between our public and private selves. One of the most powerful scenes in the episode – and the series – is Leonard Nimoy's Mr. Spock coming apart as he retreats to an empty room to wrestle with the shame of his half-breed status, and the overwhelming pain of a tidal wave of emotion. Even better, his face-off with Shatner's Kirk, also infected, who now begins to feel the ache of the loneliness and sacrifice of command. There's a lovely moment after Kirk has regained his senses and he sits in his commander's chair, eyes his pretty yeoman (Grace Lee Whitney) wistfully, and recalls what he'd said to Spock about having "no beach to walk on."

There were other gems. Some were good ol' sci fi adventures ("Balance of Terror," The Changeling"), and others were just plain fun (here you really have to give the show props; *Star Trek* did know how to loosen up and have fun in eps like "I, Mudd," "Shore Leave," "The Squire of Gothos," "A Piece of the Action," and – the best of the best – "The Trouble with Tribbles").

They were just few and far between, and as the series continued on, they got fewer.

*****

Gene Roddenberry didn't get the adult audience he'd hoped for. But the kids saved his creation. They were the ones who watched the show in syndication and grew up with it, who kept the idea of *Star Trek* – which was stronger than the show itself – alive. They were the ones who started the fan clubs and the conventions and bought the merchandise that kept the brand of a failed TV series viable until Paramount decided to resurrect it 10 years after its cancellation to capitalize on the sci fi craze ignited by the success of *Star Wars*. Finally, with the time and money and resources the series had never had at its disposal, what Roddenberry had meant *Star Trek* to be could, at long last, be.

RICHARD MATHESON (1926 – 2013): "JUST" A GREAT STORYTELLER

June 27, 2013

A week after James Gandolfini died, we lost another Jersey boy: novelist, short story writer, film and TV screenwriter Richard Matheson. His was not as well-known a name to the general public as Gandolfini's, certainly, and perhaps only familiar to sci fi and fantasy fans, the genres within which he scored some of his most memorable successes. When he died, Steven Spielberg, whose early career received a huge boost when he directed the made-for-TV movie *Duel* (1972) which Matheson adapted from his own short story, said, "For me, he is in the same category as Bradbury and Asimov."

Personally, I don't think he stood in that same tier with Bradbury, Asimov, Clarke, Robert A. Heinlein – the real sci fi giants. Nor did he stand in any rung below them. Rather, he stood off to the side.

Clarke grappled with our place in the cosmos, Bradbury used sci fi and fantasy to comment on contemporary issues, Asimov had a sense of the epic, Heinlein set the standard for a generation of space operas. Matheson – whose portfolio was more diversified than any of them – was not as high-minded nor as ambitious. He was that oft overlooked, underappreciated species of creative talent: a guy who knew a good story and knew how to tell it well. But damn, could he tell a story.

He was a born writer, publishing his first short story at the age of eight. By the 1950s, his stuff was showing up regularly in magazines and anthologies and was soon found ripe for adaptation to film. His early novel *The Shrinking Man* was turned into that classic of 1950s sci fi, *The Incredible Shrinking Man* (1957), with Matheson himself doing the adaptation, spinning what could easily have been a bit of FX corn into a surprisingly affecting, meditative piece on the value of the individual.

The obits all talk about his sci fi pieces: *Shrinking Man*, his novel *I Am Legend* which was adapted into no less than three movies (cheapie *The Last Man on Earth* [1964]; schlocky *The Omega Man* [1971]; zombified *I Am Legend* [2007]), and others, but his portfolio is dizzyingly varied: amid the vampire stories and sci fiers were westerns (besides his own short stories, Matheson wrote for many of the major cowboy shows of the 1950s/60s including *Cheyenne*, *Have Gun – Will Travel*, and *Lawman*), gothics (Matheson did five Edgar Allan Poe adaptations for Roger Corman in the 1960s, Corman claiming Matheson wrote them so well "I always shot his first draft"), and contemporary suspense thrillers like "Button, Button" (adapted into the 2009 feature *The Box*) and, of course, *Duel*.

But even within those genres the commemoratives most often touch,

Matheson brought his own, distinctive humanist flavor. He was less interested in genre trappings than in finding that relatable, identifiable, universally human element within it. He wrote one of the best and most adult *Star Trek* episodes with "The Enemy Within" where a transporter failure splits Captain Kirk into a Jekyll & Hyde twosome. His *The Twilight Zone* "Steel" (also self-adapted from one of his short stories) used a futuristic robot story to illustrate – as host Rod Serling says in the Matheson-written closing narration, "…that no matter what the future brings, man's capacity to rise to the occasion will remain unaltered."

And there's his gloss on vampire tales with the cheeky *The Night Stalker* (1972), which Matheson adapted from an unpublished novel by Jeff Price. Set in contemporary Las Vegas, leavened with *The Front Page*-styled newspaperman humor and sparked with the kind of visceral action usually lacking from big screen fang films up to that time, for years *Stalker* was the highest-rated TV movie of all time, and spawned the equally fun sequel *The Night Strangler* (1973) which Matheson also wrote.

Matheson wasn't a sci fi writer, a fantasy writer, a horror writer. He was a writer, plain and simple. A drive with a friend tickled something in his imagination and it became *Duel*. He wondered, as so many in the 1950s wondered, about the dehumanizing corporatization of America and that somehow came out as *The Shrinking Man*. That's how writers' minds work; sensing a good story and telling it well, and few knew a good story and told it as well as my fellow Jersey boy, Richard Matheson.

JACK KLUGMAN (1922 – 2012): EVERYMAN

December 26, 2012

For most, Jacob "Jack" Klugman's defining role was Oscar Madison, the quintessential white collar guy with a blue collar New York sensibility – loud, oafish, impulsive, a compulsive gambler and an inveterate slob – on the TV series adaptation of Neil Simon's *The Odd Couple*, which ran on ABC 1970-75. Those among the AARP crowd who like their vintage 1970s cop shows – stuff like *Cannon, McCloud, Barnaby Jones, MacMillan and Wife* — might also have fond remembrances of Klugman in *Quincy M.E.* (1976-1983) as a pushy, passionate medical examiner…who was also, at times, loud, oafish, impulsive, a compulsive gambler and a bit of a slob.

But when I heard Klugman had passed away on Christmas Eve, what flashed through my mind was the singular appropriateness of his passing on such a spirit-filled day, because my favorite onscreen memories of the actor were his four appearances on *The Twilight Zone*. What was the connection for me? All four of Klugman's *Zone* episodes dealt, in one way or another, with matters of the spirit: death, a meaningful life, legacy.

By the time Klugman made his first appearance on the series, he was already moving easily between stage (where he'd begun and to where he'd regularly return throughout his career), the big screen (most notably as the streetwise Juror #5 in the Sidney Lumet 1957 classic, *12 Angry Men*), and television. Evidence of his professional status: the same year Klugman showed up on *Zone* for the first time – 1960 – he received a Tony nomination for his role in the original Broadway run of the musical *Gypsy*.

With his everyman looks and the slouch-shouldered trudge of a man who always had more bills to pay than money to pay them, Klugman was a perfect choice for *The Twilight Zone* whose best stories were about little people: their frailties and foibles, their admirable if minor nobilities, their often small ambitions and hopes.

In the 1960 *Zone* episode "A Passage for Trumpet," Klugman plays a washed-up, alcoholic trumpet player who attempts to commit suicide. A visit from the best trumpet player in the universe – the angel Gabriel (John Anderson) – persuades him that even when life is at its worst, there's always something worth living for, including the ability to move people with music.

It was a bit heavy-handedly sentimental, but a virtual rehearsal for the more hard-edged "A Game of Pool" during the next season which seemed to be capitalizing on the success of Robert Rossen's big screen pool room classic, *The Hustler* (1961). In a vaguely similar plot construct to "Trumpet," instead of a down and out horn man, Klugman is a neighborhood pool ace frustrated at his second-class status in being constantly compared to long-dead pool great Fats Brown (Jonathan Winters). Klugman is visited by the spirit of Brown who challenges him to a game for the highest stakes of all: his life.

Klugman was back in "Death Ship," this time as the commander of a space exploration mission which discovers the wreck of their own ship occupied by their dead selves, and is damned to relive the inexplicable discovery time and time again.

But easily the actor's best work on the series was his last: the 1963 offering, "In Praise of Pip." Klugman plays another low-life, a bookie, whose singular positive accomplishment is his grown son, Pip. Hearing that Pip has been critically wounded in what was then a little brushfire war in a part of the world few Americans had ever heard of – Vietnam – Klugman attempts an act of atonement for his otherwise grubby little life and intercedes on behalf of one of his luckless bettors, taking a bullet from one of his boss's enforcers in the process. The wounded Klugman visits the local amusement park where he's visited by the spirit (or hallucination?) of his son as a young boy (Billy Mumy). They relive their fun days on the midway, but when young Pip disappears, the dying Klugman turns to the night sky and beseeches God to take his life in trade for that of his son. Klugman dies, Pip lives. Coincidence? Divine intervention? In the world of *The Twilight Zone*, it could be either… or even both.

With the exception of being a space commander of the future, Klugman was always eminently relatable in his Zone roles; someone who looked like us, sounded like us, and even had the same little dreams as us: a desire for minor greatness ("Passage for Trumpet," "Game of Pool"), to accomplish at least one decent thing ("Praise of Pip"), to be remembered fondly and well.

These pieces came to me when I heard of his Christmas Eve passing because they seemed to provide a kind of epitaph which, in true Klugman fashion, was something to which we could all relate and which seemed so seasonably appropriate: he had managed his minor greatness, never having been a major star, but yet becoming a much beloved Familiar Face; illustrating, in so much of his work, the decency that could be found in the most – at first glance – ignoble of souls, like a third-rate bookie or even a cigar-puffing, constantly indebted sports writer like Oscar Madison; and he will always be remembered fondly…and well.

GEORGE LUCAS: ONE (MEGA)HIT WONDER?

January 25, 2012

It's a phrase out of the music industry: one-hit wonders. Those bands that come out of nowhere, hit the top of the charts with a catchy, maybe even impressive single, or have one chart-topping album, and then never seem to be able to hit that sweet spot again. Anybody remember Boston's second album? Another hit single after "96 Tears" from Jay and the Mysterians?

But they're not alone. There's not an area of entertainment where the phenomenon doesn't exist. Rod Serling never topped *The Twilight Zone*, and Chris Carter never came up with another series as good as *The X Files*. Fitzgerald wrote a lot of impressive stuff, but never matched *The Great Gatsby*, and drank himself to death over it (well, Zelda being crazy didn't help). Michael Cimino copped an Oscar for *The Deer Hunter* (1978), and then began a long, spectacular flameout.

It happens. And maybe it's time to finally recognize George Lucas as a member of that club.

Early last year, I'd written a compare-and-contrast piece on Steven Spielberg and Lucas. I acknowledged that, of the two, Lucas probably has had the greater impact on the movie industry. Hell, Lucas has probably had the greatest impact on the industry since Griffith!

The success of the first *Star Wars* trilogy created the template for the big-budget blockbuster franchise which expands and cross-pollinates its brand across a host of platforms, from TV to videogames to merchandising. *Star Wars* moved Hollywood from the movie business into the brand name event business. All of those monster hits which dominated the 2011 box office – from *Harry Potter and the Deathly Hallows Part 2* to *Transformers: Dark of the Moon* and *Pirates of the Caribbean: On Stranger Tides* – owe more to Lucas than to Spielberg (or anybody else for that matter). For good or for ill, love it or hate it, in the 35 years since *Star Wars* opened, mainstream Hollywood has largely remade itself in Lucas' image.

The burden of phenomenal success: *Star Wars* (1977).
Mark Hamill and Harrison Ford.

And there may be no other single person since Melies for whom the expansion of film technology owes so much as well. From the original *Star Wars* on, Lucas has been a fearless pioneer in pushing back the physical limits of filmmaking. Not only do the *kinds* of movies that dominate the marketplace owe something to Lucas, but so do the way they look and sound. It might be an oversimplification to say it, but it's not hard to make a case that movies are the way they are because of George Lucas.

Successful, influential, powerful, no doubt, and in many ways brilliant and a pioneer, but as last weekend's release of *Red Tails* highlights, as a creative force – as a *filmmaker* – George Lucas has also been a disappointment. He may not *quite* be a true one-hit wonder…but he's damned close.

*****

Lucas has had other hits. Arguably, his best movie – certainly his most *human* movie — is the one whose success bought him the license to make *Star Wars* (1977); *American Graffiti* (1973). Stung by the failure of his first feature, the visually striking but emotionally aloof and dramatically opaque sci fier *TXH 1138* (1971), Lucas took mentor Francis Ford Coppola's advice to try something more mainstream-friendly, and came up with *Graffiti*. A bittersweet, warm-hearted salute to his own early '60s youth, *Graffiti* is easily one of the best coming of age films in the American canon. It was also such an enormous commercial hit that it kicked off a '50s nostalgia craze that went on for years.

Lucas is also responsible for the ginormously successful *Indiana Jones* franchise. Though Lucas friend Steven Spielberg helmed all four of the *IJ* films, and other writers penned the screenplays, Spielberg has always been open about saying (most recently in a lengthy interview in *Entertainment Weekly)* that the series is Lucas' baby, and that he directs to Lucas' vision.

Still, say "George Lucas" and the title that comes to mind — in big, bold letters, no less — is *Star Wars*. It's the franchise which launched the Lucas empire, and it's still the realm's cornerstone and main product. For decades, he's kept the franchise alive by recycling the movies through one big screen/home video release after another, in almost every possible configuration: boxed sets, new added features, re-doing the special effects on the original trilogy, etc. The film franchise has been the launch pad for toys, pricey collectibles, TV spin-offs (Cartoon Network's animated *Star Wars: The Clone Wars; Star Wars: Underworld* currently in pre-production), and any number of videogames, like *Lego Star Wars: The Complete Saga,* and *Star Wars: The Old Republic,* released late last year and proving the brand to still be unflaggingly vital *six years* after the last *Star Wars* feature hit big screens. But go into Lucas' IMDB directing, writing, and producing credits, and once you take *Star Wars*-related projects out of the mix, the pickin's get mighty thin. Take out *Indiana Jones,* and you could make a case that Lucas is a borderline failure.

His producer's portfolio outside of those two cash-cow franchises is a hodge-podge of art house ambition *(Mishima: A Life in Four Chapters* [1985], *Powaqqatsi* [1988]) and utter misfires *(Radioland Murders* [1994], *Willow* [1988], *Labyrinth* [1986], *Howard the Duck* [1986]). You can count the number of non-*Star Wars/Indiana Jones* feature successes on one hand – and still have fingers left over (neo-noir *Body Heat* [1981]; import *Kagemusha* [1980]; sugary animated feature *The Land Before Time* [1988]).

The knock on Lucas, as both a producer and a writer/director, goes back to the beginning of his career and even includes his biggest successes. He's either been dismissive of the human element in his films, and/or considers it secondary to the visual possibilities, and has been quoted as saying, "actors are irrelevant." Even on his most flesh-and-blood feature, *American Graffiti,* Lucas reportedly left direction of the actors to his dialogue coach, and on *Star Wars* the cast joked his idea of directing was simply to say, "Faster and more intense!"

After *Star Wars,* Lucas threw his DGA card away, but came back after 21 years to direct the franchise's second trilogy. After the childlike exuberance of *Star Wars, Star Wars: Episode I – The Phantom Menace* (1999), *Episode II – Attack of the Clones* (2002), and *Episode III – Revenge of the Sith* (2005), despite being box office monsters, were emotionally disappointing. The application of CGI technology was awe-inspiring, but the heart of the films, well, it's like the old Gertrude Stein line about Oakland: "There's no 'there' there."

And sadly, *Red Tails* fits all-too-well into the Lucas canon.

*****

Twenty-three years ago, an aviator friend of Lucas' told him the story of the Tuskegee Airmen; an all-black Air Corps unit fighting in the segregated military during WW II. Their feats of valor were legendary in quality, but criminally ignored for decades. Telling their story became a passion project for Lucas, and when he could find no studio backer for *Red Tails*, he finally cracked open his own checkbook and forked out $58 million for the production, and another $35 million for marketing.

If only the end product matched his obviously heartfelt commitment. Reviews have been almost unanimously negative and in agreement. Mark Jenkins of *The Washington Post* used words similar to so many of the major appraisals when he wrote, "The African American fliers' great achievement merits a great movie. *Red Tails* isn't it."

In many ways, *Red Tails* is typical Lucas. Unsurprisingly, the man who exhilarated the first generation of fanboys with the outer space dogfights of *Star Wars* provides an aerial spectacle second to none thanks to CGI. As he recently told Charlie Rose, "…this is one of the first films where we actually were able to create the dogfight the way it really would be, and get you right into the seat and get you right into the action…"

But on the ground, the film has all the grace of a concrete ping-pong ball. *Entertainment Weekly*'s Owen Gleiberman caught the critical consensus in his review writing, "As long as it stays in the air, *Red Tails*…is a compelling sky-war pageant of a movie. On the ground, it's a far shakier experience: dutiful and prosaic, with thinly scripted episodes that don't add up to a satisfying story." The film's Rotten Tomatoes rating is an abysmal 33% positives among all critics; just 25% among major reviewers.

You would expect more after 23 years of development. On the other hand, as *The Star-Ledger*'s Stephen Whitty pointed out in his write-up, "How many scriptwriters' hands has this project passed through? How many drafts have been written, rewritten, thrown out, resurrected and then thrown out all over again?…whatever the original inspiration was, it's been lost under layers, like a house's once-nice, now painted-over paneling."

Ironically, *Red Tails* was released the same week as another airwar epic, the Blu-ray refurbishment of the silent 1927 WW I classic and first Best Picture Oscar-winner, *Wings*, and looks even more dramatically anemic in comparison. Whereas *Red Tails* deflates every time it hits the ground, William Wellman's 85-year-old flicker still packs an emotional punch. According to one DVD reviewer, "*Wings* has it all – romance, drama, humor, action. And *what* action." Even the dogfight scenes have a dramatic heft missing from the admittedly spectacular combat sequences in *Red Tails*, because in Wellman's movie, they were about as close to being real as possible without using live ammo. No CGI, no green screen: that's actually stars Buddy Rogers and Richard Arlen at the controls of their biplanes, putting their aircraft through such violent maneuvers that Rogers, who learned to fly for the film, sometimes vomited as soon as he climbed out of his plane. In the end, what comes through in *Wings*, even after eighty-odd years, is what's missing not only in *Red Tails*, but so many Lucas projects: fleshed-out, three-dimensional human drama.

Red Tails is Lucas' first big screen project outside of his two big-dollar franchises since the 1994 flop *Radioland Murders*, but he's long been taking flak for his faulty storytelling even within his signature work. His last three *Star Wars* installments were all rapped for what seemed an obsession with creating alien civilizations, grand-scale action sequences, and even entire characters through the magic of CGI, but a consistent inability to make us care about any of it. Even the last *IJ* installment – *Indiana Jones and the Kingdom of the Crystal Skull* (2008) — was considered a let-down, an emotionally hollow exercise after the rich storytelling of *Indiana Jones and the Last Crusade* (1989).

Every filmmaker has his bad day, but Lucas has had an awful lot of them, and usually for the same reasons. And it may be that even his fanboy base is growing tired of his constant re-tweaking/recycling of the six *Star Wars* films that are the fuel rods for the whole Lucas enterprise. Last year's Blu-ray release of the original trilogy included changes die-hard fans furiously claimed changed entire relationships and meanings in the films.

Lucas, who has always tended to be a bit prickly over criticism, reacted by essentially saying he was taking his marbles and going home. "Why would I make any more (*Star Wars*) movies) when everybody yells at you all the time and says what a terrible person you are?" he told *The New York Times*, and then went on to make noises about backing away from the business.

But Lucas has said that before. He said it when he gave up directing after the first *Star Wars*. He has also several times said – as he told Charlie Rose recently while promoting *Red Tails* – "…there's the intellectual side of me that wants to do more experimental films which I haven't done since I did my first film, *THX*, and my student films. And I – that's now where I'm going is to try to get back to that."

Yet Harrison Ford told MTV News late last year that a fifth Indiana Jones is "on George's plate," and there's TV series *Star Wars: Underworld* in development.

The financial maintenance of Lucas' vast empire requires this kind of constant franchise stoking. One of Lucas' problems is he may very well be trapped by what's needed to keep Lucas Inc. going.

But another truth may sit out in plain sight in *THX 1138*. It's a hypnotic piece, unlike anything Lucas has made since. The antiseptically white-on-white visuals and a plot and characters suggested more than stated, offer a cold experience for the viewer. Lucas was, even as a student at UCLA – and remains a technological virtuoso. But for all of his effects skill, for all his command of the medium, Lucas hasn't been able to get that most basic requirement of memorable moviemaking onscreen since the first *Star Wars* thirty-odd years ago: heart.

STANLEY KUBRICK (1928 – 1999): STUDIO AUTEUR

March 19, 2014

Nuclear apocalypse as a wicked joke: *Dr. Strangelove or How I Stopped Worrying and Learned to Love the Bomb* (1964) with Peter Sellers as Strangelove, just one of the three roles he played in the film.

Throughout the 1960s-early 1970s, a combination of financial desperation, creative daring, and an adventurous movie-going public had produced a creative detonation in mainstream American movies not seen before or since. Each year of the period seemed to bring at least one mightily ambitious visual experiment by a new contributor to the commercial movie scene, the "look" of that effort being as much a part of its identity as its characters and story. One could pick no better representative of the trend than Stanley Kubrick, for no director of the time so extended the boundaries of mainstream commercial filmmaking, or what it meant to be a mainstream commercial filmmaker.

For the most part, Kubrick's professional ascent was built on the taking of standard genres – the war story, science fiction tale, sword-and-sandal epic – and twisting them into shapes so singular that each Kubrick outing became an acknowledged one-of-a-kind classic. *Paths of Glory* (1957) deglamorized war in the most emotionally brutalizing of fashions; *Spartacus* (1960) gave a bittersweet soulfulness to the sword-and-sandal epic as well as – finally — a dramatic heft to match the genre's grand scale; *Dr. Strangelove or How I Stopped Worrying and Learned to Love the Bomb* (1964) turned the Cold War nuclear thriller into an acrid, black-humored joke; *2001: A Space Odyssey* (1968) vaulted the sci fi "space opera" from juvenile status to that of cinematic poetry; *A Clockwork Orange* (1971) dispensed with the awe and gadgetry of most futuristic fantasies and, instead, delivered a disturbing portrait of a graffiti-marred, violence-ridden dystopia; *The Shining* (1980) took Steven King's haunted hotel novel and re-worked it into Hollywood's first intellectual horror tale, a sensory – rather than narrative – rendering of a "rotten spot" in the spiritual fabric of the world where evil seeps into this existence through the psychological fault lines of its main character, the ambivalently depicted apparitions perhaps being only the psychotic delusions of its protagonist.

A one-time photojournalist, Kubrick had begun his career with a series of small-scale, independently-produced movies the most notable of which was the time-fractured caper thriller *The Killing* (1956). *Paths of Glory* brought him to the attention of the majors, and the impressive critical and box office reception of *Spartacus* provided him with the latitude to initiate his own projects at the studio level. After directing an adaptation of Vladimir Nabokov's controversial novel *Lolita* (1962), *Dr. Strangelove* and *2001* followed demonstrating his ability to turn in pictures which, however idiosyncratic and intellectually demanding, still connected with the mainstream audience (with rentals of $21.5 million, *2001* was the 16th highest-grossing movie 1961-1970).

2001 was Kubrick and major studio moviemaking at its most courageous, the movie being a complete rejection of typical narrative mechanisms. The story, which Kubrick wrote in collaboration with noted sci fi author Arthur C. Clarke, spans millions of years, from simian pre-humans to a future where mankind takes a quantum evolutionary leap into near-godhood, always under the tutelage of never-seen alien forces. Within the grand scope of the story, the movie is virtually plotless, lacks any meaningful characters, and much of its sparse dialogue is intentionally banal and disposable. Kubrick himself described *2001* as, "…a non-verbal experience…," conveying its story in the same abstract, oblique manner of, say, a poem or piece of music; hinting, inferring, suggesting, but never explaining. One academic perhaps best described the dynamic of *2001* in a comparison with the more conventional and light-hearted *Star Wars* (1977): *"Star Wars* is like rock 'n' roll; *2001* is like a piece of classical music, a 'tone poem,' like *Also Sprach Zarathustra,"* referring to the Richard Strauss composition which became the movie's signature piece of music.

Kubrick continued to test non-traditional narrative forms throughout the remainder of his career, though he would not make another movie as non-linear as *2001* (although Vietnam War-set *Full Metal Jacket* [1987] would come close). Still, his subsequent movies remained a cross-breeding of mainstream Hollywood and avant-garde film, with the narrative and emotional "information" in his films conveyed by visuals at least equal, if not superior, to the conventional mechanisms of plot, character, and dialogue.

After the success of *2001,* then Warners production chief John Calley, intrigued by Kubrick's growing artistic prestige (and also, no doubt, by the consistent returns of the director's projects since *Spartacus),* offered the filmmaker a permanent home at the studio along with complete creative autonomy. Kubrick was allowed to develop whatever projects he chose, take as long as he wanted to bring them to fruition – which ran years in some cases — and even dictate the details of the marketing campaigns for his releases. Even amid Hollywood's creative explosion of the 1960s/1970s, it was an investment of studio faith and largesse in a maverick talent on a scale yet to be equaled, producing some of the most unique high-profile releases ever turned out by a major studio: *A Clockwork Orange,* period piece *Barry Lyndon* (1975), and *The Shining.* Although Calley left Warners in 1981, the studio continued to provide Kubrick a production home, giving him the opportunity to complete *Full Metal Jacket,* and erotic drama *Eyes Wide Shut* (1999), released just after the director's death at age 70 of a heart attack.

Other filmmakers have had the box office muscle to demand the kind of autonomy Kubrick retained (DeMille, Hitchcock), or buy it for themselves through exemplary commercial success (Lucas, Spielberg), but Kubrick's relationship with Warners remains unique because Kubrick and his work remain unique. Warners/Kubrick was a one-of-a-kind wedding – an oddity from its first day – between an art house sensibility and the production capabilities of what remains one of the biggest production/distribution entities in the world; a daring partnership only made practical by a mass audience's appetite for cinema that entertained by being challenging, even difficult. It's entirely possible, nay, probable, that such a partnership could only have happened when it happened, and is not likely to ever happen again.

BREAKING THE BANK: 6 OF HOLLYWOOD'S LOST OLD-SCHOOL EPICS

June 28, 2012

For moviegoers growing up in the last 20-30 years, big is the new normal. I'm talking about those big-budget, over-produced, effects/action-packed extravaganzas that are as expected and routine an arrival as a commuter bus, and never more so than during the summer months. Come a rise in temperatures, there's an almost ceaseless parade of these megabuck behemoths through multiplexes starting in May and continuing until the kids go back to school, one rolling out almost every week.

Consider these May-August releases and their eye-popping price tags:

5/4: *Marvel's The Avengers* — $220 million

5/11: *Dark Shadows* — $150 million

5/18: *Battleship* — $209 million

5/25: *Men in Black 3* — $250 million

6/8: *Prometheus* — $120-130 million

7/3: *The Amazing Spider-Man* — $220 million

7/20: *The Dark Knight Rises* — $250 million

7/31: *Total Recall* — $200 million

8/5: *The Expendables 2* — $100 million

For those of you who haven't been keeping count, that's a little over $1.7 *billion* in productions costs for just these nine flicks. And that doesn't include money spent on marketing. Press buzz around the time of its release was that worldwide marketing expenses for *MIB3* pushed the movie's total tab to $375 million. Based on that, it's a reasonable guess, then, that the real cost for the above nine releases is probably and easily somewhere over *$2 billion*.

What makes these gargantuas physically possible and financially affordable are technological advances in special effects, particularly CGI; and a swelling overseas audience as well as broad and deep ancillary markets.

The *amount* of bigness in today's movies may be particular to the last few decades, but bigness itself goes back to the earliest days of commercial moviemaking.

D. W. Griffith's *The Birth of a Nation* (1915) is not only the film which turned a nickelodeon diversion into a major form of serious entertainment, but with its sprawling, episodic story and its scenes of grand scale, screen-filling action, it also qualifies as the first epic.

True to what would become a standard Hollywood paradigm, Griffith was quick to outdo himself with his massive – even by today's standards – follow-up, *Intolerance: Love's Struggle Throughout the Ages*. At over three hours long, following four parallel stories set in different ages, and at a cost of a then staggering $2 million (about $460 million today), *Intolerance* was and remains truly epic. There are scenes in *Intolerance* which would remain unmatched in scale for decades (and only then through CGI magic-making), such as the Great Wall of Babylon scene boasting 100-foot high set pieces populated by thousands of costumed extras. Brag it may have been, but it was not an idle one when Griffith crowed, "Remember how small the world was before I came along?"

With the establishment of the studio system in the 1920s, most movies were made on a cost-efficient production line basis, but the studios always had an eye out for that special property it could turn into a – literally – once-in-a-lifetime screen event. When it found one, the resources poured into such a product were, even by today's lavish standards, head-spinning.

Consider *Wings*, the 1927 epic director William Wellman aimed to make the definitive statement on WW I. For one scene, Wellman had 165 aircraft dogfighting over a full-sized recreation of a sector of the WW I western front. Or 1931's *Cimarron*, based on Edna Ferber's popular (and epic in its own right) novel, where director Wesley Ruggles ran 5,000 mounted extras past 28 cameras to recreate the Oklahoma Land Rush.

Remember: we're not talking about miniatures or models or computer-generated magic. We're talking life-sized, 1:1 stuff here — 165 pilots flying 165 cloth-and-cable WW I fighter planes over real trenches manned by thousands of uniformed extras. We're talking real riders on real horses galloping hell-bent across the plains.

Every year or so, one studio or another would heave one of these Goliaths onto screens with the kind of supporting hype reserved for the Second Coming: the first version of *Ben-Hur* (1925), the WW I epics *The Big Parade* (1925) and *All Quiet on the Western Front* (1930), Western saga *The Covered Wagon* (1923), and, of course, the most memorable of the pre-WW II classic epics, *Gone with the Wind* (1939).

After WW II, the big budget spectacle evolved from a special effort to a desperate Hail Mary move to stave off the movie industry's slow-motion collapse.

As soon as the war ended, the movies began losing audience; not in dribs and drabs but in a torrent. Just in the first ten years after the war, average weekly attendance dropped from 82 million to 50 million (and wouldn't stop dropping for another two decades). Not coincidentally, the number of TV sets in the country rose over the same period, from a literal handful to almost 31 million, amounting to nearly one in every two American households.

The only way to beat the little screen, thought Hollywood, was to make the big screen bigger. That meant releasing more movies in color, more movies in stereophonic sound, gimmicks like 3-D and Smell-O-Vision (yeah, you read that right), and, as I said, by making the big screen, well, *bigger* with a variety of wide screen processes such as Panavision, CinemaScope, and the hugest of the huge, the wraparound screen of Cinerama (think of it as the Imax of its day).

But Hollywood needed big stories to fill those big screens. The 146-degree arced screen and multi-track sound of Cinerama wasn't invented for intimate human drama or cutsie heart-warmers. The idea was to outgun TV with the kinds of giant-sized storytelling TV couldn't match.

You could argue it started with Cecil B. DeMille and his Biblical epic, *Samson and Delilah* (1949), the third highest-grossing movie 1941-1950 behind *The Best Years of Our Lives* (1946) and *Duel in the Sun* (1946). DeMille had established himself as a master of Big Picture moviemaking back in the silent days, but his postwar work made his name synonymous with screen extravagance, each of his efforts bigger than the one before.

The epics played big and, when they worked, earned big. Taking their cue from *Samson and Delilah,* a string of similarly grandiose sword-and-sandal epics weaved through the list of the decade's top moneymakers: *Quo Vadis* (1951), *The Robe* (1953), *Solomon and Sheba* (1959), *Spartacus* (1960), DeMille's own *The Ten Commandments* (1956), and The Big Daddy of the toga-and-chariot gang, Oscar-winner *Ben-Hur* (1959).

One of the all-time great epic scenes from one of the all-time great epics: the chariot scene from the 1959 version of *Ben-Hur*. The film featured the largest sets constructed for a movie up to that time, and the chariot race set was the biggest of the big. The race, choreographed by master stuntman Yakima Canutt and second unit director Andrew Marton, was run in a five-story high replica of a Roman era arena populated by seven thousand costumed extras and took five weeks to shoot.

The big/bigger/biggest formula was applied against other genres as well. There were epic comedies *(Around the World in 80 Days,* 1956), epic war movies *(The Bridge on the River Kwai,* 1957), epic dramas *(Giant,* 1956), epic adaptations of epic novels *(War and Peace,* 1956), epics about great events past *(The Alamo,* 1960) and not so long ago *(Exodus,* 1960).

By the end of the decade, the big budget epic had become a regular part of the movie landscape. They only constituted a relative handful of titles each year – their tremendous expense and sheer physical demands prohibited more – but each was introduced as a singular event, their very rarity making every one of them something special and remarkable.

They would initially premiere only at high-end showcase theaters, like New York's Radio City Music Hall, playing for weeks – sometimes even months – before moving on to the neighborhood theater circuit. They would have musical preludes, intermissions, souvenir programs and sometimes other overpriced tchotkes for sale in the lobby. These weren't just movies; these were *events,* so much so that when the most popular were re-released years later, even the re-releases were considered events, a chance to revisit – or, for younger moviegoers, visit – a legend from the past.

Not unlike today, big wasn't always better, and a number of these epics were like big, beautifully-wrapped gift boxes with not a lot inside. *How the West Was Won* (1962) is a good example. Nearly three hours long and packed with stars from start to finish, *HTWWW* was supposed to portray one hundred years in the pioneering and settling of the American West, broken up into episodes, each helmed by a different director. Well, it was big, it looked great on the Cinerama screen and sounded even better accompanied by Cinerama's multi-track stereo, but each episode tended to fall into stale oater clichés imbued with a *faux* grandeur by being in an incredibly big-ass production.

Even flicks by King of the Big Picture himself, Cecil B. DeMille, don't hold up particularly well, despite having been huge moneymakers in their day and *The Ten Commandments* remaining an Easter time TV favorite. DeMille had never evolved past a silent era brand of hammy acting, he favored shooting exteriors on obviously artificial sets (this at a time when other filmmakers were increasingly moving toward location shooting), and his storytelling was grandly sentimental and as nuanced as a poke in the eye. Even other directors of his time, though impressed by DeMille's showmanship and box office muscle, didn't think much of his filmmaking. Said director William Wellman, "Directorially, I think his pictures were the most horrible things I've ever seen in my life."

But other directors found, in the big canvas, a way to draw an audience deeply into a layered, textured story in a way more conventionally dimensioned movies didn't. They found the big story for the new big screens, and delivered work with all the richness of an epic novel. Think David Lean and *The Bridge on the River Kwai* and *Lawrence of Arabia* (1962), Stanley Kubrick and *Spartacus* and *2001: A Space Odyssey* (1968), William Wyler and *Ben-Hur*, Arthur Penn and *Little Big Man* (1970), Francis Ford Coppola and his *Godfather* films (epics which combined to create a still greater epic).

Eventually, the epic, as it used to be, would be subsumed by a new, incessant kind of big budget moviemaking, the kind of moviemaking which now marks every summer and holiday season, and which turns what was once the rare and special into the commonplace.

It has also turned the epic into kid stuff. With $100-200 million or more on the line, big budget movies have to target the lucrative young audience; it's the only demographic which can possibly generate enough revenue to make such a hefty investment pay off. So, instead of *Lawrence of Arabia,* we get *Battleship;* instead of *Patton* (1970), we get *Men in Black 3*. The adult epic is dead.

Some of the best titles from the classic epic days still have an afterlife, recirculating on cable channels. You all know them: the evergreens, legendary films by legendary filmmakers still standing as cinematic milestones: *Ben-Hur, Lawrence of Arabia, 2001, The Guns of Navarone* (1961), *The Longest*

Day (1962) et al.

But there are a few I think have fallen off the popular radar for reasons I don't quite understand. They still show up, but the titles don't have the same attraction as the evergreens. If they do pop up, and you want to see Big Picture storytelling at its best, you might want to give them a watch…but save yourself a couple of hours for it.

The Sand Pebbles (1966)
Directed by Robert Wise
Adapted from Richard McKenna's novel by Robert Anderson

It's China, 1926, and Jake Holman (Steve McQueen) is a Navy fleet engineer re-assigned, at his own request, to a small gunboat patrolling China's rivers. All Holman wants is to run his engine without interference, but the great political and social forces fighting for domination in a fractured China reach even into his boiler room.

Although neither the novel nor the movie was intended as an allegory of America's then increasing involvement in Vietnam (McKenna based his novel on his own experiences in the 1930s as a "China sailor" on an American gunboat), it was understandably taken as such. Both McKenna and Anderson tapped into those universals which have dogged so many of our military involvements, from the Indian Wars of the 1880s through Vietnam to the still-unresolved conflict in Afghanistan: a lethal mix of willful ignorance and dismissal of native sensibilities, arrogance, and naïve, simplistic idealism.

Movies, it is sometimes said, takes us to times and places normally beyond our reach. Aided by renowned production designer Boris Levin, and shooting on location in Taiwan and Hong Kong, Wise delivers us into a recreation of China c. 1920s so full-bodied and textured, we feel just as dislocated and bewildered and entranced as any new sailor showing up for duty on the gunboat San Pablo.

But at the heart of all that production value is a very human, very life-sized story about one unexceptional, emotionally unanchored sailor moving from casual apathy to heartbreak to disillusionment. In his only Oscar-nominated performance, McQueen shows he was always more than the King of Cool. His Jake Holman only feels at home surrounded by machinery, but then he reaches out – violating both white and Chinese taboos – to befriend one of the coolies who do the dirty work on the ship, and suffers mightily for it.

McQueen at his best: he's just killed his Chinese friend to save him from torture by one of the many militant groups vying for power. Numbed, he retreats to his engine room, tries to bury his grief by stoking his boilers, and then suddenly slumps over his shovel as if in physical pain. Wise shoots McQueen from behind and gets more out of those slumped shoulders and bowed back then some directors get from a screen full of tears.

Barry Lyndon (1975)
Written and directed by Stanley Kubrick,
Adapted from *The Memoirs of Barry Lyndon, Esq.*, by William Makepeace Thackery

Thackery's tale about an opportunistic Candide-like character was loosely based on a real-life fortune-hunter, and is considered the first novel built around an anti-hero. Barry (Ryan O'Neal) begins as a nice enough Irish lad who missteps when he fiddles around with a British army officer's girl. On the run after a duel, he passes through one adventure after another, always looking for some way to advance his station, ultimately marrying into money which he then proceeds to squander away along with the love of his sons and wife.

At the time, *Barry Lyndon* was an underperformer and considered something of a disappointment. Audiences looking for Kubrick's follow-up to the high-energy, violence-filled antics of *Clockwork Orange* (1971) choked on the deliberately-paced elegance of *Barry Lyndon*. But with the remove of four decades, *Lyndon* seems less a follow-up to *Clockwork* than to Kubrick's similarly poetic *2001: A Space Odyssey* (1968). Pushed less by narrative than by immersion in a sense of place and time – with cinematographer John Alcott channeling the paintings of Thomas Gainsborough — one is hard put to think of another film which so completely puts the viewer in the 18th Century.

That said, *Barry Lyndon* is not without its narrative charms as well, particularly during Barry's climb to the upper classes. He's waylaid by a loquacious highwayman, captured by Prussians and turned spy, then turned again by the cool gambler he's been set to spy on, and on and on and on: an alternately mirthful/heartbreaking trek through the constantly ebbing/flowing world of European intrigue.

Most lovely moment: Barry finds himself serving in a British army unit with one of his few, true friends, Captain Grogan (Godfrey Quigley). Grogan is mortally wounded in a skirmish against the French. Barry drops out of the ranks to carry him to the safety of a gully. Grogan presses his remaining coin on young Barry, then says, "Now kiss me, me boy, because I'll not be seeing you again." Barry sets his lips to the father-like figure as the older man dies, leaving a weeping Barry alone, the intertwined tree branches overhead through which filter columns of light providing a nature-formed temple for the young man's grief.

It's a Mad, Mad, Mad, Mad World (1963)
Directed by Stanley Kramer
Written by William Rose and Tania Rose

At the time, Kramer had a reputation as one of the most socially-conscious filmmakers in Hollywood, with a body of topical, often controversial movies to his credit including the anti-racism *The Defiant Ones* (1958), anti-nuke *On the Beach* (1959), anti-Creationist *Inherit the Wind* (1960), and anti-Nazi *Judgment at Nuremberg* (1961). Having spent years depressing the hell out of people, Kramer turned around 180 degrees and set out to make the biggest, funniest movie comedy ever (he hoped) by casting every comedic performer he could think of in a big-screen, snowballing chase after $350,000 (hardly seems worth it today, but trust me, that was a lot of bucks in 1963).

Even a Kramer comedy had something more on its mind than just laughs. There may not be a funnier or more bitter indictment of greed as a small number of everyday, otherwise decent schmoes get wind of a buried cache of loot from a long-ago robbery, and devolve from reasonable people trying to negotiate a fair split into a frantic, obsessed, incredibly destructive and ever-expanding mob that seems to lay waste to a good bit of southern California in their race for the money "hidden under a big W."

The true mark of how well *Mad, Mad World* works is to look at how often its "comedy of destruction" has been copied without delivering the same quotient of laughs: think *1941* (1979) where even Steven Spielberg couldn't pull it off.

Along with all the crashing and smashing and cars careening, there are any number of hysterical comic performances: Sid Caesar as the level-headed vacationing dentist who ultimately becomes a manic Ahab-like obsessive; Phil Silvers as a fast-talking salesman who talks himself into more trouble than he talks himself out of; Jonathan Winters as a slow-burning but ultimately raging moving van driver. One could go on and on, and that's one of the charms of the movie: it's a showcase for just about everybody who was anybody in comedy in the 1950s-early 1960s, and the Roses give them just as much to juggle verbally as bonk-in-the-head slapstick (to name one: Terry-Thomas' lacerating indictment of Americans' obsession with "boosoms").

Cinematographer Ernest Laszlo gets great use out of the desert and sleepy locales of a then under-developed southern California, and the movie has an exhilarating visual sweep which complements the escalating, mushrooming chase.

But my personal favorite scene is not the wholesale destruction of a hardware store by Sid Caesar, or Jonathan Winters' razing of a gas station, or Mickey Rooney and Buddy Hackett stuck in a pilotless airplane which crashes through a billboard, but a quieter bit of verbal wit. Before the craziness takes root, Caesar gathers with Winters, Rooney, Hackett and Milton Berle to try to devise a fair split, and comes up with a mathematical formula worthy of Stephen Hawking: "You get one share for the truck, you get one share for being a person in the truck, you get one share for going down to the wreck..."

Curio note: Milton Berle was a notorious but highly skilled camera hog. If you watch closely, in every crowd scene Berle lags behind everyone else to get himself a few extra seconds of face time in front of the camera.

The Three Mustketeers (1973); *The Four Musketeers: Milady's Revenge* (1974)
Directed by Richard Lester
Adapted from Alexandre Dumas' novel by George MacDonald Fraser

A Hollywood producer's wet dream: a property of proven and perennial popularity, an immediately recognizable brand name, and it's in the public domain so the rights don't cost a dime. That's why the Internet Movie Data Base lists 29 screen and TV adaptations of Dumas' 1844 adventure novel dating back to 1914. But nobody – seriously, *nobody* – did it as well as Richard Lester & Co. in this two-part, epically sumptuous romp through 17th Century France.

Lester had originally intended *The Three Musketeers* as a vehicle for The Beatles (he had already directed them quite successfully in *A Hard Day's Night* [1964], and *Help!* [1965]), and the dry, tossed off, deadpan wit and little tickling bits going on in the margins which trademarked those Fab Four features abounds here. Example: at a lavish costume ball for the king of France, a group of dwarves carrying serving trays on their heads engage in Altmanesque mumbles as to which of their head-balanced hors d'oeuvres the king liked best.

For all of its throw-away bits of humor, Fraser stays impressively close to the plot of Dumas' novel and its tale of French royal court intrigues and derring-do, and the roles are filled out by a cast brimming with charm: Michael York as the naifish D'Artagnan, Oliver Reed as brawling Athos, Frank Finlay as clothes-hound Porthos, and Richard Chamberlain as lady's man Aramis. And behind them sits a bench equally deep in talent: the great British comedian Spike Jones, Lester favorite Roy Kinnear, Charlton Heston as the oily Richelieu, Fay Dunaway and Christopher Lee as Heston's chief henchpersons, and Raquel Welch in an unexpectedly deft turn as a clumsy, somewhat ding-a-lingy lady-in-waiting to the adulterous queen (Geraldine Chaplin).

Lester beautifully balances truly impressive swordplay with humor, maintains a buoyant tongue-in-cheekiness without ever descending into camp. And when, in the second film, the action takes a turn toward the dark, Lester manages that transition just as smoothly, having kept the film grounded enough to allow grief as well as fun.

Curio: *Musketeers* was originally shot as a single film, but producers Ilya and Alexander Salkind split the movie in two, causing such a ruckus among their cast ("Let me get this straight; I get paid for *one* movie, but you get *two* movies out of it?"), it resulted in a lawsuit and the consequent routine inclusion in actors' contracts of "the Salkind clause" to prevent future producers from pulling the same move.

The Big Country (1958)
Directed by William Wyler
Adapted from Donald Hamilton's novel by Jessamyn West, James R. Webb,
Sy Bartlett, and William Wyler

In Hamilton's grand scale novel, Wyler saw an allegory for the self-destructive Cold War dueling between East and West which had been going on since the end of WW II. Charles Bickford is Wyler's Wild West version of Eisenhower, heading a ranch clan of powerful, high-society-aspiring types who believe they're bringing civilization to the West, engaged in an on-going, escalating fight with Burl Ives' boorish, Third-Worldy bunch.

As big as the West is – and cinematographer Franz Planer catches the sense of a limitless expanse as few Western lensmen have – it seems almost paradoxical (if not psychotically obsessive) that each family is murderously committed to the idea there's no room for the other.

Between them is sea captain Gregory Peck, come west to marry Bickford's daughter (Carroll Barker) only to lose her when he refuses to indulge in typical displays of cowboy machismo. Peck finds a kindred spirit in Jean Simmons, owner of a key piece of territory Bickford and Ives both covet.

The story of feudin' ranchers is an old one, but Wyler infuses it with a sense of tragic pointlessness no John Wayne oater ever had.

One of the best moments: After having refused to publicly trade punches with Charlton Heston, Bickford's like-a-son foreman, Peck calls Heston out for a one-on-one before dawn, while the rest of the ranch is still asleep. Peck's not the coward he's been branded to be, nor a foppish pacifist; he's just not willing to spill blood for a show. The fight is filmed in long shot – in fact, often in extreme long shot, against plains which seem to roll on forever – as if to italicize just how meaningless the petty (and sometimes lethal) peacock displays by and between the dueling families really are.

MICHAEL GOUGH (1916 – 2011): "OH, YEAH! *THAT* GUY!"

March 18, 2011

Stars bring a character to life on the screen; but behind them is another kind of actor that brings life to that character's world. They are the seasoning which turns a good meal into a great meal, the chinking keeping a cold wind from blowing through the holes in a script. Call them what you will: supporting players, character actors, familiar faces, second bananas. To most viewers, their names mean nothing, and a headshot over their obituary usually draws little more than an, "Oh, yeah, *that* guy!" They rarely get their due, often only at their passing, which, sadly, makes it time to give one of the best his due: Michael Gough, who died this week at the age of 94.

All of his obits usually start with saying he was best known for his role as Batman's faithful butler Alfred in the Tim Burton version of *Batman* (1989) and its three sequels. That's often the lot of a supporting player like Gough; they're always "best known" for their most visible role. But this almost always does them a disservice. Actors like Gough are not about *a* role, but a body of work, a *function* if you will, to step in and step up, make a scene snap and pop with little direction, little instruction, knowing what they're there to do the minute they get the call.

That's how they get to have careers like Gough: 64 years long, over 100 film credits as well as work on TV, in just about every kind of story. He worked horror (genre devotees, like Burton, especially remember his work for Hammer Studios from the late 1950s into the 1960s in films like *Horror of Dracula* [1958] and *Horrors of the Black Museum* [1959]) to upscale class A drama *(Out of Africa* [1985]; a 1967 Brit TV series version of *Pride and Prejudice)*; the broadest of broad slapstick *(Top Secret!* [1984]) to the cheesiest of sci fi *(Konga* [1961]; *They Came from Beyond Space* [1967]); grand camp *(The Avengers* Brit TV series in the late '60s) to great cinema *(The Age of Innocence* [1993]).

And this doesn't count his substantial stage resume. Gough, like most of the memorable British actors of his generation, found his start in the theater. He'd studied at the Old Vic and was soon in demand for roles in London's West End theater district. Even as a film and TV regular, he never gave up the stage and copped a Tony in 1979 for his work in Alan Ayckbourn's comedy, *Bedroom Farce*.

Though his film roles tended to feature his patrician bearing and a certain silky elegance, on stage he showed how ruthlessly he could chase down a laugh. In a West End production of John Osborne's *A Patriot for Me*, Gough's Baron von Epp ruled over a drag ball as a gowned and tiara-ed Queen Alexandra, complete with handbag and fluttering fan.

Though he never gained the stature of contemporaries like Olivier, Richardson, Gielgud, it was not through lack of talent. Olivier himself thought enough of Gough to cast him in his screen adaptation of *Richard III* (1955), a veritable showcase of English theater big guns including the above named Big Three.

As is the British theatrical tradition, the material – at least on film and TV – was secondary. *Dr. Who* or *Pride and Prejudice;* no matter. A working actor works, and as a craftsman he always does his work as well as he can: big screen, little screen, schlock, high art – all done with the same commitment, the same finesse, the same class. That was Gough. Whether he was playing the mad scientist in a poor boy's *King Kong* like *Konga,* or deliciously playing the silliness straight-faced in *Top Secret,* or taking his place in the Battleship Row of class acts in the background ensemble of Scorsese's tribute to Ophuls in *The Age of Innocence,* no matter how big or how small the part, he never condescended, he never phoned it in, and, with a sniper's precision, always knew his place in the wider fabric and never showboated; Michael Gough was always *there*.

And in another grand theatrical tradition, he remained in his traces nearly to the end. When his body could no longer hold up to the rigors of the work, he still had that lovely, regal voice which enlivened animated characters in *The Corpse Bride* (2005) and *Alice in Wonderland* (2010), both from Gough fan Tim Burton.

The familiar faces, the second bananas; with a combination of talent, skill, and a certain particular charm, they keep their few lines and few scenes from being throwaways, make the smallest characters come alive in the same moment in the same world as the biggest characters played by the biggest stars. Their value is never appreciated until they're absent and then you suddenly notice a movie becomes a little less alive, a story a bit less vibrant and full, the screen a little emptier.

Michael Gough passed this week, and now we can appreciate what he gave us because our screen is now forever a little emptier.

POST SANDY THOUGHTS: 7 DISASTER FILMS DONE RIGHT

November 12, 2012

The gray rolling seas thundered through the forest of pilings under the piers, sometimes cresting enough to send a geyser of wind-whipped froth up onto the decking. Other places, the dark water poured through the gaps the wind and tide had eaten through the dunes and poured into the beach town streets. It pulled boats large and small from their moorings in the lagoon marinas and piled them like a child's toys up on the land. Some in apartment buildings would tell of the cars in their ground level garages floating against each other like bathtub playthings. But there was nothing childlike in the way the sea took away entire houses, and made seaside villages look like an extension of the ocean.

For the day and a half I watched Hurricane Sandy pound my home state of New Jersey, which was all the time I had before I lost my cable service to the storm, the pictures that most tugged at me were what the 90 mph winds and unstoppable tide did to the boardwalk cities. For any Jersey kid, The Shore is part of growing up; it's part of being a Jersey kid. When I saw helicopter shots of Seaside Heights, saw the end of one of its amusement piers ripped away and its roller coaster half-submerged in the surf, I was watching that part of me die. I could feel my eyes grow wet.

Even with all the talk about Jersey resiliency, about coming back, about rebuilding The Shore bigger and better, even if it turns out to be true – and for the sake of the state, I hope it does – it will never be the same. That will be someone else's Jersey Shore. Mine will be gone forever.

That's the thing most disaster movies miss; that human element. The pain of loss; loss of life, loss of things that have a meaning to the heart, to the memory.

One of the gifts movies give us is the ability to experience vicariously what we would never want to experience personally: war, crime, battling demons from the underworld. Disaster movies have generally been just another kind of safe thrill, with the best performance in them often that of the special effects crew.

Most – or at least the ones I tend to think of when I think of disaster movies – are all about spectacle…and only about spectacle. Part of that is by design. If you really felt the emotional impact of the wholesale destruction of a city, or, in some cases, an entire world, well, that's nobody's fun way to spend an evening. Other times it's because, to be blunt, that other than the impressive effects work, most disaster movies are just so damned bad, with tidal waves and high rise infernos and flying disasters serving as a backdrop for the soapiest, most overwrought melodramas populated with one by-the-numbers cliché character after another. Not exactly a recipe for moving drama.

And you can find it as far back as *The Hurricane* (1937) and *San Francisco* (1936) in the 1930s, *The High and the Mighty* (1954) in the 1950s, and then that tidal wave of disaster pix kicked off by *Airport* (1970) which included *Airport*'s three increasingly lame sequels, *Earthquake* (1974), *Avalanche* (1978), and a veritable parade of destruction from Irwin Allen including *The Poseidon Adventure* (1972), *The Towering Inferno* (1974), *Flood!* (1976), *Fire!* (1977), *The Swarm* (1978), *Beyond the Poseidon Adventure* (1979), *When Time Ran Out...* (1980), *The Night the Bridge Fell Down* (1983), and *Cave In!* (1983).

You could flip between any three of them on your cable box and they're all so similar you'll never be lost. There'll be some square-jawed hero type saying something about how some building/plane/bridge/resort/whatever is unsafe, gotta get the people out, yadda yadda yadda, and then there's another guy – a short-sighted greedy little prick – who says something about not starting a panic and ruining the tourist season/financial disaster/similar kind of crap. There'll be a couple of headliners to get the contemporary audience in, some kids for the kids and to give the hero something to save, and a couple of oldsters about 40 years past their career peak to get the senior crowd in.

When you actually experience something akin to a movie-type disaster, it makes you a little mad. I don't begrudge anyone the fun of watching cities crumble or disappear in a volcanic explosion. Even after Sandy, I still see the appeal. But the dramatic emptiness... That always bothered me, and now it bothers me a bit more.

But there are those filmmakers and screenwriters who have seen, in the disaster movie, an opportunity not just to thrill people, but to move them at the same time, to touch them, to awe them, to make them feel something more than, "Wow, that's cool!"

1: A Night to Remember (1958)
Directed by Roy Ward Baker
Adapted from Walter Lord's book by Eric Ambler

James Cameron's *Titanic* (1997) might have had better special effects (change that; it had incredible effects), but its gooey teen romance front story pales next to this painstakingly exact adaptation of Walter Lord's classic account of the tragic 1912 sinking of the opulent ocean liner on her maiden voyage. It's a stirring and ultimately moving account of grace under pressure, of human hubris and waste, of heroism and infuriating indifference. Cameron caught some of it, but *Night* is wholly dedicated to it and it still stands as a textbook example of how to do it right.

2: *United 93* (2006)
Written and directed by Paul Greenglass

True stories always have the advantage of being true. If a coward shirks, when a hero stands up, when a life is wasted, the idea of This Is How It Happened gives the proceedings a weight fiction rarely attains. So it is with *A Night to Remember,* and so it is, again, with Greenglass' tribute to the passengers on United 93 who rebelled against their hijackers on 9/11 and were killed when their airliner crashed into a Pennsylvania field. True, no one knows exactly what transpired on United 93, but Greenglass' depiction of life-sized heroes fits with what was known of the passengers, and he blends it with gripping recreations (using some of the real participants) of what went on that dark day at military and civilian air traffic control centers. Knowing how the story ends gives *United 93* an inevitability that works on you long before its heartbreaking finale.

3: *Fearless* (1993)
Directed by Peter Weir
Adapted by Rafael Yglesias from his novel

Jeff Bridges plays the survivor of an air crash heralded as a hero for leading a number of other survivors out of the wreckage to safety. Suffering from a form of PTSD, Bridges neither rejoices in his survival, nor broods over his friend and partner lost in the crash. He seems, rather, strangely disconnected from his loved ones (wife Isabella Rossellini and son Spencer Vrooman). Instead, his strongest connection is to another survivor, Rosie Perez, whose young son died in the crash. It takes another near-death experience to bring the catharsis that finally brings the inner man back to life.

It's a psychologically intriguing, emotionally moving movie that grapples with that moment of one's death – the clear recognition that these minutes are your last — which ascends to the poetic when Bridges, slipping toward death in an allergic reaction, relives the crash (one of the most horrifying renderings of an air crash you'll ever see on film) and then begins to "move toward the light." A hard, often tearful, ultimately rejoicing watch.

4: *Fate Is the Hunter* (1964).
Directed by Ralph Nelson
Adapted from Ernest K. Gann's book by Harold Medford

Medford's script retains only Gann's title and the idea which Gann, who'd been a pilot during the early days of commercial air travel, weaved throughout his memoir; that you can do everything right in the cockpit, and still not make it home.

Rod Taylor is a pilot taking out a routine commercial flight from Los Angeles. Minutes from the airport, his ship develops mechanical problems. Taylor is forced to attempt a belly landing on a nearby beach which goes tragically wrong and all aboard are killed. Old friend and boss Glenn Ford is tasked with investigating the crash and finds himself defending a man with a reputation for hard-living and capriciousness, but who he comes to find out was a deeply compassionate and generous human being…just in ways not obvious to those who live by first glances.

Ford carries with him a genuine sense of loss and that gives *Fate* its flavor and heft, and he's backed by fine performances from Taylor, Suzanne Pleshette, Wally Cox, Mark Stevens and others. A good, solid, often affecting drama.

5: *The Last Voyage* (1960)
Written and directed by Andrew L. Stone

In the days before CGI, you had two ways to create an on-screen disaster: fake it with special effects…or do it. Life-sized. For real…or as close to it as you could safely come. Stone used the deactivated ocean liner Ile de France as the "star" of this film about an aging ocean liner holed by a boiler explosion on her last transoceanic trip. Stone actually partially sunk this ship and shot much of the action, including flooding compartments and explosions, on the actual liner.

The story is simple. Robert Stack's wife (Dorothy Mallone) is trapped in wreckage from the explosion, and he spends much of the movie trying to free her as the ship sinks further and further into the water. Stack and Mallone lend some heart to the suspense elements in those moments when she tries to get him to leave her and look after their daughter, but the real-life setting gives it all a this-is-what-it's-like feel that even Cameron's majestic ship-sinking couldn't quite capture.

6: *The Day the Earth Caught Fire* (1961)
Directed by Val Guest
Written by Val Guest and Wolf Mankowitz

The late 1950s and 1960s saw any number of apocalyptic scenarios bred by the real-world fears of Cold War nuclear arms escalation. But *Day* took a slightly different tack; there's no atomic war, accidental or otherwise, here. Rather, an accident – but one brought out of the same east/west postwar tensions – does the dirty deed. Two atomic tests (one by the U.S., the other by the Soviets) shift the Earth's orbit just enough to push it closer to the sun and the possible extinction of the human race.

No special effects, hysterics, no marauding bands of *Mad Max*-type apocalyptic road warriors. *Day* is a drama-driven, thoughtful treatment well played by Edward Judd, Janet Munro, and the great Leo McKern. Its ambiguous ending is as haunting as any spectacular fireball. Michael Bay and the *Armageddon* (1998) gang, take a cue.

7: *Airplane!* (1980)
Written and directed by Jim Abrahams, David Zucker, and Jerry Zucker Uncredited adaptation of the 1956 Candian teleplay *Flight into Danger* by Arthur Hailey, and its 1957 feature film adaptation *Zero Hour* by Hailey, Hall Bartlett, and John C. Champion

I had to end on a high note (for my sake as well as yours), and thank God for Abrahams and the Zuckers for providing it. Think of every possible disaster movie cliché you can, and guaranteed you'll find it affectionately lampooned in this joke-a-minute laugh-fest.

The question for today's audiences is, how many will get the jokes? The writing/directing trio grounded their movie solidly in decades of disaster movie tropes cycled and recycled endlessly on TV. Even some of the casting – Robert Stack, Lloyd Bridges, Leslie Nielsen – is something of a wink-wink joke to the knowing, each of them parodying the kind of stalwart parts which comprised much of their respective careers.

But even with that caveat, well, here's a sample of some of the dialogue:
"Can you fly this plane and land it?"
"Surely you can't be serious."
"I am serious…and don't call me Shirley."
That's gotta be funny for anybody.

TRAIN WRECKS: MY FAVORITE STINKERS

November 24, 2012

Not all bad movies are equal. Some just stink; others are entrancingly awful.

I remember John Cleese being interviewed by Dick Cavett some years ago, and saying something to the effect that when you understood all that goes into making movies, the surprise isn't that so few good movies get made; the surprise is that anything gets made at all! There have always been more bad movies than good (I'm not talking about box office flops; plenty of good movies have stiffed, and plenty of turds have minted box office gold). Back in the days of the silents, not every flick which showed up at the neighborhood nickelodeon was a Charlie Chaplin gem. And during Hollywood's Golden Age, the *Casablancas* and *Gone with the Winds* were the rarities. And during that phenomenal creative explosion of the 1960s and 1970s, there was a lot more crud than cream. That being the case, with such an outrageous tonnage of junk, it shouldn't be a surprise to discover there are all kinds of bad movies.

There is, of course, the standard Hollywood bad; movies that aren't completely lousy, but just forgettable and disposable. You know; like every other Sandra Bullock movie. Like every Katherine Heigl movie.

And then there are movies that were never supposed to be good. Torture porn, splatter flicks, teen sex comedies. I guarantee you that the cinematic aspirations of the folks behind *Saw 3D* (2010) were probably less than auspicious.

Some movies are so beautifully, perfectly awful, they have a charm of their own. They become camp classics, as entertaining in their left-handed way (and in a way 180 degrees from what their makers intended) as anything that even remotely passes for good. Think *Reefer Madness* (1936), *Robot Monster* (1953), anything by Ed Wood. And just below those are duds that may not be quite as classically bad, but bad enough to be fun bad, *Mystery Science Theater 3000* bad (my personal MST fave: *Manos: The Hands of Fate* [1966]).

But there's yet another kind of bad, and I'm sure each of us has their pets in this category; the movies we know suck, can even tell you why they suck… yet we keep watching them time and again. Like some sort of slow motion train wreck, we can't turn away, we remain fascinated. These are our guilty pleasures, the junkiest of the filmic junk food, the cinematic Yodel we keep hidden away to snack on when nobody else is looking, even though we know it's bad, bad, *bad* for us.

*****

The Green Berets (1968)
Directed by John Wayne
Adapted from Robin Moore's book by James Lee Barrett

Moore did it right. He spent a year training with the Berets, then tagged along with them on a 1963 deployment to South Vietnam. His 1965 book – a somewhat fictionalized version of what he witnessed – was, as I remember, not a political polemic. Though in keeping with the temper of the times it was decidedly anti-communist, the general tone of the book was a straightforward accounting of the dirty ways in which a dirty war was being fought by an elite unit specifically trained to fight dirty wars (it probably says something about Moore's attitude that a condition of the U.S. Army's cooperation in making the movie was that Moore not be involved in any way).

But Wayne, who'd never served in the military, saw Moore's book as a vehicle to rebut all the long-haired, dope-smoking, flag-burning, unAmerican peaceniks making such a hell-no-we-won't-go ruckus on college campuses at the time. With the logistical support of an approving U.S. Army, he set about making an outrageously simplistic rah-rah picture of a war that, by the time of the movie's release, was not only going badly, but tearing the country apart.

Moore's book is constructed as a series of stand-alone stories linked only by their all involving members of the Berets. Barrett's script takes a couple of those stories, combines elements of a few more into a single, wandering plotline following anti-war journalist David Jansen as he takes up Beret colonel Wayne's invitation to go to Nam and get the straight poop on what's really happening in the war. Jansen's there for a large-scale Viet Cong night assault on an American firebase, and then later drops out of sight as the movie clumsily transitions to a behind-the-scenes mission to capture a North Vietnamese general.

To be fair about this, let's put the movie's inflammatory politics aside. Let's just talk movie-making. Even at that level, we have to talk astoundingly bad.

For a project made with expansive support from the Army, the movie, at times, looks shockingly cheap. During the attack on the firebase, even in the dark, it's obvious that a lot of those Cong storming the wire are white guys in blackface. Some of their equipment is a little dodgy, too. One of my favorites – watch the battle sequences closely, you'll see it – is one of them carrying an old-fashioned tommy gun, the kind with a pistol fore grip, but with the magazine removed in the hope (I guess) nobody'd be able to tell it's a tommy gun.

A particularly crappy part of the night battle is a scene where Wayne's chopper is hit. Even for the time, it's painfully obvious they've set a small model on fire. Then, when the movie cuts to a life-sized burning chopper for the actual crash, you can see the restraining strap unfurl as the wreck is released to the ground. That's not just bad; that's bush league.

Wayne uses a visual that didn't make much sense in his previous directorial disaster, *The Alamo* (1960); having a mass of the enemy, standing shoulder to shoulder, slowly stalk forward into blazing guns with hardly a one falling. Just as dumbfoundingly nonsensical, later, when a U.S. gunship strafes the Cong who've overrun the camp, they seem to be standing around stock-still waiting for the squibs to go off.

If you want a stark measure of how badly put-together the movie is, measure its helicopter attack sequence against a Cong bridge against the majestically terrifying chopper ballet Francis Ford Coppola put together in *Apocalypse Now* (1979).

Barrett's script, politics aside, is equally sloppy, and not just with that plotline which feels like two movies (the firebase attack; the behind-the-lines operation) shotgun-wedded together. Every tired WW II war movie cliché you can think of is hauled out and run in front of the camera: the conniving scrounger with a secret heart of gold glommed onto by an adorable orphan whose only friend is his scruffy little pooch; the burly, gruff veteran sergeant; the critical newspaperman who doesn't have to know what he's talking about to have a completely wrong opinion. Those cliches look all the more tired misplaced as they are in the context of a war that was, in every way, the antithesis of WW II. I mean, c'mon; the little orphan boy? With a puppy? The only old corndog missing from the script is the one about somebody's sister who needs an operation so she can dance the ballet again.

No matter how you cut it, no matter how politically blind you want to be, it's a dumb movie with characters saying dumb things ("Out here, due process is a bullet!"), and a director (and keep in mind, God bless 'im, I loved John Wayne) doing even dumber things.

So, what's my fascination with it? What keeps bringing me back?

Part of it is the fun of watching a 1940s kind of patriotism mash up against the war that killed that kind of sensibility. As I sit there, about every five minutes I'm compelled to say out loud, "Seriously? Seriously?" Part of it is that I've always had a fondness for old war movies, and that's exactly what *The Green Berets* is – an old war movie disguised as a Vietnam War treatise.

But undoubtedly the biggest attraction for me is watching John Wayne be John Wayne no matter how wrongheaded the context. Look, he was 30 years and 50 pounds past pulling off the part (there are scenes of him in a dress uniform where it looks like his buttons will pop so hard they'll take somebody's eye out across the room), and his take on the war came out of some *Leave It to Beaver* dream state worldview, but, ya know, he was still John Wayne…and, like I said, I loved the guy.

Mackenna's Gold (1969)
Directed by J. Lee Thompson
Adapted from Heck Allen's novel by Carl Foreman.

The pedigree promised big. Thompson, after all, was the guy who'd directed 1961's huge hit, *The Guns of Navarone*. Here he was re-teamed with Foreman who had produced and written the screenplay for *Navarone*, and was taking on the same roles for *Mackenna*. It was a big-scale production originally intended for Cinerama, and its leads – Gregory Peck and Omar Sharif – were backed by an all-star supporting cast including, among others, Raymond Massey, Burgess Meredith, Lee J. Cobb, Eli Wallach, Edward G. Robinson.

Loosely based on the legend of the Lost Adams Diggings, the story has Peck as a marshal in the Old West who learns from a dying Apache about a secret canyon loaded with gold. Peck doesn't believe the story, but everyone else does, including Omar Sharif as one of those grinning Mexican banditos who lives in a permanent state of toothy amusement over everything including theft, kidnapping and murder. Sharif forces Peck to take him to the canyon. On the way, they acquire a snowballing mob of gold-hunters.

From the first sonorous tones of Victory Jory's narration, it's clear Thompson/Foreman are out to tell an epic, definitive story about corrupting greed. Instead, what they turn out is a bloated, cliché-ridden, often silly tale – bloated, cliché and silly enough to make you forget these were the guys who turned out a classic actioner like *Guns of Navarone*.

Like *The Green Berets*, this is a flick which, despite its grand-scale production, still manages, at least at times, to look surprisingly cheap. It's bad enough the cast isn't riding real horses for their close-ups, but they're also filmed in front of an exceptionally lousy back projection.

Or take that all-star line-up, most of which are billed under the heading, "The Men of Hadleyburg." The idea is supposed to be that even all these decent folk (one's a judge, another's a preacher, etc.) can fall victim to gold fever. They show up en masse, they have one scene around Sharif's campfire where they shamefacedly admit to their greed, and then they're all – I'm not kidding, *all* – killed off in the very next scene during an Apache ambush.

One of my favorite bad scenes happens after the surviving fortune-seekers discover the secret canyon. An unarmed Peck and Camilla Sparv (the Swedish cutie is shoehorned into the love interest role looking as at-home in the Old West as a Japanese tea house) try to escape by climbing a sheer, several hundred-foot high cliff to some abandoned Indian dwellings (which, by the way, they do with a quickness I'm sure has Edmund Hillary pulling a WTF!!! spin in his grave). Sharif gives chase up the same cliff. Every time I watch this I keep thinking, Hey, Greg, just drop a rock on the guy's head! At least step on his fingers when he tries to climb up. But noooooo! That would make too much sense.

It gets worse.

Peck and Sharif fight. Peck beats the crap out of Sharif but doesn't kill him. Never occurs to him to, say, chuck him off that cliff once he's got him down. Good guys don't do that, I guess. Instead, Peck and Sparv now climb all the way back *down* that several hundred-foot high cliff. And, yeah, Sharif follows. So, scale a cliff, fight, climb back down, and none of them are even breathing hard.

Also like *Berets,* the whole movie feels old and tired. *Mackenna* came out the same year as *Butch Cassidy and the Sundance Kid* and *The Wild Bunch,* and next to these two energetic exercises in Old West revisionism, *Mackenna* comes off about 20 years out of date.

You want a Western about greed? One that's more than a half-century old yet still hasn't dated? John Huston did it with a modest budget and just three guys digging small handfuls of gold dust out of a mountain in Mexico in *Treasure of the Sierra Madre* (1948). Managed it quite well, in fact. I believe the word "classic" is usually used.

So, what keeps bringing me back to *Mackenna's Gold*? I think of the big name talent involved, look at what they wound up with, and wonder how this pool of normally capable filmmakers managed to get abso-freaking-lutely *nothing* right.

The Cool Ones (1967)
Directed by Gene Nelson
Written by Nelson, Joyce Geller, Robert Kaufman

Nothing ages more quickly and more embarrassingly than a movie or TV show which had worked so hard to be cool in its time. You disagree? Feathered hair, big lapels. Oh, God; mullets! You gonna honestly tell me that stuff still works for you as anything but a laugh-getter?

Lead times for some movies are so long, some crazes burn out between the pitch meeting and opening weekend. Roller disco was dying (if not dead) by the time *Roller Boogie* (1979) and *Xanudu* (1980) hit theaters, and did anybody still care about The Village People when *Can't Stop the Music* (1980) had movie-goers wishing they could?

The only thing even more embarrassing is a movie that's lethally uncool even before the first frame of film runs through the camera, not because it's late to the party, but because the people behind the camera are so phenomenally clueless. That in mind, there may not be a more grossly mis-titled movie to come out of the 1960s; *The Cool Ones* was about as cool, even then, as bowties and high-button shoes.

Roddy McDowall (you can tell he's supposed to be cool because he wears frock-length jackets, has long hair even though it's in that cute, unthreatening early-'60s Beatles bob, and wears tinted wire-rimmed glasses) is a manipulative music producer trying to engineer a boy-girl duet into stardom by getting them on a *Hullabaloo*-like TV show (look up *Hullabaloo*; you'll get a kick out of it – it makes *American Bandstand* look cutting edge) so they can score big with the kids.

And that's the rub with this clunker: "the kids." If you were around in those days, this flick's image of "the kids" would have had you wondering what drugs Warner Bros.' geriatric execs were on. The boys are wearing button-down short-sleeved shirts and loafers and have haircuts that make Marine recruits look shaggy. The girls are even neater. There's not a pair of jeans to be seen let alone sneakers.

The killer is *The Cool Ones* came out in 1967. The Beatles had already gone all stringy-haired and psychedelic with "Sgt. Pepper's Lonely Hearts Club Band," The Who had implied what the oldsters could do to themselves in "My Generation," The Doors' Jim Morrison had been busted for indecency and a couple of The Rolling Stones were dealing with drug charges. We had Cream ("Sunshine of Your Love"), Deep Purple ("Hush"), Creedence Clearwater Revival ("Proud Mary"), Jefferson Airplane ("White Rabbit"), The Byrds ("Eight Miles High"). But *The Cool Ones* gives us some dweeb off the set of *Ozzie & Harriett* singing the Sinatra-esque "This Town" and thinks it's hip. Next to that, the Beach Boys seem like acid rock (I take that back; by 1967, the Beach Boys had already tripped in "Good Vibrations").

I have to admit I've only seen *The Cool Ones* once, having stumbled across it recently on Turner Classics Movies, but it's now among my pet stinkers list. Why? Because I was there, folks. I may have only been 12, but I had eyes, I had ears, and this ain't the way it was. Not even close. That's what I love about *The Cool Ones*; it's so spectacularly detached from the very audience it was trying to reach, and from the time of which it was trying to be a part. It's like watching some midlife crisis case pull on his shag toupe and gold chains, and squeeze into a little red roadster next to a girl young enough to be his daughter. Maybe granddaughter. It's not cool; it's laughably pathetic.

Invaders from Mars (1953)
Directed by William Cameron Menzies
Written by Richard Blake and an uncredited John Tucker Battle

There are people who think *Invaders* is classic sci fi. There are others who think it's just another bit of run-of-the-mill corny '50s flying saucer schlock. And there's still others who think it's both. I'm in that last bunch.

That's the thing about *Invaders*; it stands as visual and conceptual brilliance colliding head-on with old school sci fi goofiness…only you sometimes wonder if the goofiness isn't a carefully orchestrated part of the brilliance.

Young David (Jimmy Hunt), son of a rocket scientist, is awakened one night by a thunderstorm. Through his bedroom window, he sees a flying saucer disappear into the sand pit behind his house. Thereafter, everyone who strays out into the sand pit, including his parents, disappears into the ground, then later appears acting oddly, taken over, little David figures out, by whatever is under the sand. A very nice lady from the health department (Helena Carter) dressed all in angelic white takes David under her wing and comes to believe he's not just paranoid. They hook up with a local astronomer (Arthur Franz) who babbles on about some theory about Martians who use "mu-tants" (that's how they say it in the movie) to do their manual labor. Eventually, the trio gets the Army to believe David's story about a buried spaceship. There's a lot of running back and forth by soldiers and mu-tants in a maze of tunnels under the sand pit, the soldiers blow up the flying saucer at which point David wakes up to find it's all been a dream. But now there's another thunderstorm and damned if David doesn't see – in a repeat of the opening scenes – a flying saucer bury itself in the sand pit behind his house.

The Blake/Battle script plays to a lot of prevalent post-WW II Cold War paranoias (invasion, infiltration, subversion) which get an additional spark when they mash up against more primal fears (isolation, alienation, some unseen thing pulling victims down into the underworld). And there's that last, great twist that it's all been a dream, but now it's a dream turned real. Or is it? Is the dream just repeating itself?

That Mobius strip cleverness bumps up against stale dialogue, stock characters, and a hoot of an expository scene when David and his protecting angel social worker confab with Franz who spiels out a "theory" so detailed and off-the-wall it sounds like one of those theories you see in the newspapers the supermarket stocks by the check-out counter, laid out in the page across from the one about the Roswell autopsies and how they're keeping Kennedy's brain in a jar somewhere.

And then there's this secret rocket project everybody knows about (including David) and that Franz easily drops in on with his observatory telescope.

But then consider this: sure, this all sounds dopey. But if a small kid were dreaming it, isn't this the kind of thing he'd dream? That's the thing about *Invaders*; it's either being dumb, or cleverly dumb.

Which brings us to William Cameron Menzies. Although Menzies directed other films, he remains more renowned for his day job as one of the most influential set designers of his time. Menzies was the first guy to be credited as a "production designer" coordinating all the design components which contributed to the look of a film, and his two Oscars include one for *Gone with the Wind* (1939).

On *Invaders*, Menzies was working with an obviously slim budget. The movie is set-bound and padded out to its 80-minute running time (if that) by reusing the same few clips of stock military footage as well as all that soldier/mu-tant running around in the tunnel maze under the sand pit. Watch close: soldiers run right, then later, it's the same clip only flipped to get the soldiers running left. Mu-tants run left, flip the clip, mu-tants run right.

And as for those mu-tants… The goggles and padded suits with the zipper visible in the back don't cut it, not by a long shot. For one shot where Menzies had a squad of soldiers grapple with one of these supposedly oversized goons, Menzies replaced his full-sized troopers with kids which explains why their helmets suddenly cover their faces.

And let's not forget that maze of tunnels. To get the right heat-bubble look, the tunnel sets were dressed with inflated condoms. But when the mu-tants go lumbering by, they create a breeze that sets the rubbers a-flutter.

Yet damned if something about it all isn't…haunting. Menzies may not have been a great storyteller, but the guy had an eye.

The sets don't always make sense…but then they do. One of the most oft-cited examples of Menzies' mind-messing is a scene in a police station: tall doors at one end of a long, narrow hall, the desk sergeant at his high desk at the other, and stark blank walls between. It's the world seen through the eyes of a little boy, of a dreaming little boy, and much of the film has that same, skewed, unsettling perspective.

Or take the sand pit set: a this-way-and-that-way sandy path between tufts of grass, lined by a few trees, running to the top of a low rise, a wood rail fence along one side, the path and fence disappearing into the sand at the top. Menzies, acting as his own production designer on the film, sculpts it as a stylized reality; looking natural yet so artfully put together and so carefully framed in his camera,that the recurring image of that path to nowhere becomes one of the most memorable icons from the movie. When Tobe Hooper made his more lavish (and flat-out bad in an unfun way) 1983 remake, he knew that image was so deeply imprinted on fans of the original that it was used as the visual for the movie's poster.

Invaders' budget-forced shortcomings play into that same dream state quality: the constantly reused footage, the goofy-looking mu-tants and squads of soldiers purposelessly loping down endless tunnels. Like a bad dream, it never completely makes sense, yet seems all of a piece.

I saw *Invaders from Mars* as a kid. Even then, the zippered mu-tant costumes and bobbing condoms ("Look! Martian grapes!") made me laugh. And yet images from that movie have never left me because they found resonance somewhere down deep inside where my own nightmares were created.

TONY SCOTT (1944 – 2012): LOVE 'IM OR HATE 'IM, IT'LL BE A LONG TIME BEFORE ANYONE FORGETS HIM

August 21, 2012

Director Tony Scott's career broke big with the success of the MTV-style *Top Gun* (1986).
In the foreground: Val Kilmer and Tom Cruise.

In the late 1970s and 1980s, composer Giorgio Moroder was often accused of trying to replace the orchestral movie soundtrack with high-energy, synthesizer-heavy disco pop laid on with a trowel in movies like *Thank God It's Friday* (1978), *Flashdance* (1983), *Scarface* (1983), and *Top Gun* (1986). I remember a magazine story on Moroder which quoted one of his many critics as saying, "The day the music died, Giorgio Moroder was brought in for questioning."

I think some people had the same opinion about movies and Tony Scott. Full disclosure: I'm one of them. But it would be greatly unfair to Scott, who apparently committed suicide Sunday after being diagnosed with inoperable brain cancer, not to admit that, for good or for ill, his 1980s feature work had an enormous impact on commercial filmmaking.

The younger brother of Ridley Scott by seven years, he was, like his brother, gifted with an outrageously good eye; a taste for the visual strong enough to earn him his master's degree from London's Royal College of Art (which he'd attended on scholarship no less). But painting didn't pay well, so he joined with his brother in Ridley Scott Associates where, from the 1970s into the 1980s, he applied that eye to moving pictures, directing thousands of commercials, some of them still-talked-about all-time classics in the UK.

His first feature was the visually sumptuous, dramatically wispy attempt at erotic vampirica, *The Hunger* (1983), and it was such a lambasted flop it's a surprise Scott's feature career didn't end right there. But three years later, producer Jerry Bruckheimer tapped him to direct *Top Gun* and movies would never be the same.

It was a perfect marriage of sensibilities (along with Michael Bay, Scott would remain one of Bruckheimer's go-to directors). Bruckheimer, whose youthful interest in photography had led him to his own career in commercials before turning to movies, had the same affinity for striking imagery as Scott.

The timing of the union was just right, too. MTV was only five years old, and the non-stop near-abstract visuals of music video were not only still hypnotically novel, but on their way to becoming the defining visual sensibility for a new movie-going generation. With Giorgio Moroder (another ideal wedding of sensibilities) supplying a Pop Top Ten-nish soundtrack, Scott put together montages that were, essentially, music videos woven into the narrative of the film (some critics carped that the whole movie was little more than an extended music video).

Striking visuals, a pulsing, toe-tapping score, and a super-patriotic story that made a hero of a young, cocky, mouthy, go-my-own-way fighter jock made for a flick which hit a big, fat sweet spot with MTV's first generation of ticket-buyers: *Top Gun* scored a whopping $176.7 million domestic. I did the math: at today's ticket prices, that would translate to almost $390 million: more than, say, this year's *The Amazing Spider-Man*, last year's *Harry Potter and the Deathly Hallows Part 2* or *Transformers: Dark of the Moon*, or any of the *Twilight* movies. Love it or hate it, you have to respect that kind of box office muscle.

Top Gun set the template for Scott: high-octane visuals, rapid-fire editing (often at the hands of Chris Lebenzon), an MTV-friendly soundtrack, and a story simple enough to absorb without having to pay too much attention.

It also set the template for so many of the box office winners of the next few decades, movies that moved fast, piled on the action, featured characters who were often little more than catch phrases with biceps, offered music video fodder (at least back when MTV still played music videos), and where plausibility – even under Hollywood's extremely elastic definition of the concept – was irrelevant. Think the *Lethal Weapons, Speed* (1994), *Twister* (1996), anything by Michael Bay.

Though his brother Ridley often took the same rap of favoring looks over substance, their styles, though both highly visual, were strikingly different.

Ridley's films, good and bad, play out like classical music: stately, elegant, unrushed, somber.

Tony's movies are rock 'n' roll: fast, loud, exhausting, sometimes painfully bright.

It's hard to imagine Tony doing something as subdued as Ridley's Napoleonic-era *The Duelists* (1977), or even pulling off the brooding sci fi Gothicism of *Alien* (1979). By the same token, Ridley would have seemed a poor fit for *Top Gun* or all the running back and forth in *Crimson Tide* (1995).

Despite being regularly slammed for his storytelling, Scott did care about plot and character. Explaining the failure of *Days of Thunder* (1990) – *Top Gun* cloned to the NASCAR circuit – Scott diagnosed the problem as having started production without a finished script. "(You) always have to get a story," he said, "and you've got to get character first..."

But it wasn't a sentiment that quite squared with his execution. In an *Entertainment Weekly* story several years ago about a trending flimsiness in big screen storytelling, *The Fan* (1996) screenwriter Phoef Sutton told the story of shooting the movie's climactic baseball game in a torrential downpour. Sutton and others tried to argue Scott out of it pointing out that baseball games are called on account of such weather. The rain stayed. Said Sutton: "...I don't think Tony cared about the plausibility of it."

In his later years, he seemed to be trying to reach for the kind of substance his early films were often accused of lacking, but he remained better at taking a good picture than giving it meaning. *Enemy of the State* (1998) was entertaining enough, but it was like Coppola's *The Conversation* (1974) with the poetry removed and replaced with explosions and chases; *Spy Game* (2001) was an anemic John Le Carre wannabe; *The Taking of Pelham 123* replaced the local color which had made the 1974 original so memorable with a needlessly busy yet flavorless plot.

Like his brother, Tony also produced, and in those projects one could sense an ambition to do something of substance. There were such laudable efforts as the HBO movie *RKO 281* (1999) about Orson Welles' fight to make *Citizen Kane;* *The Gathering Storm* (2002), another HBO feature, this about Churchill's attempts to prep England for WW II; *Gettysburg* (2001), a cable documentary about one of the most pivotal battles of the Civil War; and the lovely, elegiac (if sadly little seen) Western, *The Assassination of Jesse James by the Coward Robert Ford* (2007).

Though Scott would continue to turn out some respectable earners in his later years (*Déjà Vu* [2006], *The Taking of Pelham 123, Unstoppable* [2010]), after the 1980s, he'd never hit *Top Gun* heights again, and, in fact, after *Beverly Hills Cop II* (1987), only ever crossed the $100 million domestic mark one more time with *Enemy of the State* (1998). Perhaps the problem was that Scott's eye-tickling rat-a-tat-tat style had, by the 1990s, become so widely copied that his often dramatically weak films had little else to offer; the trend setter had become just another member of the pack.

But give him this. Few filmmakers make a lasting impact. Most directors and most films come and go, cinematic mayflies fluttering around the box office for a few weeks before disappearing. The same can't be said of Tony Scott. Love 'im or hate 'im, it'll be a long time before anyone forgets him.

MOVE OVER *TOTAL RECALL:* 10 MORE REMAKES YOU'LL WANT TO AVOID

August 15, 2012

Whether you measure your movies by box office, reviews, or popular appeal, Sony's $125 million remake of the 1990 Ah-nuld Schwarzenegger interplanetary action fest *Total Recall* looks like a strike-out. The movie opened with a lethal softness; a $25.7 million first weekend meaning *Recall* won't even come close to making back its budget during its domestic theatrical run. In fact, despite 22 years of ticket price increases, it's doubtful the movie will even match the original's $119.3 million haul.

And for those of you who think maybe the problem is *Total Recall* was outgunned opening while *The Dark Knight Rises* was still sucking up box office coin, entertain, at least for a moment if you will, the possibility the movie just plain sucks. According to Rotten Tomatoes' canvas, almost 70% of reviewers – and over three-quarters of "top critics" – gave *Total Recall* a thumbs-down. Those who went to see the movie didn't seem to care much for it either, with almost 45% panning the flick (again, according to Rotten Tomatoes). CinemaScore corroborates that general sense of viewers' collective "Meh!" reporting an audience score of just C+.

It's still early, but it looks like this one's headed for the septic tank, gang.

All of which may be a bad omen for those remakes still in the wings:

This month's $17 million remake of 1976's *Sparkle;*

A $75 million remake of 1975's *Red Dawn* for release later this year;

A $100 million remake of 1987's *Robocop,* a $127 million remake of *The Great Gatsby,* as well as remakes of *Carrie, Gambit, The Secret Life of Walter Mitty,* and a possible remake of 1982's *Poltergeist,* all in 2013;

Into 2014, look for remakes of *Child's Play, Annie, A Star Is Born, Pat Sematary,* and *The Crow,* just to name a few.

And that's just the headliners! Website Next Movie lists 50 remakes running into 2014; website Den of Geek lists *75!*

For all of Hollywood's investment in them, remakes, at least in today's theatrical dynamic, don't make much sense to me. Sequels I get: a movie hits big, and you exploit that opportunity by making another movie under the same brand…and then another…and then another…until people get tired of going to see them.

But remakes?

On the surface, I suppose there's a simple sense to it: take a past success, and repeat it.

But…

Remaking a movie from any time predating the current generation of young ticket-buyers doesn't give the title much drawing power. Today's young demo is about as intellectually connected to Hollywood's past glories as they are to the historical lessons of the Spanish-American War (we fought Spain?). I remember teaching a film class last year where I mentioned that *Rise of the Planet of the Apes* (2011) was not the first *Planet of the Apes* movie. They were all mystified except one who – very proud of himself, I might add – said, "Oh, yeah! Tim Burton made one, didn't he?"

Oof.

But what typically kills a remake – besides the very contemporary mindset that simply redoing a movie in a bigger, splashier fashion somehow makes it better – is when the makers — ...oh, what's the phrase? Ahhh: when they "make it relevant to today's audiences." That's Hollywood-speak for gutting the very elements which distinguished the original and replacing them with stuff that makes the remake look like all the other crap that's out there at the moment.

Total Recall's floundering, foundering performance provides us with an opening to talk about some other miscalculated, misconceived, and misbegotten remakes.

Oh, don't get me wrong. Some great remakes have been made.

These are not among them:

King Kong (1933)
Directed by Merian C. Cooper and Ernest B. Schoedsack (uncredited)
Written by Cooper, James Ashmore Creelman, Ruth Rose, Edgar Wallace, and Leon Gordon (uncredited)
v.
King Kong (1976)
Directed by John Guillermin
Written by Lorenzo Semple, Jr.
&
King Kong (2005)
Directed by Peter Jackson
Written by Fran Walsh, Philippa Boyens, and Jackson

Let's get this out there at the top. The original *King Kong* is a great movie...but it's not great movie-making. The acting from the human cast is hammy, there's not much in the way of character (Fay Wray, the object of Kong's affections, spends more screen time screaming than speaking), the dialogue pinballs between the clever (at Kong's New York unveiling: "They say it's some big gorilla." "Oh, geez, ain't we got enough of them in New

York?") to the cornball, there's not much plot, and the movie's treatment of supposedly South Seas natives is, at best, naively insensitive, and borderline racist at worst.

Yet, it works, and that's part of the original's magic. What it has going for it is the brute simplicity of a fairy tale, and taken as that, all of the movie's components – from its overcooked acting to its gorilla/bleached blonde romance – seem of a piece. RKO's back lot jungle isn't a *real* jungle, but the kind of shadowy jungle of a child's nightmare, and it's mix-and-match monster menagerie – giant spiders, a 50-foot gorilla squaring off with prehistoric reptiles – make an odd sort of sense in that milieu.

So does Kong's bizarre fascination with fainting-when-she-isn't-shrieking Fay Wray. At the end of the movie, when Robert Armstrong stands over the dead Kong lamenting, "It was beauty killed the beast," he's summed up all of the once-upon-a-time qualities which keep the movie vital eight decades later.

The most fully-realized character in the movie is Kong; sympathetic without playing for sympathy. We feel for Kong as a defeated majesty when he's taken from his native jungle, and then destroyed by his passion for screaming-meemie Wray, but Kong is a monster nevertheless. This is, after all, the beastie the natives have been offering local ladies to for some time (and it's not like a night with Kong ends up like an episode of *The Bachelorette*). In his pursuit of Wray on his native island, he squishes, munches, and otherwise dispatches the terrified natives, and he's just as unrestrained on the loose in New York, tearing up a subway train, and tossing a woman pulled from her high rise bedroom to her death because she has the misfortune not to be Fay Wray.

You could do an entire column on what producer Dino De Laurentiis' 1976 remake got wrong (Rick Baker in a monkey suit as Kong but acting less like a monkey than a guy out for a stroll in the park; trying to turn *King Kong* into some kind of eco-parable – and that's just for starters), but the most grievous was changing the brutish anti-hero of the original into a misunderstood pussycat. "Nobody cry when *Jaws* die," Di Laurentiis' had declared before the film's release, "but they cry when Kong die!"

Well, audiences may have cried, but that was because those were 134 minutes they were never going to get back.

You have to give Peter Jackson credit: after seeing the cloying mess De Laurentiis had made of a classic, it took a lot of nerve to give it another shot. Jackson's *King Kong* is a physically impressive film demonstrating the filmmaker's absolute command of CGI effects and grand scale movie-making, but it still gets *King Kong* wrong.

Not unlike De Laurentiis, Jackson works too hard to make Kong a good guy, more a victim than a magnificent monster brought down by his foibles.

Sentimental where the original was tough, substituting a child-like crush for animal passion, Jackson's version is a gooey, soft-edged puffball that, in its dignified, seriously-minded, superbly produced way, doesn't get any closer to the electricity of the original than De Laurentiis' manipulative (attempted) tear-jerker.

Straw Dogs (1971)
Directed by Sam Peckinpah
**Adapted from Gordon Williams' novel *The Siege of Trencher's Farm*
by David Zelag Goodman and Peckinpah**
v.
Straw Dogs (2001)
Written and directed by Rod Lurie

Williams' original novel was a worm-turns story about an American expatriate and his family besieged by brutish villagers when he shelters a child-killer who has escaped from his keepers. Peckinpah, intrigued by the writings of social anthropologist Robert Ardrey, and Goodman elevated Williams' rather superficial story about Everyman's capacity for violence to a more intellectually and morally complex story about primal territoriality. It was one of the director's most controversial works and remains one of his most provocative.

Lurie – who publicly stated he didn't think the Peckinpah original was all it was cracked up to be – nevertheless stayed close to Peckinah's plotting, but turned the story into a simplistic, heavy-handed Blue Stater's anti-Red State screed. Where Peckinpah's protagonist – a milquetoasty mathematician come to England to avoid the social conflict sweeping across the U.S. in the early 1970s – finally asserts himself for no cause more elevated than a Neanderthalish defense of territory and property (including a wife who no longer loves him and whom he no longer loves), Lurie's hero (and in Lurie's version, he's more clearly a hero) is a sensitive liberal fighting the good fight against a mob of narrow-minded rednecks.

Peckinpah turned out one of the signature films of the 1960s/70s. Lurie's version came out less like a re-envisioning of *Straw Dogs,* than a re-visiting of the ham-handed politics of the *Billy Jack* flicks; a dog, indeed.

Godzilla (Gojira) (1954)
Directed by Ishoro Honda
Written by Honda, Shigeru Kayama, and Takeo Murata
v.
Godzilla (1998)
Directed by Roland Emmerich
Written by Dean Devlin, Emmerich, Ted Elliott, and Terry Rossio

Spoiled by three decades of CGI effects, it can be hard, while watching a guy in a rubber monster suit kicking hell out of a Tinker Toy city, to remember that the original *Godzilla* was a serious response by the only country every atomic bombed to an era of nuclear threat. Godzilla is a monster awakened by atomic tests, and ultimately destroyed by an even more devastating weapon so frightening in its capacity, that its inventor elects to be killed along with the monster so that the secret of his invention dies with him.

As chintzy as the original looks today, it still stands head and reptilian shoulders above Sony's big budget ($130 million 1998 dollars), lobotmized remake.

Emmerich and his production partner Devlin had had such luck reviving the alien invasion movie with *Independence Day* (1996) there was no reason not to expect them to bring the same straight-faced-yet-fun approach to reviving the monster-on-the-loose genre. But for whatever reason, Emmerich and Devlin didn't trust the audience; they went for a wink-wink-nudge-nudge jokey approach, creating an overly busy script (government conspiracies, a finale ripped off – badly – from *Aliens)*, and then trying to steamroller their way to box office success with over-the-top CGI effects (I don't know what was the ditziest sequence: Godzilla winning a duel with an atomic submarine in the Hudson River, or leaping in a surprise ambush to eat an Army helicopter in flight).

Looking at what director Matt Reeves and producer J.J. Abrams were able to do for the monster movie with *Cloverfield* (2008), you can appreciate all the more just how dumb the Godzilla remake is.

And hey, Roland, Dean – what did you do to the Godzilla roar?

The Flight of the Phoenix **(1965)**
Directed by Robert Aldrich
Adapted from Trevor Dudley Smith's novel by Lucas Heller.
v.
Flight of the Phoenix **(2004)**
Directed by John Moore
Written by Scott Frank and Edward Burns

The original is one of the great survival adventure films. A crew of oil workers and some visitors are flying out of the Saharan oil fields when their plane is brought down by a sandstorm. Hardy Kruger is the prickly, abrasive engineer who claims a plane can be built from the wreckage to fly them to safety. James Stewart is the equally prickly veteran pilot locked in a juvenile who's-the-boss-*I'm*-the-boss duel of egos with Kruger, each of them forgetting that their competing vanities could very well cost the lives of the other survivors.

The critical reception was overwhelmingly positive, but the public didn't come. *Flight* did so badly at the box office, it sunk director Robert Aldrich's production company (he wouldn't rebound until 1967's *The Dirty Dozen*). The movie may have been too bitter a pill for audiences to swallow.

Aldrich cut against the grain of the survival genre. Stuck in oven-baked emptiness, physically deteriorating under the constant bombardment of heat, wind, and sun, his characters don't devolve into primitivism, but rather become more obsessive about their pettinesses; self-destructively so. Stewart, in one of his best late career performances, plays his grizzled age but against type as a hard-headed old-timer unwilling to cede his authority to or subordinate his experience to Kruger's slide rule. Aldrich, a master hand at ensembles (i.e. *The Dirty Dozen; The Longest Yard* [1974]), backs up Stewart and Kruger with a deep bench of character players: Richard Attenborough, George Kennedy, Peter Finch, Ian Bannen (who copped a Supporting Actor Oscar nod), and Aldrich go-to player Ernest Borgnine among them.

But, as well thought of as *Phoenix* was, why remake a flop?

I can only think some not-so-bright exec thought, "Ya know, if we just change this and tweak that so it's a less grim pic, we might have a winner here!"

They still wound up with a flop, but one that's a lousy movie.

The resurrected *Phoenix* is blandly cast with Dennis Quaid, Mirando Otto in a pointless gender switch of Attenborough's character, the usually intriguing Giovanni Ribisi replacing Hardy Kruger with a pile of ticks and mannerisms, and a rank of characterless muscle types in lieu of Aldrich's Battleship Row of supporting players.

In the original, the survivors race against their dwindling water supply. Dehydrated and sunburned, they literally begin to physically come apart. The remake provides the survivors with ample water and food, and their "survival" doesn't seem any more challenging than a few days at a fitness spa.

Without the grimness, desperation, and petty ego spats of the original (and I grant, they're probably what kept people away in 1965), the remake doesn't become a more appealing movie. It becomes a pointless one that never gets off the ground.

Charade (1963)
Directed by Stanley Donen
Written by Peter Stone and Marc Behm
v.
The Truth About Charlie (2002)
Directed by Jonathan Demme
Written by Demme, Steve Schmidt, and Jessica Bendiger

The original – often called "the best Hitchcock movie Hitchcock never made" – is a delightful confection, but a confection nonetheless. Its plot – three goons preying on a petite lovely as they try to find out where her dead husband hid a fortune in stolen gold — is an excuse to watch Cary Grant and Audrey Hepburn charmingly flirt against as romantic a setting as charming flirts could want: Paris, fetchingly shot by cinematographer Charles Lang. There's Henry Mancini's alternately lovely/thrilling score, Peter Stone's dazzlingly witty script, and a delicious rogues gallery of a supporting cast including Walter Matthau, James Coburn, George Kennedy, and Ned Glass.

Stone's script offers a pitch-perfect balance: romantic sparks between two of the most charismatic stars of the day, alternating with deepening mystery, plot twists and double-backs, and occasional bursts of violence. It's a textbook example of how to "just entertain" without treating an audience like a collection of popcorn-munching morons.

But because *Charade* is so insubstantial (its plot doesn't actually make a lot of sense), it's a bit of a puzzlement why Demme – with meaty flicks like *Something Wild* (1986), *Philadelphia* (1993), and *Silence of the Lambs* (1991) – would want to take it on.

The bigger puzzlement is how a filmmaker of Demme's caliber could so misinterpret the original. What had been a classy, slick bit of film fun becomes leaden and unnecessarily gritty. There's cinematographer Tak Fujimoto's gray, rainy Paris, a supporting cast too low in wattage (Tim Robbins, Ted Levine, Lisa Gay Hamilton, and Joong-Hoon) to provide the bright colors of the original's second tier, and while Thandie Newton captures a lot of the beauty and fragility of Hepburn, Mark Wahlberg — ... Well, great in *The Departed* (2006) and *Boogie Nights* (1997), but the guy's no Cary Grant (granted: who is?).

Demme remakes a movie that was all about fun and charm with little of either.

The Thing from Another World (1951)
Directed by Christian Nyby and an uncredited Howard Hawks
Adapted from Joseph W. Campbell, Jr.'s novel, *Who Goes There?*
by Charles Lederer and an uncredited Hawks and Ben Hecht
v.
The Thing (1982)
Directed by John Carpenter
Written by Bill Lancaster
&
The Thing (2011)
Directed by Matthijs van Heijningen, Jr.
Written by Eric Heisserer

Why settle for less than the original? Classic '50s sci fier *The Thing from Another World* (1951). Left to Right: Robert Cornwaite, Margaret Sheridan and Norbert Schiller, Everett Glass, George Fenneman, Paul Frees.

The original had novelty going for it. The idea of alien invasions was not only new, but plugged into still blossoming postwar Cold War paranoia.

That aside, the plot of the original *The Thing* is quite simple and direct. An Arctic research team finds a crashed UFO, salvages one of its crew frozen in a block of ice, the alien gets free and in a plotline to be endlessly emulated over the next sixty-odd years, the alien monster tries to kill the humans, the humans try to kill the monster.

What makes *The Thing* a classic is its exceptional execution: a wonderful ensemble cast of solid B-listers (Kenneth Tobey, Robert Cornthwaite, Margaret Sheridan, et al), a brisk, firecracker style most attribute to producer Howard Hawks rather than titled director Nyby, and Lederer's smart, sharp script (when one of Tobey's men wonders if the alien can read minds, one of his comrades replies, "He'll be real mad when he gets to me").

I'd go so far as to say the characters in *The Thing* are *so* well etched – so utterly believable in an unbelievable circumstance – that they could easily have been dropped into a more realistic context (a war movie, say), and play just as well without any changes in the writing or performance.

Carpenter's remake has quite a few devotees, and I'd be less than honest if I didn't admit to watching it every time it comes on. It's got mood, it's got suspense, and, thanks to cinematographer Dean Cundey, it's got a nice, clean look. Like the original, Carpenter, too, puts together a strong ensemble of Familiar Faces behind lead Kurt Russell including Wilford Brimley, David Clennon, Keith David, Richard Dysart and others. And Lancaster's script is actually closer to Campbell's 1938 source material with its alien which recreates itself as any life form it chooses.

Impressive in their own right are the creature effects by Rob Bottin. Even in this CGI era, Bottin's accomplishments through animatronics, puppetry, prosthetics, and make-up effects are still startling.

Yet the movie lacks something vital which the original had in abundance: heart. Too much of the movie seems an artifice: a research team that seems to do nothing but sit around bored witless waiting to be infiltrated by alien grotesques; an Antarctic research station with a well-stocked armory of flamethrowers, shotguns, and an endless supply of dynamite (what the hell kind of research are these guys doing?); characters who are barely characters, carried by the charisma of the cast but little in the script.

Example: Kurt Russell's chopper pilot MacReady. We can tell he's supposed to be a go-his-own-way maverick because he wears a sombrero in blizzards. That's the movie's idea of character.

All of that may be why the movie flopped. It's highly watchable, technically impressive, the cast engaging, but it lacks the fun, the vibrancy, and the characters-we-care-about element that keeps the original a lively watch over a half-century later.

As for Heijningen's version, the less said about it the better. Intended as a prequel to Carpenter's movie, it nevertheless plays like a remake, with the actions of the Norwegian research team referred to in Carpenter's flick generally playing out a scenario closely mirroring its predecessor. This *Thing* never finds its own, distinctive voice. Problem is Heijningen isn't Howard Hawks or, for that matter, John Carpenter. His rendering is just another in a long line of pale alien-on-the-loose clones dating back to the original, and just as valueless.

Invasion of the Body Snatchers (1956)
Directed by Don Siegel.
Adapted from Jack Finney's novel by Daniel Mainwaring, Richard Collins (uncredited)
v.
Invasion of the Body Snatchers (1978)
Directed by Philip Kaufman
Written by W.D. Richter

&
Body Snatchers (1993)
Directed by Abel Ferrara
Written by Raymond Cistheri, Larry Cohen, Stuart Gordon, Dennis Paoli,
Nicholas St. John
&
The Invasion (2007)
Directed by Oliver Hirschbiegel, James McTeigue (uncredited)
Written by David Kajganich

Siegel's original sci fi classic was a little-noticed B movie at the time of its release, but whose stature steadily grew over the years: a tribute not only to the sharply intelligent and adult treatment Siegel & Co. gave their material, but to the deeply resonant subtext which still connects today.

The perceived meaning of *Invasion*'s story of pods from space which replicate humans as emotionless copies has swung from an interpretation as a warning against communist subversion to the other end of the political scale, viewed, instead as an anti-McCarthyist alarum. But Siegel himself has stated he was after something more universal; a sense of desensitization and alienation he saw infecting the American psyche of the 1950s.

Phil Kaufman's remake is a film often cited as an example that the possibility of doing a good remake – hell, a *great* remake – is possible in the right hands. Kaufman shrewdly saw that the themes in Siegel's version were even more relevant in the woefully dysfunctional America of the 1970s. Battered by a host of disillusionments starting with Vietnam and climaxing with Watergate, stuck in an unwavering recession and what '70s pundits referred to as "a great malaise," Kaufman saw the same disaffection and personal withdrawal Siegel and his gang had seen a generation earlier, only even more entrenched.

Like Siegel, Kaufman saw that the key to the story wasn't its hook of replicating pods or even in punching up the story with a bigger budget and cooler effects. The story almost wholly relied on making the personal drama between its characters work, and, if anything, Kaufman's version drives the often affecting drama home even more solidly than Siegel's.

The same can't be said for Abel Ferrara's *Body Snatchers*. Despite a host of writers contributing to the project (or maybe because of them), Ferrara's telling doesn't seem to be about much. It's the weakest kind of remake; taking the hook, but missing the point. Reset on an Army base, replacing the central love story (which wasn't just the typical sci fi gratuitous romance, but the heart of a story about the loss of heart) with more mundane daughter/dad problems, there just doesn't seem to be much going on either dramatically or emotionally. With a '90s restlessness, the movie tips its hand so early, there's none of that creeping paranoia which plays so well in both Siegel's and Kaufman's versions; a subtlety which, in those earlier films, cleverly blurs the line between alien cooption and all-too-earthly human failing.

Give Hirschbiegel and Kajganich this much; they work up a sweat trying to make their version about *something*. The movie reeks of an earnestness in trying, as Kaufman did in his time, to make the story relevant to the modern day. The script takes a nifty twist on the old story with the infectees (in this version, they're not copies but controlled by an organism which invades the brain) making the point that their very lack of emotion can provide a more stable, peaceful, cooperative – in short, "better" – world. The provocative idea here is that our humanity is paradoxically demonstrated by our propensity for violence and chaos.

But despite that intriguing dramatic quirk, the movie comes off as slack and tired despite a lot of running around, and overly familiar. The philosophizing feels like lip service rather than, as Siegel and Kaufman were able to pull off, an integral, nay, *critical* element in their respective telling. The only message of import Hirschbiegel does successfully convey is that this is one story that's been cloned way too many times.

Planet of the Apes (1968)
Directed by Franklin J. Schaffner
Adapted from Pierre Boulle's novel *Monkey Planet* by Rod Serling and Michael Wilson

v.

Planet of the Apes (2001)
Directed by Tim Burton
Written by William Broyles, Jr., Lawrence Konner, and Mark Rosenthal

&

Rise of the Planet of the Apes (2011)
Directed by Rupert Wyatt
Written by Rick Jaffa and Amanda Silver

Let's do this one in reverse.

In *Rise,* James Franco's well-meaning doctor gives chimp Caesar (Andy Serkis, master of motion-capture performing) a serum which makes him super-smart. Caesar gets treated badly by a nasty animal-keeper, bands together with a bunch of other apes he makes super-smart, and they lead an ape rebellion against humans. Moral: be kind to monkeys.

In Tim Burton's version, astronaut Mark Wahlberg chases off after a super-smart monkey on a wayward space ship, flies through a wormhole, and winds up on a planet run by talking apes. Wahlberg eventually discovers this is the end result of a rebellion of super-smart monkeys left behind on his mother ship which crashed and spawned a planet of the apes. Moral: There probably is one but damned if I could see it. Maybe it's, Don't leave the keys to the space ship with supert-smart monkeys.

In the original, a deep space mission crashes on a planet where humans are mute beasts, and apes run the show. In one of the most iconic moments in American movies, surviving astronaut Charlton Heston discovers this ape world is actually what's left of his home planet after nuclear self-destruction.

Ok, you tell me where the meat is.

Schaffner's original was not only a scream of anti-nuke terror (in the 1960s, a very real and palpable fear; how afraid are you of a rebellion of super-smart monkeys?), but in its anti-heroic lead character – Heston's condescending, arrogant, cynical, and dismissive astronaut Taylor – it captured all of the discontents and disillusionments of the 1960s. Taylor is not a curious scientist, nor noble adventurer. He signed on for this one-way mission out of no motive higher than the belief "…there has to be something better than man. *Has* to be."

And that kind of dramatic heft makes the original better than its descendants. *Has* to be.

The Manchurian Candidate (1962)
Directed by John Frankenheimer
Adapted from Richard Condon's novel by George Axelrod
and Frankenheimer (uncredited)
v.
The Manchurian Candidate (2004)
Directed by Jonathan Demme
Written by Daniel Pyne and Dean Georgaris

Frankenheimer's original has attained status as one of the all-time classic conspiracy thrillers. Although its context is firmly embedded in the East/West Cold War duel of the 1950s/1960s, what keeps Frankenheimer's film relevant today is that the real core of the story is not the clever conspiracy by which an American Army officer captured by the North Koreans is brainwashed, re-manufactured as a hero, and then placed in a position to carry out the assassination of a presidential candidate. What drives the story – the ability of the conspirators to lay the groundwork for their plan – is the easy way fears on the left and right are exploited. In the original, those dirty commies are not the real enemy; as Pogo once famously taught us, "We have met the enemy and he is us."

In his second appearance on this list, Demme missteps the same way he misstepped on *Charade,* by mistaking the obvious for the valuable. His remake – not a badly made movie by any means – gloms on to the conspiracy aspects of the original *Candidate,* tries to contemporize the plot by turning the conspiracy into one of greedy corporations, but misses that essential element which is at the heart of the original; that the most potent weapons our enemies have are our own prejudices and paranoias. Our fears don't turn us against our enemies, according to Frankenheimer, Axelrod, and Condon, but against ourselves.

The Taking of Pelham One Two Three (1974)
Directed by Joseph Sargent
Adapted from John Godey's novel by Peter Stone
v.
The Taking of Pelham 1 2 3 (2009)
Directed by Tony Scott
Written by Brian Helgeland
&
The Taking of Pelham One Two Three (1998)
Directed by Felix Enriquez Alcala
Written by April Smith

It's said that it's the fat that gives sausage its flavor, and that's the case with the original *Pelham*. Despite the clever boldness of its plot – four armed men hijack a New York City subway car and hold its passengers for $1 million ransom – that's not what makes the movie a 1970s favorite. Peter Stone – an Oscar, Emmy, and Tony-winner – uses Godey's plot as an excuse to provide a mosaic portrait of 1970s New York in all its dysfunctional, chaotic, grimy, caustic glory (when rumpled Transit cop Walter Matthau asks fiery train master Dick O'Neill to remember the passengers whose lives are at stake, O'Neill replies, "What'd they expect for their lousy thirty-five cents; to live forever?"). New York is the real star of Sargent's *Pelham,* and it's a city performance which rates up there with *Midnight Cowboy* (1969) and *The Naked City* (1948).

Stone's script is in good hands. Sargent, with the help of New York's best cinematographer, Owen Roizman, the crisp cutting of Gerald Greenburg and Robert Lovett, and David Shire's pulsing score, takes a static situation and turns it into a suspenseful barn-burner of a flick, as funny as it is suspenseful without sacrificing credibility. Great cinema? Probably not. Great entertainment? Easily.

And yet *Pelham* stiffed at the box office despite warm reviews. The movie only performed well, oddly enough – both domestically and abroad – in cities with subway systems.

That makes the decision to remake this commercial dud another one of those bits of indecipherable Hollywood (il)logic, even though all of the creative decisions behind the remake are typical Hollywood schlock-making.

Tony Scott has always been a director of visually lush, dramatically vapid pictures. He may have one of the best eyes for pictorial beauty in the business, but Scott wouldn't know gritty if he fell in front of a street sweeper.

The original's caper, while brazen, was fairly straightforward: four guys take over a subway car and demand money. Helgeland, on the other hand, piles one unnecessarily complicated complication on top of another. This time, the caper is part of some byzantine plot to manipulate gold prices, the gang leader – John Travolta as one of those giggling, smirking, showboating master villains Hollywood has come to love over the last 20-30 years (in the original, Robert Shaw played a low-key, brutally pragmatic ex-mercenary) – has a twisty history, as does the subway dispatcher (Denzel Washington) Travolta forges a connection with (another go-to gimmick Hollywood has been enamored with since the macabre *pas de deux* between Jodie Foster and Anthony Hopkins in *Silence of the Lambs* [1991]).

It's a plot that's three times as busy yet never as suspenseful as the original, and whose biggest crime is replacing all of Sargent's/Stone's & Co.'s New York flavor with an empty, colorless hodge-podge of Hollywood formulae.

As for the 1998 made-for-TV movie, it's perhaps an even stronger demonstration of what made the original *Pelham* such a fun watch. The '98 version stays fairly close to the plot of the original, but it fails to pass off a pristine Toronto subway system as New York's, it's blandly cast, slackly paced, and, like Tony Scott's version, lacks any of that distinctive New York tang.

If you miss the first train, do yourself a favor and let these other two go by.

Dishonorable Mentions:

The Andromeda Strain **(1971) v.** *The Andromeda Strain* **(2008)**
The made-for-A&E remake turns Robert Wise's smart, disturbingly credible adaptation of Michael Crichton's equally credible story about a lethal organism from space into an overlong, under-produced numb-skulled conspiracy tale. The only strain here is the effort needed to watch the remake.

The Getaway **(1972) v.** *The Getaway* **(1994)**
The former was one of Sam Peckinpah's dramatically slightest but possibly most fun actioners, but next to Roger Donaldson's edgeless, colorless, remake, it plays like *Mean Streets*.

On the Beach (1959) v. On the Beach (2000)
Stanley Kramer presented the nuclear destruction of the world with a poignant grace. The bloated made-for-TV remake is nearly twice as long with less than half the heart or style. About halfway through, you wish the world would end a little sooner.

Rollerball (1975) v. Rollerball (2002)
Norman Jewison's flawed but compelling story of a corporatized future

where a brutal game is used to demonstrate the meaninglessness of the individual gets turned into a pedestrian number about sports fans' bloodlust. WWE fans will be shocked.

Point Blank (1967) *v. Payback* (1999)

Remaker Brian Helgeland makes the mistake of thinking the meat of John Boorman's '60s classic is in its familiar plot about a ripped-off hood on a body-strewn quest for vengeance and his stolen money. It isn't. The punch is in Boorman's stylish telling set against West Coast antisepticism which wires into a creeping, corporate soullessness which has even taken the heart out of The Mob. No wonder Tony Soprano needed therapy.

The Longest Yard (1974) *v. The Longest Yard* (2005)

The former: Robert *(The Dirty Dozen)* Aldrich; Burt Reynolds at his peak. The latter: Peter *(Tommy Boy)* Segal; Adam Sandler who has never had a peak. That's all you need to say. Blow the whistle, throw a flag, send Segal & Sandler to the showers.

MR. RICHARD ZANUCK (1934 – 2012): "GOOD" SELLS

August 1, 2012

There are all kinds of producers: hucksters, hustlers, con men and schlockmeisters. Some are in it for the glory, some like to walk the red carpet with a starlet on their arm. For some, the biggest award is a box office hit and it doesn't matter what kind of crap they throw on the screen to earn it. There are producers like Harvey Weinstein who will spend more money to promote himself to an Oscar win than he does on actually making his Oscar-winning films. And there are producers like Joel Silver who once said the only proper role for women in film was either as a dead body or naked.

And there are those who, to be honest, may also have a touch of all of this, but are mainly driven by a desire to make good movies. Like Dick Zanuck.

I don't think anyone will argue – and certainly the obits which abounded after his death from a heart attack earlier this month – that Richard Zanuck was a class act as a producer. It's there in his final score: three Best Picture Oscar nominations for *The Verdict* (1982), *Road to Perdition* (2002), and a win for *Driving Miss Daisy* (1989), as well as the Motion Picture Academy's Irving G. Thalberg Memorial Award (received with his one-time producing partner, David Brown) for the caliber of his body of work.

The movies were in Zanuck's blood. He was the son of the legendary Darryl Zanuck, longtime chief of 20th Century Fox, accompanied his dad to the studio to watch rough cuts when he was still a youth, and would even assume the senior Zanuck's studio throne in the 1960s (Zanuck, had left the studio in the 1950s, returned in 1962 after the success of his independently-produced epic, *The Longest Day* [1962], helped offset the studio's money-hemorrhaging *Cleopatra* [1963]).

As a studio chief, Zanuck blended his father's Old Hollywood sensibilities with a feel for the new young audiences of the 1960s, and was not afraid to challenge conventional wisdom. Instead of salutary war stories like *The Longest Day*, for example, there was the darker, more ambivalent war epic, *The Sand Pebbles* (1966). And when kids were in the streets protesting the war in Vietnam, Zanuck greenlit *Patton* (1970), a salute to one of America's all-time great – and greatly terrifying – warriors. He saw sci fi not as low budget drive-in fodder, but the kind of Space Age-attuned storytelling which could bring young ticket buyers out in droves, and turned out the, for the time, state-of-the-art effects fest *Fantastic Voyage* (1966), and rolled the studio's dice on what was, at the time, a daring, you-gotta-be-kidding-me project, *Planet of the Apes* (1968).

He still had a foot in Old Hollywood as well, as evidenced by *The Sound of Music* (1965), which may be one of the schmaltziest big studio musicals of all time. It's also – adjusted for inflation – one of the biggest box office hits of all time as well.

In a biographic turn worthy of Shakespeare, Tennessee Williams, and the best episodes of *Dallas,* a couple of big budget flops got Zanuck booted from Fox and replaced by his father (even more ironic, it was his father, who on his return to Fox in '62, had helped engineer Richard's ascent to the head of the company; and in another irony, Richard Zanuck would pass on the anniversary of his father's death).

After leaving Fox, Zanuck teamed with David Brown, whom he'd met at Fox, and they formed one of the most successful and respected producing entities of the last 40 years. Not every movie they produced was a gem (*The Island,* 1980), nor were they all hits (does anybody even remember *Rich in Love* [1993]?), nor were Zanuck & Brown morally immune to cashing in on a hit with a can't-hold-a-candle-to-the-original sequel (*Jaws 2* [1978], *Cocoon: The Return* [1988]). But the overwhelming body of their work, even when titles missed the mark, consisted of films which so obviously aspired to, above all things, be good: *MacArthur* (1977), *Rush* (1991), *Mulholland Falls* (1996), *Deep Impact* (1998), *Big Fish* (2003), to name just a very few.

In a business that has always been about safe choices, Zanuck and Brown consistently cut against the grain. They took a chance on a young TV director named Steven Spielberg on a serio-comic couple-on-the-run tale with *The Sugarland Express* (1974), and without waiting for the box office tally (which, despite glowing reviews, was unimpressive), turned over one of the most valued properties of the time – the bestselling novel *Jaws* – to him and, in the process, changed the direction of Hollywood forever. With most of the majors exhaustively chasing after the youth market with the likes of *Back to the Future* (1985) and *Batman* (1989), Zanuck and Brown cut against the prevailing winds with hits headlined by geriatrics with *Cocoon* (sixth top-grossing release of 1985), and the Oscar-winning *Driving Miss Daisy* (number eight in 1989). And perhaps nothing demonstrates Zanuck's willingness to see how far he could push the commercial mainstream than his six team-ups with Tim Burton including the visually deranged *Charlie and the Chocolate Factory* (2005), nightmarish musical *Sweeny Todd: The Demon Barber of Fleet Street* (2007), and Zanuck's final film, the campy *Dark Shadows* (2012).

One of my favorite stories about Dick Zanuck, and the one that I think captures what that essential part of him was as a – yes, you can call a producer this – filmmaker, is one I heard from Sonny Grosso, one of the real-life cops involved in the famous "French Connection" heroin bust.

Journalist Robin Moore had turned the case into a book, and a film adaptation had been pitched to Fox which turned it down five times. Finally,

Zanuck agreed to take the project on, but there was a hitch: some of the participants were still haggling with executive producer G. David Schine (probably better known for his role as Roy Cohn's protégé during Cohn's infamous Red-baiting days working for Senator Joe McCarthy). By this time, Zanuck knew his days at Fox were numbered. In a conversation with Grosso, Zanuck pushed him to quickly make a deal "…because I'm gonna be fired in a few weeks."

Academy Award winning *The French Connection* (1971) starring Gene Hackman as fanatical narcotics cop Popeye Doyle, the role that won him an Oscar. Richard Zanuck's name was nowhere on the film, but it wouldn't have gotten made without him.

What I like about this story is that with his exit imminent, there was nothing in *The French Connection* for Zanuck. He had begun to see the potential in the project, but he knew the credit, as typically happens in such cases in Hollywood, would go to his successor. Zanuck just thought it was a movie that should be made. *The French Connection* (1971) would win five Oscars, including Best Picture, be one of the biggest grossing movies of the decade, and become one of the all-time classic thrillers. Zanuck's name isn't anywhere on the film, but he's largely responsible for it getting made (as for karmic justice: Zanuck's name has managed to stay connected to the movies, while G. David Schine would produce only one other film – the justifiably unremembered 1977 documentary, *That's Action!* – and his connection to *Connection* is largely forgotten).

That kind of desire, that kind of belief that "good" can make money, is what distinguished Richard Zanuck throughout his career. It has always been a rare commodity in Hollywood, and now it's rarer still.

CLIFF ROBERTSON (1923 – 2011): "UTILITY PLAYER"

September 12, 2011

He played leads…but never became a star. He played supporting parts…but was never considered a second-stringer. He moved between the big and little screen easily throughout much of his career without ever looking like he'd overreached (for the former), or was slumming (in the latter). The only thing that mattered – the one thing that was consistent whatever the vehicle, whatever the medium, whatever the size of the role – was the caliber of his work. By his own description, Cliff Robertson, who passed away this week one day after his 88th birthday, was a "utility player" who shone whatever his position.

Still in his 20s, he was already working regularly on TV during those early, hectic days of live broadcasting in the early 1950s, and just as immediately demonstrating the utility that marked his career. His range was limitless as he performed in everything from heavyweight drama anthology *Hallmark Hall of Fame* to Saturday morning kiddie sci fier, *Rod Brown of the Rocket Rangers*, leading all those little junior Rocket Rangers out there with (in the words of *Variety*) "gee whiz enthusiasm" in pledging the "Rocket Ranger Code."

He began to get his first major roles in film in the mid- and late 1950s, playing opposite and losing Kim Novak to William Holden in the steamy (for its time) *Picnic* (1955), playing a humanitarian platoon leader in the bowdlerized film adaptation of Norman Mailer's *The Naked and the Dead* (1958), knocking the teen girls dizzy as The Big Kahuna surfing king in *Gidget* (1959), making them swoon again as one of an ensemble of dedicated young (and uniformly good-looking) wannabe doctors in *The Interns* (1962).

At the same time, he continued to maintain a heavy presence in TV, guest-starring on some of the most popular series of the day such as *The Untouchables, Wagon Train, Ben Casey* as well as drama anthologies like *The United States Steel Hour*.

Curiously, it was these anthologies, not his big screen work, which provided the best opportunities for Robertson to showcase just how strong and serious a dramatic actor he was. He racked up Emmy nominations for the TV versions of "The Days of Wine and Roses" and "The Two Worlds of Charly Gordon," and copped a win for "The Game."

TV also provided Robertson with the work for which most contemporary audiences probably remember him thanks to endless re-runs on cable, namely his appearances in two of the most memorable episodes of the classic sci fi/fantasy series, *The Twilight Zone*. In "One Hundred Yards Over the Rim," Robertson plays a 19th century immigrant settler, his wagon stranded in the desert of the American southwest, who sets out for help for his ailing son and finds himself mysteriously transported to the 20th century. Even stronger is one of the all-time series classics, "The Dummy," with Robertson as a tortured ventriloquist sure the little wooden figure on his knee has a malicious mind of his own.

He finally seemed to break out of the junior film ranks with *P.T. 109* (1963), a dramatized *(highly* dramatized) version of author Robert J. Donovan's account of John F. Kennedy's adventures aboard the eponymous torpedo boat during WW II. Robertson was the choice of Kennedy himself to play the lead (Jackie Kennedy wanted Warren Beatty). It's not a particularly good movie, it's lousy history, and it's not even Robertson's best work, but the high profile film boosted the actor's visibility and improved the roles coming his way. Among the best of those which soon followed was that of the vicious, back-biting presidential candidate Joe Cantwell trying to out-maneuver nice-guy candidate Henry Fonda in the film version of Gore Vidal's astute political drama, *The Best Man* (1964).

Robertson reached a professional peak of sorts a few years later with his Oscar-winning role in *Charly* (1968), a big screen redo of "The Two Worlds of Charly Gordon." Robertson had already lost one juicy role in a film remake of his TV work when Jack Lemmon had been cast in the film version of *The Days of Wine and Roses* in the role for which Robertson had gotten an Emmy nom. Determined not to lose *Charly* as well, he bought the rights to the story himself and spent years trying to get the film made. It was worth it.

It's a heart-breaking performance. Charly Gordon is an oft-teased, mentally retarded adult who volunteers for an experimental surgical procedure which transforms him into a genius. But the effects of the procedure are short-lived, and Gordon – fighting the clock trying to use his new brain powers to solve the tragic puzzle of his come-and-go mental prowess – needs to face going back to his childish state.

Despite the commercial and critical success of *Charly,* despite the Oscar, Robertson never quite made the step up to marquee value star. But the actor seemed to understand the ephemeral nature of status in Hollywood. "The year you win an Oscar is the fastest year in a Hollywood actor's life," he would later observe. "Twelve months later they ask, 'Who won the Oscar last year?'"

But if he was frustrated, he kept it to himself, and continued on as the valued utility player, showing up when called, always putting out the good work as he did as a well-meaning if prosaic CIA officer in *Three Days of the Condor* (1975), one of the signature exercises in political paranoia from the era.

His biggest career challenge came in 1977, not in a role, not in a film or TV project, but in the all-too-seamy all-too-real world of corporate Hollywood. Robertson found his name forged on a $10,000 check. Despite being advised by the power circles of moviedom to keep the issue to himself, the actor blew the whistle on what came to be known as "Hollywoodgate." The forgery turned out to be one of several traced to Columbia studio chief David Begelman who lost his job, and was convicted and sentenced to probation. Hollywood, however, having the free-spinning moral compass it does, soon welcomed Begelman back and in 1980 he became the president of MGM. Robertson, on the other hand, was tacitly punished for going public on executive suite misdoings, and didn't get another acting call for four years.

By the time the work started coming his way again, his leading man days were over, but Robertson hadn't lost a step, always bringing his A game whether it was on a high profile feature *(Brainstorm,* 1983; *Star 80,* 1983), or a switch-off-the-brain time-killer *(Escape from L.A.,* 1996), or a prime time TV soap like *Falcon Crest* where he had a recurring role in the mid-'80s.

Youngsters discovered him – and oldsters were reminded about him – when he appeared as Uncle Ben in *Spider-Man* (2002), struggling to understand his young nephew's angst, and unknowingly, through his own innate decency, giving the fledgling superhero his moral center. With all the gravitas of his years, and with a gravelly voice that sounded weighed down by the wisdom of the ages, Robertson gives his nephew his mandate and one of the all-time great lines in superhero flicks: "Remember, with great power comes great responsibility."

To the mass public, Robertson was not well-known enough, not iconic enough to be missed, his many sterling performances too poorly remembered to still be appreciated. And if that's the case for anyone reading this, than salute the survival of a quality performer who, in one of the most competitive and vicious of trades, maintained a career over six decades. That alone is worth commemorating in an arena Robertson once described thusly: "This isn't exactly a stable business. It's like trying to stand up in a canoe with your pants down."

ELMORE LEONARD (1925 – 2013): "I DON'T REMEMBER ALL THE BAD ONES"

August 22, 2013

According to IMDB, close to 40 films and TV shows have Elmore Leonard's name attached, some as creator, some as screenwriter, but about three-quarters because they're based on one of his novels or short stories. Leonard, who died August 20 of complications following a stroke, didn't like most of them. Actually, that's something of an understatement. He *hated* most of them, the distinction being he hated some more than others.

Leonard had a love/hate thing going with Hollywood. He loved taking movie money, but usually hated what Hollywood did with his material. He went public with his revulsion over Burt Reynold's thoroughly lousy 1985 adaptation of his novel *Stick*, and while I don't know this for a fact, I'm sure he was shaking his head, at least at first, when Quentin Tarantino cast Pam Grier in *Jackie Brown* (1997) to play what had been a white character in his source novel, *Rum Punch* (although he did consider the finished film one of the best adaptations of his work). The two versions of *The Big Bounce* (1969 and 2004) were a favorite whipping post for him as he labeled them the second-worst and worst movies ever made respectively.

"I don't remember all the bad ones. I know *The Big Bounce* was bad, though, and they made it twice (1969 and 2004). It wasn't bad enough the first time."

Leonard seemed to have a pretty good handle on what the problem probably was: "…when you bring a 350-page manuscript down to 120 (script) pages…a lot of the good stuff (in my books) is gone. It disappears. Because then you're more interested in plot than you are in, say, character development." And despite all the scheming and plotting and inevitable double-crossing in Leonard's novels, what made them work was his richly-developed, morally dubious characters spitting dialogue that sang like some kind of street poetry (according to Leonard, he was heavily influenced by the dialogue-heavy storytelling of George V. Higgins in Higgins' crime novel, *The Friends of Eddie Coyle*).

Personally, I never quite plugged into Leonard. His writing is terrific, his characters fun, his dialogue a joy to read, but his crime plots are a bit too clever for my tastes. I always preferred Higgins' grittier, grubbier, street-real tales. Still…

Leonard hit his stride when he turned from writing Western tales to crime stories, and nearly all the books he turned out from the 1980s on were bestsellers. But while they didn't quite play out the way he'd penned them for the page, my favorite Leonard adaptations came from his Wild West tales.

There's *The Tall T* (1957), one of the first Leonard adaptations, an intense little suspenser anchored on the psychological give-and-take between bad guy Richard Boone and hostage Randolph Scott, Boone seeing in Scott the kind of man he maybe once was, and wishes he could be again. And there's *3:10 to Yuma* (1957 and remade in 2007), another duel more psychological than shoot-'em-up with Van Heflin (in the original) as a desperate farmer trying to win himself a bounty by getting smooth-talking bad guy Glenn Ford onto a prison-bound train. And then there's one of my all-time favorite Westerns, *Hombre* (1967), a mash-up between John Ford's 1939 *Stagecoach* and the classic de Maupassant short story, "Boule de Suif," with Paul Newman as a cool-as-they-come outcast, a white man raised by Apaches that the ostracizing passengers of a stagecoach turn to for help when threatened by a band of highwaymen.

My personal tastes are just that; personal taste with all the subjectivity that goes with that. But I understand and value the standing of the man and his undeniable talent in both the literary and film worlds. Coming so soon after the death of another master storyteller, Richard Matheson, it does get one wondering if we're not witnessing the passing of an entire generation of storyteller and with them, a kind and caliber of storytelling that managed the hat trick of being deftly executed, enormously entertaining, and driven by very recognizable, life-sized human hungers and foibles.

DON AND *DIRTY:* THE CAREER OF DON SIEGEL (1912 – 1991)

August 25, 2010

Under-appreciated throughout much of his career, with his early work made up of catch-as-catch-can projects, his credits meandering from Westerns *(The Beguiled,* 1971; *The Shootist,* 1976) to science fiction *(Invasion of the Body Snatchers,* 1956), war stories *(Hell Is for Heroes,* 1962), period pieces *(The Verdict,* 1946), crime stories *(Dirty Harry,* 1971; *Charley Varrick,* 1973), and even vehicles for pop stars *(Hound Dog Man,* 1959, with Fabian; *Flaming Star,* 1960, with Elvis Presley), Don Siegel still managed to compile a body of exceptional work, always marked – usually despite limitations of budget and time – by intelligence and respect for both his material and his audience.

Critic Richard Combs, in a 1994 *Film Comment* piece on Siegel, wrote that whatever the milieu, Siegel's strongest movies – *The Big Steal* (1949)*, Riot in Cell Block 11* (1954)*, Invasion of the Body Snatchers, The Lineup* (1957)*, Hell Is for Heroes, The Killers* (1964)*, Madigan* (1968)*, Coogan's Bluff* (1968)*, The Beguiled, Dirty Harry, Charley Varrick, Escape from Alcatraz* (1979) – all shared the traits of "…strong characters, tightly contained situations, and a narrative style that is…both direct and oblique, objective and frenzied, casually realistic and coolly abstract."

The plots in Siegel's best films are remarkably simple: *The Big Steal* is one, long chase; *Hell Is for Heroes* is a basic Us vs. Them punch/counterpunch combat story; in *The Beguiled,* wounded Union soldier Clint Eastwood tries to sweet-talk the mistress of an all-girls school from surrendering him to Confederate troops; *Dirty Harry* stalks a serial killer; a handful of cons plot an *Escape from Alcatraz* in what is, essentially, a prison breakout procedural. The A-B-C simplicity of Siegel's plots grants him ample running room for complexity of character, inter-character relationships, and, that most subtle and hard-to-define aspect of cinema, tone. Siegel carries all this off with a clean, unobtrusive, yet flavorful visual style, and with both a logistical and dramatic economy which would be one of the most oft-cited earmarks of his work, making him, at his commercial peak from the late 1960s through the 1970s, something of a master of the mid-range thriller.

Even during this flush period he still had his missteps: the surprisingly bland espionage thriller *Telefon* (1977, which Siegel took over from original director Peter Hyams), the problem-plagued *Rough Cut* (1980, Siegel was one of the movie's four directors), and still another troubled production, the aptly titled *Jinxed* (1982). Still, in his better, more personally imprinted work, he typically outclassed those working on a more lavish scale.

Siegel's characteristic economy traces back to the very start of his career in the 1940s at Warner Bros. where he wound up unofficial head of the studio's Montage Department. He benefited from moviemaking advice and counsel from directors like Anatole Litvak *(City for Conquest* , 1940; *Sorry, Wrong Number,* 1948), for whose features Siegel cut trailers, and especially from conferring with his opposite number at MGM, montage master Slavko Vorkapich. Under such guiding hands, Siegel served a form of directorial apprenticeship assembling sometimes complex scripts for his montage sequences, and came to believe early on in the unlimited possibilities of a succinct form of visually-driven storytelling. He left Warners after earning his feature director's stripes on the Victorian-era thriller *The Verdict* and the drama *Night Unto Night* (1949), then spent better than a decade gypsying around the B-movie circuit and occasionally foraying into television.

As early as *The Big Steal* – only his third feature – Siegel showed a visual assurance, logistical expertise, a storytelling precision, and a penchant for the unpredictable twist in the seemingly predictable which he would carry forward throughout his career. The story (screenplay by Drayson Gerald Adams and Daniel Mainwaring, adapted from Richard Wormser's story, "The Road to Carmichael's") concerns a GI on the run (Robert Mitchum) trying to clear himself of a false robbery charge who hooks up with an at-first dubious Jane Greer on an extended chase along the back roads of Mexico, a setting neatly conforming to the movie's modest budget without betraying it. Faced with a familiar story he feared might become a standard-issue B-thriller, Siegel opted to infuse the movie with a genre-contrary sense of humor, turning *Steal* into one of the few (possibly only) comic *noirs*. In the process, the central characters are flipped from their usual genre stances: Mitchum's hero thinks of himself as a self-assured, smart cookie, but he's actually rather dim, the clever thinking getting him through one tight spot after another coming from Greer — a character who, in many *noirs,* would typically have been relegated to tag-along romantic interest. The Mexican police colonel (played by one-time matinee idol Ramon Navarro), rather than fulfilling the then prevalent below-the-border stereotype of slow-witted, comic and corrupt Mexican cop is, instead, shrewd, observant, intelligent, and scrupulously honest. The Military Policeman (William Bendix) so doggedly hunting Mitchum turns out, in a final twist, to be the unknown true culprit Mitchum has been frantically searching for.

Siegel would thereafter be regularly attracted to characters who refuted expectations (a gangland kingpin played by tweedy Vaughn Taylor in a wheelchair in *The Lineup;* Mob banker Woodrow Parfrey worried about how a recent robbery threatens his community standing in *Charley Varrick*), heroes who were not always likable (a brutalizing Clint Eastwood in *Dirty Harry;* Steve McQueen's killing machine of a GI in *Hell Is for Heroes;* the inquisitive hitmen of *The Killers)* or even particularly heroic (Walter Matthau's fast-thinking, double-dealing bank robber in *Charley Varrick)*. Siegel put a peace sign belt buckle on Andy Robinson's serial killer in *Dirty Harry* confessing he didn't quite understand the significance of doing so himself, but liked the idea of this cold-blooded killer's blindness to the truth about himself.

Though some of Siegel's Bs suffered from expected constraints – tight budgets, second-rate casting, inferior scripts – he regularly showed, as he did with *Steal*, that with the right script and able (if B-list) talent, he could turn out exemplary work: *Riot in Cell Block 11*, with its prisoners and warders both depicted as victims of a flawed penal system, remains discomforting and relevant today; *Invasion of the Body Snatchers*, shot on a skimpy $250,000, stands as one of the all-time science fiction classics.

Toward the end of the 1950s, with feature jobs harder to come by in an economically suffering Hollywood, Siegel turned more often to TV of which, with its even more threadbare budgets and fleeting shooting schedules, he thought little, declaring it "...equal to the worst 'B' pictures that one can make." He thought even less of his own work for the medium, saying his only inspiration for taking TV jobs were the paychecks. Dismissive as Siegel was, the vitality of his TV work still managed to stand apart from an endemic blandness in the medium. If for nothing else, Siegel's work in TV is worth remembering for one particular project, a TV movie which, despite the strangling limitations of TV production and Siegel's own self-deprecation, was, even at the time, taken as an extraordinary piece of filmmaking: *The Killers*.

Adapted by Gene L. Coon from a slip of an Ernest Hemingway short story and intended as the medium's first made-for-TV movie, elements of *The Killers* haven't aged well. The movie can't shed a TV "look" burdened, as it is, with the stale quality of the studio back lot and back-projection traveling scenes. Too, what seemed provocative in 1964 – the awkwardly choreographed slow-motion assassination which opens the movie – seems positively tepid next to the more graphic and elaborately orchestrated violence of the big-screen movies which shortly followed i.e. *Point Blank* (1967), *Bonnie and Clyde* (1967), *The Dirty Dozen* (1967), *The Wild Bunch* (1969). Still, thematically, the movie remains a powerful extrapolation of *noir* existentialism and nihilism: there are no heroes, only Bad Guys; there is an enveloping sense of inevitable, all-encompassing tragedy; and the movie ends with the destruction/self-destruction of every principal character.

Lee Marvin and a fey Clu Gulager play two hitmen hired by an unknown party to kill trade school instructor John Cassavetes. Marvin is intrigued by the acquiescence with which Cassavetes had given himself over to his executioners. "There's only one guy who's not afraid to die," Marvin calculates, "that's a guy who's already dead." Marvin and Gulager learn Cassavetes was a washed-up auto racer who'd been the getaway driver in an armored car robbery. As much as for the money, Cassavetes' reason for taking on the job was his interest in coquettish Angie Dickinson, the moll of gang leader Ronald Reagan (in his last movie role). Now further enticed by the still-missing robbery loot, Marvin and Gulager discover Dickinson had played both Cassavetes and Reagan to her own advantage; a betrayal which left Cassavetes emotionally gutted and ready for death. In a pitch-perfect *noir* finale, a mortally wounded Marvin faces off with Dickinson who is, once again, trying to bargain and tease her way clear. The dying Marvin looks at her over the sights of his raised pistol, rebuffs her with, "Lady, I haven't got the time," and pulls the trigger. He picks up the money-stuffed valise, staggers outside as the sound of police sirens near, finally collapses from his wounds, the money spilling free into the street.

Put off by the movie's dark themes as much as by its (for the time) brutal violence, network sponsors rejected *The Killers,* and Universal, which had produced the movie, put it into theatrical release. *The Killers* represents the beginning of a fruitful relationship between Siegel and Universal, and was the first in a series of big screen crime thrillers *(Madigan, Coogan's Bluff,* and – on loan-out to Warner Bros. – *Dirty Harry,* his first major hit) which finally upraised Siegel from the B-list.

The richness of Siegel's later work stems from the same skilled craftsman's precision exercised in his early films. His casts, both in early and later years, are generally small *(The Big Steal* rests on the shoulders of four main characters; *Dirty Harry* is primarily carried by six roles; *Escape from Alcatraz* by about the same), but the movies nevertheless feel character-rich. Siegel favored stories which, despite having a main "anchor" character, played closer to ensemble pieces, his supporting players working with clearly defined, individualized roles giving his stories a sense of being fully populated.

Similarly, his movies "feel" bigger in scope than they really are: on *The Verdict,* Siegel concealed the physical limits of his Victorian street set by having the studio fog machines produce enough mist to conceal the 1946 L.A. skyline just beyond; in *Dirty Harry,* he conveyed the air of a citywide dragnet looking for a rooftop sniper with only a roving shot from a patrolling helicopter taking in a handful of police-uniformed extras scattered about city roofs. *Riot in Cell Block 11, Invasion of the Body Snatchers, The Beguiled, Charley Varrick,* and especially *Escape from Alcatraz* are all stories which, like *The Big Steal,* organically demand very little in terms of locations and production design. Most of *The Big Steal* takes place on back roads; the bulk of *Escape from Alcatraz* plays out on a handful of locations all within the Alcatraz prison; *The Beguiled* remains mostly within the walls of an all-girls school; *Charley Varrick* is an urbane robbery thriller uniquely set against the sparse milieu of rural New Mexico.

His imparting of dramatic information is equally spot-on, often minimalistic, and it is sometimes surprising – in light of how full-bodied his stories feel – to discover how brief the running times are on his most memorable movies: *Invasion of the Body Snatchers* clocks in at a brisk 80 minutes; *The Lineup* at 86; *Hell Is for Heroes*, 90; *Madigan*, 101; *Coogan's Bluff*, 100; *Dirty Harry*, 102. Yet there is nothing in the storytelling which feels underwritten or anemic.

Siegel obviously approved of Steve McQueen's cutting down a script monologue in *Hell Is for Heroes* to a single, exasperated, right-on-the-money line – "How the hell do I know?" – following an ill-fated McQueen-led attack on an enemy pillbox. Clint Eastwood's *Dirty Harry* gains a sudden pathos with one line referring to his late wife as he explains how she was killed in an automobile accident: "There was no reason for it, really." In the same movie, after a D.A. informs Eastwood serial killer Andy Robinson is to be released from custody on a technicality, and then skeptically asks Eastwood why he is so sure Robinson will kill again, Eastwood sends a chill through the audience replying simply, "Because he likes it." In *Charley Varrick*, we find out the connection between bank robber Walter Matthau and his dead female getaway driver when – showing little outward emotion – he gives her corpse a farewell kiss, then removes her wedding ring and slips it on a finger next to his own.

The acme of Siegel's terseness is *Escape from Alcatraz*. According to Siegel, during development of the piece, Paramount executives were put off by the lack of character exposition in the script (by Richard Tuggle from S. Campbell Bruce's novel). They suggested the audience needed to know the full back-story on Clint Eastwood's character, an explanation of why he'd turned professional criminal. Siegel's response was the more the character was explained, the "…less real he becomes. The trick is to *suggest…*" So, in *Escape*, when a fellow convict asks Eastwood what kind of childhood he had, the reply is a curt, "Short." In another scene from *Escape*, convict Paul Benjamin – a "lifer" – is called to the visitor's gallery. He sits across the glass from a young woman (Candace Bowen) he does not recognize. She picks up the phone, says the single word, "Daddy…," and Benjamin hangs up the phone and walks away.

Siegel was not as ostentatiously visual a director as some of his 1950s confreres, like, say, Robert Aldrich, but he had a feel for just the right non-distracting visual accent. Shooting *Invasion of the Body Snatchers* on location in the small town of Sierra Madre grounded his fantastic story in a recognizably real-world milieu; he gained a similar edge shooting *Riot in Cell Block 11* in Folsom Prison using actual guards and prisoners as extras; his use of the still under construction Los Angeles freeway system for the finale of

The Lineup is a textbook example of making an action sequence more visually engrossing without simply piling on the careening and crashing of cars; and he similarly enhanced the climactic foot chase of *Dirty Harry* by running his protagonists through a quarry; also in *The Lineup*, he has Eli Wallach's increasingly desperate hood trying to enlist sympathy from the wheelchair-bound senior gangster known only as The Man (Vaughn Taylor), the latter shot in extreme close-up as an emotionless, silent monolith in a meeting on a roller rink mezzanine; there's the lapse into a dreamy slow motion shot of a Confederate cavalry patrol passing by in *The Beguiled* as Clint Eastwood's hiding wounded Union soldier secures the silence of a schoolgirl with a seductive kiss.

Siegel may have been at his stylistic best in *Dirty Harry*, getting impressive visual mileage – along with cinematographer Bruce Surtees – from San Francisco's unique jigsaw topography, giving the hunt for a rooftop sniper the sense of a high-rise three-dimensional chess game. There's a brutal nighttime face-off with the killer below the massive cement cross in Mt. Davidson Park; the mournful, wordless exhumation of the raped and brutalized body of a teenaged girl in pre-dawn hues at Golden Gate Park; Eastwood's torturing of killer Andy Robinson under the glaring field lights of an empty Kezar Stadium, the sequence climaxing with a helicopter shot soaring further and further back into the night until the stadium lights become a dim, diffused glow lost in the San Francisco fog; the final foot chase through a cacophonous quarry plant ending in abruptly contrasting quietude by a nearby stagnant pond.

Some of these sequences demonstrate Siegel's ever-growing reputation through the 1960s-70s as a master of action films. Film critic Andrew Sarris declared the climactic car chase of *The Lineup*, and the intense, close quarters shootout at the end of *Madigan* among "...the most stunning displays of action montage..." in American films. Yet his shootouts are, by contemporary standards, surprisingly small scale, even simple. Siegel's actions scenes are not about running up body counts or elaborately-gimmicked stunts, but of ratcheting up the emotional intensity. That intensity comes not from complex editing schemes or pyrotechnics, or grand scale combat and bodies dropping left and right, but by the emotional investment Siegel's pictures take great pains to elicit up to that point.

Like John Sturges (*The Magnificent Seven*, 1960; *The Great Escape*, 1963), Siegel's movies are often thought of as more action-heavy than they actually are. Siegel himself once – wrongly – described *Dirty Harry* as "wall-to-wall" action although there's only 10-15 minutes of action spread out through the movie's 102 minute running time. He despised excess and gratuitous violence, and violent acts in his movies tend to be limited to abrupt, short-lived bursts.

Siegel's application of action is as sparing and precise as his application of exposition and character revelations. The architecture of his best movies is typically one of long – even languid – stretches jarred by sudden, brief, emotionally intense spasms of action. Siegel uses those long lulls to let his movies breathe; to cultivate a sense of place, and to allow his characters to show their other dimensions, to fill his movies with a full-bodied life rather than meaningless kinesis.

Madigan, for example, opens with an under-the-credit sequence taking the viewer through a cop's tour of duty on nighttime Manhattan; *Charley Varrick* also begins with a montage sequence, this one a more pastoral portrait of a small New Mexico town stirring to life on a quiet, sunny morning. In *Dirty Harry,* Eastwood, tracked by Bruce Surtees' camera, slowly walks the roof of a high rise which was the source of a fatal sniper shot, San Francisco laid out below him, its jumbled buildings spilling out toward the bay; the future game board for the cop/sniper contest to come.

Despite his reputation for taut suspense, there are often throwaway scenes and bits of business in a Siegel movie which do little or nothing to advance the main plot, but do fill in Siegel's canvas by deepening his central characters, and/or bringing supporting characters and the background atmosphere to life: a pasture-side conversation between Mob banker John Vernon and his tweedy minion Woodrow Parfrey in *Charley Varrick* as they exchange woes brought on by the robbery of the Mafia money drop they administer (Vernon looking out at the pasture: "I never thought I'd want to trade places with a cow"); Paul Benjamin's heartache at meeting with the daughter he's never known in *Escape from Alcatraz;* a foiled suicide attempt in *Dirty Harry.*

Even within his action sequences, Siegel would step back and pause, refusing to let rampant action swallow the emotion of the moment. Best example: Clint Eastwood's Dirty Harry Callahan is disturbed from his lunch counter hot dogs by a bank robbery. There follows a short, explosive exchange of shots with the robbers lasting about 25 seconds. One of the robbers lies wounded and is about to receive the movie's signature, "Did I fire six shots or only five?" speech from Eastwood. But, between the last shot fired and the beginning of Eastwood's speech, Siegel gives Eastwood a slow 33-second walk across the debris-littered street.

If Siegel knew how to ease off an action sequence to let his characters breathe, conversely, he knew how to ever-so-slightly jack up the tension in what could be a simple, perfunctory scene. In *Charley Varrick,* Matthau's bank robber meets with shady gun shop owner Tom Tully to get a line on someone who can supply him with a false passport. As Matthau turns to leave and Tully asks if there's anything else he can help with, Matthau turns back to ask about the possibility of fencing money. Lalo Shifrin's quiet but urgent score slips in underneath, and the dialogue lapses into a cagey argot. Tully asks how much money is at stake: "A lot? Or a whole lot?" "A whole lot," Matthau replies, and the stakes of the exchange suddenly multiply.

Siegel's thrillers – particularly his best 1960s/1970s works – are as deserving of attention as more grandiose and artistically ambitious works of the time like *The Godfather* (1972), *Mean Streets* (1973), *The Wild Bunch*, *The French Connection* (1971), *Bonnie & Clyde*, etc. While younger, more self-consciously "arty" directors like Coppola, Friedkin, and others self-destructed almost as soon as they had risen to prominence, Siegel – in his 50s and 60s – with a balanced blend of efficient craftsmanship, professionalism, and creative insight, was turning out his best work. He confessed to little overt artistic ambition, claiming to be surprised at the fuss stirred up by a movie he'd intended as simple entertainment (i.e. *Dirty Harry*). Yet, in his unassuming way, in movies like *Invasion of the Body Snatchers*, *Hell Is for Heroes*, and *The Killers* he managed to produce a number of philosophically provocative classics.

KINGDOM OF DARKNESS: RKO AND *FILM NOIR*

August 10, 2010

While most crime movies from the 1930s were flyweight mysteries, Warner Bros. turned out a string of hard-boiled gangster films often depicting crime as a product of the poverty and frustration of urban slums. These movies made stars of Warners' stable of tough guy actors including Edward G. Robinson, Humphrey Bogart, George Raft, John Garfield and James Cagney pictured here with frequent co-star Pat O'Brien (in priest's garb).

Coming out of World War II, the major Hollywood studios had hoped to get back to business as usual. The distraction of the war was gone, rationing repealed, and the boys – 15 million of them — were coming home. But the expected upsurge in business didn't come. In fact, almost immediately box office began steadily dropping (and would continue to do so for the next two decades), and the majors found that the kind of frothy and escapist fare which had dominated the 1930s no longer worked for a new generation of moviegoers. The people the studio chiefs had made movies for in the 1930s had stopped coming, and a different audience – younger, better-educated, and possessed of a wholly different worldview – was taking its place.

There were several genres – some new — which came to be emblematic in one way or another of the new dynamics of postwar Hollywood. The sudden, surging popularity of science fiction movies testified to the demographic shift of the box office toward young ticket buyers, while the massive sword-and-sandal epics showed a desperate motion picture industry trying to compete with television by overwhelming it. But no genre is so closely associated with the period, and considered so reflective of the postwar change in the American psyche, as *film noir*.

Prior to World War II, most thrillers tended to be one form or another of crime story, and with some exceptions – most notably Warner Bros.' string of socially-conscious gangster films (i.e. *Little Caesar* [1931], *Angels with Dirty Faces* [1938]) – they tended to be routine (like the myriad formulaic mystery series i.e. *Boston Blackie, Mr. Moto, Charlie Chan, Crime Doctor*, etc.), escapist (the bubbly *The Thin Man* films), and/or simple, melodramatic morality tales (such as the aptly titled *Manhattan Melodrama* [1934]). But the global tragedy that was World War II inalterably changed the worldview of thrillers...and of their audience. French film critics, treated to a postwar backlog of American films, looked at what appeared to them to be a surge in thrillers visually and thematically darker than their pre-war counterparts and dubbed the new thrillers *film noir;* literally translated, "black film."

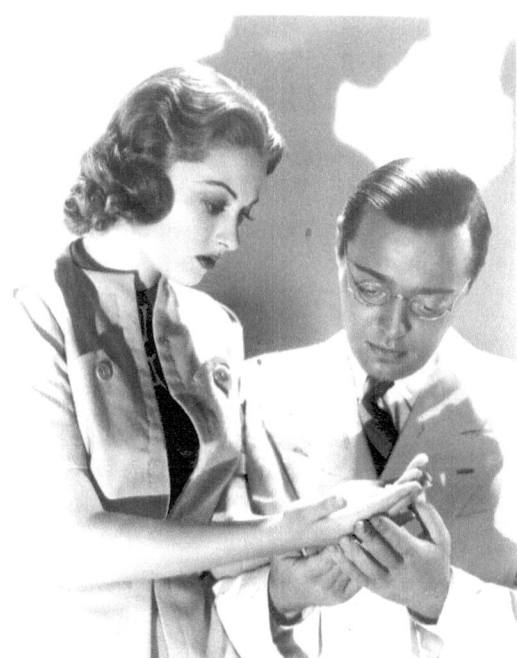

The largest share of 1930s crime stories came from long-running movie series. Often B-caliber productions, entertaining but disposable, they included the Dick Tracy, Boston Blackie, Charlie Chan, Ellery Queen, Philo Vance, The Falcon, The Saint, and Mr. Moto series. With a racial insensitivity typical of the time, Mr. Moto, pictured here, was played by Hungarian-born actor Peter Lorre.

Film noir represented the first, major maturing of the Hollywood thriller, a psychological evolution which went beyond the dramatically simplistic, morally pedantic fare of the pre-war years. *Noir* was about the flaws in the character of even the most well-meaning of people *(Scarlet Street,* 1945), about how tragedy could be visited on the undeserving through a single misstep *(Angel Face,* 1952) or even chance *(D.O.A.,* 1950). *Noir* – understandably in light of the destruction and brutality of the war – showed how thin the line could be between The Good Guys and The Bad Guys *(The Strange Love of Martha Ivers,* 1946), sometimes to the point where they were interchangeable *(Pickup on South Street,* 1953), and never guaranteed a happy ending *(The Killers,* 1946).

Although *noir* would be most closely identified with urban crime dramas, it was a sensibility and a style which spread throughout the thriller form. One could find it in hard-edged Westerns like *Blood on the Moon* (1948) and *Winchester '73* (1950), dark-hearted war films like *Attack!* (1956), and even gothic horrors like *The Body Snatcher* (1945) and sci fiers like *Donovan's Brain* (1953).

Though significant entries in the genre would come from throughout the industry, no studio would become more identified with American postwar *noir* as RKO. The company's prodigious thriller output from the war years through the 1950s, coupled with a remarkably consistent look and quality, largely defined the genre for American cinema.

RKO had experienced several successes with small-scale thrillers during the war years, particularly with the company's screen adaptation of Raymond Chandler's *Murder, My Sweet* (1944). After the war, the studio applied itself even more industriously to producing a steady stream of similarly economically produced thrillers. These thrillers would, in fact, be critical to sustaining RKO through its remaining decade as a major studio.

The company's dedication to the thriller arose from necessity. Always the most financially strapped of the majors, the studio was one of the first big movie companies to suffer – and suffer egregiously – during the postwar downturn in the industry's fortunes. Saddled with heavy debt, constrained by limited resources, its talent roster the thinnest of the majors, the elements which had made *noir* thrillers choice vehicles under wartime rationing rules – moderate budgets, limited locations, emphasis on mood and plot over action – made them even more attractive during RKO's postwar struggle to remain afloat. *Crossfire* (1947), for example, was shot for a tight $250,000 budget on a brisk three-week schedule. Production notes list only nine locations, nearly all of which incorporated standing sets.

Throughout the 1940s and into the 1950s, RKO was a virtual *noir* factory: *The Stranger on the Third Floor* (1940), *Suspicion* (1941), *Journey into Fear* (1942), *The Seventh Victim* (1943), *Murder, My Sweet, The Woman in the Window* (1944), *Cornered* (1945), *Johnny Angel* (1945), *Nocturne* (1946),

Notorious (1946), *The Spiral Staircase* (1946), *The Stranger* (1946), *The Locket* (1946), *Crossfire, Out of the Past* (1947), *They Live by Night* (1949), *The Big Steal* (1949), *The Set-Up* (1949), *Where Danger Lives* (1950), *The Woman on Pier 13* (1950), *His Kind of Woman* (1951), *The Racket* (1951), *The Narrow Margin* (1951), *Clash by Night* (1952), *On Dangerous Ground* (1952), *Macao* (1952), *Beware, My Lovely* (1952), *The Las Vegas Story* (1952), *The Hitch-Hiker* (1953), *Angel Face* (1953), *While the City Sleeps* (1956), *Beyond a Reasonable Doubt* (1956). The studio's interest in thrillers may have been primarily practical, but RKO could not have maintained such an extended commercially successful line of *noirs* without regularly turning out a popular, quality product. Despite occasional creative missteps (i.e. *The Woman on Pier 13* aka *I Married a Communist)*, the RKO thriller canon is impressively consistent in the high caliber of its execution; a remarkable achievement considering the studio's limitations. RKO was singularly fortunate in that among its thin talent ranks it had access to just the right creative personnel for the job at hand.

House cinematographer Nicholas Musuraca was a major contributor to the look of RKO's thrillers and horror films, and is often considered the "inventor" of *noir*'s expressionistic, sparsely-lit visual style, a look frequent RKO *noir* leading man Robert Mitchum dryly described as "lit by matches." In this, Musuraca was abetted by cameramen who periodically worked at the studio and shared his touch with light and shadow: Gregg Toland (famously responsible for the *noir*-like look of Orson Welles' *Citizen Kane*), Russell Metty, James Wong Howe, George Diskant, and Harry Wild. RKO also had an outstanding art department, as well as an editing department served by the likes of Robert Wise and Mark Robson, both of whom would later go on to distinguished directing careers. And then there was the studio's master of musical moods, house composer Roy Webb.

RKO also benefited from a liberal attitude toward new directors. Though a number of the company's more high-profile thrillers were directed by established talents like Orson Welles *(The Stranger)*, Alfred Hitchcock *(Suspicion, Notorious)*, and, as he entered the closing stage of his career, Fritz Lang *(Beyond a Reasonable Doubt, While the City Sleeps)*, the overall high caliber of RKO's thrillers was established and sustained by relative directorial novices. The directorial credits of the studio's thrillers indeed form an impressive list: Nicholas Ray *(They Live by Night)*, Edward Dmytryk *(Murder, My Sweet, Crossfire)*, Mark Robson *(The Seventh Victim)*, Richard Fleischer *(The Narrow Margin)*, Joseph Losey *(The Prowler)*, Don Siegel *(The Big Steal)*, Jacques Tourneur *(Out of the Past)*, Robert Wise *(The Set-Up)*, and – one of the few women ever to direct features up to that time — Ida Lupino *(The Hitch-Hiker)*. Given their creative head, and working with skilled craftsmen like Musuraca, these young, ambitious, and artistically daring directors were responsible for a string of compelling thrillers so consonant in their sensibility and look that they provided RKO with a distinct screen persona – something it had rarely had in the past – and did so at a time when bigger companies were sacrificing their own trademark identities in the pursuit of big budget audience draws.

The last necessary element for the success of RKO's thrillers was on-screen talent. RKO had historically suffered a shortage of top-flight box office draws, and that weakness became even more pronounced in the postwar period. Many of RKO's thrillers were carried on the backs of stars whose career peaks were behind them, though they usually rose to the occasion as did one-time musical star Dick Powell as Raymond Chandler's tough-as-nails private eye Philip Marlowe in *Murder, My Sweet,* ex-Warner Bros. tough guy George Raft in *Johnny Angel,* and ex-20th Century Fox leading man Dana Andrews in *Beyond a Reasonable Doubt*. However, the studio's *noir* mainstays through the late 1940s and much of the 1950s were two often underrated actors: Robert Ryan and Robert Mitchum.

Though Ryan never quite broke through to become a major box office draw, he was a fine actor who always gave an interesting performance. His emotions were never buried very deeply and he was a more fiery presence on-screen than Mitchum, his eyes quick to flash anger, despair, or glum resignation, his body, when not slumped in defeat, looking coiled and ready to explode. His range ran from heroes to villains, and sometimes characters which were a bit of both, displaying, so wrote David Thomson in a 1994 *Film Comment* profile of the actor, a "…grasp of evil (and an) affinity for men who might be heroes if they had less anger, violence, and self-loathing, and more faith in the world." His RKO gallery included the venom-spitting bigot of *Crossfire,* the ranting, self-important gangster of *The Racket,* the dogged, brutal, life-scarred cop in *On Dangerous Ground,* the desperate, noble boxer of *The Set-Up,* and, one of his most interesting RKO portrayals, the handyman of *Beware, My Lovely,* mild and deferential until something trips in his fractured psyche sending him into an escalating, potentially lethal rage.

Robert Mitchum, in contrast, was RKO's one bonafide star with marquee value during the postwar years, and became the studio workhorse, carrying the lead in an impressive number of pictures ranging from urban *noirs* to Westerns to dramas to African adventures to war stories. He exuded a jaded weariness, a sense of having seen and heard more than he wanted to. That fatalistic, been-there/done-that air served him well across a wide range of RKO thrillers. In the tongue-in-cheek *The Big Steal,* he's a dim GI on the run, falsely accused of a payroll theft, never as clever or self-possessed as he thinks he is; while in *Crossfire,* as another soldier, he's a cynical ex-newsman reluctantly drawn into helping solve a hate killing. He offers a jaded take on a world of random, pointless tragedy, where the invisible motive of the murder at hand – as investigating detective Robert Young speculates – "…is something the killer brought with him":

Soldier: What's happened? Has everything suddenly gone crazy? I don't just mean this; I mean everything. Or is it just me?

Mitchum: No, it's not just you. The snakes are loose. Anybody can get them. I get them myself. But they're friends of mine.

Eventually, the audience tired of the period's particular brand of *noir*. After so many *fatales*, double-crosses, trench coated figures walking down rain-slicked streets at night, the genre had become too familiar, had grown stale and predictable, and the classic brand of postwar *noir* died out.

But *noir* had always been about more than certain visual tropes and plot devices. A particular visual brand of *noir* might have died with the 1950s, but its world-weary, soul-sick heart continued to find a home in such neo-*noirs* as *Point Blank* (1967), *Harper* (1966), *The Conversation* (1974), *Chinatown* (1974), *Night Moves* (1975), *L.A. Confidential* (1997), *Memento* (2000), *Syriana* (2005), *The Departed* (2006).

Beyond its shadowy look, *noir* had, at its core, always been about the capacity for tragic error and outright malevolence in the human heart, and how, despite the best efforts of the best of men, sometimes heartbreak and loss were inevitable, maybe even necessary. These, sadly, are stories that never go out of date.

ROBERT MITCHUM (1917-1997): "BABY I DON'T CARE"

February 27, 2011

The title of Lee Server's acclaimed 2002 biography, *Robert Mitchum: Baby I Don't Care* (MacMillan), offers a perfect encapsulization of the eponymous actor: a hard-partying Hollywood Bad Boy who didn't give a damn what moralizing finger-waggers thought of him, or what his peers in the movie business thought, or the press, or even the public. He was going to go his own way and to hell with you, and anyone positioning themselves to make strong objection was just as likely to get a punch in the nose as shown the actor's broad back. He worked hardest at conveying the idea that the thing he did for a living – acting – was also the thing he cared least about; an impression that may have been his most convincing performance.

The Bad Boy part of Mitchum's reputation was honestly come by. As a youth, he'd been booted from more than one school, hoboed around the country, boxed (thus his distinctive battered pug's profile), and even done time on a southern chain gang. It was a background which left him with a rebellious, take-no-guff streak he never lost, even as a movie star. Two years after his star-making turn in *Out of the Past* (1947), he was famously busted for marijuana possession and even did a few months at a California prison farm (the conviction was eventually overturned although this wasn't the same thing as Mitchum being innocent; he *did* smoke grass and continued to do so well into his AARP years). On 1955's *Blood Alley*, he threw a crew member into San Francisco Bay. In 1968, as public opinion swung against the Vietnam War, Mitchum advocated a policy of "Nuke 'em all." In 1983, promoting the miniseries *The Winds of War*, Mitchum got into hot water for making anti-Semitic remarks, then refused to apologize even though they were made in jest and the actor had a number of close Jewish friends. According to Server's book, the actor smoked to his dying day—literally — although he was suffering from emphysema and lung cancer.

Sometimes his rebelliousness could take on a noble hue according to Jean Simmons, his co-star on 1952's *Angel Face*, and her then husband, Stewart Granger, both of whom told the tale in the 1987 documentary series, *Hollywood, the Golden Years: The RKO Story.*

Mitchum had a scene calling for him to slap Simmons across the face. The actor, who was often quite courtly around his female co-stars, tried to fake the slap. Autocratic director Otto Preminger demanded Mitchum slap Simmons for real, then called for take after take. As Simmons' face began to swell from the repeated blows, Mitchum decided enough was enough, turned and gave Preminger a how-does-it-feel slap across *his* face. The infuriated director stormed up to RKO's executive offices and demanded Mitchum be fired from the picture. At the time, Mitchum was the closest thing the floundering RKO had to an honest-to-God marquee-value star and it was explained to the director that if anybody was going to leave the picture, it was going to be Preminger.

But the actor had a softer side as well, one few saw. He wrote and recorded a variety of music including an oratorio produced by Orson Welles at the Hollywood Bowl. He collected quarter horses. His four-time leading lady Deborah Kerr told of Mitchum reciting self-penned poetry to her during the shooting of *The Sundowners* (1960). Dwight Whitney, in a 1969 *TV Guide* piece, sensed this something else buried behind the actor's defiantly disinterested front, writing that somewhere inside Mitchum "…lies imprisoned the soul of a poet."

As for the indolence Mitchum affected and often bragged about, and his feigned indifference to his profession ("Movies bore me, especially my own"), this, too, was true – Sydney Pollack, his director on *The Yakuza* (1974) compared him to "an extremely powerful but lazy workhorse" — but only to a point. In his tenure at RKO from the mid-1940s well into the 1950s, this "lazy" actor was a studio reliable, often pumping out several films each year, once even working on three films simultaneously. Despite making noises several times in his later years about retiring, he kept appearing on either the big or little screen nearly every year of his life.

He would say he only made movies for the money, or to meet sexy women, or to score pot, and certainly bland time-killers like *Young Billy Young* (1969), *The Good Guys and the Bad Guys* (1969), *The Wrath of God* (1972), *The Amsterdam Kill* (1977), and *Breakthrough* (1979), to name just a very few, seemed to substantiate his point. But despite claiming he just "took what came and made the best of it," he also regularly gravitated to artistically ambitious projects and their demanding directors i.e. *The Night of the Hunter* (1955) and Charles Laughton; *Heaven Knows, Mr. Allison*(1957) and John Huston; *The Sundowners* and Fred Zinneman; *Ryan's Daughter* (1970) and David Lean. The *Blood Alley* incident notwithstanding, more typically he was a no-fuss-no-muss performer, on time, not only knowing all his lines but usually the lines of everyone else. "I've survived," he once said, "because I work cheap and don't take up too much time."

Stylistically, he was, in many ways, the first "modern" movie actor which is why his performances still hold up decades later. He didn't look like other actors of his time and certainly not like those of the generation before, didn't sound like them, didn't move like them. What one actor did with a sob, he did with a small sigh; where another actor needed a few lines, Mitchum could give the same sense with a slight shrug. Look at his breakthrough performance in *The Story of G.I. Joe* (1945) as a WW II infantry officer during the meat grinder Italian campaign. Sitting over the letters he's writing to families on behalf of the dead, his broad shoulders sag just a little, his deep, slow voice gets a fraction deeper and slower — "I know it ain't my fault that they get killed," he tells war correspondent Ernie Pyle (Burgess Meredith), "but it makes me feel like a murderer" — and that's all it takes to convey a man both bone weary and heartsick over the letters he's written today, and the letters he knows he'll be writing tomorrow, and the day after that and on and on.

His pugilist's looks, a voice that could seductively purr or fall into a thick, liquory rasp, his hooded eyes looking down from atop a massive chest combined to give him an intimidating physical presence more lithely athletic actors – Fairbanks, Gable, Flynn, Lancaster – didn't have. He was threatening in a way they weren't, and, more than that, there was something unmistakably carnal about him. The sight of Mitchum, his bare skin gleaming with swamp water, shot in a severe up-angle by director J. Lee Thompson in *Cape Fear* (1962), his lazy eyes gleaming as he stalks Gregory Peck's daughter in the Georgia backwoods is a portrait of something primordial, of a walking, lusting, unrestrained id.

"Up there on the screen," he once said, "you're thirty feet wide, your eyeball is six feet high…" That in mind, few actors of his time understood, as he did, the value of stillness on the screen. He seemed fully aware of how much presence he radiated, how little he had to do to pull focus: a nod of the head, a raised eyebrow accompanied by the slightest dip in his voice. He walked off with *Cape Fear*, taking it away from star (and producer) Gregory Peck; not an inconsiderable feat considering Peck would win the Best Actor Oscar the next year for *To Kill a Mockingbird* (1962). Mitchum has a scene in a bar sitting across from Peck as he explains the why and how behind his vindictive campaign to destroy Peck and his family. The heart of the scene is two long, almost uninterrupted takes; a near-monologue done in close ups. Watch his puffy eyes switch from sadistic glee to ice cold hate, the lazy drawl of his voice slide from malicious amusement to blatant threat. The adjustments are incredibly small, yet laser-focused enough to burn a hole through the screen. In the light-hearted Western *El Dorado* (1966), using the same economical style, he was one of the few actors who could hold the screen against the iconic John Wayne. He found the humor in Leigh Brackett's spry script without ever overtly playing to the joke. In a scene largely crafted by himself, he plays against his own he-man ladykiller image as he sits in a bath embarrassed by the woman friend who must pass through the room, pulling a hat down low over his head, covering his face with his hands and muttering, "I'll close my eyes."

Throughout his career, he worked across the spectrum of genres, although never as prolifically as he did during his years at RKO: Westerns both period *(Blood on the Moon,* 1948) and contemporary *(The Lusty Men,* 1952), war movies *(One Minute to Zero,* 1952), dramas *(Till the End of Time,* 1946), romantic comedies *(A Holiday Affair,* 1949), but making his biggest impression in a series of *film noirs* which, in the late 1940s/early 1950s, had become the troubled studio's mainstay.

Characteristically, Mitchum talked them down, saying, "RKO made the same film with me for ten years. They were so alike I wore the same suit in six of them and the same Burberry trench coat." Nevertheless, he was anointed a leading man and created a never-forgotten *noir* icon in *Out of the Past* (1947). That would be how the young Mitchum would be remembered, in his fedora and trench coat, a smoldering cigarette dangling from his lips. There had been *noirs* before Mitchum, and there'd be a long parade of *noirs* with and without Mitchum after *Out of the Past,* but the movie and Mitchum's Jeff Bailey became the genre's gold standard. Addicted to one of *noir*'s most toxic *femme fatales* (Jane Greer), Bailey is doomed and knows it, is resigned to it, scratches around for whatever little triumph he can find amidst his ruination. When Greer frets, "I don't want to die!" Mitchum's Bailey replies in that resigned, prosaic way only Mitchum could, "Neither do I, baby, but if I have to, I'm gonna die last."

Because he made so many indifferent movies and his style was so minimalist, the precision of his work was often missed; Mitchum bios often use the words "underrated" and "underappreciated." But he never walked through a film (though he would often say otherwise), and in even some of his weaker movies he showed a depth he was rarely given credit for. *Not As a Stranger* (1955) was a forgettable Noble Young Doctor sudser, but Mitchum still has his moments. In his best one, he stands over an operating table, having failed to save the life of the older doctor (Charles Bickford) who has been his doting father-like mentor. Cloaked in a surgeon's cap and mask, Mitchum has nothing to work with but his eyes, but he offers up two, bottomless abysses of heartbreak.

In the first years after he left the RKO stable, he produced a gallery of solid work ranging from "merely" entertaining *(The Enemy Below,* 1957) to notable *(The Sundowners; Heaven Knows, Mr. Allison; Home from the Hill,* 1960), but chief among them were two Villain-Hall-of-Fame-caliber performances in *The Night of the Hunter* and *Cape Fear.*

Mitchum would often say his Reverend Harry Powell in *Hunter* was his favorite role, and understandably so. To truly understand his performance is to be impressed with its deftness for Charles Laughton, in his only directorial effort, is not rendering reality, but a child's fairy tale complete with guardian angel (Lillian Gish) and boogie man. Mitchum smoothly morphs from fire-

and-brimstone preacher showing the battle between Good and Evil with locked fingers tattooed "Love" and "Hate," to something less than human skulking in the shadows of Gish's yard as he stalks two children in her charge, howling like a wounded animal when he's sent running by a blast from feisty Gish's shotgun.

The Night of the Hunter has always had more artistic stature than *Cape Fear*, but the latter is surely the more viscerally delicious watch. The best way to measure Mitchum's portrayal of total depravity as vengeful convicted rapist Max Cady is to run it up against Robert De Niro's take on the same character in Martin Scorsese's 1991 remake. Brilliant though De Niro can be, his busy performance, his spindly form, his cartoonish southern accent are outgunned by Mitchum's stillness, his Tiger tank massiveness, his lazy, raspy drawl: "I got somethin' planned for your wife and kid that they ain't nevah gonna forget. They ain't *nevah* gonna forget it…and neither will you, Counseluh! Nevah!" One IMDB poster commenting on both performances put it best: "Robert De Niro *acted* scary, Robert Mitchum *was* scary. Makes all the difference in the world."

By the 1960s, a middle-aged Mitchum was getting saggier in the jaw line and thick in the middle, and the memorable roles now came few and far between. Though he'd continue to appear in film and TV shows into the year of his death, his best late career performances came in the 1970s with three aces in a row: *The Friends of Eddie Coyle* (1973), *The Yakuza*, and *Farewell, My Lovely* (1975). The paunchy Mitchum was perfect for the rumpled Philip Marlowe in *Farewell*; he could've been playing a worn-out, older version of one of his 1950s *noir* characters. And director Sydney Pollack managed to get the best out of his lazy workhorse in the Japan-set *Yakuza*, with Mitchum as a man caught between conflicting loyalties and cultures, his still broad shoulders sagging under the weight of the unintended damage he inflicted on a Japanese family during the post-WW II occupation. Mitchum's Harry Kilmer is nearly broken by the wrongs he cannot right, and the despair of trying to find an honorable end to a tragedy which seems only to compound with his each attempt to do so.

But the best of the lot, and one of his all-time great performances, was as Eddie "Fingers" Coyle, a bottom-tier Boston hood who has spent most of his life "…watchin' other people go off to Florida while I'm sweatin' out how I'm gonna pay the plumber." There may be no better portrait of life at the lowest levels of organized crime, and his Eddie Coyle is at once reprehensible yet pitiable, a small-timer victimized by big-timers, double-dealing Feds, and his own bad luck.

Mitchum worked so long – over a half-century – and made so many movies that even after stripping out the misfires and the duds, one is still left with a sizable body of impressive work representing every stage of his career, and a gallery of some of the most memorable characters in the American film canon. Not bad for an actor who never claimed more than minimal talent or interest in his profession, pretending he'd more-or-less walked through his career, a 50-odd year journey of which he said, "I never changed anything, except my socks and my underwear."

8 GREAT COPS AND CROOKS MOVIES YOU'VE PROBABLY NEVER SEEN

March 21, 2012

As happened for so many other genres, the 1960s/1970s saw a tremendous creative expansion in crime and cop thrillers. The old Hollywood moguls had died off or retired, most of the major studios were bleeding red ink, attendance had gone off a cliff since the end of WW II, and a new breed of young, creatively adventurous production executives had been tasked with trying to save their business by coming up with movies which could hook a new, young, cinema-literate audience.

It also happened to be one of the most socially turbulent times in American history. Even before the American public grew restive over the growing disaster in Vietnam, the social fabric was unraveling with self-examination and doubt. The Cold War; a certain inner emptiness that went with a period of great material prosperity; once invisible fault lines on matters of race and gender discrimination beginning to crack – all these already simmering discontents rose to a boil with the frustrations and eventual disillusionment with the war in Vietnam, a conflict which, each year, seemed only to grow larger, draw the nation in deeper, and demand ever more in blood and treasure. It was a time when we regularly asked ourselves if we were the people we had always thought ourselves to be? Were we still the Good Guys? And were the Good Guys really the good guys? Were American ideals a reality? Or an unfulfilled hope? Or a lulling, self-satisfying myth?

This unsettled sensibility began to filter into the commercial mainstream of film, sometimes covertly, sometimes obviously. Criminals became funhouse mirror reflections of American aspirations gone wrong, cops came to represent a repressive, distrusted authority, the line between Good Guy and Bad Guy grew paper thin with the wear and tear of trying to maintain a social order which seemed, every night on the evening news, to be coming apart. Out of this social maelstrom came a revitalization of the crime and cop movie forms, and a number of all-time Hollywood classics.

Francis Ford Coppola's *The Godfather* (1972) was not the first Mob movie ever made, but, together with *The Godfather, Part II* (1974), turned Mario Puzo's lurid Mafia tale into a Shakespearean tragedy about the American Dream going horribly off track told with operatic grandeur. If *The Godfather* was grand opera, Martin Scorsese's *Mean Streets* (1973) was rock 'n' roll; a brash, hyper, down 'n' dirty picture of the lowest rungs of hood-dom the movies had never seen before. Peter Yates' autumnal *The Friends of Eddie Coyle* (1973) was the crime story as John Updike novel, working class frustration and middle-aged despair transposed to the world of low-level hoods. John Boorman's *Point Blank* (1967) visually elevated a simple story about payback into an expressionist vision of a society gone heartlessly corporate.

The cops got their overhaul, too. William Friedkin's *The French Connection* (1971) brought a refreshingly gritty, near-documentary authenticity to the police procedural, while Yates' *Bullitt* (1968) rendered it as a minimalist, almost totally visual abstract. At a time of rising crime rates and riots in the streets, Don Siegel's *Dirty Harry* (1971) tapped into a popular feeling that the biggest obstacle to law enforcement was the law, while Sidney Lumet's *Serpico* (1973) showed that sometimes the problem with law enforcement was the law enforcers.

These were the biggies, the award winners, the instant classics which re-defined the crime and cop thriller genres and whose titles, even all these decades later, still stand as the milestones in the evolution of the forms. But behind them were any number of other movies, less well-remembered, but hardly lesser films.

1. *The Anderson Tapes* (1971)
Directed by Sidney Lumet
Adapted from the Lawrence Sanders novel by Frank Pierson

You can't talk about crime movies without talking about New York crime movies, and you can't talk about New York crime movies without talking about Sidney Lumet. Fun, suspenseful, and sharp, *The Anderson Tapes* may not be one of Lumet's better-remembered films, but it's easily one of his most fun.

Sean Connery, just released from prison, plans to rob an entire uptown apartment building. For Connery, this isn't just a shot at the proverbial Big Score; it's also a "Screw the Establishment!" poke in the eye at that insular, Upper East Side, hoity-toity society of one percenters he can only ever look in on as a permanent outsider.

The wrinkle to the caper, and what gives *Anderson* a lot of its bite, is that everyone Connery deals with to pull off his master caper – the "birddog" (Martin Balsam) who'll pick out and fence the building's priciest items, the Mafioso he goes to for financing (Alan King), etc. — is under some kind of surveillance. Since Connery is not the target, and much of the surveillance is illegal, and none of the agencies involved share information, it never occurs to any of the observers to flag the cops about the upcoming heist even though they've documented every step of the operation. It's a sad irony that *Anderson*'s poke at governmental intrusiveness during the paranoia politics of the 1970s feels even more resonant in today's post 9/11 climate.

Lumet's got a great cast (along with Connery and Balsam, Dyan Cannon, Ralph Meeker, a pre-*Saturday Night Live* Garrett Morris, Christopher Walken in his film debut, among others), and generously spices Pierson's smart script (Pierson would cop an Oscar for penning Lumet's better known *Dog Day Afternoon* [1975]) with the New York he loved so well in all its grit, color, danger, and absurdity.

2. *Report to the Commissioner* (1975)
Directed by Milton Katselas
Adapted from the James Mills novel by Abby Mann and Ernest Tidyman

This may be one of the best Sidney Lumet New York cop movies Sidney Lumet didn't direct, and as engrossing as *Report* is, it's hard not to wonder how much further Lumet could've went with it.

Michael Moriarity is a young, naïve NYPD detective who develops an I'll-save-you crush on a pimp's girlfriend (Susan Blakely), unaware she's an undercover cop in a maverick operation run by an ambitious police captain (Hector Elizondo), and that his well-meaning meddling can get people killed and blow the operation in embarrassing fashion.

Less a thriller than a cop drama (despite a climactic chase and tense stand-off in an elevator), Mann/Tidyman's adult script looks at a different kind of police corruption; not of crooked cops on the take, but the kind of moral corruption which goes with rampant ambition, relentless politicking, turf wars, and all the other conscience-twisting forces that go with Big City government.

Katselas fills out his cast with a gallery of on-the-money Familiar Faces (Dana Elcar, Edward Grover, Michael McGuire, William Devane, Stephen Elliott) giving *Commissioner* a rich, full-bodied feel as its plot spills from one novice cop's missteps into a major political scandal.

3. *Dead Heat on a Merry-Go-Round* (1966)
Written and directed by Bernard Girard

A flop when it came out, *Dead Heat* became something of a cult fave among the 1970s film magazine crowd and understandably so. It combines the twists of *The Sting* (1973), the exuberance of the Danny Ocean films, yet still manages to keep from floating away in fancifulness. But it also plugged into a distinctly '60s/'70s subversiveness where the Bad Guys were less bad guys than they were counterculture rebels and mavericks cutting against the grain of a suffocatingly conforming tight-assedness.

James Coburn plans to pull off a robbery at a bank on the grounds of Los Angeles International Airport. To do so, however, requires him to carry out a series of smaller scams on a cross-country trek in order to get up the money to buy the plans to the bank's alarm system. While Coburn, at his Cheshire-smiling best, charms, seduces, and cons away across the U.S. under a variety of guises, security and political bureaucrats are buzzing around LAX preparing the airport for the arrival of the Soviet premier. The two seemingly unrelated plots intersect in surprisingly organic fashion during the suspenseful third act heist.

Girard manages to keep the humor and the danger in perfect balance in a movie which stubbornly refuses to let you know where you're going until you get there. It all builds to a delicious final twist that says even when you get away with it...you still lose.

4. *Across 110th Street* (1972)
Directed by Barry Shear
Adapted from Wally Ferris' novel by Luther Davis

Though to some reviewers at the time, this was just another in the jumble of blaxploitation flicks then hitting screens in an almost unbroken parade, others picked up that there was more going on here than cheap thrills. Two-time Tony-winning playwright Luther Davis turned Wally Ferris' schlocky urban thriller into a Molotov cocktail of 1970s inner city ills: grinding poverty, racism, crooked cops, brutal cops, and despair.

Three desperate black men (Paul Benjamin, Antonio Fargas, Ed Bernard) steal $300,000 from a Mafia transfer point up in Harlem (110th Street was considered the southern border of Harlem). Somebody makes a wrong move and the robbery turns into a massacre including two dead cops. The three men are now looking over one shoulder for the Mob enforcers (led by Anthony Franciosa) out to make an example of them for their Harlem affiliates, and over the other for the cops looking to nail a trio of cop-killers.

The two pursuits are odd reflections of each other. For a past-his-prime Franciosa, this is his last chance to show his worth to the Mob. His opposite number is Anthony Quinn, a police captain also trying to prove he's not past it even as he's asked to step aside to let a young black detective (Yaphet Kotto) take the lead. Finding himself squeezed between those two, closing lines is Benjamin, a basement-dwelling janitor of a crumbling tenement up to his knees in other people's garbage with no option left but to get rich or die tryin'.

5. *The Hot Rock* (1972)
Directed by Peter Yates
Adapted from the Donald E. Westlake novel by William Goldman

Robert Redford is a (supposedly) master crime planner though he has a nasty tendency to get caught. No sooner has he been released from prison after his last miscalculation, when his brother-in-law, another con (George Segal) coaxes him into engineering the theft of a valuable diamond politically important to a pair of warring African countries. Aiding and abetting in the effort are gearhead getaway driver Ron Liebman and explosives expert Paul Sand.

So, they steal the diamond. And lose it. And steal it, again. And lose it. And steal it — … You get the picture. As their increasingly exasperated sponsor (Moses Gunn) says, "I've heard of the habitual criminal, of course. But I never dreamed I'd become involved with the habitual *crime.*"

It's not a yuk-yuk comedy caper. The humor is low-key, often dry, and sometimes oh-so-New York, but it's that tough, terse, play-it-straight approach that makes it work. At one point, Liebman, who claims he can drive anything, pilots the crew's helicopter to a raid on a police station (don't ask). As the chopper touches down on the roof, the other three leap out and begin to take their positions. Redford sees some senior citizens in garden chairs and realizes they're on the wrong roof. "Well, don't just stand there!" Liebman yells. "Go ask directions!" Redford comes back from the seniors with the news they've missed the police station by three blocks. "Hell, three blocks," Liebman shrugs, "that ain't bad."

6. *The St. Valentine's Day Massacre* (1967)
Directed by Roger Corman
Written by Howard Browne

One of King of the B's Corman's few films for a major studio, Corman's express train-paced docudrama about the events leading up to and including one of the bloodiest events in Prohibition-era criminality is an energetic, colorful, and surprisingly accurate (more or less) picture of the Chicago gang wars of the 1920s-'30s.

If there's a weak spot, it's Jason Robards heading the large cast as Al Capone. Robards doesn't have the former bouncer's heft or youth (Capone was a shockingly young 29 when he virtually ruled Chicago), and Robards seems to be trying to compensate by chewing every bit of scenery in sight.

But the rest of the cast is fun, Corman moves it all along so fast you don't notice the missing amenities you'd see in bigger-budgeted movies (there's no music score; just a piano-and-percussion main theme repeated at the close of the movie), and his staging of the regularly-spaced shoot-'em-up scenes is perfection. It ain't *Road to Perdition* (2002)…and that's a good thing.

7. *After the Fox* (1966)
Directed by Vittorio de Sica
Adapted from Neil Simon's play by Simon and Cesare Zavattini

If you're looking at those directing and writing credits and shaking your heads at such an odd marriage, it only gets odder. Burt Bacharach does the music, the cast is headed up by Peter Sellers playing an Italian master criminal, and the rest are a mix of veteran actors and – true to the nature of de Sica, the pioneering postwar neo-realist — Italian amateurs.

Sellers takes on the job of sneaking the loot from an Egyptian gold robbery into Italy, masking the effort by passing himself off as a famed de Sica-like director shooting a film in a sleepy seaside village. While the movie has a few big laughs, it's mostly a warm-hearted, gentle poke in the ribs at movie star egos, celebrity hunger (and the hunger for celebritydom), and the pretentions of certain, ahem, artsy-fartsy directors. *After the Fox* is a movie of small charms, but so many of them it's almost a crime (I had to get that in at least once).

8. *A Step Out of Line* (1971)
Directed by Bernard McEveety
Written by Albert Ruben, S. S. Schweitzer, and Steve Shagan

Peter Falk, Vic Morrow and Peter Lawford are three long-time buddies in this made-for-TV movie who regularly get together at the local stadium to watch the home team play. But it's hard times for all three: Falk can't figure out how to pay his father's medical bills, Morrow's lost his job at a defense contractor, and Lawford is dealing with some midlife appraisal of the difference between his young aspirations and his current doldrums. Falk comes up with the idea of a single bank robbery to put them right. Only it doesn't.

It's depressing how timely this movie about three Everymen victimized by circumstance remains. Narrow the lapels and it might just as well be set today.

The hook here is the very opposite of what's usually the hook in a caper film. There's nothing exceptional about these guys, their abilities, their problems, and even the robbery itself is a rather mundane affair. The hook here is the very average-ness of three men; the fact that three guys who look and sound and live just like the guys on the bar stools next to you, or in line with you at Dairy Queen getting ice cream for their kids, or who have the seats next to you at, yes, the ballgame, can be so up-against-the-wall that they *have* to try something desperate.

*****

In the years since, the capers have gotten more elaborate, the criminals more colorful, and car chases and gunplay have replaced the grind of daily police work. *Mean Streets* gave way to *Pulp Fiction* (1994); *The French Connection* to *Lethal Weapon* (1987) and *Die Hard* (1988). The crime and cop movies from that fantastically fertile period used to reflect something about us. Now, we seem to prefer a fancier frame to the mirror…and no reflected image at all.

The prevailing gritty and realistic tone of crime and cop films of the 1960s/1970s had given way by the 1980s to movies which were less concerned with plausibility then with how much over-the-top action could be packed into a two-hour running time. Shoot-'em-up *Lethal Weapon* (1987), starring Danny Glover and Mel Gibson, set the pace for the likes of the Die Hard, Beverly Hills Cop and Bad Boys franchises as well as its own increasingly out-sized sequels.

SIDNEY LUMET (1924 – 2011): THE QUINTESSENTIAL NEW YORKER

April 11, 2011

One of the true giants passed away this week: filmmaker Sidney Lumet, dead at 86 of lymphoma.

He was one of an incredibly talented class of directors who graduated from the early days of TV; a group which included such august talents as Arthur Penn *(Bonnie and Clyde,* 1967*)*, George Roy Hill *(Butch Cassidy and the Sundance Kid,* 1969*)*, John Frankenheimer *(The Manchurian Candidate,* 1962*)*, Arthur Hiller *(The Hospital,* 1971*)*, Franklin J. Schaffner *(Patton,* 1970*)*, Norman Jewison *(In the Heat of the Night,* 1967*)*, Robert Mulligan *(To Kill a Mockingbird,* 1962*)*, Martin Ritt (*Hud,* 1963*)*, and Sam Peckinpah *(The Wild Bunch,* 1969*)*. Only Jewison is left, now, and as each member of that fraternity has passed, mainstream American moviemaking has gotten a little louder, a little emptier, and a little dumber.

TV drama in the early days was almost like good theater: it was usually live, smart, provocative, rich with real-world character and sharp dialogue. Very early on, Lumet was considered one of the more important directors in the new medium, and he worked on many of the milestone shows of the era: *You Are There, The U.S. Steel Hour, Studio One, Kraft Theatre,* and *Playhouse 90* among them.

It was a performance-driven medium then, and Lumet loved actors; always would. Maybe because he'd been one himself, starting out as a child actor in Yiddish theater, studying acting at Columbia University, working his way up to off-Broadway and film. He knew how to talk to actors, what was important to them. Actors appreciated his love of rehearsal; nailing down the essence of roles, scenes, and the thesis of a film in that process allowed him to move remarkably fast once on the shoot where he rarely called for more than two takes. Look at his cop drama *Prince of the City* (1981): 130 roles, 135 locations, yet shot in a breezy 52 days. "I call him Speedy Gonzales," Paul Newman once said of him, saying Lumet was "…the only man I know who'll double-park in front of a whorehouse."

All that pre-shooting prep paid off producing 17 Oscar-nominated performances from among his body of work.

He wasn't afraid of dialogue; big, choking blocks of it, and his movies, as a body, are as textually dense as any in the American canon. About half of his forty-odd films were adapted from stage plays. Yet, for all that gab – often, *because* of that gab — his best movies still crackle. Lumet could do with great dialogue what lesser directors failed to do with a screen filled with pyrotechnics. Think Ned Beatty's soliloquy on "the immutable bylaws of business" in *Network* (1976, written by another TV alum, Paddy Chayefsky); the one, long verbal shootout that is *12 Angry Men* (1957) – "You don't *really* mean you'll kill me, do you?"

He was sometimes faulted for not having a particularly distinctive visual style, but that wasn't quite fair. Like Arthur Penn, he believed it wasn't the director's job to intrude, to show his hand, but to serve the material. Ron Fortunato, Lumet's cinematographer on his TV series *100 Centre Street* and on his last film, 2007's *Before the Devil Knows You're Dead,* said "Sidney flips if he sees a look that's too artsy."

Not that Lumet didn't know how to give a film a look: city grit in *The Pawnbroker* (1964); the harsh black and white cinematography, and smash cuts and brutal close-ups of *Fail-Safe* (1964); picturing Ned Beatty as the center of a dark corporate universe in *Network*.

If there was one thing he loved more than actors and a script rich with sparking dialogue, it was New York. Woody Allen – perhaps the only other American director as culturally embedded in The City as Lumet – called Lumet the "quintessential New York filmmaker." It was his favorite setting, and, unsurprisingly for a filmmaker at his best when his stories were most grounded in the real world, most of his best movies are set in The City: *12 Angry Men, The Pawnbroker, The Anderson Tapes* (1971), *Serpico* (1973), *Dog Day Afternoon* (1975), *Network, Prince of the City, Q & A* (1990), *Night Falls on Manhattan* (1997). "New York is filled with reality," Lumet said, "Hollywood is a fantasyland."

Which explains why, when once asked how he wanted his passing marked, he said, "Burn me up and scatter my ashes over Katz's Delicatessen."

Some of Sidney Lumet's best:

12 Angry Men: Adapted by Reginald Rose from his 1954 teleplay, this was Lumet's feature film debut. Mostly taking place in a jury room, it should be a drab, boring, tedious slog instead of a classic legal drama.

The Pawnbroker: One of the first American features to deal with the Holocaust, Lumet lifted the idea of flash cuts from Alain Resnais' 1961 *Last Year at Marienbad* to show the unhealed psychological wounds of a concentration camp survivor (Rod Steiger).

Fail-Safe: Lumet's take on a nuclear nightmare brilliantly played out in just four locations; an exercise in claustrophobic suspense to rival Wolfgang Peterson's *Das Boot* (1981).

Serpico: One of the all-time great cop stories is Lumet's true-life account of one cop who bucked a tide of corruption in the NYPD.

Murder on the Orient Express (1974): Normally, Lumet floundered with lightweight material (see 1978's *The Wiz* or 1980's *Tell Me What You Want* for proof), but for once he hit the mark turning an Agatha Christie trifle into a showcase of brilliant performances and another demonstration of his ability to work with a story set in confined spaces.

Network: Lumet firing on all cylinders in a bitter black comedy that's even darker today in the way it anticipated TV's descent into reality programming luridness and sleaze.

The Verdict (1982): Lumet guided Paul Newman to an Oscar nom in what the American Film Institute judges to be among the 10 best courtroom dramas of all time.

JAMES GANDOLFINI (1961 – 2013): ONE OF OUR OWN

June 19, 2013

James Gandolfini died yesterday of an apparent heart attack, and in the short space of time since his passing, enough has been said about this intimidating-looking actor many called, in reality, "a gentle giant," that there's little I can add without seeming lamely repetitive. Parts large and small, before *The Sopranos* and after, will always be eclipsed by his role as Mob boss Tony Soprano; as perfect a melding of performer and portrayal as has ever graced the small or big screen. All the obits and commemoratives say as much, usually in the lead.

So, what's left to say?

That for those of us on this side of the Hudson – particularly those of us who, like Gandolfini, are of Italian descent – the loss is particularly acute, almost personal…because he was one of ours. He was one of us.

For all the praise his Tony Soprano garnered, for all the fans the character brought him across the country and even around the world, I don't think anybody appreciated how on-the-money Jersey-born Gandolfini was more than his Garden State people. Tony may have been a boss, but he was blue collar, working class, Jersey working class. He sounded like us, he looked like us, when he lost his temper he said, "Are you outta your fuckin' mind?" like us. And he mourned the loss of the old neighborhoods, the old times like us. David Chase – another one of ours – provided Gandolfini with the sheet music, but it was Gandolfini's native-tuned voice that made it sing.

I happened to have been working at Home Box Office throughout *The Sopranos'* 1999-2007 run. I never met the man, but I would hear stories. He was the bane of the publicity people assigned to the show, greatly shy as he was and hating to sit for interviews, saying more than once, "I just don't think I'm that interesting. I don't think what I have to say is that interesting."

I also heard that when he came back from a 2004 USO tour, having visited U.S. troops in Kuwait and Iraq, his feeling for those young men and women – particularly the ones coming home damaged in body and mind – was sincere and deep. He executive produced the Emmy-nominated 2008 HBO documentary *Alive Day Memories* as his personal tribute to those who'd served and come home scarred and maimed, and as a pointed, pained reminder to the rest of us of the true cost of a war too many of us had grown numb to over the years.

I remember in interviews of the time he was asked why he didn't appear on-screen during the doc; surely that would pull in more viewers. Gandolfini's stand was the film belonged to the men and women who appeared sharing their painful memories of the day death brushed by them, close enough to steal some part of them away. It was times like that it was hard not to puff up a little and say to somebody, "He's from Jersey, ya know."

And that's the difference for us. Show business lost a fine actor, a performer equally adept on stage, film, and TV. But we lost one of ours.

Ciao, Giacomo.

DENNIS FARINA (1944 – 2013): COMING BY IT HONESTLY

July 28, 2013

When the news of Dennis Farina's death by cancer at age 69 came through early this week, I think I felt a particularly sharp pang because it came so soon after the passing of James Gandolfini. I hadn't thought of it before, but with Gandolfini still fresh in my mind, when I heard about Farina's death I had a sense of connection between the two actors, and the same sense of having lost "one of our own."

As actors, they were poles apart. Gandolfini was the trained actor, the skilled artist, somebody who had found his calling young and applied himself to perfecting his instrument. Farina's was a case of fortunate circumstance, natural ability, and working from the gut.

But what they both shared – and what I'd always responded to in both men – was an Italian-American blue collar-dom, a sense of being one of the guys, of being like people I recognized from the neighborhoods in which I'd done my growing up, and whose memory I still carry. The Chicago-born Farina may have been stuck with those squashed Chicago vowels while Gandolfini was from my home turf, but in every other way they seemed, to me, to inhabit the same onscreen world. When Farina died, it belatedly occurred to me that considering all the great character actors who'd thugged their way through *The Sopranos* – Joe Pantiolono, Robert Loggia, Burt Young et al – it surprises me Farina never got a chance to face off with Big Tony. I would've loved seeing that duet.

Getting into a who's-the-better-actor game is always a tricky, dangerously subjective business, and I wouldn't presume to do it here. Gandolfini was more of an artist; Farina more of a journeyman. But when it came to playing tough guys, you have to give Farina this: he came by that toughness more honestly.

After serving three years in the Army, Farina joined the Chicago Police Department, spending some of his 18 years on the force in the department's burglary division. When he played cops and when he played the hoods cops chase, he played from memory.

The cops was where filmmaker Michael Mann found him when he was looking for a cop consultant for his first theatrical feature, *Thief* (1981). There was something about the non-actor Mann liked; he gave him a small role in the movie, then a few years later awarded him a larger, supporting role in *Manhunter* (1986), and not long after that, the lead in the short-lived, neon-lit neo-*noir* series *Crime Story* (no doubt it helped Farina's casting that the creator of *Story* was Chuck Adamson, a close friend of Mann's, and an ex-cop himself who had once been Farina's partner back on the Chicago P.D.).

Like Gandolfini, Farina is best-remembered for his tough guy roles. All his obits point to his performance as Jimmy Serrano, the funny/frightening Mob boss from *Midnight Run*. The commemorations talk about Farina's way with a line, making you laugh at the same time you believed he wasn't exaggerating his threat. My favorite line: exasperated with two bumbling henchman, Farina tells them, "You and that other dummy better start getting more personally involved in your work, or I'm gonna stab you in the heart with a pencil."

And then later in the movie, just to remind you he's not there for the laughs, Farina chills your blood when he sits across from his on-the-run-now-recaptured accountant (Charles Grodin) and tells him, "I stopped by here to tell you two things. Number one is that you're gonna die tonight. Number two, I'm gonna go home, have a nice hot meal, I'm gonna find your wife, and I'm gonna kill her, too."

While the obits all talked about his Jimmy Serrano, I always thought his best moment was in the pilot episode for *Crime Story*, for which Mann was fortunate to have Abel Ferrara (*Bad Lieutenant*, 1992) directing. Farina plays Chicago cop Mike Torello who becomes obsessed with nailing Ray Luca (Anthony Denison), an ambitious young hood on the way up. In the opening episode, after a department store robbery goes horribly bad, Farina confronts the man behind it – Denison – at a social club, knocking him out of his chair, standing over him and putting a .45 slug into the floor by his head (ironically, Farina was such a bad shot in real life he claimed other cops called him The Great Wounder). With eyes as cold and dark as a coal bin, Farina says in a quietly icy voice, "See how easy it is? How really easy it is?"

Like Gandolfini, Farina seemed to easily, disturbingly access an inner darkness, but in Farina's case, it was a darkness he'd learned about on the job.

And yet, also like Gandolfini, there was something about the man that made you want to see other colors, brighter colors. He had that quality any successful actor has; something that can't be taught, can't be learned – you liked watching him.

When he showed a flare for comedy, it was a relief to laugh with him. He had a charm, a warming smile, a twinkle in his gimlet eyes he was rarely given a chance to showcase. When he showed up on the sitcom *New Girl*, playing Nick Miller's (Jake Johnson) unreliable, con artist dad, you wanted to believe he'd turned himself around, you wanted to believe he was going to try to be the dad he'd never been for Nick…or be any kind of dad at all!

I would like to have seen more of that kind of work, see him playing the kind of guys I remember from the neighborhood, mowing their lawn wearing Bermuda shorts and black socks and shoes, working behind a counter slicing bologna, fixing the plumbing. Still, for a guy who came out of nowhere acting-wise, he did ok.

He was unpretentious about his standing as an actor, made no big deal about his work and maybe that's the thing I most liked about him. "I don't know if I have a technique," he said when asked, "I'm just trying to remember the words."

8 COUNTS OF GRAND THEFT CINEMA

October 30, 2012

We love crime movies. We may go on and on about Scorsese's ability to incorporate Italian neo-realism techniques into *Mean Streets* (1973), the place of John Huston's *The Asphalt Jungle* (1950) in the canon of postwar *noir*, *The Godfather* (1972) as a socio-cultural commentary on the distortion of the ideals of the American dream blah blah blah, yadda yadda yadda…but that ain't it.

We love crime movies because we love watching a guy who doesn't have to behave, who doesn't have to – nor care to – put a choker on his id and can let his darkest, most visceral impulses run wild. Some smart-mouth gofer tells hood Tommy DeVito (Joe Pesci), "Go fuck yourself," in Scorsese's *Goodfellas* (1990), and does Tommy roll with it? Does he spit back, "Fuck me? Nah, fuck you!" Does he go home and tell his mother?

Nope.

He pulls a .45 cannon out from under his jacket and empties it into the kid. C'mon, be honest: some jackass cuts you off on the highway, somebody runs over your foot in the supermarket with their cart and doesn't even say, "Sorry," somebody steals your yogurt out of the office fridge, are you going to look me in the eye and say that somewhere way down in some deep, dark, highly societally-repressed part of you – the barbaric part buried under millennia of that increasingly complex and organizing thing we call civilization – wouldn't want to pop the guy?

Heist flicks gain a special affection. When we're talking about The Big Job, The Big Heist, The Big Caper, The Big Score, we're not talking about hoods, strong-arms, goons, stick-up men, smash-and-grabbers, kick-in-the-door-and-yell-"Grab-some-sky" types; we're talking about artists.

The thief – the good thief, the expert thief – actually looks to avoid violence. He's relying on brains and skill rather than muscle and guns, and there's something about that to respect, even for the law-abiding, comfortably repressed good citizen. You have to admire the imagination of the job, the timing, the expertise.

And of course, there's the lure of the money, too. It's the rare person sitting in the seats who isn't tantalized by the money; a big bucket of it scored in one, fell swoop. A suitcase full of green opens up on the screen, a case full of gleaming bullion, a satchel upends and glittering diamonds spill out onto a tabletop like stars in a black velvet sky…don't you, at least sometimes, turn to your movie mate, and share a grin that says, "Imagine."

Smarts, skill, nobody gets hurt (if you're lucky), and walking out saddled with a dream's worth of loot. That's why we like a good heist flick.

The devoted cineastes know the classics: the *noirs* like *The Asphalt Jungle*, or expatriate Jules Dassin's French-made *Rififi* (1955), its half-hour heist sequence daringly shot in total silence; the Anglophiles might talk about the charming black comic capers that were part of the great parade of Ealing comedies in the 1950s, flicks like *The Ladykillers* (1955), *The Lavender Hill Mob* (1951), and *Kind Hearts and Coronets* (1949); the more cosmopolitan types will fondly remember the hysterical Italian-made *Big Deal on Madonna Street* (1958), and Dassin's frothy Turkish caper, *Topkapi* (1964), as light as his *Rififi* was dark.

If you prefer your thievery with a more contemporary taste, you've got a rich buffet to choose from as well. Like your heist flicks light and easy going down? Steven Soderbergh's *Ocean's Eleven* (2001), *Twelve* (2004), and *Thirteen* (2007) mix *Topkapi*-like fun with a heavy swirl of The Big Con a la *The Sting* (1973) for more laughs than thrills. Like your capers dark and hard? You can't do better than modern day crime flick master Michael Mann and *Thief* (1981) and/or *Heat* (1995). Unless you want to go for Ben Affleck's *The Town* (2010).

But, as with any genre, there are the lesser-knowns, the cult flicks, the unjustly forgotten. Not to remember them and, by the grace of Netflix, not to give them a look…that would be a crime:

Thunderbolt and Lightfoot (1974)
Written and directed by Michael Cimino

The descriptives one usually associates with heist flicks are "suspenseful," "gripping," "nerve-wracking," and the like. What you usually don't hear are, "affecting," "touching," "moving," but those are the words that come to mind watching Michael Cimino's directorial debut, a heist flick unique in structure, feel, and look.

Clint Eastwood plays a con on the run from the gang that mistakenly thinks he double-crossed them on a previous job, and who hooks up with amoral drifter Jeff Bridges. Both rootless, drifting somewhere between something and nothing, the laconic Eastwood and hyper Bridges (in an Oscar-nominated Supporting Actor performance) become friends. They later partner up with two members of Eastwood's old gang – thuggish George Kennedy and frog-eyed Geoffrey Lewis – to redo an earlier depository robbery which involves blasting through a vault door with a 20 mm cannon.

Unlike most heist flicks, the robbery is not the heart of the story. *T&L's* first act, played in an easy pace against the rolling hills of Montana, has more in common with such odd couple flicks as *Midnight Cowboy* (1969) and *Scarecrow* (1973) than with hard-edged crime thrillers, and that, paradoxically, is what invests you in the caper. This is the rare crime flick where you care. The memorable moments from *T&L* are not from the job, but the small moments that bring Cimino's characters to life-sized life: the crappy jobs they take to raise their stake money, Lewis and Kennedy crammed in the small cab of an ice cream scooter, Kennedy's paunchy con gasping through a punch-up with Eastwood as his asthma kicks in.

All of that makes the movie's melancholy epilogue all that more moving. *Thunderbolt & Lightfoot* ends not with giddy triumph (Soderbergh's *Oceans* flicks) or even ironic defeat (*The Asphalt Jungle*), but with a true sense of loss, and gives Eastwood one of his finest moments.

Best moment: Lewis and Kennedy pull over to a kid on a suburban street with their ice cream scooter. When the kid mouths off about how a competing ice cream wagon has better product, Kennedy snarls, "Hey, kid: go fuck a duck!"

Charley Varrick (1973)
Directed by Don Siegel
Adapted from John Reese's novel by Howard Rodman and Dean Riesner

As lean and taut as *Thunderbolt & Lightfoot* is amiably ambling, Varrick is one of the oft-underappreciated Siegel's best. Walter Matthua is Varrick, a one-time stunt flyer turned crop duster who indulges in the occasional small-time bank robbery with his wife and two accomplices to get by. But their latest caper goes wrong, and Varrick's wife and one of his gang are killed. Worse, the innocuous bank they knock over turns out to be a Mafia drop. While Matthau's remaining partner (Andy Robinson) thinks of this as a lottery win, Matthau realizes they are in deep doo-doo: "I'd rather have ten FBIs after me."

The clever caper here is not the straightforward bank robbery, but Matthau's trying to figure out a way to navigate between the belligerent Robinson, the cops, and sadistic Mafia hit man Joe Don Baker to find an out.

It's a movie of small, clever moves (you may have to go back and re-watch the movie to figure out how Varrick throws each of the players at each other and arranges his own eventual disappearance), precisely etched performances, a gallery of indelible characters, and the kind of hardboiled dialogue that Matthau and company deliver done to a turn.

Favorite moment: Mob money exec John Vernon meets with his underling, banker Woodrow Parfrey, by a pasture to talk about the suspicious shadow cast over them by their Mafia bosses. It's a great pas de deux of acting, shot almost entirely in a single take. At one point in the conversation, Vernon looks out at the cows in the pasture, and says to Parfrey, "Check out the brown one. Man, what a set of jugs."

The Thomas Crown Affair (1968)
Directed by Norman Jewison
Written by Alan Trustman

Crown is probably better-remembered for the 1999 remake with Pierce Brosnan and Rene Russo than for the original with Steve McQueen and Faye Dunaway, and that's a shame, because as much fun as the remake is – and it is – it doesn't have the soulfulness of the original.

Self-made millionaire Tommy Crown (McQueen at his coolest) doesn't have a second act for his life. A success at everything but his marriage, he's faced with no worlds left to conquer, the only challenge left to him, so he tells a girlfriend, being "Who am I going to be tomorrow?"

His answer is to plan a bank robbery which leaves him pitted against equally sharp and clever and self-made insurance investigator Dunaway. Their duel of wits escalates/evolves into erotic feint-and-parry and from there into a love affair, but one always dogged by the question of how each will play the final hand.

The remake is a lighter piece about one of those too-clever-for-real-life heists and a happy, neatly-wrapped ending. But the original came out at a time when Hollywood happy endings not only seemed phony, but offensively so when it seemed there were no real-life happy endings to be had. The most delicious moment in the movie is its teasingly ambiguous ending which leaves the questions, Did McQueen's Crown ever really love Dunaway? Or was it just another challenge to stave off suffocating ennui? Or maybe was it a little bit of both?

With a great look from Haskell Wexler, one of the all-time cinematographic greats, and sharply cut by future director Hal Ashby (the chess scene between McQueen and Dunaway is classic), and a haunting score by Michel Legrand, the original tends to leave the remake looking like petty theft.

The War Wagon (1967)
Directed by Burt Kennedy
Adapted by Clair Huffaker from his novel.

"It's a Western!"
"No, it's a heist flick!"
"No, it's a Western!"
"It's two, two, two movies in one!"
And so it is.

By the mid-1960s, John Wayne was well-ensconced as, well, John Wayne. He'd become that rarity of rarities among actors: a brand name. All the public had to know was John Wayne, cowboy hat and a horse, and they knew what they were going to get. Thankfully, on a regular basis, a director and a script would come along that seemed to know how to get the most out of such a popular commodity. *The War Wagon* was one of them.

Wayne plays an ex-con who unfairly did time after nasty ol' Bruce Cabot framed him then stole Wayne's rather nice ranch and the profitable gold mine therein. Wayne's revenge plan involves knocking over one of the regular shipments of gold out of the ranch made on the horse-drawn armored car known as the War Wagon. He teams up with womanizing hired gun Kirk Douglas for whom Wayne is a sore spot ("You caused me a lot of embarrassment. You're the only man I shot that I didn't kill."), drunken demolition man Robert Walker, Indian tribal liaison Howard Keel, and bellicose inside man Keenan Wynn.

There's nothing novel in a motley group coming together for a big score, but Huffaker's script is heavily and delightfully laced with a droll wit that keeps the movie a fun watch throughout.

Favorite moment: two of Cabot's men draw on Wayne and Douglas which, as one might expect, leaves the two overreachers dead in the dusty street. Douglas, with the kind of smirk only Douglas could pull off, says, "Mine hit the ground first." To which Wayne drawls back as only the Duke could, "Mine was taller."

Gambit (1966)
Directed by Ronald Neame
Written by Jack Davies, Alvin Sergeant, and Sidney Carroll

Jules Dassin's *Topkapi* kicked off a wave of similarly buoyant, light-hearted caper flicks set amid exotic settings, movies like *How to Steal a Million* (1966), *Hot Millions* (1966), *After the Fox* (1966), and *Duffy* (1968), to name a few. For my money, the best of the lot is *Gambit,* starring a still-a-star-on-the-rise Michael Caine with an equally ascendant Shirley MacLaine.

Caine is, as we come to find out, a wannabe master thief who has concocted with his partner (John Abbot) an elaborate charade to gain them entry to the private art collection of jillionaire Herbert Lom. The object of Caine's maneuverings: an invaluable ancient Chinese statue which Lom also values for its resemblance to his deceased wife…who bears a striking resemblance to the bubbly Hong Kong dancer Caine persuades into baiting Lom's interest.

This one is just about fun, with a great cast with both Caine and MacLaine showing why they became stars, Lom as a heavy with a heart, and Neame and his writers laying out some bait of their own with an early-film tease showing how the caper is *supposed* to work which only barely matches the climactic heist.

Stay to the very end and the last, final twist, and ask yourself: is Caine turning good? Or does he *know?*

Heist (2001)
Written and directed by David Mamet

You can't just watch a Mamet movie; you have to listen to it as well. Mamet plays with words in a WTF fashion the way a juggler keeps a chainsaw, an apple, and a bowling ball in the air at once: remarkably. Example: says one of the movie's bad guys: "Everybody needs money. That's why they call it money."

Gene Hackman is a master thief arm-twisted into a big caper by double-dealing Danny DeVito. Hackman only agrees once he figures out how to put this heist through a few pretzel twists to both protect his ass and insure that this time around he comes out ahead.

As he proved with *House of Games* (1987) and *The Spanish Prisoner* (1997), Mamet knows how to put together a twisty-turny plot so convoluted it makes *The Sting* look as complicated as *The Cat in the Hat*, and it helps that he's got a deep-bench of a cast who know how to dish up those aural ballets of Mametesque dialogue: Hackman, DeVito, Delroy Lindo, Sam Rockwell, Mamet favorites Ricky Jay and Rebecca Pidgeon (Mrs. Mamet).

Favorite moment: after a climactic shootout, Hackman, gun in hand, stands over the wounded DeVito who has given him so much trouble. DeVito, looking to buy himself a few more seconds on this earth, gasps out, "Don't you want to hear my last words?" Says Hackman just before he pulls the trigger, "I just did."

The Pope of Greenwich Village (1984)
Directed by Stuart Rosenberg
Adapted by Vincent Patrick from his novel

At the time, there were those who wrote *Pope* off as a *Mean Streets* wannabe, and it's not hard to see where they were coming from. Mickey Rourke plays the Harvey Keitel part, a guy with an honorable if self-destructive commitment to look out for his impulsive, hot-headed cousin (Eric Roberts pushing a little too hard to be Robert DeNiro), each hustling to fulfill a dream: maitre d' Rourke wants (like Keitel in *Streets)* a restaurant of his own one day, and Roberts, well, he just wants to be the guy that can plunk down the money to sit front row at a Sinatra concert.

But when Roberts' finagling of checks at the restaurant where they both work lands them out on the street, Roberts comes up with a caper to put them both where they want to be. They enlist an aging locksmith/ex-con (the great character actor Kenneth McMillan) to crack a safe supposedly holding a boatload of bucks. But along with the money, they find the safe is holding a stash of tapes made by a crooked cop of brutal local Mob boss, Bed Bug Eddie. With a psycho like The Bed Bug, simply giving the money back isn't going to be enough to get the trio out from under.

If *Pope* suffered, at the time, from comparison to Scorsese's then recent classic, time has been good to the movie. Free of Scorsese's shadow, it's a fun bit of New York grit, flavorful, giving us a Mickey Rourke who was still a star-in-the-making at the time (and making us wonder what the hell happened since), backed by an ensemble of top-notch character actors besides McMillan including M. Emmet Walsh, Jack Kehoe, Philip Bosco, Tony Musante, and, utterly chilling as the animalistic Bed Bug Eddie, Burt Young.

The Happening (1967)
Directed by Elliot Silverstein
Written by Ronald Austin, James D. Buchanan, and Frank Pierson

Be forewarned: *The Happening* isn't for everybody. Frankly, I'm not sure who it is for. But it's still worth a watch as a heist flick trying to go someplace heist flicks don't usually go.

Faye Dunaway, Robert Walker, and Michael Parks are a bunch of '60s-style flower kids drifting from one eventful time-killer to another who fall in with too-cool-for-school George Maharis and then fumble their way into kidnapping Mafioso Anthony Quinn. The problem is, nobody wants to pay Quinn's ransom: not his wife, not his Mob colleagues, not even his mother. To them, Quinn's not coming back is actually the more attractive option. Quinn takes command of his own kidnapping to get revenge on those who cut him loose.

But *The Happening* is after more than just a triple-reverse take on a kidnapping tale. It strains – and it does often seem like a strain – to be after something more. Trying to plug into the late 1960s sense of disillusionment and disappointment, the movie flounders its way toward some sort of climactic existential finale without quite pulling it off.

Look, what was hip in 1967 seems corny now (actually, the movie's interpretation of 1967 hip was a bit corny then), and what at first seems a fun premise goes off the rails in its grab for substance, but it's worth watching – once – to see something truly (if not totally successfully) different in the genre. And in a genre with a rather limited menu – you either get away with it or you don't – different is a noble aspiration.

PETER FALK (1927 – 2011): WORKING HARDER THAN EVERYBODY ELSE

June 26, 2011

It is to be expected that the obituaries and commemorations for Peter Falk, who passed away last Thursday, would center on his four-time Emmy-winning starring role in the long-running series *Columbo* (the character was first introduced in a 1968 TV movie, it was turned into an NBC series running 1971-1977, then ABC revived the brand in 1989 for 24 TV movies, the last airing in 2003). His role as the perennially rumpled, misleadingly bumbling, "Ahhh, just one more thing…" homicide detective was not only his most famous and memorable character, but one which achieved that rarified altitude of "iconic." Think Falk; think Columbo.

And as deserving as the tributes are, as laudatory as the valedictories have been, they still don't do justice to the range and power Falk demonstrated throughout his career as an actor on both large and small screen.

Even the laurels thrown on his work in *Columbo* focus on the visible elements, the "easy" part – the pretense of messy, shuffling ineptitude – and not the slyer, sometimes surprisingly darker elements Falk, in collaboration with series creators William Link and Richard Levinson along with their stable of writers, occasionally injected to keep the formula fresh and the character intriguing.

The show was always fun, but every so often it would hit some resonating chord, something hearkening back to J.B. Priestly's 1945 play, *An Inspector Calls,* the pointed prototype for *Columbo,* which brought a human element to a TV genre that, then and now, was often about no more than putting a puzzle together, and forgetting the tragedy behind it. In some of those episodes where Falk was matched with a performer of equal power, there was an element of real pity (opposite Donald Pleasance as a desperate winery owner who murders his crass brother to save the family business; Patrick McGoohan as a starchy military academy commander fighting to save his beloved institution) and tragedy (Janet Leigh as a past-it movie actress slipping into senility and not even remembering her crime; symphony conductor John Cassavetes' humiliation of wife Blythe Danner when she learns he murdered to conceal an affair) that, at best, seems only perfunctory in today's *CSI*s and *Castle*s and the like.

Perhaps one of the most intriguing episodes was the awkwardly titled, "The Bye-Bye Sky High I.Q. Murder Case," written by Robert M. Young, in which Falk goes up against Theodore Bikel as head of a Mensa-type organization of certified geniuses. There's an absolutely chilling scene before the final reveal where Falk and Bikel sit together during a power failure, and as they pass the time in conversation – what the screenwriting gurus would maintain was a throw-away scene, but stands as one of the most memorable moments in the series – Columbo, for the only time in the series, explains himself:

> "You know, sir, it's a funny thing. All my life I kept running into smart people. I don't just mean smart like you and the people in this house. You know what I mean. In school, there were lots of smarter kids. And when I first joined the force, sir, they had some very clever people there. And I could tell right away that it wasn't gonna be easy making detective as long as they were around. But I figured, if I worked harder than they did, put in more time, read the books, kept my eyes open, maybe I could make it happen. And I did. And I really love my work, sir."

It's not just Young's on-point dialogue, but Falk's delivery that sends a chill through the scene: the sense of a committed obsessive, the slight touch of vindictiveness toward all those "very clever people" he's outdone, and finally, the malevolent – maybe even slightly sadistic? – declaration that nothing gives him greater satisfaction than the way he toys with and manipulates and finally lowers the boom on a killer.

But anyone who knew Falk's work before he landed *Columbo* should not have been surprised at what he could do with the part. He'd already been moving easily between film and TV and the stage, had been twice nominated for a Best Supporting Actor Oscar, picked up a Tony for his lead role in Neil Simon's *The Prisoner of Second Avenue*, and had already copped an Emmy for the 1961 TV movie, *The Price of Tomatoes*. He'd even already played a Columbo-esque character in the short-lived but critically-acclaimed early '60s lawyer series, *The Trials of O'Brien*. There was a reason he was considered worth the then considerable amount of $250,000 per *Columbo* episode, and that NBC and the producers were willing to accept his demand of doing the show on a rotating basis with two other 90-minute mystery series rather than as a weekly.

Throughout his career, Falk was a utility player, carrying leads (dim-bulb planner of one of the biggest robberies in U.S. history in the true-crime-inspired *The Brinks Job* [1978]), supporting roles (the loving grandfather who narrates *The Princess Bride* [1987], or working in an ensemble (as a high-strung cabbie in the all-star comedy epic, *It's a Mad, Mad, Mad, Mad World* [1963]). He played broad comedy (Jack Lemmon's inept henchman in *The Great Race* [1965]), domestic drama (the frustrated husband who doesn't understand the how or why of his wife's breakdown in *A Woman Under the Influence* [1974]), heroes (the war-loving corporal of *Anzio* [1968]), or villains.

His breakout role had been in the true-crime-inspired *Murder, Inc.* (1960) playing Mob contract killer Abe "Kid Twist" Reles. *Murder, Inc.* had been one of a stream of punchy "B" caliber gangster flicks *(I, Mobster* [1958], *Al Capone* [1959], *The Rise and Fall of Legs Diamond* [1960], *Portrait of a Mobster* [1961]) filling out double bills at the time, and *Murder, Inc.* shared all the same limitations of its contemporaries: obviously tight budget, colorful but hardly memorable second tier cast, clearly back lot locations. But Falk's performance as the ice-blooded sociopathic Reles is from some other A-caliber universe. Every scene he's in is electric; and every scene without him suddenly feels leaden. A *Murder, Inc.* with a full cast equal to Falk would have been an all-time gangster classic.

The very next year Falk earned another Oscar nod playing the Dr. Jekyll version of his Mr. Hyde/Reles in Frank Capra's adaptation of Damon Runyon's Depression-era Mob comedy, *Pocketful of Miracles*. Tweaking the same kind of character that, in *Murder, Inc.*, had sent a shiver down spines, he now charmed and tickled as the exasperated gangland secretary of state for Mob boss Glenn Ford, watching his carefully arranged deal for Ford with a bigger Mob go down the tubes as Ford attempts to do an ever-more-complicated good deed for a street corner apple-seller (Bette Davis).

It seemed there was no genre or style beyond Falk. In Sydney Pollack's surreal antiwar story *Castle Keep* (1969), Falk hit the perfect note for Pollack's dreamy, highly symbolic vision; he was a flat-out hoot in his largely ad libbed cameo in *It's a Mad, Mad, Mad, Mad World*; he was painfully life-sized in the TV movie *A Step Out of Line* (1971) as a financially-strapped working man looking to a bank robbery not out of greed, but for survival.

Along with friends Ben Gazzara and John Cassavetes, he would sometimes work just for a paycheck (the impressively bad Italian-produced *Machine Gun McCain* [1969]) to help Cassavetes raise financing for his independently-produced films in which Falk did some of his best work: *A Woman Under the Influence* (with Cassavetes' wife Gena Rowlands), and maybe Cassavetes' most accessible work, *Husbands* (1970), with Falk, Cassavetes, and Gazzara as three friends on a midlife crisis-fueled bender following the death of a fourth buddy.

Watching Falk in Cassavetes' largely improvised dramas back-to-back with him pulling off with equal adeptness the straight-faced silliness of *The In-Laws* (1979 – his explanation of "The Guacamole Treaty" which protects the giant flies preying on Amazonian natives is an exquisite piece of deadpan comedy) is a better appreciation of the breadth and depth of the actor than simply to tout how beautifully he pulled off *Columbo*.

Like the good lieutenant once said, "I figured, if I worked harder than they did, put in more time, read the books, kept my eyes open, maybe I could make it happen." And every time Peter Falk stepped on a stage or in front of a camera, he made it happen.

MR. COOL: BLAKE EDWARDS (1922 – 2010)

December 26, 2010

When the news of Blake Edwards' passing at age 88 broke earlier this month, it stood to reason his obituaries would mandatorily lead off identifying him as the writer/director behind the *Pink Panther* movies and as a "master of sophisticated slapstick comedy." After all, the *Panther* films may not have been his best work, but, in a career marked by as many flops as hits, they were his most recognized and consistently popular efforts with six films spanning 20 years (excluding 1993's execrable post-Peter Sellers *Son of the Pink Panther*).

In the longer obits, it was nice to see his more sophisticated work also remembered like romantic comedy *Breakfast at Tiffany's* (1961), another iconic rom-com for another decade in *10* (1979), his 2/3 brilliant and 100% brutal skewering of Hollywood in *S.O.B.* (1981), and an early turn at drama with *Days of Wine and Roses* (1962), still one of the most disturbing portraits of alcoholism in a studio film.

What wasn't acknowledged – and, so long after the fact, might not even be remembered – is Blake Edwards' role in bringing the element of *cool* to the big and little screen.

By the late 1950s, Edwards knew the stodgy, blocky '50s were giving way to a jet age/jet setting vision of something sleeker, smoother, tougher: shoebox Chevys ceding the road to low-slung, bullet-shaped T-birds, poodle skirts surrendering to obscenely snug pencil skirts punctuated with sky-high stiletto heels, broad lapels and fat ties retreating in front of a narrower, more tapered look fitting like a second skin on suave yet diamond-hard Edwards heroes like Peter Gunn, Richard Diamond, Mr. Lucky.

Edwards had tapped into the chrome-sheathed vein of cool even before Sinatra & his Rat Pack turned Vegas into a private playground, before James Bond and Derek Flint did the same for much of the rest of the world, before Newman, before King of Cool McQueen. On TV, Edwards' footsteps would be followed by the globe-trotting antics (with studio back lots standing in for the globe) of the agents of U.N.C.L.E and *I Spy*, of The Saint and the light-fingered Alexander Mundy of *It Takes a Thief*, of the millionaire cop of *Burke's Law* ...but Edwards had already been there; he'd been the pathfinder.

Breakfast at Tiffany's Holly Golightly (Audrey Hepburn) was New York cool, an aspiring socialite in Givenchy dresses who played outside social conventions to rub elbows with mobsters and princes; *Mr. Cory* (1957) was slum cool as Tony Curtis' wannabe gambler romanced his way up the social ladder at a Wisconsin resort; and even amongst the hilarity of the original *The Pink Panther* (1963), David Niven's jewel thief was the epitome of early '60s jet setting, skiing-in-Gstaad-summers-on-the-Riviera cool.

Edwards' cool wasn't just about fulfilling male persistently-adolescent fantasies, although that was undoubtedly part of its appeal. It was a recognition that that 1950s air of innocence was falling away; an acknowledgment that the world was a bigger, more textured, more complicated, more violent and certainly sexier place than movies and TV had previously acknowledged. To this day, the *noir*ish jazz bounce of Henry Mancini's "Peter Gunn Theme" still brings back the vibrancy of something new; the death of the lush, oozy orchestrals of Old Hollywood and the soft-edged sensibility that went with it, and the onset of something more dynamic, more carnal, more deadly.

Consider Edwards' most popular TV venture, *Peter Gunn* (1956-61). The image of private eyes before *Gunn* was one of work-a-day gumshoes like Bogart's Sam Spade in *The Maltese Falcon* (1941), or rumpled two-suits-in-the-closet types like Dick Powell's Philip Marlowe in *Murder, My Sweet* (1944). They were nondescript men of modest means working out of nondescript offices scuffling from one hopefully paying job to the next. *Kiss Me Deadly*'s (1955) strutting Mike Hammer (Ralph Meeker) was the exception, but managed it only by being an absolute and totally amoral heel.

But Craig Stevens' Peter Gunn drove a cool car, lived in a cool apartment, wore cool clothes, dated cool-looking women and, instead of working out of some grubby office, picked up his calls at a cool jazz club. He flashed neatly-creased five-dollar bills at his informants, knew how to mix a cocktail, seemed as at home with the very very rich as with the very very poor.

It wouldn't be long before Edwards' brand of cool – in fact, the whole concept of cool – became steamrollered by the tragedies and countercultural tides of the late 1960s. The supposed sophistication of Peter Gunn and Mr. Lucky seemed paradoxically naïve and clueless as assassination piled on assassination, the Vietnam War grew from back page item to consuming the national consciousness, and cool was replaced by a proudly grubby look of long hair, tie-dyed T-shirts, and ragged bell bottom jeans.

Edwards seemed at a loss as to how to respond to the new cultural milieu, and began turning out a string of clunkers like *Darling Lili* (1969) and *The Tamarind Seed* (1974). He didn't get his commercial feet under him again until he returned to the innocent, timeless fun of the *Panther* movies with *The Return of the Pink Panther* (1975).

That late '50s/early '60s brand of cool may seem quaint now, innocent in its own way, maybe even flat-out corny from a remove of forty-odd years. But in an era of trashy *Housewives from Wherever* and the prime time cable cavorting of the spoiled rich, reality shows where teen pregnancy has become the aspiration of trailer park wannabe celebs, where hip-hop and pop stars brag about dragging their street cred into the Hollywood hills rather than graduating past it, there is something to be said for Blake Edwards' cadre of cool dudes who knew a good wine from a bad, held the door for a lady stepping into their T-bird, and always knew the right fork to use.

7 GREAT REBEL PORTRAITS OF THE '60s AND '70s

May 27, 2012

The French gave us the word "demimonde" – literally, half the world. But what it has come to mean in English, or so says Webster, is "a distinct circle or world that is often an isolated part of a larger world."

Storytellers have always held a fascination with the dark side of human nature; that part of the psyche which is normally restrained and leashed, taught to be obedient, held in check, as Conrad wrote in *Heart of Darkness*, by the reproving looks of our neighbors. After all, what was Robert Louis Stevenson's *The Strange Case of Dr. Jekyll and Mr. Hyde* but a probing of that other, id-driven half and the entrancing appeal of doing what one wants instead of what one should.

Film is no different than literature, and from its beginning the movies have produced a rich vein of stories about society's fringe dwellers, those who operate beyond the realm of the law abiding by necessity, desire, or sociopathic carelessness. Often in the movies, they are criminals, pure and simple: thieves, killers, brutes.

But the blossoming of *film noir* in the 1940s and 1950s seemed to uncork something among more audacious moviemakers; an interest not simply in the lawbreaker, but a creature who lived in a gray place between the socially acceptable and the outright criminal. Perhaps many moviemakers – people operating out of the mainstream of American life themselves – identified with these rogues and hustlers for whom the social norms didn't apply.

This became especially true in the 1960s and 1970s. It was a time when American movies were at their most daring, and moviemakers were being granted a then unprecedented creative freedom.

It was also a time of great social upheaval and social rebellion, and the maverick, the rebel, those who lived beyond the rules in a shadow world which often had few rules of its own, became an attractive, intriguing figure.

Some were criminals, some only semi-so, but all lived in a place most of us suspected existed…but never ourselves saw.

Herewith some of the best portraits from the '60s/'70s of that demimonde and its most colorful denizens:

The Hustler (1961)
Directed by Robert Rossen
Adapted from the Walter Tevis novel by by Rossen and Sidney Carroll

Throughout his career first as a screenwriter than as a writer/director, Rossen had a fascination with characters operating where the normal rules of behavior didn't apply i.e. the psychotic sea captain of *The Sea Wolf* (1941), soldiers trying to survive "just another day" in WW II in *A Walk in the Sun* (1945), the amoral political kingpin of *All the King's Men* (1949), and the strangely corrupt heroes of *They Came to Cordura* (1959). But he never captured the idea as well or in so exquisitely seamy a fashion as in *The Hustler*.

Paul Newman is Fast Eddie Felson, a pool hustler on the come looking to take down the king of the pool rooms, Minnesota Fats (Jackie Gleason). Felson is broken by Fats in a brilliantly staged opening pool duel, then scuffles around trying to put together a big enough stake to take on the Fat Man once again.

It's a movie of bus station bars and cheap saloons, wheelers and dealers, and the kind of smoke-filled dives where a misplaced hustle gets your thumbs broken. And somewhere in all the cigarette smoke and all-night pool contests Felson finds, much to his own surprise, there's still one bit of heart to him.

Aided and abetted by cinematographer Eugene Shuftan and the great editor Dede Allen, Rossen gives the bookending pool marathons an electricity even Martin Scorsese couldn't quite match in his more upscale sequel, *The Color of Money* (1986), but then Scorsese's movie is in color and set when pool had become – shudder – respectable. As no other movie before or since, Rossen's flick captures the seedy sexiness of old time, men-only pool halls and the men who made their disreputable living and sought an even more disreputable glory off a green felt tabletop.

Taxi Driver (1976)
Directed by Martin Scorsese
Written by Paul Schrader

Enough has been written over the years about *Taxi Driver* that anything said here could only be redundant. Suffice to say that Scorsese/Shrader's tale of a disaffected, totally socially disconnected Viet vet prowling the scummy streets of 1970s New York is, for many, the ultimate outsider's story.

Photographed with a they-only-come-out-after-dark neon-lit gloom by the brilliant cinematographer Michael Chapman, *Taxi Driver* captures New York when it was at its worst; it's an alien nightscape populated almost entirely by the bizarre, the deadly, and the perverse.

It's not for all tastes, and may make you want to take a long, hot shower afterward, but for those not weak of heart, turn down the meter flag and take a Boschian ride through downtown hell.

Midnight Cowboy (1969)
Directed by John Schlesinger
Adapted from the James Leo Herlihy novel by Waldo Salt

From the 1960s into the 1980s, the Times Square/42nd Street area of New York was, sadly, an internationally recognized image of urban decay and decadence. Tawdry, dirty, filled with the lava-lamp glow of neon and flickering grindhouse and porn theatre marquees, and populated by the most garish of hookers and hustlers, The Deuce, as the natives called 42nd Street, was the beating dark heart of what, at the time, seemed a dying, utterly corrupt city.

And amidst the abandoned tenements and curbside heaps of trash, John Schlesinger and Waldo Salt told a surprisingly touching story of human connection. Even those at the bottom, they said, even the utter, most self-deluded losers get lonely and hunger for a friend.

Jon Voight is one of the self-deluded, a young Texan who comes to New York thinking he can score as a stud. And Dustin Hoffman, in one of his early, signature roles ("I'm walkin' heah!"), is one of the losers. There's no driving plot; just the day-to-day hustles they pull off to barely stay alive in a city which seems an urban Darwinesque exercise in survival of the fittest, but it's memorable, melancholy theme, its time capsule images of a New York long gone (some might say thankfully), and its bittersweet ending will hang with you for days.

Footnote: *Midnight Cowboy* is the only X-rated movie ever to win the Academy Award for Best Picture (the movie was later re-rated R in 1971).

Bring Me the Head of Alfredo Garcia (1974)
Directed by Sam Peckinpah
Written by Peckinpah and Gordon Dawson
from a story by Peckinpah and Frank Kowalski

There are those, like Roger Ebert, who consider *Alfredo Garcia* among the controversial director's best work and a genuine piece of cinematic art. There are others, like Michael Medved, who consider it among the worst movies ever released by a major studio.

Either way, I think anyone would agree this is easily one of the most audacious movies, with the possible exception of *Taxi Driver*, to go into the American commercial mainstream.

Warren Oates is Benny, a down-at-the-heels piano player in a cheesy tourist bar somewhere in Mexico. He has a chance at a $10,000 payday when he learns there's a bounty on the head of Alfredo Garcia for knocking up the daughter of a mysterious jefe's daughter. Benny learns from his hooker girlfriend (Isela Vega) that Garcia is already dead, killed in an automobile accident. They have only to drive to Garcia's hometown in the Mexican boonies to retrieve his head. But any quest so perverse and morally corrupt can come to no good end, and this one is no exception.

Alfredo Garcia is about losers holding on to society's lowest rung by their fingernails, being given a one-time-only Faustian deal to climb up. By turns disturbing, ethereal, nightmarish, and occasionally even touching (Oates and Vega have a roadside scene which may be one of the most affecting in all of Peckinpah's movies), *Alfredo Garcia* – love it or hate it – is one of a kind.

Right down to its brazen title, few films have pushed the limits of commercial filmmaking as hard or as far as *Bring Me the Head of Alfredo Garcia* (1974). Pictured: *Garcia* lead Warren Oates leaning against a car.

Hard Times (1975)
Directed by Walter Hill
Written by Hill, Bryan Gindoff, and Bruce Henstell

This forgotten first feature by Hill is easily his best. It has all the entrancing simplicity of a barroom ballad, and much of the same flavor.

Charles Bronson is a drifter who comes to Depression-era New Orleans and hooks up with hustler James Coburn to make some money in backroom bare-fisted fights.

It's a lean, almost wisp of a story, told with an appropriate terseness and a clean, Spartan style Hill rarely matched afterward. Hill gets more mileage out of Bronson's weathered face than other directors can get out of a page-long monologue.

When asked what he does for a living, Bronson plainly replies, "I knock people down." And that's how the movie works: plain, direct, and on target.

The Cincinnati Kid (1965
Directed by Norman Jewison
Adapted from the Richard Jessup novel by by Ring Lardner, Jr. and Terry Southern

What *The Hustler* is to pool, *The Cincinnati Kid* is to poker.

In another tale set in Depression-era New Orleans, Steve McQueen is the heir presumptive in the world of backroom high-stakes poker, looking to topple The Man: Lancey Howard (Edward G. Robinson). Not quite as grim as *The Hustler*, nor as period flavorful as *Hard Times, Cincinnati Kid* is still a terrific piece of hustlers-on-the-make entertainment.

Part of its rich feels comes from being perfectly cast from McQueen and Robinson down to the smallest parts (filled by such great character actors as Jack Weston, Jeff Corey, Milton Selzer, among others).

And Jewison manages the impossible: he turns the static sit-down of a days-long poker contest into an edge-of-seat third act fraught with suspense and an explosive climax. Less disturbing than most of the movies on this list but one of the most fun watches, deal yourself in.

The Flim-Flam Man (1967)
Directed by Irvin Kershner
Adapted from the Guy Owen novel by William Rose

Long before *The Sting* (1973) and the elaborate cons of the *Ocean's 11* movies, there was George C. Scott flim-flamming his way across the small towns of the American rural south hustling a living off small, deft cons and preying on the greed and foibles that seem to be an inherent part of the human design. Scott takes a young Army deserter under his wing (Michael Sarrazin) who begins to despair of his mentor's constant success.

"You can't cheat an honest man," Scott rationalizes, suggesting that – as he proves time and again – there are no honest men, but Sarrazin can't let himself go there.

"I gotta believe in somethin'."

Perhaps a bit sentimental at times, but great fun and with a wonderful sense of place, it's not a bad antidote for the more grim entries on this list.

As a matter of fact, I can send you the DVD right now. All I need is access to your checking account… Oh, come on, you can trust me.

BEN GAZZARA (1930 – 2012): GREATER THAN THE SUM OF HIS PARTS

February 4, 2012

Ben Gazzara died on February 3 of pancreatic cancer. An alumnus of the famed Actors' Studio, he had a long career on stage, TV, and film. Not just long, but accomplished.

On Broadway, he was the original Brick in the Tennessee Williams' classic, *Cat on a Hot Tin Roof,* and then he eclipsed that triumph with another powerful stage performance as a junkie whose habit poisons his relationships with everyone who loves him in *A Hat Full of Rain.*

His TV career launched in the early 1950s and extended through the next five decades. His small screen credits included roles on the landmark live drama anthologies of the '50s, such as *The United States Steel Hour, Kraft Theatre,* and *Playhouse 90,* and such acclaimed productions as cop drama *A Question of Honor* (1982), one of network TV's first attempts to address the then detonating AIDS epidemic in *An Early Frost* (1985), and the epic mini-series, *QB VII* (1974). He starred in one of the classics of 1960s TV, *Run for Your Life* (1965-68), earning two Emmy nominations as a successful lawyer trying to live life to the fullest after learning he has just two years to live.

On the big screen, however, he never quite achieved the same stature he did on TV and the stage, in large part because – by his own admission – "I didn't really take advantage of the opportunities," though late in his career he became a valued character actor (he was a particular hoot as a porn king in the off-kilter *The Big Lebowski* [1998]). But his best film work may have been in some of his least-seen films; the movies he made for John Cassavetes, and the most popular of the three films they made together was *Husbands* (1970).

Cassavetes was a true art house renegade, taking acting roles in commercial movies to put together enough money to make his own, highly personal films. In *Husbands,* Cassavetes, Gazzara, and Peter Falk play three long-time friends who react to the death of another buddy with a midlife crisis bender of booze and a jaunt to London. Think *The Hangover* – but serious and for grown-ups.

Like much of Cassavetes' work, *Husbands* has the shapelessness and shambling pace of life, the same sense of spontaneity, the same chaotic tumbling of the comedic into the tragic. It's a demanding watch, but a rewarding one, almost uncomfortable at times in its feel of intruding into the real.

The heart of the movie is the give-and-go between the three leading men, and it may be one of the most honest and vibrant portraits of male friendship – with all its awkward intimacy and macho bullshit – captured on film. The bond between the three seems so damned *real*, it's a surprise to find out that the three hadn't known each other before *Husbands*.

Watching the film, seeing how open and vulnerable the three made themselves to each other, at the obvious chemistry among them, it's no surprise they came out of the project friends. Gazzara would act for Cassavetes twice more, in *The Killing of a Chinese Bookie* (1976) and *Opening Night* (1977), and direct several episodes of Falk's hit TV series, *Columbo*, including one starring Cassavetes as a philandering orchestra conductor.

But if you really want to see how closely tied the film brought them, go to YouTube and find them on an episode of *The Dick Cavett Show* being interviewed about *Husbands*. It puts Danny DeVito and his limoncello hangover on *The View* to shame. On the one hand, it's appalling to see three grown and obviously half-crocked men cackling and falling over themselves on network television like kids farting in the back pew during mass.

On the other hand, it seems almost a scene from *Husbands,* and shows just how right the three of them had gotten it on film. Some things you can't create; you can only hope to capture.

Husbands, Chinese Bookie, et al was not work Gazzara or the others did for fame and fortune. These were art house films before there was much of an art house circuit. Most people didn't hear about them, even fewer went to see them. It was work done for the sake of doing; art for art's sake. Film actors tend to be judged by their commercial successes and their visibility; not their willingness to explore the art. In that sense, Gazzara's artistry was bigger than his career.

LEE REMICK (1935 – 1991): "UNCOMMONLY GIFTED"

August 2, 2011

When it comes to actresses, the movie business has always had an eye for beautiful faces. Unfortunately, it has often only been an afterthought as to whether or not that beautiful face could do anything other than be beautiful. Leaf through the archives of any of the movie glamour magazines from long ago and you'll find them a cemetery of beautiful faces primped and hyped by the Hollywood PR machine to be The Next Great Thing. Some never made it past a screen test, while others managed to survive a few screen roles, but through lack of talent, charisma, the right roles — whatever mysterious magic it is that causes a performer to click with an audience — soon disappeared, never to be heard of again. It's a long, *looong* casualty list of forgotten pretties like Merrilyn Grix, Eleanor Counts, Kathy Marlowe, Myrna Dell, Sandra Giles, Jean Colleran, Sunnie O'Dea, Eve Whitney, Helen Perry, Colleen Townsend, Dawn Addams, Ina Balin, Nicole Maurey…and on and on and on.

But sometimes Hollywood gets it right.

Lee Remick was beautiful. Petite, with an hourglass shape, devastating blue eyes, and the delicate features of a porcelain doll under a cascade of honey-blonde hair.

She was, in fact, beautiful to the point of distraction, considered early in her career as "America's Answer to Brigitte Bardot." Until she began her fight with cancer in 1989, the years remained kind to her throughout her career, allowing her an elegant, mature beauty every bit as eye-catching as the sex kitten allure of her early professional years. John J. O'Connor, reviewing the 1980 TV movie adaptation of Marilyn French's novel, *The Women's Room*, wrote of Remick that she was an "…uncommonly gifted actress whose somewhat fragile, almost stereotype good looks tend to distract one from that fact."

"Uncommonly gifted actress." That was the kicker. Right out of the gate, with her debut role in Elia Kazan's prescient expose of media power, *A Face in the Crowd* (1957), she demonstrated a powerful, first rank talent.

She never managed to be called "great," the way Bette Davis, or Joan Crawford, or Rita Hayworth were considered great, but then she never had that kind of iconic star aura to her either. For stars, what makes them stars is something familiar which surfaces in every role: Davis' brassiness, Crawford's stridency, Hayworth's sexual heat. Remick didn't have that; she was too good at what she did. When she finally passed in 1991, the most common word which showed up in her obituaries was "versatile."

Born in Quincy, Massachusetts of an actress mother and a department store-owning father, she had trained for modern dance and ballet but, by her own admission, wasn't particularly good at either. She studied acting at Barnard College and then moved on to the legendary Actors Studio, becoming part of a generation of one-of-a-kind AS alums which included Marlon Brando, Montgomery Clift, James Dean, Shelley Winters, Rod Steiger, Eva Marie Saint, Dennis Hopper, Steve McQueen, Paul Newman, Joanne Woodward… That the list doesn't end there sends one's head reeling, and Remick was as good at her craft as any of them.

She had been working on stage and in live TV drama when AS co-founder Kazan caught her on TV and cast her as the bimboesque baton twirler who turns the head of TV personality Lonesome Rhodes (Andy Griffith). In true AS fashion, she lived with a local family during the Arkansas shooting and practiced baton twirling so she'd come off natural on camera. And she did. When the cameras rolled, there was nothing of the well-educated young woman from Massachusetts up there, but a leggy, backwoods teen easily enthralled by a big-time TV star.

If she had a trademark that was it; that she had no trademark. *The Los Angeles Times'* Charles Champlin wrote of her that in every role she "…ceased to be the actress acting and became the character."

Her range was limitless. There was the simple, small town Texas girl of *Baby, the Rain Must Fall* (1965) trying to reboot a life for herself, her daughter, and husband Steve McQueen just released from prison; which was 180 degrees away from the uptown Manhattan sophisticate sexual compulsive of *The Detective* (1968), married to hard-bitten cop Frank Sinatra. There was her Oscar-nominated turn as the farm girl turned partying alcoholic housewife of *The Days of Wine and Roses* (1962), riding a wave of booze to oblivion; which was equally distant from her swivel-hipped trailer camp trash whose questionable rape puts vengeful husband Ben Gazzara (another AS grad) on trial for murder in the deliciously torrid *Anatomy of a Murder* (1959).

She was as adept at straight drama *(Wild River,* 1960, her self-professed favorite role, opposite Montgomery Clift) as broad comedy (playing a militant Prohibitionist in the comedy Western, *The Hallelujah Trail,* 1965). She never gave up the stage, becoming good friends with tune-meister Steven Sondheim after appearing in his short-lived *Anyone Can Whistle* in 1965, and copping a Tony nod two years later for Frederick Knott's taut thriller, *Wait Until Dark.*

The 1960s and especially the 1970s were not generous ones for actresses, particularly those moving into their 40s. It sometimes seemed the Academy Awards had to beat the bushes to come up with 10 nominees for Best Actress/Supporting Actress categories (Example: Beatrice Straight won her Supporting Actress statue for 1976's *Network* with less than six minutes of screen time; the smallest Oscar-winning performance on record). With good women's roles dwindling, Remick smoothly transitioned back to TV continuing to turn out high caliber work racking up seven Emmy nominations in TV movies like *The Women's Room* and mini-series like *QB VII* (1974), *Jennie: Lady Randolph Churchill* (1975), *Ike: The War Years* (1978).

When asked why she now appeared so rarely on the big screen, Remick replied, "I make movies for grownups. When Hollywood starts making them again, I'll start acting in them again."

My personal favorite wasn't one of her award-nominated parts, nor the touchstone roles talked about in her obits, terrific as they all were. It was her turn in the 1968 comedy thriller, *No Way to Treat a Lady*, adapted from William Goldman's novel by John Gay, and directed by Jack Smight. I remember it because it seemed to capture all of what she could do in the character of a self-possessed sophisticate and wickedly sly big city survivor who, underneath all that urban savvy, was a vulnerable, lonely, emotionally bruised girl.

She plays Kate Palmer, an independent, city-smart Lincoln Center tour guide – kind of an ancestral *Sex and the City* urban single – who may have caught a glimpse of a killer (fellow ASer Rod Steiger) who's been strangling little old ladies. George Segal is menschy NYPD detective Morris Brummel still living at home, harangued every day by a doting mom (a hilarious Eileen Heckart) about his lack of a college diploma, wife, children, and how poorly he stacks up against his doctor brother.

From the moment she opens her door to him, Morris is smitten. She's still half asleep, her tousled hair tumbling down unheeded into her face, and other parts of her also in danger of tumbling out of her nightgown, but she's too damned tired to care. But, bit by bit, she awakens to the inherent decency of the cop in her doorway.

What plays out is a romance so lovingly pieced together, it's a shame it hadn't been lifted out of a wry serial killer thriller and dropped into a true big city romance. We see Remick – ably matched by Segal – sweet, sly, goofy, comically cunning in the way her shiksa goddess converts Momma Brummel to her side by pretending to boss her son around the same way Momma does.

But the highlight of their *pas de deux* takes place on Morris' "yacht" – a police patrol boat. The relationship teeters on the brink of turning from dating to something deeper. She senses Morris' reluctance (he's not commitment-shy, but feels unworthy) and John Gay gives her a lovely speech: "I've had him already," she tells Morris.

"Who?"

"Randy Beautiful." She's had the nights filled with hunks and little else, cavorted with the beautiful people who were only beautiful on the outside.

In Morris, she sees the proverbial inner beauty. "Are you gentle, Morris?" she asks him, her voice a mix of hope and plaintiveness. "You can have me if you say yes."

It's the kind of grownup moment one rarely sees in major films these days, and even more rare is to see it done so well, with an achingly sweet honesty, and an equally sweet simplicity.

Perhaps if she had lived longer, pulled a Meryl Streep or a Glenn Close, surviving to nab the juicy mature roles that have come to both actresses, she might finally have been tagged "great"…because she was.

But whether anyone said it or not, the greatness was there, for like any great performer, she had her own voice, her own unique gifts. Said Charles Champlin, "…her beauty, both perky and patrician, and her obvious intelligence were hers alone."

JOHN CALLEY (1930-2011) – "A CLASS ACT"

September 20, 2011

Hollywood joke:
A writer, a director, and a producer are crawling across the desert without water, dying of thirst. They look up and sticking out of the sand is a nicely chilled bottle of apple juice. Before the writer and director can grab it, the producer is on his feet, unzips his pants and starts peeing into the bottle.

"What're you doing?" the writer and director cry.

"Fixing it!" says the producer.

So, that attitude in mind, when I tell you John Calley died last Tuesday at age 81, and if the name is unfamiliar and I try to enlighten you by saying he was a producer and – worse – a *studio executive*, no doubt at least a few of you who regularly patronize this site out of your love for film and filmmakers might shrug and say, "So what?" A dead studio exec? That's like that other joke, the one about lawyers:

"What do you call 5000 lawyers on the bottom of the ocean?"

"A good start."

Studio executives. Ew. Often referred to with sneery repugnance as, "The Suits." Ugh. Five thousand of them on the bottom of the ocean would be a *great* start. They're the Enemy, the Others, the antithesis of the creative impulse embodied by the noble filmmaker, the antichrist to the artistic spirit. Anybody who thinks Hollywood just plain, flat-out sucks with its pandering, market research, four-quadrant development and fear of the new, horror at the original, and absolute paralyzing terror of the untried, points a finger quivering with rage at the office suites and shouts, "*J'accuse!*"

So. Who cares some old, ex-studio biggie died?

Well, not that it means much, but *I* do.

I became a fan of Calley's after reading Peter Biskind's *Easy Riders, Raging Bulls: How the Sex-Drugs-and-Rock 'n' Roll Generation Saved Hollywood*, a dizzying, sometimes hysterical, sometimes heart-breaking account of the movie industry's bumpy transfer of power from the moguls of old to a new, young generation of studio chieftains in the 1960s/70s.

In part, I liked Calley because he was one of "us," another Jersey boy like myself, originally being from Jersey City. I always root for the home team.

Jersey City wasn't exactly a bastion of the arts. It had been a mill town back in Calley's day, rough-edged, blue collar – was, still is. If Calley picked up any creative sensibilities in those days, it was the art of the deal from his dad, a used car salesman.

What his background told me was Calley – the erudite, scholarly, well-spoken production chief who screened Kurosawa and Fellini and Truffaut flicks for his execs – was a self-made man. He learned what he learned and knew what he knew because he'd seeded and cultivated and watered that gray matter between his ears, and considering what he'd learned and knew, you couldn't *not* be impressed by the accomplishment.

But just as impressive to me was that he was that rarest of rare gems in studio executive circles: he was one of the few studio bosses who'd actually *made* movies; good movies, *smart* movies. By the time he was tapped to head up production at Warner Bros. in 1969, he'd spent a few years at Filmways working as a producer or associate producer on a number of films, some of them quite impressive, like Blake Edward's brilliant, bitter antiwar comedy *The Americanization of Emily* (1964, associate producer); Norman Jewison's memorable tale of a young poker hustler on the rise, *The Cincinnati Kid* (1965, associate producer); and Mike Nichols' grand and ambitious if flawed rendering of Joseph Heller's classic antiwar novel, *Catch-22* (1970). In fact, Calley was on the set of *Catch-22* when he got the call from Ted Ashley, a one-time talent agency honcho who Warners' new owner – Steve Ross and his hodge-podge of funeral homes and parking lots called Kinney National Service – had put in charge of the studio, giving him a free hand to clean house. Once the house was cleaned, Ashley tabbed Calley to be Warners' new production chief.

It was a unique time in Hollywood; the old rulers had faded away, a new breed was replacing them eager to re-write the rule book on movies and movie-making, and Calley caught the wave. "We were all young," he told *The Los Angeles Times* in a 1999 interview, "it was our time, and it was very exciting."

This is from Biskind's book:
> "*Under Calley, Warners became the class act in town… He was so hip he didn't even have a desk in his office, just a big coffee table covered with snacks, carrot sticks, hardboiled eggs, and candy. Lots of antiques.*"

Even at the time, Calley stood apart from the rest of the new execs. According to Biskind, under Calley the production offices became a place of jeans and sandals with "…the aroma of marijuana wafting down the first floor." He wasn't a glitzy, self-promoter like Paramount's Robert Evans; in fact, according to friend Candice Bergen, while he was always quite charming and could be great company, he was also somewhat withdrawn, spending his weekend nights at home, in flannels and a nightcap reading scripts. He had a soft spot for expensive cars and yachts, and yet generally lived a life –as producer Tony Bill said at a recent memorial service – "unattached to material things." Bill recalled Calley buying a 65-foot Swedish yawl, spending a few years fixing it up, then, after enjoying it a while, selling it off. He *enjoyed* things; he didn't *amass* them.

Calley was a director's exec and he started reaching out to filmmakers who interested him, among them: Sydney Pollack who turned out *Jeremiah Johnson* (1972) and *The Yakuza* (1974) for Calley's Warners; John Boorman *(Deliverance,* 1972)*;* William Friedkin *(The Exorcist,* 1973)*;* Martin Scorsese *(Mean Streets* [1973] and *Alice Doesn't Live Here Anymore* [1974])*;* Robert Altman *(McCabe & Mrs. Miller,* 1971)*,* and Stanley Kubrick to whom Calley gave a remarkable *carte blanche,* granting him a free hand to pursue his own projects.

He generally stayed out of the way of his filmmakers, believing in giving them the freedom to indulge the creativity he'd hired them for. He would complain about the Hollywood penchant – then and just as much now – for hiring a filmmaker for his unique talent, then turning around and "…(doing) everything you possibly can to neutralize him so that he can't do what you've hired him to do in the first place." An impressive number of the signature movies from one of American cinema's most expressive periods came from Warners thanks to Calley's laissez-faire attitude: *Woodstock* (1970)*, Klute* (1971)*, All the President Men* (1976)*, Chariots of Fire* (1981)*, A Clockwork Orange* (1971)*, Dog Day Afternoon* (1975)… The list goes on.

He loved fine cinema, he loved fine filmmakers, but Calley was not oblivious to the fact he had a studio to run. As much as he liked a certain kind of cinematic artistry, he also had a feel for what was going to mint money, like Mel Brooks' hysterical *Blazing Saddles* (1974), or disaster pic *The Towering Inferno* (1974), or kicking off the superhero movie craze with *Superman: The Movie* (1978). And, like his wheeling-dealing dad, he knew how to cut a deal, joining with 20th Century Fox on *Inferno* so the two studios – which had been developing similar high-rise disaster projects – wouldn't mutually destruct in a head-to-head competition; or milking *Dirty Harry* (1971) through four sequels. Better: correctly reading the tea leaves left behind by *Star Wars* (1977), and understanding that the opportunity George Lucas' mega-hit had provided wasn't in jumping on the sci fi bandwagon, but in tapping into that same mix of boomer nostalgia/budding fanboy geekdom which he did with *Superman.*

Sitting with Peter Bart and Peter Guber on AMC's *Sunday Morning Shootout* in 2003, Calley remembered "…making *Dirty Harry*'s for $3-3.2 million. That was a great business. It was almost impossible to lose money." That, perhaps was the key. Costs weren't as extravagant as they are today, and Calley rarely went the big budget route *(Superman* and *Exorcist* were rare exceptions). In the main, he forged an admirable balance between his creative wish list and hard dollar earners, bringing both prestige and financial stability to Warners throughout his tenure.

Calley's read on the audience of the time was astute enough that he managed to hit, with enviable regularity, that sweet spot where fine filmmaking and commercial success walked hand in hand. Kubrick's *The Shining* (1980), Alan J. Pakula's *All the President's Men* (1976), Boorman's *Deliverance,* and Sidney Lumet's *Dog Day Afternoon* were not only critical and commercial hits, but were actually among the top eighty-odd earners of the 1970s.

And then, another rarity of rarities. In an industry in which doors are something executives usually get pushed out of, Calley left Warners of his own volition. By his own admission, after 13 years at the studio he was burned out. "I wasn't enjoying it," he would say later, "I had lost myself." So, he walked away, not only from Warners, but from the business, spending the next 10 years traveling, sailing (which was one of his passions).

A decade away from the business and he was recharged, but when he came back – as a producer partnered with his old *Catch-22* collaborator and friend, Mike Nichols – he wasn't completely sure of his footing. The business had changed, the audiences had changed. "I made dopey mistakes," he later appraised, "like *Tank Girl* (1995), not getting it, thinking, 'Is this the world I've re-entered? Does everybody have a safety pin through their tongue now?"

But whatever Calley's doubts were, mixed in with *Tank Girl* were more notable efforts like *Postcards from the Edge* (1990, directed by Nichols) and the Merchant/Ivory classic, *Remains of the Day* (1993) for which he received his only Oscar nomination.

Now firmly back on the movie scene again, Calley was asked to head up the United Artists side of a floundering MGM/UA. The once great pair of studios were now one broke company desperate to establish some kind of credibility as a still viable movie-making enterprise. He revived the James Bond franchise with Pierce Brosnan taking over the iconic role in *Goldeneye* (1995; the series' highest-grossing installment). The studio's Americanized version of French farce *La Cage aux Folles* (1978) became the $124 million-grossing hit, *The Birdcage* (1996; again, with Mike Nichols at the directorial helm). Never giving up his penchant for artier fare, Calley's MGM/UA also turned out critics' darlings like *Leaving Las Vegas* (1995) and Sir Ian McKellan's *Richard III* (1995).

In 1996, Sony Pictures Entertainment (which owns Columbia Pictures) brought him on board to head up the company which was also going through rocky times. Again, for seven years, Calley mixed big earners *(Spider-Man,* 2002) with more substantial fare *(As Good As It Gets,* 1997), and sometimes rolled the company's dice on something delightfully, bizarrely, exhilitaringly unique *(Men in Black,* 1997). By the time he retired from SPE, the company was again on firm footing.

He went back to producing and as per the usual, blended big box office

(*The DaVinci Code* [2006] and sequel, *Angels and Demons* [2009]) with more substantive fare (the Mike Nichols-directed drama, *Closer* [2004]).

He was not flawless. There are those who thought they'd caught a raw deal from him, and certainly Calley turned out his share of clunkers, both as a producer (turgid historical drama *Fat Man and Little Boy*, 1989) and as a studio boss (Sony's bloated *Godzilla* remake, 1998). And let us not forget *Tank Girl*. But if you view a life on balance, John Calley's moviemaking cred weighs overwhelmingly to the positive, and for that the Motion Picture Academy of Arts and Sciences gave him, in 2009, the Irving G. Thalberg Memorial Award. The MPAA cited his "…intellectual rigor, sophisticated artistic sensibilities and calm, understated manner," and declared him "…one of the most trusted and admired figures in Hollywood."

But it was for those years at Warners that I was a fan; that pitch-perfect blend of the commercial and the compelling, the entertaining and the engaging. I never saw anything about him that said this, but I suspect that in his years at SPE and afterward, seeing at how audiences and tastes had changed, he must've – *must* have – missed those days when today's art house fare could be a mainstream hit.

He said he'd had two passions: to make movies and to run a studio. I suppose his great strength was his ability to combine both sensibilities in each passion, having a nose for a hit as a producer, and providing filmmakers not with a boss but with a colleague in a studio's front office.

And now he's gone. Maybe, sadly, a kind of moviemaking with him. But for those of you who might still not see cause to bow your head just a little out of respect because he was one of The Suits, remember: he didn't wear one.

NORA EPHRON (1941 – 2012): SHE WAS HER GREATEST WORK
July 4, 2012

I have to admit – somewhat sheepishly considering the outpouring of commemoratives since Nora Ephron died of myelodysplasia on June 26 – that I was never particularly a fan of her movies. But as I've read those commemoratives, it's come to me – another sheepish admission – how little I knew of her work.

Perhaps because I'd only initially become aware of her name through *Sleepless in Seattle* (1994), which she'd written and directed, that film forever colored my judgment of her output; a judgment reinforced by the fact that she happened to be working her way through a streak of similarly flyweight romances at the time including *Michael* (1986, a bit of sugary goo about an unconventional angel [John Travolta] manifested on earth apparently for the sole reason of bringing tabloid reporters William Hurt and Andie MacDowell together), and *You've Got Mail* (1998), the thematic rom/com bookend to *Sleepless* starring the same Valentine's dream pairing of Tom Hanks and Meg Ryan.

But Ephron's career is about more than one work, or even any few of her works. Like any writer – particularly screenwriters whose vision is under constant onslaught from "creative executives," studio marketing mavens, and any number of other people who, to lift a line from Paddy Chayefsky, think knowing the alphabet gives them license to meddle in the development process – she had her hits and misses. *My Blue Heaven* (1990) was a *huge* miss although its intriguing culture clash concept of Mafiosi completely misplaced in white bread middle America under the witness protection program may have been sunk as much by woeful miscasting (Steve Martin as an over-the-top guido?) as any creative misstep on Ephron's part. And *Bewitched* (2005)? Well, maybe trying to turn a one-joke TV show from the '60s into a movie for the 2000s was just doomed from the start.

But then there was her Oscar-winning screenplay for nuclear industry expose *Silkwood* (1983, co-written with Alice Arlen), which managed the deft feat of making whistle-blower Karen Silkwood a hero without sanctifying a tremendously flawed character. And, of course, there's *When Harry Met Sally…* (1989).

In his tribute to Ephron, *Entertainment Weekly*'s Mark Harris called the film "…the gold standard for modern romantic comedies…," and while I – in my typically male when-is-something-gonna-blow-up way – usually can't even stand the *idea* of rom/coms, I have to agree. It's up there with *Annie Hall* (1977) and *(500) Days of Summer* (2009) as one of those romances where its sincerity and honesty trumps romantic contrivance, and where the sharpness of its wit, the intelligence of its characters, and the sheer *knowing* behind it ("This is how it is, people; I know it, you know it, and now we *all* know it") breaks it out from the crowd of by-the-numbers *awww*-inducing sugar cookies which have so repeatedly and so vainly tried to capture the same magic.

It took Harris' piece to remind me that Ephron had begun as a journalist and essayist (only in reading Harris' obit did I remember reading one of Ephron's most well-known pieces: "I Feel Bad About My Neck"), had turned out one bitterly funny novel (*Heartburn*, inspired by her marriage-gone-wrong to journalist Carl Bernstein), and was even a respectable hand at writing for the stage (2002's *Imaginary Friends;* 2009's *Love, Loss, and What I Wore)*.

But as I've gone over her obituary pieces in doing my homework for this piece, the thing I'm probably most impressed with – and perhaps the thing for which she should truly be saluted – is that she *survived*. In a notoriously brutal profession, and one famously even harder on women who take a place behind the camera, Nora Ephron survived. I don't just mean she stayed bankable (2009's *Julie & Julia* not only recaptured a lot of that *Harry/Sally* sparkle, particularly in its Julia Child chapters, but was a deserving $94 million hit to boot), but neither she nor her work ever descended into a darker, melancholic cinematic menopause.

Creatively and personally, there always seemed to be another chapter for her. "You can always change your mind," Harris quotes her. "I know. I've had four careers and three husbands."

Say what you will about *Sleepless in Seattle* being contrived, dramatically manipulative, and about as predictable as the sweep of a minute hand, its irrepressible (if grating) optimism and belief in romantic kismet has to be admired coming from the heart of someone who, at the time, had already suffered two failed marriages (and one of them – to Bernstein – crashing and burning in spectacular fashion).

"(Be) the heroine in your life," she told the 1996 graduating class at Wellesley College, "not the victim." Nora Ephron didn't just say it; she lived it. And perhaps that was her greatest work.

PETER YATES (1929 – 2011): WE ARE WHERE WE LIVE

January 11, 2011

Peter Yates, who died this past weekend at age 81, was one of several British directors invited to make movies in The States in the 1960s, all of whom had a particular and rare filmmaker's gift for capturing a sense – the *feel* — of a setting often better than native-born filmmakers could. Yates' obits talked about the car chase in *Bullitt* (1968), the Oscar nods for *Breaking Away* (1979) and *The Dresser* (1983), but they missed how this gift he shared with his UK colleagues was such a critical part of what made his best work so special.

Think of the hundreds – the *thousands* – of American-helmed movies set against the country's great metropolises where the city sits inertly behind the action, as undistinguished and indistinguishable as a generic theatre backdrop. Then compare them to the almost hallucinogenically surreal Los Angeles of John Boorman's *Point Blank* (1967), Manhattan's desperate, grubby demimonde in John Schlesinger's *Midnight Cowboy* (1969), or the sun-burnished San Francisco of *Bullitt* — probably Yates' best-remembered film. It may very well have been their stranger-in-a-strange-land distance which gave these Brit émigrés the ability to appreciate what was so distinctive and unique about American locales in a way the inured natives couldn't.

Yates and the others understood, as few filmmakers did (and do), the powerful interplay there could be between plot, place, and people; the idea that *this* story could only play out with *these* characters and only in *this* place. And *place* – that feeling of *there* belonging to no other location – is one of the most intangible, ephemeral, and difficult sensations to conjure in cinema.

The car chase in *Bullitt* – still one of the classic sequences in American thrillers – wasn't Yates' most deft accomplishment in that film, but how he used so many tools to capture the San Francisco vibe. William Fraker's crisp, golden cinematography; Lalo Schifrin's jazzy score; the terse and opaque Alan Trustman/Harry Kleiner screenplay; the hard, low-key performances led by a tight-lipped Steve McQueen as the eponymous well-dressed, Mustang-driving cop; the little fill-in touches like a corner market, a jazz club luncheon for the culturally smart set — Yates pulled it all together to create a San Francisco that was the quintessence of late '60s California cool.

Thank of how *un*memorable *Bullitt* might have been had it adhered more closely to Robert L. Pike's source novel, *Mute Witness,* with Bullitt as an aging, nondescript, ice cream-loving, blue collar Boston cop. Good or bad, it would've been a more *familiar* movie; more *expected*. *Bullitt* is *Bullitt* because no other cop movie looks – or *feels* — like it.

What Yates managed with *Bullitt* was no fluke as he demonstrated four years later in the New York-set caper comedy, *The Hot Rock,* with screenwriting ace William Goldman adapting Donald E. Westlake's novel. Yates held the comedy back from silliness, with him and his actors playing it straight so the laughs seemed to come not from constructed jokes but from a credible urban lunacy organic to the sprawling, chaotic character of an off-kilter Big Apple. *The Hot Rock* is *The Asphalt Jungle* (1950) getting off at the wrong subway stop, its supposedly deft criminals now a step off their rhythm, stepping in dog doo-doo instead of the winner's circle. Only in New York, Yates seems to say, only in crazy, weird Gotham with its endless supply of loons, losers, and wannabes, could the supposed mastermind of a crack heist team get mugged while casing a joint for their next job.

After Yates had hit West Coast chic and East Coast nuttiness, he went for The Middle with *Breaking Away*, showing himself just as deft at capturing heartland Americana as Big City glitz. Set in Bloomington, Indiana, Steve Tesich's semi-autobiographical screenplay combined coming-of-age-awareness with sports-underdog-triumph for one of the all-time great American movies of adolescent passage. For those who remembered *Bullitt, Breaking Away* seemed a surprising about turn for the director, but Yates nailed perfectly the petty prejudices of a little burg, its insularity and familiarity, and the supreme frustration of big dreams stuck in a small town.

But in no film did Yates get it down as well as he did in the film criminally absent from most of his obits: the Boston-set crime flick, *The Friends of Eddie Coyle* (1973), with Paul Monash adapting the novel by one-time Boston criminal attorney George V. Higgins. *Eddie Coyle* presages the Beantown *noirs* Ben Affleck would make his specialty 35 years later i.e. *Gone Baby Gone* (2007) and *The Town* (2010), and no movie, with the possible exception of Martin Scorsese's *Mean Streets* (1973), has ever delivered so acutely and despairingly a gutter-level view of the penny-grubbing day-to-day at the bottom rungs of the Mob hierarchy.

Set against a naked-treed Massachusetts autumn rendered with beautiful bleakness by cinematographer Victor J. Kemper, *Eddie Coyle* has no master criminals, no elaborate heists, no car chases, no gunfights, no Last Capers. There is only Robert Mitchum's schlumpy Eddie Coyle (Yates, as good with actors as action, draws out one of the actor's best late-career performances), being played by double-dealing Feds and bad guys further up the ladder as he frantically tries to hustle his way out from under a pending prison wrap, and make a few dollars to keep his family off welfare should he have to do the time.

Yates had too many fizzles in his resume to be considered a great director, but he turned out a number of films made great by his remembering and deftly capturing the idea that who we are and what we do comes very much from the place where we live.

ELIA KAZAN'S *AMERICA, AMERICA* AND *MAN ON A TIGHTROPE*

Posted June 1, 2013

Author's Note: These were my contributions to a group piece ranking the films of the noted filmmaker.

America, America (1963)

It's no surprise this is one of the few films Kazan wrote himself as it is easily – confirmed by his own admission – his most personal film. It's right there in the movie's first words, a voiceover spoken by Kazan himself: "I'm Elia Kazan. I am a Greek by blood, a Turk by birth, and an American because my uncle made a journey."

Based on Kazan family stories, *America, America* tells the saga of Stavros Topouzogloum, Kazan's real-life uncle, and his Sisyphusian efforts to make passage from Turkey to the U.S. in the 1890s. Played by non-actor Stathis Giallelis, Stavros' story is a constant one of one step forward, two steps back as he begins to put together the money for the trip, then loses it, makes it again, loses it again, etc.

Topouzogloum's story is about more than leaving for a better life; it's about leaving for *any* life. The Greeks and Armenians of Ottoman Turkey's Anatolia region are treated so brutally it conjures up images of Russian pogroms, Klan lynchings in the American south, Serbian ethnic cleansing, the persecution of the Jews under the Nazis. Topouzogloum is looking for survival as much as opportunity.

The passion Kazan put into the film is clear and sincere. In scenes like the torching of an entire village and the killing of women and children by trapping them in a burning church, Kazan's outrage is as apparent and hot as the flames on-screen. Kazan manages to capture more than the singular experiences of his ancestor; he captures what the immigrant experience was for so many who were disenfranchised in their home countries, who saw America as a near-mythic Eden offering safety along with possibility.

Yet for all its heartfelt emotion, *America, America* is more a movie to be appreciated than enjoyed. Neither as compact as such Kazan films as *On the Waterfront* (1954) or as electric as *A Streetcar Named Desire* (1951), the deliberate pace of the film over its 168-minute running time, combined with the rough-hewn look which came from shooting on-location in Greece, takes a toll on the average viewer. The film's not helped by the casting of Giallelis, an energy-sapping black hole of an actor.

America, America is an essential chapter in the cinematic chronicling of the country's immigrant heart, but one you only want to read once.

Man on a Tightrope

There should be more to this effort than there is considering the pedigree here: Kazan directing a script by one of the best screenwriters of the period (among his many accolades, Robert E. Sherwood had won an Oscar for his screenplay for the touching WW II coming-home drama, *Best Years of Our Lives* [1946]), working from material inspired by a true-life escape from behind the Iron Curtain, shot on location in Europe.

Frederic March is Karel Cernik, manager of a family circus now nationalized and used as a propaganda vehicle in communist-controlled Czechoslovakia during the grimmest years of the Cold War. Tired of watching his circus wither day by day under the strictures of the repressive authorities, Cernik executes a daring escape for his crew across the border into West Germany.

All the earmarks of a strong Kazan production are there: it's well cast in depth with March backed up by Gloria Grahame as his trampy wife, Adolphe Menjou and the great character actor John Dehner as slimy commie honchos, a pre-*Have Gun -- Will Travel* Richard Boone, and providing the young love interest, Terry Moore and Cameron Mitchell. Having gotten a taste for the kind of authenticity location shooting could lend a film with his plague-in-New-Orleans thriller, *Panic in the Streets* (1950), Kazan shot on location in Bavaria which, thanks to lenser Georg Krause, has an appropriately who-wouldn't-want-to-escape-from-here bleakness. Trying to give the story still more of Kazan's Method school reality, Kazan filled his movie circus with acts from Circus Brumbach, an East German circus whose escape to the west not only inspired the Neil Paterson source novel, but whose real-life border-leaping machinations were incorporated into the script.

Yet the movie lacks the spark of Kazan's best and it's hard, knowing Kazan's bio, not to see the movie as more of an overly earnest effort to demonstrate true-blue loyalty to the good ol' U.S. of A. than to tell an effective drama. The year before, during the height of the country's McCarthyist paranoia, Kazan had testified in front of the House UnAmerican Activities Committee, reversing his earlier stand of not naming names when one studio boss told him such a refusal would guarantee he'd never work in Hollywood again, and named a number of high profile talents as communists ruining a few careers in the process. March, too, may have been trying to get out from under a cloud having been considered for blacklisting in 1949. Adding to the movie's flag-waving bonafides is the presence of Menjou who had not only cooperated with HUAC, but was one of the more active members of the Motion Picture Alliance for the Preservation of American ideals, a right-wing group dedicated to opposing communist influence (whatever that meant) in Hollywood.

With a half-century remove from the politics of the time, *Man on a Tightrope* loses its sense of the imperative and comes off, instead, as a well-performed but routine escape drama.

GREAT LOCATIONS: *THE PRISONER* AND *LOCAL HERO*

April 5, 2013

>*Author's Note: This was written for a monthly theme of writers' favorite film locations.*

On a number of past occasions, I've written, in various contexts, about what I consider to be that most elusive of on-screen elements: a sense of place. "Sense of place" is the difference between a location serving as mere background, and being a character in its own right. It's about getting the viewer's head *there*, getting us to feel like we know what it's like to walk that ground, smell those smells, feel the chill or suffocating heat in the air. When I talk "sense of place," I think of the autumnal Boston of Peter Yates' *The Friends of Eddie Coyle* (1973), the bracing, exhilarating chill of the Rockies in Sydney Pollack's *Jeremiah Johnson* (1972), the urban grit I feel on the back of my neck watching John Schlesinger's *Midnight Cowboy* (1969), the musty, dusty stale-beer-and-cigarette-smoke feel of Robert Rossen's *The Hustler* (1961). It's a special gift to create that magical sense of having taken us to someplace else in a movie, and it's something few directors can do, something even the best can't do every time.

The key is there is no key. There's no guaranteed, go-to strategy to pull it off. The right director + the right material + the right crew + the right setting + some other God knows what ingredient, and something alchemical happens where what appears on the screen is more than an image. It's a portal, and sometimes what we see and feel through that portal is so vivid, so real, it can haunt us, beckon us, entice us.

I have a special fondness for films and TV shows that pull that off, but I've never been as enraptured by a setting as I have by those of two UK productions: the 1967 cult series *The Prisoner*, and the 1983 Bill Forsyth movie, *Local Hero*.

*****

The Prisoner, which aired in the U.S. as a CBS replacement series during the summer of 1968, is one of the all-time great mystifiers. Patrick McGoohan – who, along with George Markstein, created the series – plays an unnamed spy who resigns for unknown reasons and is soon abducted by agencies unknown and taken to The Village where, like the other residents, all one-time spies, he is assigned a number; in his case, Six. Episode by episode, the mysterious masters of The Village seek to break down Number Six's resistance, but his independence and rebelliousness always prove too strong.

With its highly symbolic yet dauntingly opaque storytelling, and an adamant refusal on the part of the show and its creators to explain themselves, *The Prisoner* was, and remains, a polarizing bit of television, splitting audiences (unevenly, I should point out) into those who absolutely hated it, and those who, to this day, consider it some of the best and most adventurous commercial television ever made (can you guess which side I'm on?).

Key to making the show work was its major setting: The Village. For its exteriors, the production used the Hotel Portmeirion, an isolated resort on the coast of Wales. Designed and built bit by bit between 1925 and 1975 by Sir Clough Williams-Ellis, McGoohan remembered the locale from shooting some of his previous series *Danger Man* (shown in the U.S. in syndication as *Secret Agent*) there, and thought its fanciful mix of styles and settings would be perfect for a site that was, in *The Prisoner*, supposed to have been expressly designed to lull its prisoners into complacency and docility.

From its secluded gardens to its reflecting pool promenade to its dominating domed main building to its haunting tidal flats, there's a certain semi-fairy tale quality to Portmeirion – and The Village – I'm hard put to find anywhere else on celluloid. Sorry to say, Mr. McGoohan, I wouldn't mind being a prisoner there myself.

****

In *Local Hero*, Peter Riegert plays a Houston oil company sharpie sent to the fictional Scottish village of Ferness to negotiate the purchase of the village from the locals so it can be razed and replaced with a mammoth oil storage facility. The twist is that while Riegert expects resistance from the natives, they *want* to sell and are just trying to massage Riegert into providing them with as big a payday as possible. While Riegert doesn't sway from his mission, he nonetheless falls victim to the entrancing, quiet charms of the place and becomes ever more rueful about what's in store for quiet little Ferness.

It's hard not to be as bewitched by Ferness as Riegert's Mac. Cuddled between rolling green hills and the sea, Ferness is a cozy huddle of cottages and small walk-ups, removed from the chaos, the crowd, the frenetic pace, the noise of modern living elsewhere. Ferness is neither some isolated bit of the past nor forgotten bit of the present, but its own little self-contained bubble of sweetness and gentility and ease.

Alas, there is no real Ferness. Writer/director Forsyth used several locations to form a composite, but most of the village exteriors were provided by Pennan on Scotland's Moray Coast.

As it happens, I saw *Local Hero* after my first trip to Maine to visit a friend acting at a small theater near Berwick. Berwick had the same unwinding effect on me that Ferness had on Mac, and flying back into Newark Airport I felt much as Mac does when he flies back to hustling bustling Houston.

I'm not sure if *Local Hero* is why I've maintained such a strong affection for Maine or the other way around, but every time I catch the movie on TV I ache to walk Ferness' quay, smell the sea roll in, watch the aurora blossom in the evening sky.

SOFIA COPPOLA'S *LOST IN TRANSLATION*

Posted June 22, 2013

Author's Note: This was another group piece, this time ranking the work of filmmaker Sofia Coppola.

Few movies have more exquisitely captured that sense of isolation and loneliness of strangers in a strange land, of the melancholy ennui of those stuck, literally and figuratively, between here and there, as *Lost in Translation* (2003). Coppola's biggest success (*Lost* grossed more than her four previous films combined), it taps that teasing, haunting question which dogs us all late at night, staring at the ceiling, running down the navigational decisions of our lives and wondering about the road not taken, the door not opened, the connection not made: what if?

It is the wispiest of stories: Bill Murray is Bob Harris, a movie star on the downhill side of his career in Tokyo to pick up a paycheck shilling for a Japanese liquor company, and Scarlett Johansson is newly-married Charlotte, idled in the same hotel as Murray by her knothead photographer husband (Giovanni Ribisi) off on a shoot. Bob and Charlotte cross paths in the hotel bar, help each other kill time, and bit by bit begin to connect in a subtle, soulful way.

Soulful is the right word: they're both lost souls. "I just don't know what I'm supposed to be," Charlotte confesses, a young woman whose life has yet to start, while Bob ("I'm just completely lost," he tells his wife on a long distance call, she thinking he's talking about carpet samples) has that creeping midlife sensation his might be over. But for a few days, in each other's company, they are no longer lost.

A love story marked only by a goodbye kiss, a romance with nothing more passionate than pleasantly shared time, *Lost* is more poem than narrative; an ode to regret, to lost possibilities, to the words of the 19th century poet, John Greenleaf Whittier: "For of all sad words of tongue and pen, The saddest are these: 'It might have been'."

ANNE BANCROFT (1931 – 2005): "THE CONSUMATE EVERYTHING"

August 14, 2011

Before we called them MILFs or cougars – *long* before – there was only Mrs. Robinson. She was a mid-1960s adolescent fantasy come true; the sexy, available, older woman/housewife next door with an appetite for young not-quite-men/not-quite-boys. She became so indelibly, boldly etched in the public consciousness that the name became a noun – and, for young males, a hope – and the referenced fodder for a thousand if-only-they-were-true Letters to *Penthouse*.

But the character in the movie *The Graduate* (1967) was no exercise in wish fulfillment, no *Weird Science* (1985) or *Risky Business* (1983) teen's wet dream. Rather, Mrs. Robinson was a devouring suburban nightmare, a paean to unmoored youth and disillusioned adulthood and life-draining, soul-killing upper middle class ennui.

Over four decades later, the name still resonates, her portrait so deeply carved into the pop culture by Anne Bancroft's letter perfect Oscar-nominated performance that Mrs. Robinson remains the proto-MILF/cougar; the root of that particular sexual anthropological tree. Throughout her career, Bancroft would be approached by admirers to be told that, as young men, her Mrs. Robinson had been their first sexual fantasy. That unending tribute demonstrated how well she had captured the undeniable casual eroticism of the character.

And it irritated the hell out of her because it sometimes seemed as if she'd done nothing else…and that was hardly true, hardly true at all.

She'd been born Anna Maria Louisa Italiano in the Bronx of immigrant parents, attended the American Academy of Dramatic Arts and almost immediately found work in the early years of live TV.

A friend of hers was called for a screen test at 20th Century Fox, and Bancroft followed along to read opposite. Fox passed on the friend but offered Bancroft a studio contract. She jumped at the opportunity, later admitting she had wanted not to be an actress, but a movie star. Fox chief Darryl Zanuck thought her name "too ethnic," and gave her a list of possible alternatives. She picked "Bancroft" for its dignified sound.

At Fox, she became neither an actress nor a star. She might have had a new, dignified name, but the career Fox handed her was hardly comprised of classy stuff. The studio ran her through one forgettable flick after another; pictures like *Gorilla at Large* (1954) and *New York Confidential* (1955). "Every picture I did was worse than the last one," she would later say. The parade of junk took a toll on her spirits and her personal life; her first marriage foundered.

As soon as her Fox contract expired, she high-tailed it back to New York to study at the legendary Actor's Studio. She would come to the attention of Arthur Penn and later say the director was probably the single individual who'd had the greatest impact on her career.

Penn put her through a series of top-of-the-line performances which effectively re-minted Bancroft as an actress of the first order rebooting her career. On stage, she copped back-to-back Tony wins under Penn's direction, first in the 1958 romantic comedy/drama, *Two for the Seesaw,* and then the following year for what would become one of her signature roles, that of Helen Keller's tutor, Annie Sullivan, in *The Miracle Worker.* Penn would tap her again for the 1962 film version which would put an Oscar on her mantelpiece next to her two Tonys.

It would, over the years, become a rather crowded mantel.

For the next few years she split her time between stage and screen, consistently turning in acclaimed work and winning another Oscar nomination in 1964 as the dissatisfied housewife of Peter Finch in the Brit drama, *The Pumpkin Eater.*

But if Penn had been her first-stage booster rocket, Mike Nichols put her career in orbit with what is easily her best-remembered role as Mrs. Robinson in the screen adaptation of Charles Webb's novel, *The Graduate.* She was 35 at the time, made up to play 40, while Dustin Hoffman was 30 playing painfully awkward 20-year-old Benjamin Braddock, freshly graduated from college, trapped between the great expectations of family and friends, and his own utter cluelessness as to what to do with his life. He finds a comfortable numbness in the seducing arms of family friend Mrs. Robinson.

As it turns out, Mrs. Robinson is looking for some numbness of her own. She's never more sexy than her initial, liquory come-on ("Mrs. Robinson, you're trying to seduce me…aren't you?"), their later encounters becoming as erotic as a root canal. Mrs. Robinson isn't there for romance or even for sex. She's killing time, hitting on Benjamin the same way she hits on a bottle of booze. At one point, Benjamin, frustrated by the emptiness of their robotic trysts, presses her for conversation. For once, her self-control falters, and she allows herself one, pained rumination on her long-ago, dead dream of being an artist. For that moment, the gray-templed sex icon reveals the wounded soul under the well-coifed, immaculately posed exterior, and the predatory lady next door becomes both pitiful and pitiable. Benjamin is hiding from the terror of an unknowable future; Mrs. Robinson from the terror of her unbearable present. Said Bancroft of the character: "(We) reach a point in our lives, look around and realize that all the things we said we'd do and become will never come to be – and that we're ordinary."

She was a star now, but didn't play the star game, didn't make star choices, was even willing to pull back on her career a bit in favor of time at home. That stability and independence seemed to be directly tied to the stability she now had in her personal life.

In 1961, she met then comedy writer Mel Brooks while rehearsing for a TV show. According to Brooks, it was love at first sight, and three years later they were married. They seemed, to outsiders, the oddest of odd couples: the svelte, classy-looking, dark-haired Italian Catholic, and the short, homely, shtick-dishing Jewish schlub. But, according to director Robert Allen Ackerman, they made "…one of the great show business love stories of all time…They were madly in love with each other…," and they would laugh and love until her death.

If Bancroft sometimes chafed at how Mrs. Robinson overshadowed her later career, it's understandable. The body of work she produced over the next thirty-plus years is impressive in its breadth and outstanding in its consistent quality. She moved between the big and small screen and the stage, gracefully aging from leading lady to character actress, piling on the critical plaudits year by year. She played drama *(Young Winston,* 1972; *'night, Mother,* 1986), she played comedy *(The Prisoner of Second Avenue,* 1975; *Honeymoon in Vegas,* 1992); she played cultured upscale ladies *(The Elephant Man,* 1980), she played noodgy yentas *(Broadway Bound,* 1992). She would add another Tony nomination to her tally playing Golda Meir on Broadway in 1977's *Golda,* and run her Oscar nomination score to five with her portrayal of a fading prima ballerina in *The Turning Point* (1977), and the tough-minded mother superior of *Agnes of God* (1995). She increasingly turned to television where there were better roles for mature actresses, amassing five Emmy nods and wins for *Annie, the Women in the Life of a Man* (1970), and *Deep in My Heart* (1999), making her the 15th performer to take the Triple Crown of Oscar, Tony, and Emmy wins.

Though much of her work had an upscale prestige to it, she was not above knocking herself off her classy pedestal, buffooning around in her husband's *Silent Movie* (1976), his remake *To Be or Not to Be* (1983), and his parody *Dracula: Dead and Loving It* (1995). She even turned up as a shrink in a 1994 episode of *The Simpsons,* trying to cure Marge of her fear of flying.

She kept her private life private, not sharing her battle with uterine cancer, working nearly to the end, picking up her last Emmy nomination for the Showtime TV movie, *The Roman Spring of Mrs. Stone* (2003), and then cutting up with her husband in a 2004 episode of the HBO comedy series, *Curb Your Enthusiasm,* with her and Mel Brooks goofily parodying a scene from his 1968 classic, *The Producers.* For many, then, her death was unexpected and a tragic surprise.

She wanted it otherwise, but even if she were only remembered for *The Miracle Worker* and *The Graduate,* there's many a lengthy filmography which can't boast even one work of that caliber. For those who knew her – and particularly, those who knew her well – her legacy consists of so much more. Said David Geffen, "She was the consummate everything. Actress, comedienne, beauty, mother and wife. She made it all look easy."

ANDY GRIFFITH (1926 – 2012): THE YOKEL AS SHREWDIE

July 7, 2012

Andy Griffith was understandably defined by his most popular role: Sheriff Andy Taylor on the early 1960s series, *The Andy Griffith Show*.

Because of that, it sometimes seemed, in the years after – at least to those of us who'd grown up watching Sheriff Andy — Griffith was working awfully hard to show there was more to him than the genial, sage, small-town sheriff on what was easily one of the gentlest and most sweet-natured (without being saccharine) shows in TV history. I remember his racist murderer in the true crime-inspired *Murder in Coweta County* (1983), still defiant and unapologetic as he's being strapped into an electric chair for execution; his caustic, hard-drinking, and ultimately thieving Hollywood cowboy extra in the overlooked cult favorite, *Hearts of the West* (1975); his neo-fascist general in the 1979 TV mini-series redo of *From Here to Eternity*.

This was, in fact, the reason he'd left *Andy Griffith* with a year left on his contract: "I wanted to prove I could play something else."

The sad irony was that Griffith had proved it long before; it was just that people had forgotten.

He'd gotten his start as a stand-up comic, had become particularly well-known for his piece, "What It Was, Was Football," an uninformed rube's attempt at deciphering the tangled mess on the gridiron. His rustic naïf persona landed him the lead and the first of his two Tony nominations in the 1955 stage play, *No Time for Sergeants*; a role he repeated first on TV and then in the feature film version.

Director Elia Kazan saw an opportunity for Griffith to put a nightmarish twist on that same cracker barrel yokel character when he cast him in the searing, frighteningly prescient indictment of media manipulation, *A Face in the Crowd* (1957). Griffith plays Lonesome Rhodes, a back roads drifter with a gift for spinning homey little homilies which turn him first into a local radio star, and eventually into a media giant. But behind the friendly grin and the small town airs is an arrogant, conscienceless, self-indulgent s.o.b. whose very success, in his own eyes, is a testament to the gullibility and malleability of that mass audience which has embraced him as one of their own.

It's a powerful, disturbing performance in a powerful, disturbing film which seems all the more relevant with each political season…and it stiffed. Maybe it was too on the money. Maybe people just didn't want to see that likable country bumpkin guy who was showing up on talk shows doing that funny bit about football be a prize prick.

In any case, it was the likable picture of Griffith from *Sergeants* which carried over into *The Andy Griffith Show*. But even then, the laid back, low-key tone of the show belied just how deft Griffith was.

Spun off from an episode of *The Danny Thomas Show*, Griffith's character was initially a broad, joke-trawling variant on his *No Time for Sergeants* character, but, as the series progressed, his Sheriff Andy Taylor became more sophisticated, less caricatured. As Griffith began to exert more creative control over the series, he realized that despite his name in the title, this was an ensemble show, and it wasn't about jokes as much as creating a fully-realized, three dimensional idyll of small town living. Mayberry – inspired by his own North Carolina hometown of Mt. Airy – was a place (to borrow from the Cohen Brothers' *Raising Arizona*), "Where all parents are strong and wise and capable and all children are happy and beloved."

Griffith was the sane anchor and he deliberately positioned himself as straight man for a constellation of delightfully quirky town characters: Don Knotts' high-strung Deputy Fife, Frances Bavier's meddling Aunt Bee, Howard McNear's off-center Floyd the barber, Jim Nabors' backwoodsy filling station attendant Gomer Pyle (who was spun off into his own hit show), and a host of others. For all their quirks and sometimes small towny parochialism, the tone of the show was always one of affection, not lampoon.

It was not life as it was, but life as it could be. People fumbled with their foibles, sometimes fell victim to their pettiness, but in the end, they atoned, they redeemed, they re-heard the voices of the better angels of their natures. The situations were almost painfully life-sized (like frugal Aunt Bee trying to avoid paying full price for a new refrigerator), and the rhythm of the show almost pastoral. Griffith had deliberately decided against playing the show in front of a live audience; he didn't want the cast playing to the crowd. Some of the funniest moments on the show are the ones that capture a sleepy, warm Mayberry afternoon, with a few of the locals parked in front of Floyd's barbershop, a listless conversation slowly taking an odd turn – a kind of below-the-Mason/Dixon-line version of Paddy Chayefsky's, "Whaddaya wanna do tonight, Marty?" "I dunno, Ang; whadda you wanna do tonight?"

And Griffith fought hard to maintain the integrity of that show. In real life, and by his own admission, he could be terribly short-tempered. During several episodes of the second season, you can see Sheriff Andy's hand is bandaged; the result of a Griffith tantrum ending with him punching a wall.

He left the show to return to movies but he never gained much traction on the big screen, and returned to TV where he worked steadily. Griffith had a second, late career success with the less substantive *Matlock*, a one-hour legal drama where the actor chortled and dropped rustic one-liners as a lawyer who played the country bumpkin to camouflage a shrewd courtroom operator. He claimed *Matlock* was his favorite character, but, popular as it was, it was almost indistinguishable from such geriatric-skewing flyweight mysteries as *Murder, She Wrote* and *Diagnosis Murder.*

Like many – maybe most – actors identified with a single success, Andy Griffith was a much better actor than he was often given credit for. Given the chance, he was able to take that Carolina drawl and tweak it for a laugh or adjust it to send a shudder down your spine. And if he had been trapped or restricted by the success of *The Andy Griffith Show*, it was only because he'd done his job on the show so well.

BARBARA STANWYCK (1907 – 1990): THE DAME FROM BROOKLYN

April 2, 2011

A classy dame. A dynamite broad. A tough cookie. The language is definitely un-PC…and yet, it seems not only proper but singularly apt when talking about Barbara Stanwyck. It was the language of the day when her star soared off into the ascent, and it would remain so *her* over the course of a 60-year career on stage, film, and TV, it would be criminal to clean it up for politeness' sake. It was the kind of language she unabashedly used herself in her later years, describing herself frankly, bluntly, and with characteristic modesty, as was her wont, as "…a tough old broad from Brooklyn."

And, kiddo (as she'd probably say), she *was*. She *had* to be.

She was four-year-old Ruby Stevens when a drunk pushed her mother off a streetcar killing her, and her father, unable to cope, ran off. She bounced from one foster home to another, often running away. At nine, she was on the road with her sister, a showgirl, and by 16, she was a showgirl herself. By the time she was 19, she'd scored her first dramatic role on stage in *The Noose*, cast as – with a logic usually rare in show business – a showgirl. The raves she got for *The Noose* took her to Hollywood.

Determination and raw talent: that was what she had, that was *all* she had. She was, after all, a school dropout who'd never had any formal performance training. Early in her career, that posed a problem for her directors.

Ladies of Leisure (1930) was only her third film, and she was working under the guiding hand of the great Frank Capra. Capra found her prone to a rookie mistake: she always went full out on the first take, even in rehearsal, and could never match it thereafter. Capra learned not to rehearse her, but talk her through the scene in her dressing room before she hit the set. Wrote Capra in his autobiography, when it came time to step in front of the cameras, "She remembered every word I said – and never blew a line."

She may not have been *taught* how to act, but she *knew*. The noted film critic Pauline Kael once wrote of Stanwyck that she "…seems to have an intuitive understanding of the physical movements that work best on camera," and said of even her early performances that the actress's work was marked with a "remarkable modernism." Those instincts would earn her four Oscar noms and three Emmys for her trophy case.

She had the magic every great actor has: the ability to make you believe she was what she wasn't. She was not a classical beauty by any means, but in one of her iconic roles – the *femme fatale* of *Double Indemnity* (1944) – she threw off enough sexual heat to burn a hole in the screen. Neither was she a particularly curvy gal, yet in another of her memorable parts – goodtime showgirl Sugarpuss O'Shea in the screwball comedy *Ball of Fire* (1941) – you could believe a room full of encyclopedia-writing eggheads would trip over their tongues to get a little closer to her.

Film crews loved her. She never forgot it was their work that put a picture on the screen and was famous for her easygoing, ego-less ways on a set. She knew their names, the names of their wives and kids. As she grew older, her stature in the business greater, it was a generosity of spirit she extended toward young performers cast opposite her.

The most famous story, of course, concerns William Holden on the 1939 film, *Golden Boy*. It was Holden's first role, and at the beginning of the shoot he was coming off so badly director Rouben Mamoulian wanted to fire him. Stanwyck saw something in the young Holden, and managed to persuade Mamoulian and the producers to keep him on, launching a career as memorable as her own. Holden would never forget what she'd done for him, sending her flowers every year on the anniversary of the first day of filming, and even thanking her on-stage at the 1978 Oscars.

Watch her in *Executive Suite* (1954). She plays the newly-minted widow of a driven furniture company exec, her grief exploding in rage at the man who loved his company more than his wife. But then, a young, idealistic exec makes a pitch at a board meeting to take the company on a more humane, more dignified course. Holden, now an established and respected star, played the young exec, and in Stanwyck's admiring gaze in that scene, it's hard not to see a more personal pride, a sense of, "This is what I knew you had in you."

But Holden's story was hardly singular. After working with Stanwyck on 1952's *Clash by Night*, ever-fragile Marilyn Monroe would say Stanwyck had been the only one of Hollywood's older generation to treat her kindly, and on the TV series *The Big Valley*, she became something of a surrogate parent for Linda Evans when the young actress' mother passed away.

By the 1950s, her big screen career was winding down and she successfully transitioned to the small screen, playing the iron-willed head of a ranch family in the successful *The Big Valley*. It introduced her to a whole new generation of fans, which turned out to be something of a mixed blessing. She made so many notable films – *Stella Dallas* (1937), *Meet John Doe* (1941), *Ball of Fire*, *The Lady Eve* (1941), *Double Indemnity*, *Christmas in Connecticut* (1945), *The Strange Love of Martha Ivers* (1946), *Sorry, Wrong Number* (1948), *Titanic* (1953), among others – it seems something of a shame that she's probably best remembered by anyone not a very senior senior citizen for a backlot TV Western.

But then Stanwyck's great strength as an actress was her tremendous versatility. She wasn't like a Crawford or a Davis where an image came immediately to mind. It seemed there was nothing she couldn't play. She could be the *femme fatale* of *Double Indemnity*, the cold, bitter manipulator of *The Strange Love of Martha Ivers*, the pitiable victim of *Sorry, Wrong Number*, the self-sacrificing mother of *Stella Dallas*, the free-spirited chorine of *Ball of Fire*, disappearing completely into each of them.

How she would be remembered didn't matter to her; by her own request, there was not even a service to mark her passing. She was a trouper, a tough cookie, and all that mattered was the work. "'Career' is too pompous a word," she once said, describing her long professional journey through show business, "It was a job and I have always felt privileged to be paid for doing what I love doing."

See? A classy dame.

WILLIAM HOLDEN (1918 – 1981) AND GLENN FORD (1918 – 2006): GOLDEN BOYS

June 21, 2011

By most accounts, Harry Cohn was a royal son of a bitch.

For the uninformed, Harry Cohn was co-founder of Columbia Pictures, and the autocratic ruler of the studio from its founding in 1919 until his death in 1958. He was vulgar, crass, tyrannical, a screaming, foul-mouthed verbal bully i.e. a royal son of a bitch.

He was also a *cheap* son of a bitch.

Originally considered a "Poverty Row" studio, Cohn's Columbia, at least at first, refused to build a roster of salaried stars as the other studios did. Cohn didn't want the overhead or the headaches he saw saddling other studio chiefs with their contract talent. Cheaper and easier was to pay those studios a flat fee for the one-time use of their marquee value stars to give Columbia's B-budgeted flicks an A-list shine. Columbia was considered such a nickel-and-dime outfit at the time that other studios often loaned their stars to Columbia as a form of punishment; Columbia as a penal colony.

By the late 1930s, though, even Cohn saw the benefit in having his own on-tap stars and began to build a stable, but even then he wanted a configuration which would minimize the problems he saw other studios having with rebellious stars. A favored Cohn tactic: hire one actor as an always threatening waiting-in-the-wings replacement for another – hire a Kim Novak to keep a Rita Hayworth in line, for example. Start mouthing off you were unhappy with your salary or with the pictures you were being assigned or the directors working with you, and on suspension you'd go, your name growing colder in the public consciousness while your salaried clone got all the parts – and the public attention that went with them — you would have gotten.

And that was Cohn's thinking in 1939 when both William Holden and Glenn Ford were put under contract to Columbia. Cohn envisaged them as fit for the same kinds of roles and, as such, saw the opportunity to play them against each other.

But the actors fooled him. Instead of cutthroat competitors, they became good friends and remained so until Holden's death in 1981.

Oh, they did sometimes compete for the same parts but it was hardly the kind of manipulative managerial power play contest Cohn had hoped for. Rather, it was one even the two friends had to laugh at. Ford would later tell of both he and Holden stuffing paper in their shoes to boost their heights as they went after the same role. "Finally, neither of us could walk, so we said the hell with it."

Fittingly as friends, the course of their separate careers mirrored each other to an almost *Twilight Zone*-y degree:

Holden's family had moved to southern California from Illinois while Ford's had migrated to the same part of the country from their native Quebec. They were both discovered about the same time on the west coast theater circuit, put under contract about the same time (Ford originally to 20th Century Fox, Holden in a deal which split his services between Columbia and Paramount), and both won their first starring roles in 1939 — Ford in the Western *Heaven with a Barbed Wire Fence*, Holden in the melodrama *Golden Boy*. And each came damned close to blowing his chance as a film actor first time out.

Ford only landed at Columbia after Fox cut him loose following a dud of a screen test. And Holden's career came even closer to ending before it had begun.

Holden had been given the lead in the screen adaptation of Clifford Odets' stage play about a young man torn between boxing and the violin, but the novice film actor's work during the first days of *Golden Boy*'s shooting had been so underwhelming the producers had decided to can him. But co-star Barbara Stanwyck saw something in the young actor the execs didn't, and she lobbied forcefully for him until she convinced the chiefs to keep Holden on. The actor's work grew more assured over the course of the picture, his career was launched, and thereafter he was known as Golden Holden or, appropriately enough, Golden Boy.

For the next few years, Ford and Holden worked regularly building up their resumes with solid work in mostly minor films until the outbreak of World War II. Holden went into the Army Air Corps, Ford into the Marines, and when they came back to Hollywood after the war, they found themselves, like so many actors who'd gone into military service at the time, having lost much of the commercial traction they'd built up in the pre-war years. In another eerie parallel, each would find their stalled careers rebooted in spectacular fashion with a breakout performance in a film classic.

Ford hit pay dirt first in the 1946 *noir Gilda* as a silky ne'er do well grifting about South America who teams up with an even silkier and more of a ne'er do well in George Macready. Macready coos, Ford purrs, and it's a surprisingly unsubtle and – still to this day — daring bit of mutual homoerotic seduction which brings the two men together, making the ensuing love triangle when Macready's new wife shows up (Rita Hayworth in her own iconic star-making turn) a true three-way. When Ford falls for Hayworth's Gilda, it's hard to tell if Macready is more burned his friend is running off with his wife, or that his wife is running off with his boyfriend.

The 1946 audience may not have picked up on the boy-boy subtext, but

Ford's steamy coupling with Hayworth (the two would pair up onscreen in four more films) made *Gilda* a hit, and vaulted the actor instantly into leading man ranks.

Holden's big break didn't come until 1950, but it happened with an even more memorable *noir*, Billy Wilder's horror show about past-it Hollywood glamour, *Sunset Boulevard*. It's a brave performance in a brazen film, Holden playing a flat-busted screenwriter who leaves his integrity at the door to hustle his way into the favors of a reclusive, forgotten, frightfully deluded silent film star (real-life silent great Gloria Swanson). Scandalous in its time, still creepy today, *Sunset,* like *Gilda,* became one of the touchstone movies of the postwar period and put Holden into the orbit of bonafide Hollywood A-list stars.

Though Holden would land a greater number of major hits and be the bigger commercial star, both actors would consistently rank among the top box office draws of the 1950s. Between them, they compiled a truly outstanding body of work including the social-commentary-camouflaged-as-romantic-comedy *Born Yesterday* (1950 – Holden); the *Dirty Harry*-esque classic *noir The Big Heat* (1953 – Ford); WW II POW camp drama *Stalag 17* (1953 – Holden); the movie that brought both rock 'n' roll and the postwar juvenile delinquency crisis to the big screen in *Blackboard Jungle* (1955 – Ford); a blazing indictment of the demeaning corporatization of the American worker in *Executive Suite* (1954 – Holden); pressure cooker Western *3:10 to Yuma* (1957 – Ford); Korean War classic *The Bridges at Toko-Ri* (1954 – Holden); one of the most authentic portrayals of life on the cow trail in *Cowboy* (1958 – Ford); the steamy *Picnic* (1955 – Holden); a sly skewering of Ford's own Western image in *The Sheepman* (1958 – Ford); Frank Capra's last film, the Damon Runyon gangster comedy, *Pocketful of Miracles* (1961 – Ford); and one of the all-time classics of American cinema, David Lean's epic war film, *The Bridge on the River Kwai* (1957 – Holden).

Though Cohn had intended to threaten each with their interchangeability, Holden and Ford were hardly that. They were two distinctive brands of actors which was only natural as, despite their close friendship, they were two distinctive brands of people.

Holden (born William Beedle), the son of a well-to-do family, was a bit of a sophisticate and globetrotter for much of his life. He collected fine art, kept a second home in Switzerland, and perhaps most famously, founded a game preserve in Kenya which was often a gathering place for the good-timing jet set crowd.

There was also something melancholic to Holden, at least in his later years. At some point, by his own admission, he lost his passion for acting, staying with it simply to maintain his lifestyle. He was an alcoholic for much of his life, was hit with a suspended sentence for being involved in a fatal drunk driving accident in Italy in the 1960s, and apparently died bleeding out from a head wound from a fall, too intoxicated to call for help.

He was also, to be blunt, the prettier of the two actors. He had the kind of manly good looks tailor-made for movie magazine covers and one-sheets. One could argue *Picnic* was largely sold on the power of its iconic beefcake poster featuring a bare-chested Holden being pawed by a lusting Kim Novak.

Though he played a variety of roles, always with distinction, it's no surprise, then, that the roles which best suited Holden were savvy guys, sophisticates and/or street-smart guys, men who'd seen the world, knew how it worked, and knew how to work it. He may have sent ladies' hearts fluttering as the virile but aimless drifter of *Picnic,* but he always looked more at home in a suit or a uniform i.e. the wastrel playboy younger brother of uptight Humphrey Bogart in another teaming with Wilder in the romantic comedy delight, *Sabrina* (1954); the slick ladies' man competing with David Niven to deflower virgin Maggie McNamara in the – for its time – titillating *The Moon Is Blue* (1953); the idealistic intellectual of *Born Yesterday* trying to open ditzy Judy Holliday's eyes to the law-bending practices of her boorish businessman boyfriend; the equally idealistic junior exec of *Executive Suite* trying to save his company's soul; the brutally judgmental cavalry officer of *Escape from Fort Bravo* (1953); the world-seasoned correspondent in the three-hankie soaper *Love Is a Many Splendored Thing* (1955); the equally world-seasoned expatriate in the equally soapy *The World of Suzie Wong* (1960); the forceful Broadway director of *The Country Girl* (1954); the conniving POW of *The Bridge on the River Kwai*. It is equally unsurprising that of his three Oscar nominations, one was for the fast-talking, fast-pitching, self-hating de facto gigolo of *Sunset Boulevard,* and his one Best Actor win was for the caustic, cynical, barracks black market maestro of *Stalag 17*.

There was always something more proletarian about Glenn (born Gwyllyn) Ford. Ford's father, a railroad man, had early on advised him to develop a practical trade to have something to fall back on should acting fail him, and even after he became a major star Ford was known to do his own house repairs: plumbing, wiring, the whole blue-collar working man shebang. If there's anything to the idea that the character of the man influences the character of the role, it was probably clearer in Ford than Holden. Ford certainly thought so saying, "I've never played anyone but myself on screen."

Like Holden, Ford played a wide range of roles, usually acquitting himself well, but despite his career breakout as a smoothie casino operator in *Gilda,* he would become better remembered for his Everyman-flavored characters. In fact, Ford would take a critical drubbing for being painfully miscast in the 1962 remake of *The Four Horsemen of the Apocalypse* in the playboy role first done in 1921 by Rudolf Valentino. The actor himself admitted, "I'm out of place doing sophistication. I'm so uncomfortable in a tuxedo."

It would be hard to picture Holden the glib smoothie as the tentative, frustrated inner city schoolteacher Ford played so memorably in *Blackboard Jungle,* or the constantly befuddled fish-out-of-water public relations officer of *Teahouse of the August Moon* (1956). While Holden could be the seasoned globe-trotting correspondent involved in a hot-and-heavy affair with a Eurasian doctor during the Chinese revolution in *Love Is a Many Splendored Thing* or fall for a Hong Kong prostitute in *The World of Suzie Wong,* he couldn't be the guy-next-door Ford played as a widower fumblingly trying to find the proverbial "nice girl" in *The Courtship of Eddie's Father* (1963), or the small-time salesman trying to connect with the spinster postmistress of *Dear Heart* (1964). Holden tries to reinvigorate the heart of a furniture company in *Executive Suite,* while Ford only wants to save the reputation of his friend, a dead pilot accused of negligence in *Fate Is the Hunter* (1964). If Holden was in a corner, his was the kind of character who tried to fast-talk his way out, whereas Ford floundered and flustered. Watching Ford overwhelmed by the culture clash of *Teahouse,* lost in the inanity of military public relations in *Don't Go Near the Water* (1957), caught up in a laughable blackmail scheme in *The Gazebo* (1959), or watching his smooth-running bootlegging operation unravel in the course of his trying to do one good deed in *Pocketful of Miracles,* it's clear no actor could flounder, fluster, stammer, and comically collapse as well as Ford.

As much as their personas, their acting styles were radically different as well. Holden's emotions were right *there;* where he raged (the climax of *Executive Suite),* Ford simmered (the Ahab-like sub skipper of *Torpedo Run* [1958]); when Holden wrestled with fear *(The Bridges at Toko-Ri),* Ford fell into a quiet sweat that made you feel the knot in his stomach *(The Fastest Gun Alive* [1956]). It was, perhaps, Ford's more low-key approach which might've been responsible, despite a host of acclaimed performances, for his never even being nominated for an Oscar; his work was too subtle to be appreciated. Holden, whatever the emotion, was certain in what he felt – love, sadness, anger — while Ford had an ability to show a half-dozen different emotions at war with each other.

In *Cowboy,* his veteran trail boss tries to let down his shell to connect with his young upstart partner (Jack Lemmon) who has mistaken callousness for toughness ("You haven't gotten tougher," Ford tells him later, "you've gotten miserable") and offer some solace over the Mexican woman who's jilted Lemmon. It all flickers across Ford's face; the awkwardness, the embarrassment, the knowing the advice will be unwelcomed yet the urge to reach across to the young man, the realization that any words will only sound lame. Or in *Fate Is the Hunter,* as Ford, at a safety hearing trying to explain that a devastating air crash may have been more about fate than human error, he fumbles for words, knowing how insane his story sounds, how lacking in solace it will be for the kin who've come to hear why they've lost their loved ones; it is a beautifully played scene of a man grasping for words to describe something beyond words. And there's *The Fastest Gun Alive* (Ford, in real life, was reputedly one of the fastest draws in Hollywood, able to draw and fire in 0.4 seconds) where soft-spoken store clerk Ford brags to being a speedy draw, then later, when being pushed into a shootout to save his town threatened by gunslingers, must chokingly confess to his own fear, having never drawn against a man. The quivering tone, the catch in his voice, the glum, unheroic resignation are all pure Glenn Ford.

Heading into the 1960s, the careers of both actors continued to parallel, but now unhappily, as their marquee value began to decline with their middle years. But Holden was given a late career gift which bypassed Ford.

In 1969, Holden was cast by director Sam Peckinpah in the classic deconstructionist Western, *The Wild Bunch*. Holden was 51 by then, and the years of alcohol made him look older, but that was perfect for the role of a fading legend of an Old West bandit being pushed to extinction by New West progress (there's a story Peckinpah considered Ford for the role played by Robert Ryan, an old riding partner of Holden now forced by circumstance to hunt him down; Ryan did an excellent job but it's tantalizing to consider the added dynamic which might've been gained if the part had been played by Holden's real-life friend Ford) . The movie rekindled Holden's career (ironically at a time when he was less committed to it), and led to an Emmy-winning turn in the cop drama TV movie *The Blue Knight* (1973), and one of the best roles of his career, an Oscar-nominated turn as a TV news division chief trying to stave off the debasing rising tide of reality TV in the frighteningly prescient Sidney Lumet/Paddy Chayefsky black comedy, *Network* (1976). With his fading good looks and seen-it-all world weariness, Holden became the go-to guy as an emblem of a kind of dignity and class and honorability which seemed to be falling beneath a steamroller of raucous, cacophonous sensationalism.

Ford, who kept acting until his health began to fail him (a supporting role in the 1991 cable movie *The Final Verdict* was his last screen work), never got that Third Act spike. There were a series of minor Westerns (one of his favorite genres; he did two dozen over the course of his career, more than any other single type of film on his resume), sometimes made overseas, and he also found work on TV, some of it memorable *(The Brotherhood of the Bell* – 1970), some of it less so *(The Disappearance of Flight 412* – 1974). But no matter how large or small the part, how large or small the screen, Ford always brought his A-game.

One of the brightest spots in his late career was no more than a cameo as Pa Kent in *Superman* (1978). He has only two scenes: where he and his wife (Phyllis Thaxter) discover the toddler from space who will grow up to be Clark Kent/Superman, and a scene with teenaged Clark (Jeff East) where, in that wonderfully stumbling Ford fashion, he grapples with trying to explain to his adopted son his grand if yet undefined, undivined purpose. The brackets of those two scenes tell us everything we need to know about a decent, hard-working man always trying to do right without always being sure of what it is, and hoping he has passed those same qualities on to his son. The scene ends with Ford done in by a failing heart, and for a second – in that way only Ford seemed to be able to do – a host of emotions rush across his face, he quietly utters "Oh, no," and we see the great pain of his knowing he's leaving his struggling, confused son just when he knows the boy needs him most.

William Holden and Glenn Ford: each barely made it out of the Hollywood starting gate, each was launched on a stellar career by a studio manipulator bent on turning them against each other, each ended with a body of work any dedicated performer has to envy. But what the bigger accomplishment might have been for both men is that in an industry infamous for double-dealing, back-stabbing, bad-mouthing, and for the *schadenfreude*-esque mantra, "It's not enough for you to do well, but for your friends to do badly," that not Harry Cohn or the inherent competition of the business or their own differences ever got in the way of a friendship they maintained all their lives.

THE MAGNIFICENT SEVEN

November 18, 2011

*Author's Note: Contributors were asked to write about their "gateway" films: the movies that made them fall in love with the movies.

The Magnificent Seven (1960)
Directed by John Sturges.
Written by Walter Newman (uncredited) and William Roberts
Based on the 1954 Japanese film, Seven Samurai

There was no a-*ha!* moment, no seeing of the light, no epiphany. I'd loved movies since I was a kid, had been a buff since my early teens, but there was no one, shining instance of enlightenment where my relationship with film graduated to something — ... Well, the kind of thing my *Sound on Sight* colleagues have been talking about this month with their "gateway" films. Instead, it was a cumulative experience for me; my road to that point was a long, winding, gradual one. Here and there along that road something would lodge in the ol' gray matter, tickle at some deep place, until enough of those somethings gathered up over the years finally coalesced into a critical mass.

But I can tell you where that first turn in that road was; that first stop where I picked up that first something. I was six years old, it was 1960, and the movie was *The Magnificent Seven.*

It's the waning days of the Old West and gunfighters are going the way of the dinosaurs. Chris (Yul Brynner) is approached by some Mexican farmers hoping to hire gunmen to protect them from the predations of a bandit gang led by Calvera (Eli Wallach). Though the farmers can only offer a mere pittance in payment, Chris takes the job and enlists six other gunmen: Vin (Steve McQueen), O'Reilly (Charles Bronson), Britt (James Coburn), Lee (Robert Vaughn), Harry (Brad Dexter), and young Chico (Horst Bucholz), most of whom are down on their luck, and who would rather be gunfighters for another day on the farmers' few dimes than face alternatives like clerking in a grocery store. Once in the village, they begin to bond with the *campesinos* and train them to work in their own defense. They fend off one attack by Calvera, but then, when they leave to raid the bandit camp, they are betrayed by one of the villagers. Rather than kill the Seven, Calvera sends them packing, but the Seven return to the village, and the farmers help them kill or run off the remaining bandits. In the final battle, four of the seven are killed. Afterward, Chico elects to stay with a local girl he's fallen in love with, and Chris and Vin – realizing that, with the job done, they have no place in the village – ride off.

Though it's now looked on as a classic Western, it was hardly considered such at the time. An Old West re-working of Akira Kurosawa's 1954 masterpiece, *Seven Samurai,* it was often judged a poor relation to the original, and its director, John Sturges, hardly in the same league as Kurosawa, or even among the notable American directors of the day for that matter. At best, Sturges rarely rated in the critical community as more than a craftsman-like entertainer. At worst… In his seminal *The American Cinema: Directors and Directions 1929 – 1968,* film critic Andrew Sarris dismissed Sturges' work with, "…it is hard to remember why Sturges's career was ever considered meaningful." Ouch.

And that cast which, by the end of the decade, would be viewed as an action-adventure dream team? At the time, it was one big star (Brynner) backed up by what was then a strictly B-list roster.

Even the public didn't take to the movie at first. Domestically, *The Magnificent Seven* was a so-so performer on its initial release, doing far better for overseas audiences than it did at home.

But something in it – all those things designed and accidental which, over the years, have come to be recognized in the movie – worked on me.

It was not my first movie, not by any means. My cousins and I, practically since the day we'd graduated from our strollers, had been regularly taken to Disney movies and cartoons as well as been dragged along to more adult fare which bored us to tears because we didn't get most of it, like – and don't ask me why I remember this one – the Lana Turner/Anthony Quinn meller, *Portrait in Black* (1960).

But *The Magnificent Seven* got to me in a way the Disneys and the drippy dramas didn't. I still remember the way it resonated in my head on the way home, the way I could still see it in my mind when I closed my eyes that night in bed. Part of it was certainly that I was a six-year-old boy, and here was a cowboy adventure full of cool, gun-totin', eminently quotable tough guys, and always that twain shall meet…at least in the early '60s. But there was something else…

I've come to believe that we "serious" film folk don't always appreciate how much serendipity plays in making memorable films memorable. Like *Casablanca* (1943) and Bogart and Bergman being third choice leads working with an unfinished script based on a lousy unproduced play being adapted on the fly. Or *Jaws* (1972) and Steven Spielberg using that gnaw-at-your-vitals shark-POV shot only because that damned mechanical shark rarely worked. Like the poker players say: sometimes you just get lucky.

Not to diminish what Sturges brought to *The Magnificent Seven,* but there were a number of elements on that picture where luck was with him.

Take that classic score – da daaaah…da da da daaaaaaaah — surely among the most memorable in movie music. The great Dmitri Tiomkin had been Sturges' go-to music guy for several years. But Tiomkin had wanted to lay in an Old School Hollywood song over the opening credits as he'd done for Sturges' *Gunfight at the O.K. Corral* (1958). Sturges said no, they argued, and Tiomkin was axed. Enter Elmer Bernstein and his New Hollywood, high energy dynamic which earned the film its only Oscar nod. Almost 20 years later, the music was still echoing so clearly in the pop culture zeitgeist, John Barry could get a laugh by lifting a few bars for a quick, jokey homage in the James Bond flick, *Moonraker* (1979).

Then there's that once-in-a-lifetime all-star-before-they-were-stars cast. Brynner had an ego as big as the strutting royal he'd played in *The King and I* (1956), and saw *Seven* as a star vehicle. As the project's one headliner, he retained casting approval and tried to engineer a supporting line-up he could easily overshadow. At the time, on first glance it looked like he'd gotten exactly what he'd wanted: Dexter (treasure-chasing Harry) was a reliable but unexceptional supporting actor, and German-born Bucholz (as Mexican-born gunfighter wannabe Chico) was a non-entity in his first American film. As for the rest of the Seven...

McQueen, Bronson, Coburn, and Vaughn had been bouncing between TV and movies for several years. McQueen's most visible feature work had been in the teen-targeted sci fi cheapie *The Blob* (1958), and his career had only recently gotten traction with his starring role in the popular Western TV series, *Wanted: Dead or Alive*. Vaughn's film credits ranged from supporting parts in B-flicks like *Good Day for a Hanging* (1959) to the lead in schlockmeister Roger Corman's *Teenage Cave Man* (1958). With the exception of McQueen's TV show, not one of them had a resume worth a damn.

And yet...

Brynner had pitched the project to Sturges, an understandable choice as the director had turned out a string of successful adult Westerns throughout the '50s i.e. *Escape from Fort Bravo* (1955), *Bad Day at Black Rock* (1956), *Gunfight at the O.K. Corral*, *The Law and Jake Wade* (1959), *Last Train from Gun Hill* (1960). As it happened, on one of Sturges' recent non-Westerns, the 1958 WW II actioner *Never So Few*, the director had been impressed by the work of two young, struggling actors in the supporting cast — McQueen and Bronson – so much so that he tapped them again for *Seven*. Sterling Hayden had originally been cast for the part of the Zen-flavored, knife-wielding Britt, but when Hayden dropped out, Sturges couldn't find a replacement. Robert Vaughn, who'd already been cast, recommended his good friend James Coburn.

Sometimes you just get lucky.

Brynner had judged them by their status, not their talent, nor had he anticipated how damned *hungry* they were. They seemed to know, small as most of their parts were, they'd each been given a hell of a showcase. Instead of a one-man show, every time Brynner turned around he saw them all blatantly trying to steal focus every time they got within camera range. There's a story about shooting a very simple shot – the Seven riding across a shallow stream – but behind Brynner in the lead there's a six-act play going on: who's fussing with his hat, who's wiping at sweat, etc. Maybe with a less talented cast or a different director it might've come off as showboating, fussiness, too much business in the background. Instead, they came off as a full-bodied ensemble.

And for that they all owed Walter Newman because they'd been right: his screenplay would boost almost all their careers with what would forever remain among their best- and most fondly-remembered parts.

Walter Bernstein had originally gotten the job of adapting Kurosawa's film but his script was tossed. The job then fell to Newman (William Roberts was later brought in to tweak the screenplay on location; in a dispute over credit, Newman took his name off the film and Roberts' remains, although supposedly *Seven*, as shot, is substantially the movie Newman wrote).

The challenge for Newman was to bring the *full* ensemble to life. He couldn't give them all the same amount of screen time (Brynner would've popped a vein), but he did work out a rather elegant construction for his screenplay for the supporting tier (Brynner and McQueen – as his #2 in the group – are present throughout). Each of them has at least – for lack of a better word – three "anchor" scenes: their introduction, their death scene (for four of them), and somewhere in the middle at least one scene which gives the character room to breathe; to *be*. Then, sprinkled here and there between those anchors, a line or two here, a small action there…just enough to convey the *impression* of a movie-long presence. Coburn's indelible character – beating a braggart to the draw with his knife; studying the petals of a flower with Zen-like focus while waiting to ambush some of Calvera's men – speaks less than 100 words in the whole movie (I counted them). Vaughn's silky Lee has only 16 lines. Yet, you feel them present throughout the movie. It's the writer's version of a magician's illusion, offering just enough suggestion for you to believe something is there when it isn't.

But for that construction to work, *everything* has to work. The writer has to *nail* it; the performer has to *nail* it; and the director — … Well, you get the picture.

On *Seven*, they did, and it's that part – not the beautifully choreographed gun battles, but the *human* part of the story – that hit me and hung with me, even as a kid. I'd seen people die in movies before: shot, stabbed, drowned, beaten, drained by vampires, eaten by monsters. But *Seven* was the first time I'd felt *loss*.

While the Seven may be master gunmen, these are not the steroidal superheroes that would dominate action movies from the 1980s on, trying to pass off quirks as character ("I got it! We'll have the one guy always eating! And this other guy, we'll have him always eyeballing women!"). They're human with all the limitations that infers.

With the exception of Chris, who seems touched by the *campesinos'* initial request, none of the others take the job out of the better angels of their nature. They're out of work, broke, some of them literally hungry. Chris and Vin find O'Reilly chopping wood for his breakfast. When Vin recounts the monster paychecks O'Reilly's been paid in the past, he sums up with, "You cost a lot."

"That's right," O'Reilly replies. "I cost a lot."

"The pay's twenty dollars," Chris tells him.

O'Reilly turns his back on them…at first. And then, "Twenty dollars? Right now, that's a lot."

Those middle anchor scenes are just as pivotal, and just as vivid, probably none more than Robert Vaughn's revelation that he's taken the job not because he's on the run from the law or his enemies as he originally implied, but because he's lost his nerve. Newman gives him a wonderful, melancholic monologue. "The final, supreme idiocy," he tells the *campesinos* who come to his aid when he awakes thrashing from a nightmare, "a deserter hiding out in the middle of a battlefield."

Even when they come back for the climactic battle, they don't all come back to do good by the villagers. Harry belatedly comes back to save his friend, Chris; Lee in a last attempt to dignify himself; and Britt out of pride. "Nobody throws me my own guns and says run," he coldly declares. "Nobody."

If they'd all been generic do-gooders, well, I'd seen *those* heroes in movies before, and they all blurred together. But these weren't heroes. They were men – unnaturally skilled, granted – who got scared, humbled, vain, horny, shy around women just like anybody else. They were also not invulnerable. They bled, they died.

Sturges' strength – Andrew Sarris' opinion notwithstanding – was, in his best films, that he was quite content to spend as much time as he felt was needed in character. In movies like *Escape from Fort Bravo, Last Train from Gun Hill,* and — his best effort – *The Great Escape* (1964) there's surprisingly little action, yet gobs of time are invested in getting *us* to invest in the characters. Of *Seven*'s 123 minutes, less than 15 are devoted to action. What made Sturges a top action director, and what distinguishes him from most of what has passed for action fare over the last 30 years, wasn't his flair for action, but in knowing action had more impact if it *mattered,* and what made it matter was that the characters mattered.

And that's where Sturges got lucky again.

Newman hadn't written in the final battle in any detail. Sturges worked that out during filming. Each actor, striving to make the most of his big exit, made sure his last seconds on film were memorable. Vaughn's death scene I never forgot. He's just freed the imprisoned farmers, tipping the final fight against the bandits, when he's shot and flies against an adobe wall, sliding down, the rough brick pulling at his face until he dies on his knees. That's precision filmmaking: relying on three key scenes, Sturges, Newman and Vaughn introduce us to a character who initially gives off an unsettling, off-putting vibe, then turn him pitiful, and then finally, sympathetically, bittersweetly heroic.

That night, trying to go to sleep, those death scenes – Vaughn at the wall, Harry shot down trying to save a cornered Chris, Britt trying to make one, last knife throw as he dies, and O'Reilly, surrounded by the village kids who've adopted him, acknowledging with his last breath the Mexican side of the heritage he's denied ("What's my name?" "Bernardo! Bernardo!" "You're damn right!") — haunted me because the characters had seemed so alive, so heroic, yet utterly life-sized.

In time, the popularity of *The Magnificent Seven* would grow; enough so to spawn three embarrassingly bad sequels and a misguided TV series. For years, the original would remain among one of the most consistent performers first on network TV, then later in syndication and, still later, on cable. It would grow from middling hit to one of the most prominent entries in the American canon of Western movies, and its plot of disparate characters coming together for an impossible mission against overwhelming odds one of movies' most imitated.

For me, it became a gold standard, even decades later as my interest in film, both academic and professional, grew deeper and more serious. When CGI effects came to mean more than story, when heroes came to be defined by their superpowers or super gadgets or super abs rather than their recognizably human limitations, when the ratio of character and story to action reversed itself to turn out two-hour pyrotechnic fests which still left me feeling, "So what?" I would think back to *The Magnificent Seven,* and say to myself, "Now *that's* how it's done."

Was it great cinema? Probably not. Just entertainment. But with the kind of heart "just entertainment" doesn't often seem to have these days.

All I know is when it still occasionally reruns on cable – and maybe it's just because I'm older, more nostalgic, and will get teary over ASPCA commercials – I can still feel what I felt 51 years ago: the same building excitement at the beginning, the same mournfulness at the close. When

Britt, Lee, Harry, and O'Reilly die, I still sigh.

As opposed to what happens when I come home from a movie these days, and put my head on the pillow at night and remember what I'd seen. Oh, I still sigh, but it's more of a, "I spent $10.50 on *that?*"

JANE RUSSELL (1921 – 2011): THE GOOD GIRL

March 2, 2011

When Jane Russell died at home earlier this week at the age of 89 from respiratory failure, it was the passing of a Hollywood myth. Not a legend, but a myth, for the Jane Russell we remember, the images of Jane Russell we carry in our heads, were wholly Hollywood magic: making us believe in something that wasn't really there. Consider: Russell's obits all use the same words—"sex symbol," "provocative," "sensual," "pinup girl." For the viewing public, she was all these things, and that was Hollywood smoke-and-mirrors at its best for the woman behind the image that steamed up camera lenses and burned through movie screens and left many an American male tossing and turning restlessly in his bed after a night at the movies was, in the end – as they used to say in her day – a good girl.

Without taking anything away from her, that she is so well-remembered at all is a triumph of Hollywood imagery over substance. She was sold as a sexpot and though inarguably voluptuous, she was, on close inspection, attractive but not overly so. She had only a moderately long career, was making only a few sporadic film appearances by the 1960s, her last in *Darker Than Amber* (1970), before she walked away from movies for good. Few of her nearly two dozen films are particularly memorable, and in that strange, weird way peculiar to Hollywood, the film which launched her career – *The Outlaw* (1941) — is remembered more for forever defining her as a Movietown sex goddess than for being any good.

Even the truth of her can read like a hackneyed Hollywood fable. Though she had been going to drama school, she was discovered by that most eccentric of eccentric billionaires, Howard Hughes, while she was working as a receptionist for his dentist. Despite her never having been in front of a movie camera, Hughes immediately cast her as the female lead in his production of *The Outlaw*, a highly *highly*-fictionalized Billy the Kid tale. When strong-willed director Howard Hawks tired of Hughes' constantly meddling and walked off the picture, Hughes himself took the reins which, according to Russell, resulted in a marathon nine-month shoot, and an even longer marathon to get the movie in front of a paying audience.

In Hughes' hands, the movie didn't feature Russell as much as it featured Russell's undeniably eye-catching physical endowments. One of America's great oddballs was so impressed with them, he designed a special seamless "cantilever bra" to further enhance his leading lady (which she claimed she never wore; a secret she said she kept from Hughes). Hollywood censors were also impressed with her, ahem, gifts (it was impossible not to; they're the center of focus in nearly every scene she's in), but not in a good way. Though the movie would barely rate a PG today, in its time it was considered too steamy for release, and Hughes wound up battling with censors for two years before managing to gain the film even a limited distribution, and it wouldn't be until 1946 – five years after its completion – that *The Outlaw* would finally gain wide release.

Russell would not appear in another movie during all that time, yet she was a star and a sex icon before *The Outlaw* hit screens. Crazy or not, Hughes understood the movie's selling point was its very taboo-ness. During the time it was banned, the billionaire shrewdly built up interest in the film by marketing the hell out of it which he did by marketing the hell out of Russell. According to the actress, "…Howard Hughes had me doing publicity for *(The Outlaw)* every day, five days a week for five years."

And, like much of the movie, most of *The Outlaw*'s relentless promotion centered around the two real stars of the film: Jane Russell's breasts. Garson Kanin once wrote about walking along Broadway with George S. Kaufman and passing no less than five billboards for the movie featuring Russell with peeping cleavage and come hither gaze. Kaufman's reaction: "They ought to call it, *A Sale of Two Titties.*"

That would be the prism through which Russell would be viewed throughout much of her career, although every so often she would catch a role showing there was more to her than a healthy set of curves. She was a capable tough-gal foil for lily-livered Bob Hope in the Western farce, *The Paleface* (1948), and in her best film, *Gentlemen Prefer Blondes* (1953), she sang, danced, charmed, made funny, and easily held her own against the Death Star of sex bombs: Marilyn Monroe.

The bulk of her movie career, however, was rather undistinguished although if anyone was bothering to look past her décolleté, they'd have been able to see that while she wasn't a great actress, she could hold the screen against some impressive presences. She did two films playing opposite Robert Mitchum, the best of which is the delicious mess, *His Kind of Woman* (1951). Like Mitchum, she came across with an attractive blend of sexiness and toughness, not unwilling but picky. Where Monroe came across as a whispery fragile flower playing against Mitchum in *The River of No Return* (1954), Russell stood her ground, matched him bedroom eye for bedroom eye and a look that said, "Well, maybe if you're a good boy…"

She showed the same tough-but-sexy moxy in the Western *The Tall Men* (1955) with Clark Gable. Russell's Nella Turner would never have stood for being whisked up a set of stairs to the boudoir the way Gable had done with Vivien Leigh in *Gone with the Wind* (1939). More likely, she would have kicked him in the nuts, then stood over his writhing body telling him,

"When *I* say; not *you!*"

In one way, she was a better actress than most thought because she made it all so convincing…and it was as removed from her true self as the sun from the moon. She may have played the loose-hipped sex bomb in the movies or when guest appearing on TV, but she managed something in her decades in Hollywood few other Tinsel Town pinup queens managed then or since: a scandal-free life. Her first marriage was to her high school sweetheart and it lasted 24 years. Privately, she was a devout Christian reading the Bible every day, held Bible studies in her home, recorded gospel records, and founded the World Adoption International Fund which placed over 51,000 kids with adoptive families.

That's the magic of Hollywood, the kind of dream-making the Dream Factory excels at. Jane Russell will always be remembered laying back on a bed of straw, dress slipping off her shoulder revealing a bit of cleavage, hair tousled, looking as if she's just had a roll in the hay and is ready for another. But behind the sultry gaze and dark, kissable lips she was a good girl.

9 OVERLOOKED (ALMOST) CLASSIC WESTERNS

January 3, 2013

One of the best films to come out of the '60s/'70s torrent of Westerns was Sam Peckinpah's demythologizing masterpiece, *The Wild Bunch* (1960).

The Western was a movie staple for decades. It seemed the genre that would never die, feeding the fantasies of one generation after another of young boys who galloped around their backyards, playgrounds, and brick streets on broomsticks, banging away with their Mattel cap pistols. Something about a man on a horse set against the boundless wastes of Monument Valley, the crackle of saddle leather, two men facing off in a dusty street under the noon sun connected with the free spirit in every kid.

The American movie – a celluloid telling that was more than a skit – was born in a Western: Edwin S. Porter's 11- minute *The Great Train Robbery* (1903). Thereafter, Westerns grew longer, they grew more complex. The West – hostile, endless, civilization barely maintaining a toehold against the elements, hostile natives, and robber barons – proved an infinitely plastic setting. In a place with no law, and where will and desire and ambition could, and usually were, enforced at the point of a gun, there seemed no story which couldn't find a malleable setting in the Old West, from plain ol' rootin' tootin' adventures to political allegories, social commentary, and revisionist reconsideration of American mythology.

The genre reached a creative peak during the 1960s and 1970s. At a time when America seemed to be questioning all of its creation myths, there seemed no better place for that examination than in one of its most persistent myths — the West – and Western movies poured out in a flood. Some 200 Westerns hit U.S. screens between 1960 and 1978, with over 70 turned out 1969-1972 alone. This was the era of *Hombre* (1967), *McCabe & Mrs. Miller* (1971), *A Man Called Horse* (1970), *Jeremiah Johnson* (1972), *Butch Cassidy and the Sundance Kid* (1969), *Little Big Man* (1970), *Pat Garrett and Billy the Kid* (1973), *The Wild Bunch* (1969), and Sergio Leone's cycle of Clint Eastwood-starring "spaghetti" Westerns culminating in *The Good, the Bad and the Ugly* (1966).

But by the late 1970s, after seven decades of remarkably consistent popularity, the genre was fading. Maybe it was the glut of men-on-horseback flicks, maybe too many of them had been just plain bad, maybe an overdose of revisionism had made the form too unpalatable; too much social commentary, not enough fun. Certainly by the 1980s, key to the audience's waning appetite for the Western was that the form simply didn't work anymore. It was too sedate, the action too small in scale. A man fending off hostile Indians with a lever-action Winchester didn't cut it next to screen-filling intergalactic battles, wizardry and magic, rampaging monsters, and all the other effects-fed forms which came to dominate the box office. Maybe the Old West had simply gotten too old; too far back in antiquity to resonate with a young audience characterized by a cultural disconnect with the times and tastes which predated them.

Oh, there would still be the occasional, notable hit: Eastwood's melancholy *Unforgiven* (1992); Kevin Costner's sledgehammer of noble revisionism in *Dances with Wolves* (1990); the flyweight goof, *Maverick* (1994). But the Western, as a box office cornerstone, as a persistent audience favorite, as a broomstick-riding young boy's fantasy-feeder, had lost its place.

There are still Westerns we remember, and Western filmmakers – like a John Ford, a Howard Hawks – that still stand high in the American canon. Serious cineastes still salute Ford as a master and never better than when he reveled in the legendary West of *She Wore a Yellow Ribbon* (1949) and *The Searchers* (1956). Hawks had *Red River* (1948) and *Rio Bravo* (1959), Delmer Daves had *3:10 to Yuma* (1957) and *Cowboy* (1958), Budd Boetticher had his tight, little Randolph Scott Westerns, and Anthony Mann his psychologically heated collaborations with James Stewart. We remember the allegorical *High Noon* (1952), and the epic sweep of *How the West Was Won* (1962) and the brooding melancholy of *The Ox Bow Incident* (1943).

In their shadow, but riding high in the saddle nonetheless, were others. Perhaps they never attained the status of classics, they never had the poetic resonance of a Ford, the compact cohesion of a Boetticher, the he-man myth-making of Hawks. But something still happened for you when you saw their heroes climb up in the saddle, give their mounts some heel, and head off in a cloud of dust.

1. *The Professionals* (1966)
Directed by Richard Brooks
Adapted from Frank O'Rourke's novel by Richard Brooks

I don't know why *The Professionals* isn't remembered as well as, or rated among the all-time great Westerns. I'd go one step further; it should be among the all-time great action/adventures with possibly one of the best Western ensembles since *The Magnificent Seven*. The credit goes to Brooks, always an intelligent, creatively ambitious filmmaker interested in serious, adult stories. Despite its rip-roaring nature, *The Professionals* is no exception.

The Mexican-born wife (Claudia Cardinale) of a Texas millionaire (Ralph Bellamy) has been kidnapped by a bandito/revolutionary (Jack Palance) and taken south of the border. Bellamy hires a crack team of specialists led by ex-soldier Lee Marvin (backed by Burt Lancaster, Robert Ryan, and Woody Strode) to get her back. The trek south is grueling, the raid on Palance's camp daring, and the long ride back marked by as many plot twists as there are bends in the road.

What distinguishes *The Professionals* from most actioners is the history Brooks gives his principals: Marvin, Lancaster, and Palance had once fought side-by-side in the Mexican Revolution. Disillusioned, Marvin and Lancaster had left and have been scratching around ever since for a quick buck. That undertone of rueful melancholy gives *Professionals* an emotional hue few action flicks even attempt.

Facing off with his friend-now-foe Lancaster, Palance understands Lancaster's cynicism while trying to explain his own tattered but undying commitment:' "We stay because we believe. We leave because we are disillusioned. We come back because we are lost. We die because we are committed."

2. *El Dorado* (1966)
Directed by Howard Hawks
Adapted from Harry Brown's novel by Leigh Brackett

Rio Bravo is considered one of Hawks' best and it may be the better piece of cinema, but this *de facto* remake is, I think, immensely more fun.

Gunfighter John Wayne and town marshal Robert Mitchum are old buddies. Wayne has been approached by nasty land grabber Ed Asner to work for him in a range war, but Wayne won't go up against his friend and leaves town. Some months later, he hears Mitchum has become a laughable drunk and a new ace gunman is being brought in to take care of him. Wayne rides back to help Mitchum, in turn helped by a rather inept James Caan who owes Wayne for saving his life.

That's the key to Brackett's story; criss-crossing moral debts: Wayne owes Mitchum and the family Asner has been trying to run off; Caan owes Wayne; Mitchum owes his own self-respect to try to gather himself together and become the man he once was.

While Brackett's script gives the proceedings enough dramatic heft to get us caring about how it all plays out, it's also funny as hell. *El Dorado* doesn't take itself nearly as seriously as *Rio Bravo* does, and Brackett composes a perfectly balanced piece of action (choreographed with characteristic flair by Hawks) and wit. Take this bit where Wayne — chasing a gunman with a bad leg who has run by the shotgun-armed Caan – comes across Caan in the street:

"Did you get him?" Wayne asks.
"Who?" Caan blithely replies.
"The fella that ran outta the church!"
"Well, yes and no."
"Yes and no? Did you or didn't you?"
"I hit the sign, and the sign hit him."
Exasperated, now: "Well, that's great."
"He was limping when he left!"
"He was limping when he got here!"

3. *Escape from Fort Bravo* (1953)
Directed by John Sturges
Written by Frank Fenton, Phillip Rock, and Michael Pate

You can't talk about Westerns without mentioning at least one cavalry v. Indians pic. I know Ford's cavalry films – particularly *Fort Apache* (1948) and *She Wore a Yellow Ribbon* – are considered the gold standard, but Ford's penchant for the sentimental and the romantic never sat quite well with me. My favorite is *Escape from Fort Bravo,* a movie as tough and hard as the sun-baked desert where it takes place.

It's the Civil War, and Fort Bravo is an undermanned Union prison for Confederates far out on the southwestern frontier surrounded by hostile Mescalero Apaches. While the fort commander (Carl Benton Reid) always has it in mind that he may one day have to arm his rebel prisoners to fight off the Apaches, his subordinate, William Holden, is an unbending, unyielding warden with no qualms about bringing back runaways in humiliating fashion.

Holden's hard shell finally gives way when Eleanor Parker comes to town. When it turns out she is part of an escape plan involving her rebel lover (John Forsythe), Holden vows to bring the escapees back for a harsh justice, including – and especially — Parker. But on the return, they are ambushed by a band of Mescaleros. In the bare shelter of a small hollow, the small band, fighting together, try to hold off the Apaches until help comes. With only the barest of elements – a shallow hole, empty ground, some far off rises– Sturges' creates a masterful bit of action movie-making in the third act fight between Holden and his small band and the Apaches.

Ford was in love with the *idea* of the West, but Sturges saw that the scabrous outlands of the southwest were no place for romanticism and soft hearts. His men are hard; not macho, strutting hard, but hard out of necessity, hard from the personal armor they build around themselves as a means of survival.

Best moment: Half of Holden's people are dead, the others wounded, and there's Powell. In an attempt to save the still-living by having the Mescaleros think he's the lone survivor, Holden climbs out of their little shelter and suicidally walks toward them. As the cliché goes, the silence, broken only by the wind, is deafening. The Mescaleros come out of their distant positions, small figures on the white bluffs outlined against a startlingly blue sky, and then there's the exquisitely unbearable suspense of waiting for the inevitable first shot to be fired.

4. *Rio Conchos* (1964)
Directed by Gordon Douglas
Adapted from Clair Huffaker's novel by Joseph Landon and Huffaker

The Civil War is not long over. Richard Boone is a one-time rebel officer obsessed with killing Apaches to revenge the wife and child lost in an Indian massacre. Stuart Whitman is a cavalry officer responsible for losing a shipment of new repeating rifles. Boone is not-so-gently coaxed into helping Whitman find a Confederate renegade who has set up camp in Mexico and plans to give the repeaters to Apaches and set them loose north of the border to avenge the South's defeat.

What breaks *Rio Conchos* out of the usual "impossible mission" genre are the roiling inner lives of its principals. Caustic, bitter, and brutal, Boone is a classic anti-hero, so filled with hate for the killers of his family that he blows his group's cover when he attacks a similarly hate-filled Apache chief during their south-of-the-border meet. And there's Edmond O'Brien's psychically fractured renegade reb officer, babbling his insanely grandiose plans for a southern resurrection as he dodders around a half-finished recreation of a plantation house.

With not a Good Guy in sight, and a violent, tragic ending in which obsession and hate trump common sense, *Rio Conchos* passes as a Western *noir*. As good as this flick is, I'd recommend watching it just to see the closing crane shot: as deft a "money shot" and "button" as you're likely to see.

5. *The Fastest Gun Alive* (1956)
Directed by Russell Rouse
Adapted from Frank D. Gilroy's story, "The Last Notch," by Gilroy and Rouse

They called them "psychological Westerns"; Westerns where the threats were as much inside a man's head as they were out in the dusty streets and arid badlands. The grandfather of the form is Henry King's 1950 *The Gunfighter*, but this one's a worthy descendant.

Glenn Ford is a nice-guy store-keep, but he's starting to bridle at the constantly rehashed story of a gunfight in a nearby town. When Ford mouths off that the blatherer doesn't know what he's talking about, his friends and neighbors are dismissive until Ford returns with a gun of his own and puts on a display in the street which leaves the townspeople judging him to be – you guessed it – the fastest gun alive. But that shooting in the next town was by ruthless bank robber Broderick Crawford who thinks *he's* the fastest gun alive. When Crawford and his gang pass through Ford's town and Crawford hears word of Ford's feat of speed and marksmanship, he threatens to burn down the town unless Ford faces him in the street. Ford may be fast, but now he confesses what's really been eating at him: he's never drawn down on a man, and still carries the guilt of his town marshal father's death.

There's not a lot of action here, but a slow, deliberate, ultimately relentless build-up to the final confrontation. It's a fine cast that sells this: Crawford's psychotically obsessed gunman, his deliciously droll back-up John Dehner, but especially Glenn Ford. After one of his neighbors (Leif Erickson) has offered to take his place against Crawford, Ford takes his gun and tries to ready himself to go out into the street. As Erickson starts to tell Ford he doesn't need to do this, Ford, his voice tight with fear, says, "Don't say a word…because a word is about all it'd take."

6. *Invitation to a Gunfighter* (1964)
Directed by Richard Wilson
Written by Hal Goodman & Larry Klein, Alvin Sapinsley, Elizabeth Wilson and Richard Wilson

And speaking of psychological Westerns, damned near everyone in this flick could do with some time on a shrink's couch. That also makes this, for the patient viewer, an unusually emotionally dense oater.

Just after the Civil War, reb soldier George Segal has returned to his hometown to find his girlfriend married to another man and his family farm confiscated and sold off by Pat Hingle, the Bible-quoting, string-pulling, manipulative power in town. Hingle puts out a call for a gunfighter to rid the town of this last rebel and inadvertently winds up with Yul Brynner, an ice-blooded killer who seems to see through to each individual's flaws... then enjoys poking at them. But behind Brynner's cool exterior are his own demons.

Invitation is a stew of prejudice, guilt, obligation, false faces and spiteful hate. It might be a little too soapy for some, too deliberate in its pace for others, but for someone wanting a little bit more than dust and bullets, you might want to take up this *Invitation* (ok, groan, yeah, I know, but I couldn't resist).

7. *The Scalphunters* (1968)
Directed by Sydney Pollack
Written by William W. Norton

A comic Western about racism. That's right; you saw all those words in the same sentence: "comic," "Western," "racism." Comedy Westerns are tough enough to pull off without becoming exercises in plain silliness, but to throw a hot button social issue into the mix compounds the challenge several fold. Norton's script is up to the mark, and Pollack – always an intelligent director who liked his movies with some kind of meat on their bones – does its mix of action, humor, and barbed comment justice.

In pre-Civil War Texas, Burt Lancaster is a trapper on his way to town with a load of valuable pelts. One of the local Apaches (Armando Silvestre) takes umbrage that Lancaster has been trapping on tribal land and takes Lancaster's furs. Not a completely unreasonable guy, the Apache pays Lancaster with an escaped slave (Ossie Davis). Lancaster tracks the Apaches but before he can steal his furs back, Silvestre's band is attacked by "scalphunters" – a band of murderers who slaughter and scalp the Apaches for bounty money. Davis falls into the hands of the scalphunters, led by Telly Savalas, and tries to play

Savalas and his girl (Shelley Winters) off each other to gain his freedom. Meanwhile, Lancaster dogs Savalas' caravan, trying to get back his furs and Davis who, to Lancaster's frustration, has no wish to be "liberated" back into slavery.

Refreshingly, the script doesn't ennoble anyone, including Davis. In fact, the moral of *The Scalphunters* may be that all men are created equal, the proof being that all men, whatever race, creed, or color, are equally susceptible to the same dumbassedness, and a blindness to it.

That goes for Lancaster, too, even though he holds what loosely passes as the hero role. As his furs are being taken away by Silvestre: "You're all right, Two Crows. You oughta be a white man. They'd make you captain of the steamboat and president of the bank. Just because you own this damn country!"

8. *Bite the Bullet* (1975)
Written and directed by Richard Brooks

Not as punchy as *The Professionals,* but an admirable flick nonetheless, *Bullet* is about a grueling, big-money, 700-mile cross-country horse race.

Gene Hackman is an apathetic cowboy who gets swept up in the enthusiasm for the race and decides to enter even though it means going up against James Coburn, an old friend and Spanish-American War buddy. As the motley (maybe *too* motley) assortment of riders pounds their way across boulder-strewn hills, woodland back roads, and cruel desert, Brooks takes swipes at prejudice (in any number of forms), animal cruelty, empty-headed machismo, and the American obsession with winning at any cost.

As he did with *The Professionals,* Brooks gives his characters a history; they carry with them the weight of their memories. A particularly strong piece is Hackman's monologue about how he met – and lost – his wife during the war with Spain.

And also as he did with *The Professionals,* Brooks exercises a gift for a choice *bon mot*. Hackman leaves Coburn to keep an eye on Jan-Michael Vincent, a self-styled Stetson-wearing tough-guy, after he's beat hell out of him for calling a miscast Candice Bergen a whore. Says the curious Coburn: "Why don't you tell me the story of your life. Just leave out everything but the last five minutes."

It's not always a particularly subtle film, and it goes *waaay* off the rails for a bit about three-quarters through with some half-assed subplot about a prison break, but it gets back on track for a finish that's triumphant, and, without cheating, touching.

9. *Waterhole #3* (1967)
Directed by William A. Graham
Written by Joseph T. Steck and Robert R. Young

Ok, you've had your social commentary, you've had your frontier angst, you've had your cowboy hearts of darkness. Now, you just want to kick back and have some fun.

James Coburn, in the kind of role he practically patented in the 1960s, plays a wolfish, fast-talking, quick-thinking, conniving gambler who comes into possession of gold from an Army payroll robbery. Then the stolen gold is stolen from him by hot-headed marshal Carroll O'Connor, then stolen back by the original thieves which prompts Coburn and O'Connor to team up to steal it back and — ... Well, you get the picture. There's gunfights in a whorehouse, more lying than a presidential debate, and O'Connor's daughter (Margaret Blye) claiming rape (although even she's not sure that's what it was) to anybody who'll listen only to be ignored, even by her own father (who seems more concerned with Coburn's having stolen his prized horse) in the chase after the loot.

A lot of it, admittedly, is un-PC by contemporary standards, and it does fizzle out toward the end, but if you can give in to it, and enjoy Coburn, O'Connor, Claude Akins, Joan Blondell, James Whitmore, Bruce Dern, and the always-scary Timothy Carey playing the hell out of the goofiness, it's a fun watch, particularly if you buy into the pic's philosophy, sung by Greek chorusing balladeer Roger Miller: "Do unto others before they do it unto you."

THROWBACK: CLINT EASTWOOD

September 16, 2010

There are two timely justifications for revisiting the career of Clint Eastwood at this particular moment. The most obvious is the premiere of Eastwood's latest directorial effort, *Hereafter,* at the Toronto International Film Festival earlier this month. The other is his appearance on the Beloit College Mindset List for the Class of 2014 which came out in August.

Beloit College has issued its Mindset List each August since 1998. They describe it as "…a look at the cultural touchstones that shape the lives of students entering college (in the fall)…" According to an Associated Press story on the issuance of the most recent list, the idea behind it "…is to remind teachers that cultural references familiar to them might draw blank stares from college freshmen born mostly in 1992."

This year's list includes items like:

"Item #15. Colorful lapel ribbons have always been worn to indicate support for a cause…

"Item #28. They've never recognized that pointing to their wrists was a request for the time of day…

"Item #68. They have never worried about a Russian missile strike on the U.S.…"

And, more to the point at hand, Item #12: "Clint Eastwood is better known as a sensitive director than as Dirty Harry."

The AP story emphasized this last point, speaking with one Seattle 18-year-older who said of Eastwood, "I know he directed movies, but I also know he's supposed to be sort of bad-ass."

To Eastwood fans of a certain age, that this one-time movie bad-ass is now a regular feature of the film festival circuit accompanying sensitive directorial efforts like *Hereafter, Million Dollar Baby* (2004), *Changeling* (2008) et al, and is among one of the most respected filmmakers in mainstream films, is nothing short of mind-boggling.

Sort of bad-ass? Indeed, back before the Class of 2014 was born, he was considered one of the baddest bad-asses on the big screen.

* * * * *

With an early *curriculum vitae* including stints as a logger and gas station attendant, and then, eventually, bit parts in movies like *Tarantula* (1955) and *Revenge of the Creature* (1955), there is little from the beginning of Clint Eastwood's career portending the eminent status he would be granted as a director with *Unforgiven* (1992), cement with *Mystic River* (2003), and entrench with *Million Dollar Baby* and the bookend pieces, *Flag of Our Fathers* (2006) and *Letters from Iwo Jima* (2006).

Eastwood's movie career began as a contract player for Universal in the 1950s, but his first major break – and minor star status – came with his casting as a regular on the popular Western TV series, *Rawhide*. He stepped up to the big screen when Italian director Sergio Leone, looking for an American actor as a "hook" to gain U.S. distribution for his "spaghetti Westerns," cast Eastwood as The Man With No Name in three increasingly popular oaters, *A Fistful of Dollars* (1964), *For a Few Dollars More* (1965), and *The Good the Bad and the Ugly* (1966). The Leone successes led to offers to Eastwood of leading roles in American movies, though they were often B-caliber actioners such as *Hang 'Em High* (1968), and *Where Eagles Dare* (1968), which rarely did little more than milk the laconic gunman persona Eastwood had established in his Italian features. However, with the breakout success of *Dirty Harry* (1971), Eastwood finally took a place among the ranks of major action stars, and quickly began to exploit the power of his newly bankable status by negotiating for his first feature directorial effort (Eastwood had initially tried his hand at directing on *Rawhide*), the psychological thriller *Play Misty For Me* (1971), a critically well-received story of a stalker's obsession which essentially presaged *Fatal Attraction* 16 years later.

As actor and director, Eastwood early on displayed an admirable tendency to use his growing commercial value as a consistently popular action hero to, in effect, cross-collateralize creative risks both behind and in front of the camera, resulting in a body of work (much of it made through his Malpaso production company) which, while often dominated by routine action thrillers of one sort or another, was salted with a wildly eclectic mix of more personal endeavors. In terms of sheer creative guts if not quality, Eastwood's against-type projects showed more nerve than evidenced in the oeuvres of talent of greater critical standing.

There was, for example, his departure from cool, dead-shot San Francisco loner cop Dirty Harry Callahan with his portrayal of less assured New Orleans detective Wes Block in *Tightrope* (1984), a single father pondering his own repressed sexual kinks as he tracks a serial killer through the city's demimonde; he played broadly against type (co-starring with an orangutan, no less) as a happy-go-lucky bare-knuckle boxer in the loopy comedy *Every Which Way But Loose* (1978) and its sequel, *Any Which Way You Can* (1980); Eastwood poked gentle fun at his Western persona in *Bronco Billy* (1980), playing the star of a cheesy modern-day traveling Wild West show whose deep, dark secret is that he is really a shoe salesman from New Jersey; and then there was his doomed hillbilly crooner bonding with his runaway nephew on a cross-country trek in the Depression era drama, *Honky Tonk Man* (1982). His willingness to occasionally try significant departures from his commercially proven personas comes from a Zen-like simplicity of purpose he explained in a 2004 interview with British journalist Michael Parkinson where he discussed his decision to do *Every Which Way But Loose* against his agent's advice after having done a series of action thrillers: "... they said, 'That's not you,' and I said, 'Well, what is me? I don't know'."

Similarly, while his directorial credits prior to 1992 show a preponderance of routine actioners like *Dirty Harry* sequel *Sudden Impact* (1983), *Heartbreak Ridge* (1986), *The Eiger Sanction* (1975), *The Gauntlet* (1977), and *The Rookie* (1990), among them are also *Bird* (1988), his brooding biography of jazz great Charlie Parker; *Honky Tonk Man* and the Capra-esque *Bronco Billy;* and *White Hunter, Black Heart* (1990), with Eastwood also starring as a John Huston-like movie director in a story inspired by Huston's carryings-on during the production of *The African Queen* (1951). Still, for all his genre dabbling and occasional genre inversions, a number of box office successes and the occasional critical tip-of-the-hat, by the mid-1980s Eastwood's directorial reputation was that of a solid but unexceptional craftsman generally known for turning out the same kind of action thriller fare which had launched his career, but often failing to live up to the creative promise of *Play Misty For Me*. With a streak of disappointing or middling returns for *The Dead Pool* (1988), *Bird, Pink Cadillac* (1989), *White Hunter, Black Heart,* and *The Rookie*, and with Eastwood approaching 60, there was even some question as to whether or not he had passed his box office peak.

The best mile markers of Eastwood's career through *Unforgiven* are his self-directed Westerns. Westerns had launched his big screen career, and they usually demarcated phases of his Hollywood passage. As well, Eastwood is as much a part of Western movie iconography as he is a part of the Dirty Harry-like rogue cop genre, considered by some as much a Western standard as John Wayne. His lanky frame, trademark squint, laid-back and often terse way with dialogue, an acting style the late actor Richard Burton described as "dynamic lethargy," has always provided a natural fit for the saddle.

Play Misty For Me had made a bigger impression with critics than at the box office, so, understandably, for his second directorial effort, Eastwood fell back on what had, to that point, proven to be one of his more reliable commercial vehicles: the Western, with *High Plains Drifter* (1973) (*Misty* had a domestic gross of about $10 million vs. $19 million for *The Good, the Bad, and the Ugly,* and $36 million for *Dirty Harry. Drifter* did about $14 million domestic).

Eastwood has always counted Sergio Leone and *Dirty Harry* director Don Siegel as the two greatest influences on his directorial career, but it is Leone's spirit which dominates *High Plains Drifter*. The Italian director's operatic style is stamped all over the movie, from the near-surreal imagery Eastwood concocts with cinematographer Bruce Surtees (Largo, a collection of raw-finished and half-built buildings with a bare toehold on strip of desert shore alongside a lifeless lake, painted a Satanic red at Eastwood's order, the town's "Welcome" sign amended to read, "Welcome to Hell"), to Dee Barton's ethereal soundtrack (channeling Leone's usual composer, Ennio Morricone), to the dramatic histrionics (snarling pit bull Bad Guys; spineless and transparently conniving Largo elders), and especially in the movie's rather obvious morality tale (by *Shaft* scribe Ernest Tidyman and an uncredited Dean Reisner) about a — literally — avenging angel gunfighter come to town. This broad stylization and overt symbolism makes *Drifter* – like Leone's movies — something of a kabuki Western, but it is a tone that fits the *Twilight Zone*-ish, not-quite-real-not-quite-unreal feel of the picture.

The Outlaw Josey Wales, coming just three years later, represents a substantial change for Eastwood. His career more firmly established, he begins to experiment, leaning away from Leone and more toward a Don Siegel aesthetic in attempting a story (Phil Kaufman and Sonia Shernus adapting Forrest Carter's novel, *Gone to Texas*) more naturalistic and true-to-life (priming him for such subsequent life-sized projects as *Bronco Billy* and *Honky Tonk Man*). Eastwood is Josey Wales, a neutral Southern farmer during the Civil War who joins a Confederate guerilla band after raiders aligned with the Union ("Redlegs" for the identifying stripe on their trousers) torch his farm and slaughter his family. At the end of the war, Wales and the other guerillas prepare to lay down their arms at an arranged surrender only to be ambushed by the Redlegs. Wales escapes and winds his way west dogged by bounty hunters and a Redleg posse.

In contrast to *High Plains Drifter*'s aggressive visuals of a sun-baked hell, under the hand of Eastwood again working with Bruce Surtees, *Josey Wales* is a more visually subdued, often pastoral piece, set first among the quiet greens of Southern farmland, then moving on to the Western spaces. This is not the bleached-bone West of *Drifter*, but a softer-hued expanse, a limbo land with islands of promise for the cast-off and on-the-run. Eastwood's eye here eschews Leone's visual hysteria in favor of Siegel's low-key approach; clean, straightforward visuals, letting the story, the characters, and the scenery speak for themselves within a relaxed frame, adding only sparingly the smallest of visual flourishes. *Josey Wales*' strongest moments are its quietest: the "orphan" Wales' gradual assembling an *ad hoc* family of fellow drifters (an aged Native American highwayman; a Native American woman liberated from sexual slavery; a pair of stranded lady settlers); the plain language eloquence of Wales' face-to-face meet with Indian chief Will Sampson to strike a deal for peaceful coexistence; and especially in a melancholic coda where a wounded

Wales finds himself face-to-face with the guerilla leader (John Vernon) he mistakenly assumed had arranged his unit's massacre, each pretending not to recognize the other as they obliquely strike a peace and recognize that, finally, "The war's over."

Whether it was by inclination or for box office insurance, *The Outlaw Josey Wales* still regularly strays into the shoot-'em-up Eastwood formula first staked out in the Leone movies. Like clockwork, Wales constantly bumps into a bounty hunter (more often, bounty hunter*s*) or his Redleg pursuers, delivers a zingy this-means-war one-liner or two ("Dyin' ain't much of a livin'," he says, trying to dissuade one gunman from taking him on), there's a fast draw, a blaze of gunfire and Wales, no matter how badly outnumbered, emerges victorious, intact, and unmoved (after killing one pair of would-be assassins, he punctuates the episode by disdainfully spitting a large gob of tobacco juice on one corpse's forehead). The movie seems caught between two poles: a routine Eastwood exercise in body counts on the one hand; a mournful, ruminative Western ballad on the other.

Eastwood would not venture another Western for 12 years, but when he did, there was more than a little gumption involved, for in those post-*Heaven's Gate* (1980) years simply making *any* Western was an act of daring, let alone turning out one as retro as *Pale Rider* (1985). The Eastwood/Surtees combine takes *Rider*'s visuals beyond those of *Josey Wales*, pushing for a greater texture, testing the camera's tolerances for shadow, particularly in the dim natural light schemes of the movie's interiors (perhaps a test run for the dark palette of *Bird*). Eastwood and Surtees manage a visual *authenticity* – that hardest of screen sensations to capture: the *feel* of a place — in *Pale Rider* which Michael Cimino couldn't match in *Heaven's Gate* (1980) with five times Eastwood's budget. One can almost smell the dankness and raw wood and mud chinking of the cabin household of struggling small miner Michael Moriarity and his wife Carrie Snodgrass; feel the damp chill of a strip mine where ore is blasted out from open rock face with water cannons.

But, as visually striking as *Pale Rider* is, to the same degree so is it dramatically pallid. The screenplay by Michael Butler and Dennis Shryack is nothing more than a re-hashing of the 1953 classic *Shane* – and not a particularly imaginative rehashing — which also cuts and pastes from earlier Eastwood works. Eastwood's nameless gunman (his clerically-garbed character known only as, "Preacher") is just another – and by now, tired – variant on his Leone era Man With No Name, and his role of other-worldly avenger is a lift from his own *High Plains Drifter*. *Pale Rider* is so painfully familiar that from its opening moments, the audience is simply marking time to the predictable Eastwood-defeats-a-small-army finale. Still, perhaps Eastwood understood the importance of Western rituals to Western fans – or at least Eastwood fans:

Pale Rider was a respectable performer, with a domestic gross of $41.4 million against a lean $6.9 million budget.

In the years following, Eastwood seemed stalled. Much as *Pale Rider* had been an unimpressive rehash of *Shane*, *Heartbreak Ridge* was a similarly uninspired reworking of *The Sands of Iwo Jima* (1949). He reached far afield from his usual beat with *Bird* and *White Hunter, Black Heart*, but while the first gained him a fair measure of critical respect, both performed abysmally at the box office. A return to the action genre with *The Rookie* seemed a tired *pro forma* effort. Then came an offering some would come to consider to be among the best American movies of the last few decades as well as one of the all-time classic Westerns: *Unforgiven*.

When compared to Eastwood's previous work, the artistic maturity of *Unforgiven* is startling. Though one can easily see Eastwood's technical prowess evolve over the course of his directorial career, there's been less of a discernible evolutionary line in his handling of drama. His previous directorial effort – *The Rookie,* released just two years earlier – is pedestrian in every way; Eastwood turning out a by-the-numbers Eastwood actioner long after the appeal of the formula has waned. On the other hand, everything about *Unforgiven* is fresh, yet assured, as if coming from another part of Eastwood's movie-making soul where it had been percolating for years and was only just now ready to appear fully formed. Said *Rolling Stone* at the time, *Unforgiven* was, "A polished piece of rawhide revisionism, it's antiromantic, antiheroic and antiviolent…if it's not recognized right away as a classic, it will be."

There is much about *Unforgiven* which feels a product of aspects of Eastwood's moviemaking process now honed to a fine edge. By 1992, Eastwood had established a work pattern that was, according to a *60 Minutes* profile, "…a study in efficiency, consistently bringing his films in ahead of schedule and under budget"; budgets which, from the outset, nearly always fell below the blockbuster era's vertiginous median. On the set, director Eastwood rarely devotes more than two takes to a scene. Generally working with the same crew time and again, the consequent familiarity produces shoots that are surprisingly speedy and economical. Director Sam Mendes *(American Beauty* [1999]; *Road to Perdition* [2002]) would, 12 years after *Unforgiven*'s release, still marvel in an interview with Charlie Rose at how Eastwood could turn out a movie of such quality after a shoot of only five weeks or so – unheard of for most major studio productions whose shoots routinely run into months.

Yet the shoots themselves, for all their speed, are easygoing, in part because of Eastwood's own laid back, even-toned manner. Along with a crew familiar with Eastwood's needs, what also comes into play is the cast preparation which goes on beforehand. In a 2003 interview, Eastwood himself explained the process as it worked on *Mystic River*, saying how most of his directing of the actors happened long before filming. As each member of the cast was brought on to the project, Eastwood would discuss the material, then send them to Boston – the story's locale – to get a feel for the neighborhoods in which the story played out. He also arranged meetings for the cast with Dennis Lehane, author of the novel upon which the movie was based. Said Eastwood, "….by the time we started everyone was really well schooled on what they wanted to do…"

Nor does Eastwood allow himself to be distracted by the non-essential. If the weather takes an unwanted turn, an effect doesn't come off, an actor fumbles a prop or a move, Eastwood either incorporates the unexpected into the scene providing a sense of spontaneity for his actors, or drops the element altogether.

Having established a system composed of talent Eastwood could trust – crew members with a long, established working relationship with him; actors who already know what is expected of them — Eastwood comes to a shoot like the designer of a finely engineered car whom only ever has to lightly lay his fingertips on the wheel on occasion to get the car to go where he wants it. That "light touch on the wheel" manifests itself on-screen as what Sam Mendes described as "certainty"; a visual economy which says Eastwood knows exactly what he needs to tell his story, and has put a team together who knows how to give it to him.

This presents on-screen as visuals which, while never bland, are simple and clean. The camera in *Unforgiven* almost never moves rapidly, generally avoids zooms and pans, rarely moves in for extreme close-ups giving his actors room to interact, and allows beats for Jack N. Green's autumnal cinematography to bring something to every scene. Dialogue-heavy scenes play out at a natural rhythm with minimal interruption by cuts or distracting camera moves.

The two most significant differences elevating *Unforgiven* far beyond Eastwood's previous attempts at heavier dramatic fare are the principal actors, and David Webb Peoples' Oscar-nominated screenplay.

Prior to *Unforgiven*, Eastwood vehicles – whether directed by the actor or not – were populated with second tier performers, some of which, like Geoffrey Lewis *(Every Which Way But Loose; Any Which Way You Can; Pink Cadillac* [1989]*)*, John Vernon *(Dirty Harry; The Outlaw Josey Wales)*, Bill McKinney *(Thunderbolt and Lightfoot* [1974]*; The Gauntlet* [1977]*; Bronco Billy; The Outlaw Josey Wales)*, and John Mitchum *(Dirty Harry; Magnum Force* [1973]*, The Enforcer* [1976]*; The Outlaw Josey Wales)*, were part of a John Ford-like stock company Eastwood regularly drew on to fill supporting parts. While many of Eastwood's "company players" were quite fine performers, they also, unfortunately, often gave Eastwood's pictures – especially his more "serious" dramatic efforts like *Honky Tonk Man* and *White Hunter, Black Heart* — a

B-caliber air. *Unforgiven* marked the first time Eastwood surrounded himself with actors of comparable stature – Gene Hackman, Morgan Freeman, and Richard Harris – an ensemble which gives the picture a dramatic *gravitas* Eastwood's earlier serious efforts never managed.

The real strength of the movie, though, is David Webb Peoples' screenplay. At first, *Unforgiven* offers all the elements of another Eastwood-as-avenger yarn: Eastwood is a retired gunman turned failing pig farmer who, out of economic necessity, takes up his gun again to become one of a trio trekking to the far-off town of Big Whiskey, Wyoming, in pursuit of a bounty on a pair of cowboys who mutilated a prostitute. Peoples' plot is a twisting, turning, eel-like thing, though, worming away from genre-conditioned expectations to deliver, in the words of *Entertainment Weekly* reviewer Chris Willman, "…a compelling sermon on how even the best-intentioned justice gets messy and inexact." "In this film," says Eastwood, "the punishment never fits the crime." *Unforgiven* is unconventionally structured, defying the oft applied Hollywood canard that every scene should propel a movie's plot forward. Instead, *Unforgiven* digresses, it pauses for throw-away scenes and sub-stories having little or no connection to the central plot, it switches focus between its two principals (Eastwood's gunman William Munny and Gene Hackman's autocratic Big Whiskey sheriff, Little Bill) and follows them off on tangents, even shifting emphasis from the plot which kicked off the movie to the spun-off tale of vengeance that concludes it. The movie plays, then, less like the typical Hollywood construct than a disease vector study, tracing the virulent, corrupting toxicity of the movie's initial, priming act of violence as it passes by contact randomly but naturally from one character to another, killing souls as lethally as people as it goes along. There is, by the movie's end, no vindicating act, no resolution restoring the scales of justice, no catharsis, no uplifting epiphany, nothing even remotely resembling triumph. Instead, the innocent have died along with the guilty, and there has been little clear demarcation between the Good Guys and the Bad Guys, between victims and victimizers. Often, characters are both. Peoples says, "I have a hard time being on anybody's side in anything. I'm inclined to see everybody's point of view," which makes *Unforgiven* one of the most provocative of morality plays; one in which it becomes nearly impossible to divine rightness of action, of how to do good without also doing harm. "(It's) easy to imagine," wrote Willman, "the 'bad guys' killed by Eastwood (in *Unforgiven*) as heroes in some other movie." "The world of *Unforgiven*," said *Rolling Stone*, "is a complicated world. It's an adult world. It's a world where violence doesn't solve any problems, it just changes the problem."

Eastwood's gunman William Munny sums up the movie's ethos with one of *Unforgiven*'s signature lines. As wannabe gunslinger The Schofield

Kid (Jaimz Woolvett) tries to drown his self-disgust over his first killing with liquor, he tries to ease his conscience by the idea that the man he'd killed "… had it comin'." Eastwood's scarred and time-ravaged face looks out at the messenger carrying the whores' bounty toward them and says, "We've all got it comin', Kid."

Unforgiven was as un-Hollywood a major studio Western as had appeared on big screens since *The Wild Bunch* (1969). It also marked a maturing in the sensibility of its star and director. "(It's) the first time," Eastwood would say at the time of the movie's release, "I've…been able to interpret it in a way that death is not a fun thing." The Eastwood persona of old – the Dirty Harry-esque avenger who "…just 'removed' …" the opposition -- was gone.

Unforgiven, with its acclaim and awards, announced a new stage in Eastwood's career. He was no longer an actor/director, but a director/actor, and a "serious" director at that.

He came to seem to prefer being behind the camera rather than in front of it. Eastwood's turn as an aging Secret Serviceman – one of his best performances – in the Wolfgang Petersen-directed *In the Line of Fire* (1993) was, as of this writing, his last time in front of the camera on an actor-for-hire basis. He was no more than a supporting player in *A Perfect World* (1993), and didn't appear at all in *Midnight in the Garden of Good and Evil* (1997), or *Mystic River.* Regularly, now, learning one of the lessons of *Unforgiven,* his movies would be cast with an eye toward dramatic heft, i.e. Kevin Costner and Laura Dern in *A Perfect World;* Meryl Streep in *The Bridges of Madison County* (1995); Kevin Spacey and John Cusack in *Midnight in the Garden of Good and Evil;* Gene Hackman, Ed Harris, Scott Glenn, Laura Linney, Judy Davis, and E.G. Marshall in *Absolute Power* (1997); James Woods and Anthony Zerbe in *True Crime* (1999);Tommy Lee Jones, James Garner, Donald Sutherland, David Cromwell, Marcia Gay Harden, and William Devane in *Space Cowboys* (2000); and Jeff Daniels and Angelica Huston in *Blood Work* (2002). Yet, by the time of *Blood Work,* one might have been inclined to wonder whether or not *Unforgiven* had been a fluke, or, at the very least, Eastwood's come-and-gone creative peak.

Eastwood's directorial craftsmanship was as solid as ever, and he would turn out major commercial successes with *Bridges* and *Space Cowboys.* And, there is something memorable in each effort even if the whole was often less than the sum of its parts: Kevin Spacey's magnetic performance as a snobby, gay, antique dealer in *Midnight in the Garden of Good and Evil;* sparkling scenes between Eastwood and Ed Harris in *Absolute Power,* and with James Woods and Denis Leary in *True Crime;* capturing the heartbreak of the last hours of a family's death row vigil in *True Crime;* bare-bottomed Tommy Lee Jones, James Garner, Donald Sutherland and Eastwood gamely playing their ages as a quartet of decrepit astronauts assembling for one, last mission in *Space Cowboys;* Eastwood inverting his macho image as a retired FBI agent who has received a heart transplant, his face twisting in fear as he covers up his scarred chest when fists start flying in *Blood Work;* distilling the syrup out of novelist Robert James Waller's *The Bridges of Madison County* with the help of screenwriter Richard LaGravenese to turn out a rare, grown-up romance for a grown-up audience featuring grown-up characters.

Yet the sensibility of *Unforgiven* – morally complex, dramatically provocative and resonant – only arose in fleeting moments. His post-*Unforgiven* resume reads like that of one of the studio contract directors of the Old Hollywood mogul era; disparate, eclectic, executing with equal polish whatever the studio chiefs hand his way. Only here, Eastwood was the studio, and the disparate, eclectic choices were his own and, after *Unforgiven,* disappointing. Despite William Goldman's Herculean efforts at streamlining David Balducci's unfocused thriller novel about murder and the White House, *Absolute Power*'s picture of the upper echelons of government is painfully naïve and simplistic, paling next to any random episode of TV series *West Wing; Blood Work*'s tale of a taunting serial killer is a tired hike down an already too-familiar *Silence of the Lambs* (1991) path; *True Crime*'s race-against-time story of a crusading reporter trying to save a man unjustly convicted of murder is a creaky throwback to the newspaper dramas of the 1930s.

Nowhere does Eastwood show his limitations as a director more clearly than in the failed adaptation of John Berendt's non-fiction book, *Midnight in the Garden of Good and Evil.* Eastwood and screenwriter John Lee Hancock are at a loss as to how to handle Berendt's deftly-sculpted collection of what at first seem random tales of the Savannah elite and not-so-elite, disparate threads which slowly coalesce into an account of a scandalous sex-and-murder trial. Eastwood and Hancock respond to the challenge by force-fitting Berendt's material into a more conventional, straight-forward form – including a contrived romance for its narrator hero — that costs the story much of the book's unique charm and enrapturing mystique.

Eastwood came closest to *Unforgiven's* dramatic accomplishments with the half-brilliant *A Perfect World,* also scripted by John Lee Hancock. In what was, at the time, brazen casting, Eastwood took Kevin Costner – then coming off a streak of squeaky clean Good Guy roles – and had him play viciously against type as escaped felon Butch Haynes who takes eight-year-old Phillip (T.J. Lowther) hostage with him on a rambling road trip across Texas. The story could easily have tipped into treacle, a bonding story between surrogate father and surrogate son that, in typical Hollywood fashion, results in the moral rehabilitation of the hard-boiled Haynes, but the movie refuses the trap of audience-satisfying sentimentality. As Hancock discretely alludes to

Haynes' own scarred childhood, the convict's role doesn't so much develop into that of protective father figure as much as Haynes' living out the fantasy of a childhood he never had through young Phillip. Hancock adroitly walks a dramatic high wire in the Haynes/ Phillip plot, balancing between moral lights and darks until in the movie's climax, the story tumbles into a hellish blackness. While sheltering in the home of a family of sharecroppers, Haynes' past dysfunctions are triggered, and, in one of the most chilling scenes Eastwood has ever put on film, the felon prepares with practiced efficiency to murder the farmer in front of his wife and son. As a scratchy country tune plays and repeats on an ancient turntable, Haynes binds the man with duct tape, then his wife and child, then seals the family's eyes shut before turning to Phillip – and in a horrifying corruption of the father/mentor role Haynes has flirted with – tells Phillip he can either watch or leave; "You're old enough to decide for yourself." Eastwood and Hancock deliver, wrote *Film Comment*'s Kent Jones, "…the *ultimate* life lesson: that the same person can be nice and frightening, wise and murderously crazy, all at once."

But, the movie is crippled by a parallel story; the pursuit of Haynes by Texas Ranger Red Garnett (Eastwood). Where the Haynes/Phillip story is bold and complex, the chase is strictly formula; a few cheap jokes, stereotypically sun-glassed government killers, and the sentiment so neatly avoided on one side of the movie is here tripping up the tale of a Texas Ranger with a burdened conscience and a past connection to Haynes.

But then, in 2003 came *Mystic River*, a movie some critics have hailed as one of the best American films in years; to some, in decades.

All of the certainty and assurance marking *Unforgiven* is back in full force in *Mystic River*; in its text (adapted from Dennis Lehane's acclaimed novel by Brian Helgeland who had shared an Oscar with Curtis Hanson for adapting James Ellroy's similarly layered neo-*noir*, *L.A. Confidential* [1997]), its visuals, and its powerful ensemble of principals (Sean Penn, Tim Robbins, Kevin Bacon). Though a modern-day dramatic thriller, *Mystic…* takes on many of the same themes of *Unforgiven* and mines still deeper into their core, particularly that of the toxic quality of violence. When one of three childhood friends is abducted and abused, the incident leaves all three scarred; emotional fault lines which, decades later, fracture in a dominoes-fall series of compounding tragedies Eastwood describes as "…an unraveling." And, also like *Unforgiven*, *Mystic* is a devastating attack on the Hollywood revenge myth; according to *Entertainment Weekly*'s Jeff Jensen, how "…the aching need for justice and closure can cloud wisdom and curdle compassion." Instead, *Mystic* resurrects *Unforgiven*'s thesis that violence is an uncontrollable demon, and that, as William Munny tells a dying Little Bill, "Deserve's got nothin' to do with it."

On balance, one might argue Clint Eastwood is not a great director, but a director capable of great movies. Still, in this — his latest, post-*Unforgiven* incarnation — even in his weakest work, he is a standard bearer for a kind of mainstream movie-making that has become exceedingly rare at the major studio level; one driven not by spectacle, effects, or action, not breathlessly paced, but carried by drama and characters Eastwood aspires to reflect some real aspect of the Everyman, whose stories unspool with an unhurried dignity. Wrote one French critic of Eastwood after *Mystic River*'s screening at the 2003 Cannes film festival, "(He's) a director who has placed himself in the grand Hollywood tradition so cruelly neglected by American cinema." His protagonists from *Unforgiven* on are flawed, limited, often haunted characters, fallible, and still more poignantly, often aware of their fallibilities.

There's a lovely scene in *True Crime* (another example of his ability to instill memorable moments in routine projects) between Eastwood – as a burned-out, divorced, ex-alcoholic reporter trying to get his career back on track – and Denis Leary, his supervising editor who has discovered Eastwood has been having an affair with his wife. No shouting, no histrionics; just two pained and awkward men who realize this is a situation made of their own failings, and who can't find the words to indict (Leary) or to apologize (Eastwood).

His work since *Mystic River* evidences a filmmaker unafraid to challenge himself: first came the heart-breaking Academy Award-winning boxing drama, *Million Dollar Baby* in 2004; in 2006, his depiction of the brutal Battle of Iwo Jima from both the American and Japanese sides with *Flag of Our Fathers* and Oscar-nominated *Letters from Iwo Jima* respectively, the latter brazenly filmed almost entirely in Japanese; 2008's *Gran Torino* which turned his tough-guy, narrow-minded *Dirty Harry* persona on its ear; the South African-set sports drama *Invictus* (2009); and his latest, *Hereafter*, possibly his most spiritual film to date.

It is worth pointing out that there's many a director who has been more qualitatively consistent and more stylistically expansive than Eastwood, yet has never turned out a movie as memorable as *Unforgiven*, or *Mystic River*, or *Million Dollar Baby*, or *Letters from Iwo Jima*. His post-*Unforgiven* works represent a welcome throwback predating an era in American cinema Eastwood once described as being one in which "…there's an awful lot of people hanging on wires and floating across things and comic book characters…"

ARTHUR PENN (1922 – 2010): "…A REALLY NICE GUY"

October 3, 2010

In considering the passing of Arthur Penn last Tuesday, it embarrasses me to admit how little credit I gave him at one time.

It was the mid-'70s, I was a young, arrogant, know-it-all film student at the University of South Carolina. Like so many of us who had newly-found serious study in film, I pontificated at the drop of a hat on great *cinema* and Hollywood dross, like a Columbus endlessly crowing about this New World he'd just discovered…oblivious to the fact the Vikings had beaten me there by centuries, and centuries before *them* the natives had built great empires. Like all the rest of my fellow young film study Turks interested in "serious" moviemaking, I didn't know just how incredibly much I didn't know.

I'd been too young to see *Bonnie & Clyde* when it had been released in 1967, and when I finally got the chance years later, I didn't think much of it. The slow motion violence of its death ballet climax – so shocking in its time – seemed positively tame as slo-mo shoot-'em-up scenes had since become a numbing action movie ritual. And, being as young as I was, I didn't appreciate the *context* of the film; how its outlaws-on-the-run story had, in 1967, plugged into the disillusionment, the rebellious outsider-ism, the angry sense of oppressive Establishment conformity roiling the young people of its day. I was like a naïve archeologist on his first dig, looking at the skeleton of some pre-human, unable to understand where it fit on the evolutionary parade, able only to think, "Jeez, they looked stupid."

Ahh, youth.

By the time I did see *B&C* – and having suffered through the mess of Penn's *Missouri Breaks* not knowing how unmanageable Brando had gotten by that time – I'd come to think of him as a one-hit wonder (well, two: *Little Big Man* – ok, three: *Alice's Restaurant*). He'd gotten lucky, the timing was right, he'd been bailed out by a good script, a good editor, etc.

What I'd missed and had never really understood was that Penn was not a film director. He was a storyteller. Or, if you want to give it a fancy name, a *dramatist.* He moved between TV and film and the Broadway stage, and was accomplished in each. On TV, his career stretched from the days of live drama to *Law & Order.* In film, he'd been three times nominated for Oscars, and he was a Tony Award-winning stage director whose credits included *The Miracle Worker* (which he also directed for the screen earning his first Oscar nod), *Wait Until Dark,* and *An Evening with Nichols and May.*

I used to hold it against him that he didn't have a distinctive visual style. You could look at the work of his fellow live TV grads and could always tell a Frankenheimer film, a Lumet, an Altman. Nor could he hold a candle to the new film brats coming into the Hollywood mainstream with him: Coppola, Scorsese, DePalma et al.

But that *was* Penn's style. Not to let you know that he was there; just to produce good work. It wasn't about *him;* it was about the *work.*

Look at *Little Big Man.* It's a filmic novel with a hundred chapters, each invaluable, each perfectly cast, perfectly told, each a tile perfectly placed in a grand, epic mosaic about an entire people falling under the steam roller of the white colonization of the Old West. There are scenes that are no more than a shot or two, parts with no more than a few lines. Knowing he would often have little more than seconds to establish character in his breakneck-paced epic, Penn cast actors familiar (Martin Balsam, Jeff Corey ad infinitum) and unfamiliar who could make their stamp immediately, deliver their few lines just *so,* producing, in the end, a movie of a thousand memorable moments.

If Penn didn't produce many big screen hits, it may have been that he was just too damned smart for commercial moviemaking. I began to re-think my opinion of him as, over the years, I'd see him pop up in documentaries about the movie business, or about particular stars or other directors, certain films, and the like. I was always struck in those instances by his obvious intelligence, his insight, his sense of how the subject at hand fit into a bigger picture, and yet he didn't pontificate or pronounce. There was always a certain unpretentiousness to him, an earthiness.

An acquaintance of mine, Stephen Whitty, the lead film critic for *The Star-Ledger,* had interviewed Penn on occasion. Along with all his other attributes – his sharpness of mind, his perception, and so on – the two things Whitty was most impressed by was that "…Penn was not one to promote himself…" Talking to Penn about his biggest hit, *Bonnie & Clyde,* Whitty was struck by how Penn talked about what star/producer Warren Beatty, rewrite artist Robert Towne, and damned near everybody else brought to the project – but nothing about his own role in helping it all come together.

And the other thing Whitty remembers is something one rarely hears about the major players in Hollywood, and would serve as a welcome valediction for any passing: "He just seemed to me like a really nice guy."

ERNEST BORGNINE (1917 – 2012): "KEEP GOING"

July 11, 2012

When the drama *Marty* won the Academy Award for the Best Picture of 1955, it was a win of many wins, and not just because the movie walked off with three other Oscars.

It signaled that the balance of creative power in Hollywood was shifting; that the monopoly of the major studios was fading, and that a new breed of independent companies – often formed with or by the stars who had, at one time, been held in bondage to the majors under long-term contracts – were now serious players in the industry *(Marty* had been produced by Hecht-Lancaster which had been formed by Burt Lancaster and producer Harold Hecht).

It was a victory for a new kind of anti-Hollywood storytelling; unglamorous tales about unglamorous people, *real* people. Postwar Italian neo-realism had demonstrated the power of the drama of everyday people just trying to get through a day, and *Marty* and other films like it *(The Catered Affair* [1956], *Edge of the City* [1957], etc.) took up that torch here in America.

It was also a win for a new kind of leading man, because *Marty* didn't star some lantern-jawed, brilliantined matinee idol, but dumpy, broad-faced Ernest Borgnine.

At the time of *Marty*, Borgnine had already been kicking around for quite a few years, and then only after getting a late start in acting. He'd come out of ten years in the Navy in 1945 when his mother pushed him toward acting. He made his Broadway debut with a small part in 1949's *Harvey*, then relocated to Los Angeles and landed his first movie roles in 1951.

His career took off in 1953 with *From Here to Eternity* and his role as sadistic stockade sergeant "Fatso" Judson who beats weedy little Frank Sinatra to death. *Eternity* kicked off a host of roles as heavies for which Borgnine – with his bulk, gap-toothed alligator smile, and wide eyes which seemed to dance at the prospect of inflicting pain – was a natural, such as the bully who gives a one-armed Spencer Tracy such a hard time in *Bad Day at Black Rock* (1955).

Eternity may have been a career booster, but Borgnine always felt he owed his career to director Robert Aldrich. After Aldrich cast him in the boisterous Western adventure *Vera Cruz* (1954), Borgnine became one of the director's go-to performers, appearing in five other features for the director including *The Flight of the Phoenix* (1965) and action classic *The Dirty Dozen* (1967).

But Aldrich's biggest contribution to Borgnine's career was in recommending him to director Delbert Mann for *Marty*. Mann didn't want him; Borgnine played thugs and bone-breakers, but the titular character of *Marty* was a lonely, thirty-something Brooklyn butcher still living with his mother. Aldrich lobbied, Mann gave in, and the movie walked off with Oscars for Best Picture, Borgnine as Best Actor, Mann for Best Director, and Paddy Chayefsky for the screenplay based on his 1953 live TV drama.

Borgnine would never again catch a role as rich as Marty Piletti, but then most actors go their entire careers without ever getting one. And Borgnine nailed it: his awkward first date with Betsy Drake, his wincing discomfort as his friends castigate him for going out with "a dog," his painful self-awareness of his utter ordinariness. *Marty* and Borgnine's performance still stand as one of the most moving paeans to the average everyday guy to ever make it to the big screen, and his defiant rebuttal to one of his denigrating friends is their anthem:

> "She's a dog. And I'm a fat, ugly man. Well, all I know is I had a good time last night. I'm gonna have a good time tonight. If we have enough good times together, I'm gonna get down on my knees. I'm gonna *beg* that girl to marry me. If we make a party on New Year's, I got a date for that party. You don't like her? That's too bad!"

The movie's impression on popular culture of the time can be measured in how its bits and pieces echoed in the culture-sphere for years. Twelve years later, it still resonated enough to be lampooned in a scene from Disney's 1967 *The Jungle Book* as a pair of vultures gave their spin on one of the most memorable bits of dialogue from *Marty*: "...so what're we gonna do?" "I dunno. Whadda *you* wanna do?"

Marty may have been Borgnine's artistic acme, but he still had a long, productive career ahead of him. He was not only ripe for character parts, but he had that unteachable, unlearnable, undefinable gift all long-lasting actors have: people enjoyed watching him. Whether he played a heavy or a hero, bigger than life or slice of life, people enjoyed him.

Marty established his artistic bonafides, but the early 1960s slapsticky sitcom *McHale's Navy* did more for his popularity than a decade's worth of solid work and an Oscar had. For the remainder of his incredibly long (61 years) career, Borgnine moved easily between the big screen and small, amassing an astounding range of roles, sometimes in classics (Sam Peckinpah's revisionist Western *The Wild Bunch* [1969]), sometimes in mainstream hits (disaster flick *The Poseidon Adventure* [1972]), sometimes in the most forgettable of celluloid junk (horror clunker *The Devil's Rain* [1975]).

Good or bad, he didn't care. All that mattered was the work. He would often say acting was his greatest passion: "I don't care whether a part is ten minutes long or two hours, and I don't care whether my name is up there on top, either."

As he grew older, his ongoing presence seemed to be one treasured by young directors: John Carpenter cast him as the garrulous Cabbie in *Escape from New York* (1981); Joe Dante used his voice in *Small Soldiers* (1998); and still going strong in his 90s, Borgnine found himself in the geriatric-skewed actioner *Red* (2010).

And, in a delightful inside joke for parents of *SpongeBob SquarePants* fans, Borgnine was re-teamed with his *McHale's Navy* co-star and friend, Tim Conway, in the recurring parts of semi-senile superhero Mermaid Man and his more able sidekick, Barnacle Boy.

"I think you have to keep going," Borgnine once said when asked about possibly retiring. And he did: through over 100 feature films, three TV series, countless guest appearances and voice roles, working almost up until the last with a part in *The Man Who Shook the Hand of Vicente Fernandez* which completed filming this year.

In a way, perhaps the greatest disservice Ernest Borgnine did to those of us who grew up watching him was to last so long. His constancy made him seem a permanent fixture of the film universe, and now it seems as if one of the stars in that universe has, at long last, winked out and left the sky just that little bit darker.

5 FORGOTTEN GEMS FROM FIVE GREAT MOVIE MUSIC COMPOSERS

January 14, 2013

Anybody who has ever been to a high school reunion (and I've been to my share) will tell you that the calendar and the clock can be incredibly cruel (particularly when combined with the long-term effects of gravity, but let's not go there).

Time punishes creative works as well. Some work grows dated, stale, stiff. Time and the evolving form of the given art can leave a once vibrant and exciting work behind looking dead and obsolete.

More cruel, perhaps, is work that is simply...forgotten. Not for any good reason. Good as it was, maybe it was simply not successful enough to lodge very deeply in the popular consciousness; working well enough in its day, but soon lost among the ever-growing detritus of a lot of other pieces of yesterday.

Movie music is particularly vulnerable to the cruelties of time. Outside of the form's devotees, it rarely makes much of an impression with the general public at all. Beyond John Williams or, in his day, Henry Mancini, it's hard to think of a film composer whose name ever meant much to the average moviegoer. They might even be able to whistle the "Colonel Bogey March" from *The Bridge on the River Kwai* (1957), la-daaaaa la-da-da-daaaaaa their way through the theme from *The Magnificent Seven* (1960), but mention the names Elmer Bernstein or Malcolm Arnold (who adopted the 1914 march for *Kwai*) and you're likely to get a blank stare.

But even those of us who consider ourselves students of The Cinema, well, we're not always the discerning gourmets we like to think we are. We forget, too. We remember the greats for their great work which, in turn, is what makes the greats great. But we often forget the work they did – sometimes dues-paying work, sometimes part of their creative evolution – on their way to greatness (quick: how many of you know Elmer Bernstein scored *Robot Monster* [1953], maybe the only movie that can give *Plan 9 from Outer Space* [1959] a run for the money as worst movie of all time?).

Here's five scores by five top-of-the-line movie music kings that most of us probably don't remember...but should.

Seven Days in May (1964)
Music by Jerry Goldsmith

Until John Williams bombasted his way to the top of the heap, Goldsmith (1929-2004) was the the gold standard. He began writing music for radio dramas in the 1950s, crossed over to TV before the decade was out, and became a recognized name in the movie industry with his melancholic, rustic score for the contemporary Western *Lonely Are the Brave* (1962). He quickly became a go-to composer for A-features and was particularly recognized for demonstrating – in atonal, avant garde-styled scores for *Freud* (1962), *Planet of the Apes* (1968), and *Alien* (1979) — that a good movie score didn't particularly have to be hummable.

One of Goldsmith's hallmarks was his restraint. Even in his lush scores for *The Blue Max* (1966) and *Patton* (1970), Goldsmith reined in his brass, let his strings flex their muscles, holding his horns in reserve to take heightening emotion that one last step to the peak.

He could also find the gold in the mournful wailing of a single, lonely trumpet, a signature he used to great effect in *Lonely Are the Brave*, and even better in one of his best scores: *Chinatown* (1974, composed in just 10 days to replace a pre-existing score, and rated #9 on the American Film Institute's list of Top 25 film scores).

Goldsmith also knew when to shut up. The first half-hour or so of medical thriller *Coma* (1978) has no music at all, Goldsmith only stepping up when the movie moves from its more naturalistic first act deeper into its mystery plot.

But nowhere did Goldsmith exercise as tight a discipline, or as innovative a concept, as he did in his score for John Frankenheimer's 1964 political thriller, *Seven Days in May*. There are less than eight minutes of music in the 118 minute movie. Goldsmith trusted what was on the screen, saw the strength in Frankenheimer's clean black-and-white visuals, in the gallery of strong performances led by Kirk Douglas and Burt Lancaster, in the literate, compelling script by Rod Serling.

For a movie about a planned military coup to take over the government of the U.S., Goldsmith found the movie's sound in a score composed completely for percussion. The movie's main theme is simply a series of building drums beating out the same, unstoppable march, rising to a crescendo topped off by metallic-sounding xylophone strikes.

It's a tight, minimalist, militaristic, surprisingly powerful score, and like the best movie scores, a perfect fit.

None but the Brave (1965)
Music by John Williams

Today, he's one of the most recognized, financially successful, and awarded movie music-makers on the planet. But, in the 1950s, John Williams (b. 1932) was working as an orchestrator and pianist for other movie composers (including his good friend, Jerry Goldsmith). That's Williams you hear pounding out that pulsating piano rhythm for Henry Mancini's iconic TV theme for *Peter Gunn*. By the 1960s, he'd become producer Irwin Allen's go-to guy for a slew of energetic, TV sci fi juvenilia i.e. *Lost in Space*, *The Time Tunnel*, and *Land of the Giants*. Allen liked Williams pushy, brass-heavy scores enough that when the producer stepped up to be the Master of Disaster with big screen FX-fests like *The Poseidon Adventure* (1972) and *The Towering Inferno* (1974), he took Williams with him.

But undoubtedly one of the biggest catalysts in Williams' career was when Steven Spielberg tapped him to score his 1974 thriller/drama, *The Sugarland Express*. *Express* didn't light up the box office, but Spielberg had found a creative partner and took Williams with him to his next project: *Jaws* (1975). The movie's two-note leitmotif was an instant classic and Spielberg hasn't made a movie without Williams since. When George Lucas was putting together *Star Wars* (1977), Spielberg recommended Williams to his friend and another iconic collaboration was born.

Since then, Williams has composed almost exclusively for big-budget flicks which provide a perfect growth culture for his penchant for neoromantic fullness. Whereas Goldsmith tended to hold his brass back, Williams often leads with it, lets it carry the day, starting strong and ending stronger. Williams has done so many of these epic-sounding scores, it's hard to remember, if remembered at all, that he has other colors.

One of Williams' earliest feature scores – and, I think, one of his best – was for the 1965 WW II film *None but the Brave*, remembered by trivia nuts as the one film directed by Frank Sinatra. The movie concerns a plane-load of Marines who crashland on a long-bypassed island still occupied by a small unit of Japanese soldiers. It's an impassioned if pedantic anti-war plea as the two groups of antagonists slowly learn to co-exist on the island, but ultimately are compelled by duty to engage in a final, pointless fight.

Sinatra was much better on-camera or crooning into a microphone than he was in the director's seat, and the movie emerges as an earnest, watchable, but not overly memorable effort.

But Williams' score beautifully captures the spirit of the film, its well-intended grasping for that grand idea synopsized by the movie's closing shot of the island and the superimposed line: "Nobody ever wins."

Unlike Williams' later, brass-heavy works, the opening theme, after an initial, announcing single horn, is driven by a Goldsmithesque swelling of strings which continue to carry the score. Even better are the melancholy closing minutes: the strings, now gentle, and a single, sad trumpet commemorate the wasted dead. As the few surviving Americans await a rescue pick-up on the beach, the voice of the dead Japanese commander (Tatsuya Mihashi) – his prescient words those of a manuscript written to his wife, now carried by American commander Clint Walker – intones, over Williams' beautifully understated but mournful music, that "There is no death where the spirit lives. So this was just another day, and I say to you good night."

Few of the films Williams has worked on over the last 30 years have given him the opportunity to so deftly capture the sense of loss, of tragic waste, of aspiration toward something better granted him by *None but the Brave*.

The Taking of Pelham One Two Three (1974)
Music by David Shire

Shire (b. 1937) may not have the name recognition of John Williams or Jerry Goldsmith, but in a career spanning more than five decades, he's amassed a body of impressive and respected work. His earliest professional compositions were collaborations with lyricist Richard Maltby on stage musicals (he continues to go back to the stage regularly and has been nominated for the Tony several times for his Broadway work). Within a few years, he was composing scores for TV and by the 1970s he was working on big screen projects as well.

His range is dazzling: from the original music for the movie that kicked off the disco craze, *Saturday Night Fever* (1977), to David Fincher's dark, disturbing true-life thriller, *Zodiac* (2007).

But of all his work, perhaps most distinctive is his score for the original *The Taking of Pelham One Two Three* (1974). While the film about the hijacking of a New York subway train, in time, would become one of the more memorable thrillers of the 1970s, it was a flop in its day, but no one who saw the movie could forget Shire's pounding, pumping main theme. With an urban jazz-funk beat, a rolling rhythm that caught the metal-on-metal movement of a train, it's a seamless melding of music and movie.

For all that, it's a restrained score, intruding rarely. But when it's there, it juices a non-stop thriller into hyper drive, as it does during a frantic money-counting sequence driven largely by a frantic piano.

Once you listen to Shire's main theme, Harry Gregson-Williams' score for Tony Scott's 2009 remake seems all the more characterless and as detached from the gritty heart of the Big Apple as its host film. Shire's music, on the other hand, is as New York as, well, "New York, New York," so much so that it was adapted as the unofficial theme of the New York subway system's #6 line (the line supposedly shown in the movie).

Marathon Man (1976)
Music by Michael Small

Ironically, Small (1939-2003) did his most memorable work...small. His signature scores are wonderfully atmospheric yet thinly orchestrated. There's almost something Brian Eno-esque about his best work, and *Marathon Man* is no exception.

Small began his career doing background music for New York stage productions. But when film producer Edward Pressman heard his work and asked him to score the teen pic *Out of It* (1969), Small made the jump to the big screen.

Like any film composer worth his or her salt, Small was wonderfully versatile. Bob Rafelson would hire him for his broody 1981 remake of the classic *noir*, *The Postman Always Rings Twice*, as well as for his capacity for more expansive, soaring work for the period adventure, *Mountains of the Moon* (1990).

But his trademark scores were his low-key, moody compositions for thrillers like *Klute* (1971), *The Parallax View* (1974), and *The Star Chamber* (1983). His best: *Marathon Man* (1976).

Dustin Hoffman is a Columbia grad student dragged into a shadowy underworld of fugitive Nazis and government dirty goings-on through the murder of his brother. The big villain, played by Laurence Olivier in an Oscar-nominated role, had been a dentist in a wartime concentration camp, and Small shrewdly introduces, as a recurring motif, a drill-like trill into his score.

Small works more with mood than melody: a few well chosen low notes, the thin trickle of a piano, that whining, whirring trill, the low thrum of heavy strings. Dark, rain-slicked streets become darker, the whole film feels appropriately damp and melancholy, autumnal. Yet one of Small's best moments is his more fluid, rising passage for a montage sequence tracing the romance between Hoffman and Marthe Keller – a romance which, like all of the relationships in the movie, is both tainted and doomed by its connection to malevolent forces of which Hoffman is, for the moment, ignorant.

As a thriller, *Marathon Man* was one of the best for its very human character; Hoffman is no superhero, the plot involves no super villains or grand master plans. All of its characters have a heft rarely seen in thrillers, and Small captures that gravitas, all those sad histories which seem to have fore-damned *Marathon Man's* characters, and the loss which ultimately hangs over its one survivor.

Straw Dogs (1971)
Music by Jerry Fielding

Jerry Fielding (1922-1980) started out as an arranger during the Big Band era of the 1930s and 1940s. His work with the Big Bands led to music jobs on radio which, in turn, led him to TV where he did the music for the Groucho Marx quiz show, *You Bet Your Life*. But headstrong and combative and, by his own admission, "a loudmouth," Fielding fell afoul of the McCarthy era blacklist and was banned from film and TV until hardheaded producer/director Otto Preminger tapped Fielding for his first big screen assignment, scoring the 1962 political drama, *Advise and Consent*.

His blacklist status now broken, Fielding worked heavily in television for much of the 1960s, providing music for everything from the original *Star Trek* series to slapstick sitcom *McHale's Navy* to thriller *Mission: Impossible*. His biggest break came in 1969 with his acclaimed and rousing score for Sam Peckinpah's classic Western, *The Wild Bunch*.

Fielding became Peckinpah's go-to guy and he would compose three more scores for the filmmaker. He would also establish long-running and fruitful relationships with Clint Eastwood and Michael Winner.

The Wild Bunch remains one of Peckinpah's most-beloved films which is probably why Fielding's other work for the director is not as well-remembered. I would argue that as good as his work on *Bunch* is, his more nuanced, more atmospheric work on *Straw Dogs* is even better.

Dustin Hoffman is an academic hiding from the social unrest of the time by removing himself to the Cornish countryside with trophy wife Susan George. But Hoffman can't avoid strife and he finds himself on the wrong side of a vigilante mob during the film's shattering climax.

Fielding's score is a brooding piece of mellow, atonal horns and woodwinds, and subdued strings which capture the damp, lonely emptiness of the Cornish moors, and the pagan, barbaric feel of a place that's never completely let the outside, modern world in. As pensive as *The Wild Bunch* was cathartic, as aimed at the intellect as *Bunch* was at the gut, Fielding's score for *Straw Dogs* was one of his smartest, bravest pieces of work.

HOLIDAY THOUGHTS: *IT'S A WONDERFUL LIFE* AND *MIRACLE ON 34TH STREET*

December 24, 2012

    I hadn't moved out on my own yet, so it must've been the late 1970s. It was still the early days of cable. I think we had maybe two dozen channels, a number of them being out-of-town local stations like WGBH out of Boston, and WGN out of Chicago, as well as a handful of PBS stations we'd never been able to get via our old rooftop antenna.

    The cable spectrum was growing rapidly, but faster than the amount of programming available to fill it. And that was when America re-discovered *It's a Wonderful Life* (1946).

    The movie's copyright had run out and the film had fallen into public domain. That meant that anybody and his brother who could get their hands on a print could air it…and they did. For a few years there, you couldn't punch your way through the buttons on your cable box without bumping into *Wonderful Life* a couple of times on damned near every night in the week or so leading up to Christmas.

    My brother, six years younger than me, was always a bit of a sentimentalist. After the first time he'd gotten a taste of Capra's paean to the underappreciated value of human decency, he took to it like some kind of fanatical new convert to a newborn faith. He would make us watch it whenever it was on, summon us from wherever we were in our small four-room apartment to plop together on the sofa and boo-hoo our way through the finale…together.

    And whenever he wasn't making us sit through *Wonderful Life*, he was making us sit through *Miracle on 34th Street* (1947). *Miracle* wasn't in the public domain, but because we were getting all these out-of-town channels and, apparently, they all had a license for *Miracle*, we wound up sitting through it as much as we did *Wonderful Life*.

    Which wasn't nearly as boring as it might sound.

    Maybe it was the distinctive magic of each of those movies: one reminding us that what we'd forgotten still mattered, the other rekindling a childhood belief we'd always regretted losing. Maybe it was the simple act of watching them together. I don't know.

    What I do know is that each year, while my mother and I joked about my brother's annual corralling of us on the sofa (my father had passed away some years earlier), and we'd grumble when he did it, we still fell into line, did as we were bade, and participated in the annual tearing up.

    Eventually, I would move out, and so would my brother, and *Wonderful Life* was withdrawn from public domain, re-copyrighted, and has since only run once a year on NBC. My brother lives in Virginia, my mother passed away earlier this year.

As many times as I've seen both movies, I still get misty at their finales. I get teary when George Bailey finally, belatedly, almost too late realizes just what a great life he has, and I get teary when judge Gene Lockhart says there really is a Santa Claus, but I get the biggest lump in my throat for the memories those movies stir; of a crowded sofa in a small apartment, a mother and her sons, and a lovely, lovely bit of Christmas.

MEMENTO MORI: REMEMBERING THOSE WE LOST IN 2011

December 24, 2011

In October of 2010, *Sound on Sight* asked me to do my first commemorative piece on the passing of filmmaker Arthur Penn. I suspect I was asked because I was the only one writing for the site old enough to have seen Penn's films in theaters. Whatever the reason, it was an unexpectedly rewarding if expectedly bittersweet experience which led to a series of equally rewarding but bittersweet experiences writing on the passing of other filmdom notables.

I say rewarding because it gave me a nostalgia-flavored chance to revisit certain work and the people behind it; a revisiting which often brought back the nearly-forgotten youthful excitement that went with an eye-opening, a discovery, the thrill of the new. Writing them has also been bittersweet because each of these pieces is a formal acknowledgment that something precious is gone. A talent may be perhaps preserved forever on celluloid, but the filmography now had a terminus; no additions, no more new chapters.

Some of the losses get by me. As I was thumbing through the most recent issue of *Entertainment Weekly*, a year-end "Best & Worst of 2011" edition, I was surprised at how many familiar names showed up in the issue's "Late Greats" section having passed without my knowing it. With your permission, I'd like to pay a quick homage to some of them; for all the entertaining hours they gave me in front of both the big and small screen, it would seem ungrateful on my part not to acknowledge their departure.

I grew up watching **Harry Morgan** (b. 1915). His was one of those Familiar Faces which seemed a permanent part – a Rushmore – of the entertainment landscape. When I was a kid, I watched him steal scenes as the next door neighbor in syndicated re-runs of 1950s sitcom *December Bride,* and then there he was, back again, in the 1960s revival of the granddaddy of all police procedurals, *Dragnet,* playing Jack Webb's head-nodding partner. Seemingly eternal, he came back yet again in the 1970s as the grandfatherly commanding officer on the TV adaptation of *M*A*S*H.* And there were a hundred other guest appearances, other series, and God knows how many movies. That flat Midwestern nasal twang of his was pitch-perfect for the often caustic, wry pitch which was his trademark. He was a hoot the minute he opened his mouth in movies like *The Flim-Flam Man* (1967), *Support Your Local Sheriff* (1967), and what seems like a million others. Because he was so closely associated with comedy, few knew how much dramatic muscle he could muster, and if you really want to see Morgan's range, watch him as Henry Fonda's brooding sidekick in *The Ox-Bow Incident* (1943). "I didn't really start out to be an actor," Morgan once said, "I just sort of fell into it. I've had a good career, a lot of laughs. I don't know if that's enough, but it beats coal mining." Amen and thanks for a million laughs and a few lumps in the throat, Harry.

G.D. Spradlin (b. 1920) was another Familiar Face we lost in 2011. Most probably remember him as the slimy, corrupt senator in *The Godfather: Part II*. With his tall, lean, erect frame, Spradlin was often cast as stern authority figures: the coach in *North Dallas Forty* (1979), the patrician commanding officer of a military school in *The Lords of Discipline* (1983), and the like. But Francis Ford Coppola saw something in Spradlin most directors never asked for, and gave him the mold-breaking part of a compassionate, troubled military man in *Apocalypse Now* (1979). You want to see a pro at work? Watch the look in Spradlin's eyes, hear the softening in his voice as he tells assassin Martin Sheen how his one-time friend (Marlon Brando) has given in to the insanity of the Vietnam War and gone bloodily insane himself.

Dana Wynter (b. 1931) holds a special place in the hearts of sci fi fans of which I consider myself a member of the club. She co-starred with Kevin McCarthy in the original *The Invasion of the Body Snatchers* (1956). I can never forget that close up director Don Siegel gives her near the end of the film when she's kissed by McCarthy who realizes – looking into her flat, cold eyes – that he's lost his beloved to the invading pods.

When it comes to *Star Trek*, I'm a purist; it's the original 1960s series for me and the rest can be beamed elsewhere. As such, I couldn't help but feel a pang at the passing of **William Campbell** (b. 1923), another one of those, "Oh, *that* guy!" supporting players. Campbell never graduated past the B-list, and was usually cast as some kind of silky slimeball. But, like most character actors, he had more range than he was usually given credit for. I remember him as the brash-talking Confederate trooper father-son bonding with crusty William Demarest in *Escape from Fort Bravo* (1953), and his disturbing scene in the WW II actioner *Breakthrough* (1950) where he's unable to pull himself clear of a burning tank because "I got no legs!" But the Trekkie in me remembers him best for his role in the episode, "The Squire of Gothos," one of the original series' best. Cambell eats up the part of the foppish alien Trelane with a spoon, the torments he inflicts on Captain Kirk & Co. turning out to be the pulling-the-wings-off-flies sociopathology of a child masquerading as an adult.

Brit **Pete Postlethwaite** (b. 1946) already had an extensive resume, particularly in UK TV, when I first noticed him, as most American audiences did, as the mysterious Kobayashi, minion of the feared master criminal, Keyser Sose, in *The Usual Suspects* (1995). But I didn't appreciate the range and depth of the guy until I later caught on cable his earlier performance in the true-life drama, *In the Name of the Father* (1993). Kobayashi is an austere, still pillar in an immaculately tailored suit, an agent of unbounded malevolence, the high priest of bad guys' boogeyman Sose. Giuseppe Conlon from *Father*, on the other hand, is a hunched, frail and fearful figure, whose one, great strength is his love for his bedeviled son (Daniel Day-Lewis). In the British tradition, he was a pro who brought dignity and class to whatever set he stepped on, from sci-fi like *Inception* (2010), to a hardboiled contemporary *noir* like *The Town* (2010).

Composer **John Barry** (b. 1933) may have had as much to do with turning James Bond into an international, inter-generational brand as anybody involved with the franchise. Barry was the composer on all of the early Bonds, and his brassy, kinetic scores were a signature of the series. He may have been most closely identified with the Bonds, but Barry had other colors, too: epic grandeur in *Zulu* (1964) and *Born Free* (1966), faded romance in *Robin and Marian* (1976), neo-*noir* sultriness in *Body Heat* (1981). My personal favorite: the melancholy, harmonica-carried theme from *Midnight Cowboy* (1969) which so painfully captured the isolation and disillusionment of souls lost amid the neon-lit canyons of a (then) decaying New York City.

I had an incredible crush on **Susannah York** (b. 1939) in the 1960s. She was a perfect Carnaby Street icon of the time with her lithe, short-haired, mini-skirted casual sexiness. It didn't hurt that she was also a hell of an actress, something she would prove time and again in films like *Tom Jones* (1963), *A Man for All Seasons* (1966), and, in most harrowing fashion, the Depression-era drama, *They Shoot Horses, Don't They?* (1969). Nobody got as much mileage out of York's wide blue eyes as director Sydney Pollack, shooting them through a shower's spray as the fragile psyche of her wannabe actress Alice shatters from the exhaustion and heartbreak of a desperate dance marathon.

But there was an earlier heartthrob: **Anne Francis** (b. 1930). If York was late '60s mod, Francis was good ol' fashioned Hollywood: blonde, curvy, brassy (in her best parts), and with the sexiest facial mole this side of Marilyn Monroe. In retrospect, she may have been too pretty. It was hard, particularly in that era, to get producers and casting people to see past her looks to the strong actress she was. "Most young blondes in those days ['50s] were not taken too seriously," she once explained. "I had wanted to work on a project [directing] all my own from beginning to end for many years. I had managers who said, 'Look, you're an actress. You're not supposed to do that other business.'" She could play girl-next-door, like the goody-two-shoes wife of inner city teacher Glenn Ford in *Blackboard Jungle* (1955); the intimidated bad guy's girl (*Bad Day at Black Rock* [1955]); and sci fi/fantasy buffs probably remember her from the classic *Twilight Zone* episode, "After Hours," playing a woman trapped in a closed department store, haunted by mannequins come to life, only to realize that she, too, is a mannequin who has been on leave in the human world. But she was at her best, and never more alluring, then when she played strong: the free-spirited Altaira in the sci fi classic *Forbidden Planet* (1956), or – my favorite – as the lead in the mid-'60s TV series, *Honey West*, playing a tough, independent, karate-chopping, guys-can-just-kiss-my-perfect-ass private eye before most people had heard of Women's Lib.

There was a time it looked like whenever a producer needed someone to play the wide-eyed naïf, **Michael Sarrazin** (b. 1940) seemed to get first call. There was something about those big, blue eyes, the babyish cast of his full-lipped face, his soft voice that spoke of vulnerability and innocence. But Sarrazin was a good enough actor to keep himself from becoming an empty type. As similar as many of his characters were, he made each distinct, alive: Army deserter Curley, frantically fighting off the cynicism being preached by George C. Scott's con artist in *The Flim-Flam Man*; the aimless Robert caught up in the misery of a relentless dance marathon in *They Shoot Horses, Don't They?*; the angry prodigal who returns to his lumberjack family in *Sometimes a Great Notion* (1970).

One of the funniest men who ever hit the screen was the great **Kenneth Mars** (b. 1935). He was a master of absurd, ridiculous accents, and at his best when a director stood back and let him loose on his ruthless pursuit of a laugh. Few directors knew how to do that. One was the equally ruthless laugh-chaser Mel Brooks who unleashed Mars in *The Producers* (1968) as Franz Liebkind, an atrocious playwright who pens a virtual "love-letter to Hitler" with his appalling play, *Springtime for Hitler*; and then again in his spot-on parody, *Young Frankenstein* (1974), playing a Transylvanian constable whose accent is so thick even the locals can't understand him!

Of all The Little Rascals, **Jackie Cooper** (b. 1922) was my favorite next to Spanky. I grew up watching Rascals re-runs on local TV, blissfully unaware that, by that time, the Rascals were all middle-aged. Cooper was the rare child actor who managed to maintain a career – not only as an actor, but as a producer and director — throughout his life. I thought he was a stitch as a cheap, loud Perry White in the first *Superman* movie (1978), rattling off zingers in screwball comedy style: "Lois, Clark Kent may seem like just a mild-mannered reporter, but listen: not only does he know how to treat his editor-in-chief with the proper respect, not only does he have a snappy, punchy prose style, but he is, in my forty years in this business, the fastest typist I've ever seen!" But my strongest memory of him will always be as little Jackie, fumbling through a crush on his school teacher ("Gee, Miss Crabtree…"), ridiculously competing for her attention against fellow Rascal Chubby.

Aussie actress **Diane Cilento** (b. 1933) had an impressive filmography including roles in such high-profile flicks as *Tom Jones*, *The Agony and the Ecstasy* (1965), and cult horror fave, *The Wicker Man* (1973), but my favorite was as the tough-hided dispossessed housekeeper in the equally tough-hided Western, *Hombre* (1967). She's the movie conscience, its referee between what we'd like to do, and what we should do. It's a rich, full-bodied performance, her Jessie a mix of the melancholic weight of her emotional scars, and her stubborn if battered sense of decency. In a genre which often shorts its women folk, Cilento in *Hombre* stands far above the crowd.

In my younger days, I wasn't always sure what director **Ken Russell** (b. 1927) was trying to do. Looking back, I'm not sure Russell always knew what he was trying to do…other than see how far he could go. Russell once said, "I don't believe there is any virtue in understatement," and he filmed accordingly. I was introduced to his work in my college days when I saw his screen adaptation of The Who's rock opera, *Tommy* (1975). After over 30 years of numbingly over-the-top music videos, it's hard to appreciate how novel Russell's visually flamboyant rendering of the rock milestone was at the time. Intrigued by the eye behind *Tommy*, I began backtracking its director, was struck by the seething eroticism of *Women in Love* (1969), appropriately disturbed by the fever dream visualization of *The Devils* (1971). I didn't always like Russell's work; there were times I thought him so obsessed with pushing limits that he forgot to tell his story as in *Crimes of Passion* (1984) and *Valentino* (1977). But I was always impressed with his audacity, his willingness to see how far off-center he could pull the commercial mainstream…and then try to tug it a little further.

And now they're all gone. It's a hell of a movie they'd make: a cast comprised of Jackie Cooper, Diane Cilento, Anne Francis, Michael Sarrazin, Kenneth Mars, Dana Wynter, Harry Morgan, Susannah York, G.D. Spradlin, William Campbell, and Pete Postlethwaite, scored by John Barry, and directed by Ken Russell. It's a shame that such grand cinema is reserved only for the next world. We here will have to make do with something less.

ACKNOWLEDGEMENTS

Along with the books and articles mentioned in these essays, a number of other sources provided me with a wealth of information, both specific and as background, and it would be horribly remiss of me not to give them their due here.

Bach, Steven. *Final Cut: Dreams and Disaster in the Making of Heaven's Gate.* NY: Plume, 1985.

Badger, Steve. "Remembering John Sturges: A Guide to the Films of John Sturges." www.playwinningpoker.com, Feb. 11, 2013.

Baldwin, Dave. Executive Vice President of Program Planning, Home Box Office, NY. Interview, August 19, 2002.

Balio, Tino, ed. *The American Film Industry.* Madison, WI: University of Wisconsin, 1976.

Barnouw, Erik. *Tube of Plenty: The Evolution of American Television.* 2nd ed. NY: Oxford University Press, 1990.

Bart, Peter. *The Gross: The Hits, the Flops – The Summer That Ate Hollywood.* NY: St. Martin's, 1999.

Bart, Peter, and Peter Guber. "Sunday Morning Shootout." "John Calley." American Movie Classics, Dec. 21, 2003.

Baxter, John. *Science Fiction in the Cinema.* 2nd Printing. NY: Warner Books, 1974.

--. *Sixty Years of Hollywood.* Cranbury, NJ: A.S. Barnes & Co., 1973.

Berman, Pat. "A Strange Fascination for Violence." *Columbia Record* (Feb. 1, 1975): 1-B+.

Biskind, Peter. *Down and Dirty Pictures: Miramax, Sundance, and the Rise of Independent Film.* NY: Simon & Schuster, 2004.

--. *"Easy Riders, Raging Bulls: How the Sex-and-Drugs-and-Rock-'n'-Roll Generation Saved Hollywood.* NY: Touchstone, 1998.

Bold, Alan (ed.). *The Quest for Le Carre.* NY: St. Martin's, 1988.

Box Office Mojo: www.boxofficemojo.com.

Bracourt, Guy. "Interview with Don Siegel." *Image et Son* (April 1970). Rptd. in *Focus On: Science Fiction Film.* Ed. William Johnson. Englewood Cliffs, NJ: Prentice-Hall, 1972: 74-76.

Brady, John. *The Craft of the Screenwriter.* NY: Touchstone, 1981.

Brooks, Tim, and Merle Marsh. *The Complete Directory to Prime Time Network and Cable TV Shows, 1946-Present.* 6th ed. NY: Ballantine, 1995.

Brownlow, Kevin. *The Parade's Gone By.* L.A.: University of California Press, 1968.

Burns, Kevin, and David Comtais (d). *Behind the Planet of the Apes.* 20th Century Fox Classics for American Movie Classics: 1998.

Byron, Stuart. "I Can't Get Jimmy Carter to See My Movie." *Film Comment* (March-April 1977): 46+.
Donovan, Hedley., ed. *Life Goes to the Movies.* NY: Time/Life Books, 1975.
Douglas, Kirk. *The Ragman's Son: An Autobiography.* NY: Simon & Schuster, 1988.
Dunne, John Gregory. *Monster: Living Off the Big Screen.* NY: Random House, 1997.
Ehrenstein, David. *The Scorsese Picture: The Art & Life of Martin Scorsese.* NY: Birch Lane Press, 1992.
Emery, Robert J. (p/d/w). *The Directors.* "George Romero." Media Entertainment Inc., for Encore (2003).
--. *The Directors.* "Oliver Stone." Media Entertainment Inc., for Encore (2001).
Evans, Robert. *The Kid Stays in the Picture.* NY: Hyperion, 1994.
Everson, William K. *The Bad Guys: A Pictorial History of the Movie Villain.* NY: Citadel Press, 1964.
--. *A Pictorial History of the Western Film.* Secaucus, NJ: Citadel Press, 1969.
Fine, Marshall. *Bloody Sam: The Life and Films of Sam Peckinpah.* NY: Donald I. Fine, 1991.
Finler, Joel W. *The Hollywood Story.* NY: Crown, 1988.
--. *The Movie Director's Story.* NY: Crescent, 1985.
Folsom, James, ed. *The Western: A Collection of Critical Essays.* Englewood Cliffs, NJ: Prentice-Hall, 1979.
French, Philip. *Westerns: Aspects of a Movie Genre.* Cinema One. NY: Viking, 1974.
Froug, William,, ed. *The Screenwriter Looks at the Screenwriter.* Los Angeles: Silman-James Press, 1991.
Gianetti, Louis D. *Understanding Movies.* 2nd ed. Englewood Cliffs, NJ: Prentice-Hall, 1976.
Gifford, Denis. *A Pictorial History of Horror Movies.* NY: Hamlyn, 1973.
Goldman, Andy. Director of Program Planning and Scheduling, Home Box Office, NY. Interview, August 29, 2002.
Goldman, William. *Adventures in the Screen Trade: A Personal View of Hollywood and Screenwriting.* NY: Warner, 1983.
--. *The Big Picture: Who Killed Hollywood? and Other Essays.* NY: Applause, 2001.
Greenberg, James. "Western Canvas, Palette of Blood." *The New York Times.* (Feb. 26, 1995): 19+.
Harlan, Jan. (d). *Stanley Kubrick: A Life in Pictures.* Warner Bros.: 2001.
Higham, Charles, and Joel Greenberg. *The Celluloid Muse: Hollywood Directors Speak.* NY: Signet, 1972.
Hodenfield, Chris. "Alfred Hitchcock." *Rolling Stone* (July 29, 1976). Rptd. in *The Rolling Stone Reader: The Best Film Writing from Rolling Stone Magazine.* NY: Pocket, 1996: 343-353.

Humphries, Patrick. *The Films of Alfred Hitchcock.* London: Bison Books, 1986.
Internet Movie Database: www.imdb.com.
Jennings, Gary. *The Movie Book.* NY: Dial, 1963.
Jenson, Paul M. *Boris Karloff and His Films.* Cranbury, NJ: A.S. Barnes, 1974.
Johnson, William, ed. *Focus On: The Science Fiction Film.* Englewood Cliffs, NJ: Prentice-Hall, 1972.
Jones, Ken D., and Arthur F. McClure. *Hollywood at War: The American Motion Picture and World War II.* Cranbury, NJ: A.S. Barnes, 1973.
Kemp, Philip. "The Story of All Wars." *Film Comment.* (July-August, 1996): 50+.
Linson, Art. *What Just Happened? Bitter Hollywood Tales from the Front Line.* NY: Bloomsbury, 2002.
Lyman, Rick. "Fewer Soldiers March Onscreen." *The New York Times* (Oct. 16, 2001): E-1+.
Manvell, Roger. *Films and the Second World War.* Cranbury, NJ: A.S. Barnes, 1974.
Medved, Harry, and Randy Dreyfuss. *The 50 Worst Films of All Time.* NY: Warner, 1978
Medved, Harry, and Michael Medved. *The Golden Turkey Awards – Nominees and Winners – The Worst Achievements in Hollywood History.* NY: Perigee, 1980.
Munn, Michael. *Gene Hackman.* London: Hale, 1997.
Parish, James Robert, ed. *The Great Movie Series.* Cranbury, NJ: A.S. Barnes & Co., 1971.
Parkinson, Michael, and Clyde Jeavons. *A Pictorial History of Westerns.* London: Hamlyn Publishing, 1973.
"Ridley Scott." Hollywood.com: www.hollywood.com, May 26, 2004.
Rose, Charlie. *Charlie Rose.* "Peter Bart." Jan. 1, 2004.
Rotten Tomatoes: www.rottentomatoes.com
Sarris, Andrew. *The American Cinema: Directors and Directions 1929–1968.* NY: Dutton, 1968.
Scanlon, Paul. "The Force Behind George Lucas." *Rolling Stone* (Aug. 25, 1977): Rptd. in *The Rolling Stone Reader: The Best Film Writing from Rolling Stone Magazine.* NY: Pocket, 1966: 118-130.
Scherman, David E., ed. *Life Goes to the Movies.* 2nd Printing. NY: Time-Life Books, 1975.
Server, Lee. *Robert Mitchum: "Baby, I Don't Care."* NY: St. Martin's Griffin, 2002.
Seydor, Paul. *Peckinpah: The Western Films.* Urbana, IL: University of Illinois Press, 1980.
Siegel, Don. *A Siegel Film.* London: Faber and Faber, 1993.
Sklar, Robert. *Movie-Made America: A Cultural History of American Movies.* NY: Vintage, 1975.
Smith, Roger. "Why Studio Movies Don't Make (Much) Money." *Film*

Comment (March-April 2002): 60-61.

Smith, Sean. "Periscope: Westerns – Riding Into the Sunset." *Newsweek* (March 22, 2004): 14.

"Symposium on Violence: Rites of Collective Ignorance." *Osceola* (Feb. 7, 1975): 8-9.

Terrill, Marshall. *Steve McQueen: Portrait of an American Rebel.* NY: Donald Fine, 1993.

Thomas, Bob. *King Cohn: The Life and Times of Hollywood Mogul Harry Cohn (Revised and Updated).* Beverly Hills, CA : New Millenium, 2000.

Von Gunden, Kenneth, and Stuart H. Stock. *Twenty All-Time Great Science Fiction Films.* NY: Arlington House, 1992.

Webb, Michael, ed. *Hollywood: Legend and Reality.* Boston: Little, Brown, 1986.

Weddle, David. "Dead Man's Clothes: The Making of *The Wild Bunch.*" *Film Comment* (May-June 1994): 44+.

Wright, Will. *Six Guns & Society: A Structural Study of the Western.* Berkley and Los Angeles: University of California Press, 1975.

Research Assistance:
Steve & Madeline D'Alessio.
Ron & Carol Kochel.
Bill Maass

Photographs Courtesy of Jerry Ohlinger's Movie Material Store, Inc. Except for *Path to War*, courtesy of Home Box Office.

And a special note of appreciation to Dr. Benjamin "Bernie" Dunlap; the guy who taught me how to see.

About the Author

Bill Mesce, Jr. is a screenwriter, playwright, and author of fiction and nonfiction. He spent 27 years in the Corporate Communications area of pay-TV giant Home Box Office, and is currently and adjunct instructor at several colleges and universities in his native New Jersey.

From August 2010 to February 2014, he regularly wrote about film and television for the award winning online magazine, *Sound on Sight,* which is where these pieces first appeared.

www.ingramcontent.com/pod-product-compliance
Lightning Source LLC
Chambersburg PA
CBHW020355080526
44584CB00014B/1028